Walter Thornbury

Cross country

Walter Thornbury

Cross country

ISBN/EAN: 9783337235024

Printed in Europe, USA, Canada, Australia, Japan

Cover: Foto ©Andreas Hilbeck / pixelio.de

More available books at **www.hansebooks.com**

BY

WALTER THORNBURY,

AUTHOR OF "BRITISH ARTISTS FROM HOGARTH TO TURNER."

LONDON:

SAMPSON LOW, SON & CO., 47, LUDGATE HILL.

1861.

PREFACE.

THE following chapters are chiefly reprints; they represent a campaign of some ten years in periodicals.

The scenes I have sketched are to me pleasant reminiscences of artist tramps in various English counties (especially Wiltshire, my foster mother), of many enjoyable rides and walks on the coast of Antrim and round the arbutus-woods that fringe with evergreen the beautiful shores of Killarney. As for the Somersetshire Rambles, they carry me back to some ten years ago, when I was a reporter and sub-editor of Felix Farley's Bristol Journal, a paper now dead, but which in its time had nursed the genius of Chatterton, and of nearly all the Lake Poets, and to my connection with which I look back with pleasure.

This volume preserves many memories that are dear to me of green English hedge-rows, now wildernesses of flowers and labyrinths of sweets—of Irish lakes, mirror-clear and ever fairy-haunted—of old castles not untenanted by

grim Puritan ghosts, shrouded Banshees rocking themselves to and fro—money-hiding dwarfs and clurichauns
ever busy at their magic shoes—of lonely moors where the
Grey Man walks—of white sea-shore cliffs, pale through the
gloom of storms — of silent mountains, on whose tops
forsaken Druid altars in the sun and rain gather moss—but,
above all, of a certain pleasant stone cottage, not a hundred
miles from Salisbury, up to whose mullioned windows the
roses of York and Lancaster now climb with offerings of
perfume—and above whose doorway by day in the fluid gold
of sunshine, and by night in the molten silver of the moon-
shine, the well-remembered dial still holds out its old monastic
legend as the warning shadow passes over it—*Ita vita.*

WALTER THORNBURY.

Fonthill, Wiltshire.

CONTENTS.

'CROSS COUNTRY.

CHAPTER I.

THE POETRY OF RAILWAYS.

POETRY used to sing in the hedge and on the roof-top—now it hisses in the boiler of Number Three engine, Slough station, and is audible even in that demon scream, terrible as the shriek of death to tardy pointsmen and blundering old men, with shaky hands or rusty switches. " Voices of steam," I burst out, as I unconsciously seized an angry stoker's hand at the Didcot junction the other day, " ye are many-tongued prophecies of a coming age—perhaps a golden one, perhaps, rather, one dyed all crimson with the blood of nations—." I might have gone further, had not my sable friend's " Darn your nonsense, here's the three-fifteen starting !"—cut me short.

If my friend had remained, I should have questioned him of many things of much importance to transcendental poets, but not much so to the railway share market. However, disgusted with the world in general, and stokers in particular, I ran for a ticket, which the angry tooth of the clerk's cork-presser only bit a hole through, and tumbled, meditative and poetical, into the stuffed and wadded chair of a first-class carriage.

Before me sat an old port-wine-coloured gentleman, with a bow-window stomach, and a bunch of watch-seals as large as a baby's head ; said old gentleman being wrapped up as if for a

B

north-pole voyage, and having an apoplectic voice that forbad all conversation as at once presumptuous and dangerous. After a treaty of legs, I fell a-musing again on poetry, bygone and present. You may talk as you like, I said to myself, I believe it is all here, just as much as ever it was; for look you, call the world a box, and the poetry so much gold, it doesn't matter whether I have it in gold or copper or paper—it is still the same five pounds ten, and of the same value; or call it, mind you, a close drawer and the poetry a grub I put into it; whether it is cocoon, chrysalis, or black and yellow moth, still there's the thing safe. It's like a plant, this poetry—now leaves, now mist and gases—now away in the clouds, now down again to rain. It can't escape, there's the same amount of matter. And so in poetry. The poetry's here still; and if I were to cut open a hole in the floor of my friend Atkins's shop and show him Erebus, he would believe it; as for volcanic sunsets and colour feasts of sunrises, he doesn't see much in them. So it is with railways. Men see no poetry in being shot as from a cannon, or passing from Bath to Bristol with the speed of a planet on a tour, or a fallen star bent on pleasure.

Listen, friend of the port-wine countenance and the redundant stomach.

"O! that noise, I want to go to sleep. Here's the Times; wonderful article on Palmerston!—great man, Palmerston!—great age, Palmerston!—great man of a great age!"

Very well, go to sleep. O! snore as thou wert wont to snore! But know, O insensate man, that that sound of the engine is like the champ and trample of a thousand horse: it might be Tamerlane riding to conquest; it might be Alaric thundering at the gates of Rome.

Dear me, that shutting off steam, do you know, sir, always suggests to me the sudden hissing simmer of a piece of cold lard in a hot frying-pan. It may be I am hungry, but deuce take me if I thought of anything else but a tremendous stew in a gigantic pan. Look out now, friend of the exuberant bowels, and tell me what thou seest.

"A confounded ugly country and six iron rails, like six black lines ruled in my ledger."

Behold, then, the vision of the son of faith. We are gliding on golden rails that the sunset shines on, and we are just about to thread an arch. When we lean back, and the great smoke-clouds that roll round us grow crimson in the sunlight, we shall seem as if we were in the aerial car of the Indian mythology, and were gliding away to Paradise.

My friend suggests that I am a Londoner, and that the fresh country air has rather got into my head.

Insulted at this, I leave him to apoplexy and the Times newspaper, and at the next station change to a coupé-carriage close by the stoker, to watch him stab the red furnace till it roars again. I mark, when he opens the door with a sudden, rough hastiness, the great orange flame shine out upon his Othello-like face, and turn him into the semblance of a ministering demon stirring up a kettle of stewed stock-brokers in a purgatory kitchen; I like to see him roll in the coals, and turn and twist those taps as if they were as many organ-keys.

Away with a battling tramp, and scurry, and whistle, and whiz, we go, past astonished labourers in green meadows, past telegraph-wires, on which as on interminable washing-lines sit wry-necked sparrows, who look at us as we fly past, as much as to say, " that's an odd sort of bird, but I don't think much of his plumage;" for critics who praise, have generally some compensating clause by which to make up for their moment of good-nature. Like a white banner flies the engine's smoke, —and away it rolls—stooping to join the great white fog that has no wings, and sits and broods yonder about the damp autumn fields. Through dark caves of tunnels—through dull barrennesses of high and bare embankments we rush with the force of a steam-catapult or a huge case-shot that is never spent—like a battering-ram—in a long race, for this steam-horse, with fire for blood, never wearies, never tires. Swift round curves, and swift up low hills—swift past village church and park, and farm-house, and wood—over river—along moor—past fat and lean, rich and poor—rock and clay—meadow and street; for this mad horse never wearies —never tires.

I try the second-classes, and find much eating and much merriment. They are more easily amused than the more conceited first, and are less afraid to show their honest feelings. Perhaps they have more feeling—who knows? Do they see more of the poetry of the railroad? are they listening with rapt ears, or gazing with steadfast eyes—not a whit! No, a gentleman with a brick-red colour on his high cheek-bone, a hard pincher-mouth, red hungry whiskers, and a strong whining Aberdeen accent, reads of a "Dreadful railway accident near Lewes—fourteen lives lost—list of sufferers." I look out and wonder at the horizontal lightning-fashion in which we tear into the tunnel and dig into the viaduct's doorways.   *   *   *

"First-class, ma'am, this way. No, second-class."

"Why did you say first, then?"

"There's the bell!"

"O my box!—where's my luggage? Porter!"—(in a tone of hysterical anguish)—"give me my box."

"Too late, marm—next train at 4·32,—five hours to wait, marm. Waiting-room?—yes, this way."

That is a lady's ideal of railway poetry.

"Damp seats! oh dear,—why don't they wipe the seats? this a carriage—it's a horse-box. Here, guard! do you call this a carriage? Infernal line—give me the broad gauge! Window won't go up. D—n the window—door won't shut—curse the door! whish! here's a draught enough to cut your head off. Guard! what does the company mean by this draught? Won't let a man smoke!—give me coach travelling, say I."

That is the commercial gentleman's ideal of the poetry of railroads.

"O Lor! such a hissing, and squeaking, and clatter, and then that whistle—like a devil's baby! O dear, law, it went through my poor head. And then the getting out at the wrong station to wait five hours for the next train. What I say is, Betty, give me a good jogging market-cart."

That is a country-woman's ideal of railway poetry.

"Why, I remember, sir, when I was a boy, being three days and nights on a journey that you do now in four hours. Those were the times; no hurry-scurry, helter-skelter—no chopping up decent people with trains, no gambling shares, and rascally share-market, with all the bullying and overbearing you hear of."

That is the old gentleman's ideal of railway poetry.

None of these, I am afraid, would listen to me were I to say I saw poetry in a stoker's life. On rough days, for instance, when he cowers behind his screen of giant glass spectacle, and looks out long and steadily through the sand and mist.

He is no divinity, bless you, no! Lord bless you! Nor no Diomed nor Hector, but only plain Jack Watford, of Number four, Blue Anchor. Yet he knows every crimson star that shines at stations, every emerald fire, and every white circle and red globe that stare at you for three hundred miles of line. He grasps that handle there, when the great wind blows enough to lift the train in the air like a feather, only it doesn't. Firm he holds that helm on those noisy nights, when he drives his strong, swift steam-ship on its flaming path, scattering the red-hot ashes of its rage as it ploughs on. And when the rain drives its liquid arrows at him, he only wipes his great eyeglass, and looks out a-head, or screws the engine up till it gives a long startling shriek of pain, that wakes up the sleepers in the next town, and makes them mutter and turn again to sleep.

Another generation, and the sense of novelty and poetry will have left railroads for ever. The long tearful stare of rural wonder, as the train grows small as a fly, or a black caterpillar in the distance, will be no more observed.

The sight of a train growing out of a cloud of smoke, the terror of its march, the rumour and battling of its rush, will have grown as familiar as the careening and rumble of the Royal Blue, bound to 'Ornsey or 'Ighgate. The instantaneousness, the obedient readiness of a train, already seem to us things of course. The propulsion of lightning, the comet speed, the strange contrast, such spiritual power controlled by a black fellow in fustian, Caliban ruling Ariel, is never thought of by such turtle-eating materialists, so grossly sunk in dirty three per cents. are we. But how many steps must we go back before we can return to our childish wonder at the crimson drop in a cowslip-cup, at a dark green fairy ring, or the dead men's flesh that has turned to mushrooms. As for Dryads, you can still hear their voices in windy nights, [even in Kensington Gardens,—when the rooks caw restlessly in their sleep, as if a worm had turned cold on their stomachs, and when the black leaves of the Hyde Park elms flutter and talk of what they shall do in the merry autumn time, when they once get loose from their governors, and start in life on their own account, these young things, not yet believing in winter,—not they.

What do we believe in? Look you here, friend, great on 'Change,—three weeks hence, you'll drop down at the Mansion House turtle-feast, and the alderman next you, absorbed in green fat, will not observe you taken out when he calls for a clean plate and a cold chair, to give him a zest for his sixth course. You will soon after, when a certain black gentleman shakes his head, turn pale, and in fact die. A week later, after a week's silence in a room with the blinds down, you will be carried out after a jostle down stairs to that dull Kensington churchyard, where an epitaph recording your mayoralities is already cut, to put over your head. Of what use, then, the snug detached villa, the crusty port, and the natty phaeton— olive green picked out with white—Answer, fool, of what use?

Had it not been better to have done good, and been kindly and open-hearted, and to have seen some poetry in life, and not called the air blue fog, and the rose a vegetable? Why, if that railway whistle could have been interpreted to you by an angel you might have known that it had a meaning prophetic and dreadful as the Judgment trumpet. That nettle your Malacca cane cut in two yesterday was a beautiful thing God made. No, man! 'Change is not the end of life, gold is not the old road-dust of Eden, and by no means the thing Apollyon lost Heaven for. Wake up, then! unlock your cellar, send a dozen of port to poor old Binns, the poor old head-clerk, who is so weak and threadbare. Release the orphan from Chancery, do something for the widow's son you ruined,—above all, look reverently henceforth at stokers and at all humanity, —and peace be with you at the last.

CHAPTER II.

ON THE WILTSHIRE DOWNS.

DOWNSHIRE, in the map of England, stands in a quiet neighbourly unobtrusive way, next to Ramshire, with Hillshire and Hogshire north and south of it.

Like Ramshire, it is a great sheep-breeding county; and its annual sheep fair is the largest held in Great Britain. I love every inch of Downshire; its dun-coloured and emerald downs, its lanes walled with honeysuckles in summer, and starred with primroses in spring. I like the way the white roads climb, with straightforward boldness, up the steep shoulders of the sloping prairie country. I like the floating blue of the distance, I like its lines of soldiery firs, I like its very weeds, I love even its molehills, the warts and wens, as it were, on its broad, honest, sunny face.

I write from Downshire now, for I am chasing Health, at a hand gallop, all over the tawny downs where the grizzled scorched grass is but a mere dry hide over the winter-chilled earth. The saddle is not cold yet upon which I have been scouring all this end of Downshire, from Crockerton Furze to Stanton Corner. Jingling over the little grey bridge opposite my country inn, jolts one of those country tilt-carts, with strained white awnings over them, which look like eggs, in the centre of which, having first scooped out the yolk and the white, sits the crimsoned-faced driver, whistling a country tune, almost as pleasant as that of the blackbird's that sits on the apricot-tree at my window. That is the carrier (I know him well), for he passes here every morning at ten, and is on his way from Spireton to Deverton St. Mary's.

Oh, that cart and its singing blithe driver have had a pleasant trip of it since sunrise, passing fields all of a transparent emerald flicker with the thin curling tender blades of spring wheat, among which strut, and plume themselves, and hover, and flutter, the rooks, who are engaged in entomological

researches, and large and glossy as black kittens!   They have
stirred lazily as the cart approached, have thrown out their pendent legs behind them, have worked up and down their wings
ragged at the edge, and have then resumed their studies almost
before the cart has well jogged past the milestone, orange and
black with twenty years' lichens.   Young orchards, where tiles
are hung to the top boughs to bend them over to a basket shape ;
fields spotted with flint heaps; folds full of the voices of sheep
waiting to be fed, has the old cart passed by.   Many long processions of waggons, baled with hay, or dark with faggots, has it
passed, many horses proud of the crimson and yellow shaving-
brushes on their heads, and of the sharp tingling bells upon
their harness that chime far along the glaring white road along
which they trample smokingly, the boiling dustclouds following
them as if the roads were on fire.

But let the egg-shell jog on the pleasant road, dappled as it
passes under the Deveril Park trees, and let me sketch a
Downshire village with its russet thatch roofs, and here and
there, at the post-office or the farrier's, a blue slate or a red
tile one, for the thin blue plumes of wood-fire smoke to feather
over.   There is something to my mind specially sheltering and
cozy in the look of thatch, cut away over the windows, level
yet spiky like a rustic's hair on a fair-day or holiday ; nor do I
like it the less if it be sponged and padded here and there with
green crystalled moss.   Greek and Roman workers are all very
well, but they seem fools, in my Downshire mind, to the brave
souls that devised those hearty lovable Tudor cottages, built of
stone, warm and lasting, scornful of the weather, that mellows
them to the exact tone and crustiness of the outside of a
Stilton, and covers them with lichens all in orange blots, and
frosty patches, and grey scales and shadings up to the top ridge
of the breathing chimney where the starlings chatter and twist
their glistening necks in a coquettish and fantastic way.   I
honour those wise and comfortable thinkers in ruffs and
doublets, who devised the Tudor cottages of Ramshire, with
their porches so hospitable and kindly in cold and rain, and
their strong mullioned windows so free to the air and light
yet so lordly-looking, so good for children to look out of, and

old men to bask in. I like to see the little cottage beehives in the gardens, among the cloves, carnations, and roses, with their little bee merchants dragging down all the flowers around. I like too to hear, in the evenings when the moon has a golden halo round it, as if it were melting into shapeless brightness, the drag and tinkle of the spades at work in the cottage gardens, just beyond the vicar's laurels, where the thrushes are rehearsing for their daybreak concert.

The high downs, moreover, are my special delight ; not those that rise in broad green shoulders on either side the road, shutting out all horizon ; not those, though they are in places as high as sea cliffs, sown and bunched with thousands of primroses, and pendent with long deer's-tongue or the branching feathers of fern, where the twisted beech-roots are velveted with green moss, and where the violets carpet the ground under the pied hazel-boughs which just now are tasselled with catkins. No ! those are the low downs that rapidly turn into the trim fields and cattle-dappled pastures of ordinary civilisation, and from them, down in the low country, you may in the distance see the train, which four hours hence will be in London, passing along, with a running smoke of steam like fire running along a train of gunpowder. I myself like the high downs where the horizon is a dim blue one of twenty miles' distance, far as a ship can be seen at sea. I like the prairie grasp and comprehension of those high Ramshire Downs, black with furze, lined with plantations, studded with sheep, alive with rabbits ; their keen, thin blue air vocal with plovers, and blithe choruses of larks.

You are not in solitude or uncheered there, for on the high roads you meet the Autolychus tramp on his eleemosynary progress from Deveril to Todminster ; now and then, some soldiers on leave, with their wallets behind them ; carriers and flour-waggons, and that scarlet-runner, the reckless mail cart ; not to mention chance travellers, clergymen on their rounds, and, often in the season, red scuds of fox-hunters on their way to covert—to Railton-Spinney, or Waterdyke Corner. Nor can you go half a mile without some dozens of rabbits charging with timid temerity across the road, so swiftly that you see little but a flirt of white tail near a furze-bush, as they disappear like Roderick Dhu's clansmen. You know that every thorn-bush you pass is peopled. Then the blackbirds run like rats about the thorn-bushes, or break out with a chink and fluster, as if in their conceit each bird thought the whole world specially in pursuit of him. Or perhaps, if you tread softly on the turf, you will be amused by coming on one of those blind diplomatists, the mole, like a little roll of black velvet. Then, on the fallows beyond the downs, you will surely see the crested plover, with his white belly and dark wings, swooping about, and making signals of distress with that strange "peewit" note which I think I could imitate exactly on the violin; and then, like a dark star, falls the lark from heaven, or rises, trembling, to the cloud; while the new-come cuckoo echoes his own Indian name in the fir wood that pulses with the lulling murmurs of the wild doves, where the squirrel curls in his nest, and the great black raven tolls out his sullen croak, as if a friendly lamb were seriously ill in the neighbourhood, and his (raven's) benevolent mind were troubled by his friend's indisposition.

But these are all episodical pleasures of the high downs, for the standing dish of delight there is the incomparable glory of the far distance, with its heavenly radiance of cloudy blue, and its softened glimmer of pearly colour, neither grey, nor blue, nor opal, but a union of all, with its many inner depths and glories to be wrought out only by the patient and loving eye.

I am no great believer in the poetry of sheep (uncooked), nor in lamb (without mint-sauce), but in Ramshire the sheep do throw themselves about the landscape as if they were trained to group themselves effectively—as my friend Mediocre, R.A., says. They sprinkle down the dun slopes, they cascade down the sides of the lanes, they come smoking along the dusty roads, they bleat in great multitudes. They are seen melting away in little yellow and brown spots, into the fairy azure of that magical distance through which glimmer pieces of green corn, brown fallows, golden stacks, white veins of chalks, grey-stone patches, emerald pastures, dun mounds of firs, and dark thickets of almond-scented furze, that, gradually getting thinner and thinner, break at last into single specks and dots of bushes which variegate the down as with an eruption of molehills.

Add to these variations of surface, some firs in the foreground, even as the teeth of a small tooth-comb; some round chalk basins cut by the shepherds to catch water; some grassy mounds of an old Roman camp, rising in triple terrace one above the other; and you have some idea of the higher downs taken in their generalities. To describe them, indeed, in detail would take a year: for the beauty of their atmospheric changes alone are infinite and wonderful.

But can I leave the Down country, with its quivering blue horizon, out of which the eye gradually evolves long funeral processions of firs; little toy farm-houses, so small in the distance that they are no bigger than a giant could carry on the palm of his hand (I mean a small giant, because, of course, a great giant like Brandyborax or Aldeboron has a palm to his hand as big as Salisbury Plain); grey spires, sharp and small as darning-needles; black specks of furze and bramble; and lesser specks, where glossy crows feed, or vibrate their wings—must I, I say, leave the high downs without describing the little stone tea-caddy of a Downshire church, built by that worthy but noseless man whose battered mummy of an effigy still lies, in a patient but ill-used way, on a flat tomb in the chancel?

I like the simple church, with the dial over the porch, erased by time. It is old as the Normans, I should think, that square tower, so massy and low; it is firm as the rock, so phalanxed and solid is its imperturbable immovability. The sunshine wanders over it, the rain beats it, the wind torments it, but it still remains as it has stood for centuries. The green waves of that dead sea around the yew-tree, rise and fall, century after century, but the tree is fixed as the good ship's mast: and daily casts its moving shadow into the chancel to flicker about the latticing sun and shade, as from the movement of passing wings.

There are many country moments when the songs of birds sound sweet from their very strangeness, and arrest the attention from their intrusion on scenes with which they have never been

associated. I like to lie abed early on a spring morning, and
hear all the sounds of life outside the window that cheer but
do not disturb you, so that you fall into a doze of spring-time
thoughts, as you are trying to listen, until you are roused broad
awake by the fuller chorus of young thrushes in the laurels,
who seem to be practising in a Hullah class, perpetually put
right by the fuller voices of the parent birds; but, best of all,
I like to hear on Sunday, in the Downshire church, between
the pauses of the psalm and the hushes in the Litany, the
response of the vicar's blackbirds coming in as if they had
been trained, like little choristers, in God's great open-air
cathedral.

Your contemplative Jacques can find pretty employment
in the oak coverts that here and there strew the surface of
Downshire, very aviaries of song in the pleasant May-time,
when even at noonday the nightingale may be heard gurgling
out rich soprano passages. There, the negro blackbird, with
the orange-bill, repeats his musical monotones, and the thrush
flings forth his lavish, careless carolling upon the blue spring
air. There, the robin, with breast stained ever since that
"dreadful murder" of the Children in the Wood, bides his
time, when in autumn he shall flaunt it on the Downshire
lawns. Let us enter the covert through a fir wood, where,
between straight rough-scaled stalks, that ooze balmy tears, spots
of moving sunlight flicker about on the dry pale leaves of last
year, here and there brightened where an angel's visit of clear
light from Heaven pours through and irradiates some churlish
bramble, for all the world like woman's love hallowing some
unworthy object: some Caliban of a husband, some Quilp,
some rude Cymon.

From these delights, I stroll botanising to the fretful nettles
—their white flowers soon to be black with bees—that edge
the outer skirts of the fox covert, where the waterproof buds
of the chesnut are throwing off their mackintoshes, and the
beech is unrolling his sharp-spiked buds; where the pied hazel
is fluttering its green-winged rods, and the banks are strewn
with primroses—those daylight stars, soft green where the
transparent leaves hood them in like nuns, soft gold in the

sunlight and paler in the shadow; where radiant bunches of violets purple the moss that wads the walks and velvets it for little fairy feet. Or, I find amusement in tracking the wood-pigeon to his nest by the piles of split beech-nuts under the selected fir; or, in judging that I could find a squirrel in his hammock up aloft when I see a plateful of nibbled nut-shells under the tall larch, gay with its tender pink blossoms; and, could I pursue the brook that lurks reedily among the trees, I might discover that eccentric angler, the heron, sitting on his nest, with his two legs hanging through, like a wooden-legged midshipman up in a man-of-war's cross-trees. If I had ornithological skill, I would may be seek out that feathered attorney, the cuckoo, and turn him out of the hedge-sparrow's estate that he has unlawfully seized; or, I would hunt for rare birds. Then there are broader tracks of the covert, where the grim oaks stretch out their muscular arms defiantly, and tie themselves in robust knots, where the clean-rinded beech has belts of dark moss and spots of feathery emerald, which look like the green plush stolen from a duck's neck, mixed up with snatches of the living emerald from the eyes of a peacock's fan. Then, there are huge antlered bushes of ash, strong and vigorous, butting aside the meek dog rose and the scrubby elder; and here and there among the spiked thorn-bushes whose snow is not yet in the bloom, there are flowers of burning gold, kingcups whose nectar the bee drinks thirstily; and when you turn the corner of a wood walk, there is a stinging buzz of startled flies, and a great black humble-bee flies at you like a bullet; and this gay buzz and sense of life in every square inch of air, is, I think, one of the most joyous and delicious symptoms of warm spring weather, especially when you add to it over and above, a perpetual pulsation of cooing doves, a singing contest of birds, and a general unfurling and unpacking of the little green fairy dresses that are hereafter to be called leaves, and will eventually club together to form the shroud of poor dead King Summer.

Then perhaps you startle a great raven from a tree where he sits complaining of the exorbitant price of mutton at Ramsbury market, and you come out in the open where some moles are making a small parody of that useful but mouldy institution, the Thames Tunnel, or you emerge in a small glade, with a view through oak boughs, barred with sun and shadow, of a great slope of down, miles away, with a long slate roof shining in the sun, a cascade of sheep, and in front a green square of meadow where some cows are on their knees in flowers, that look from here like a gold carpet, woven without seam, perfect from the top throughout.

It has been a glorious day in Downshire; the merry wind driving about the cool wavering shadows; the cuckoo echoing in the woods at Colonel Hanger's, where the pheasants cluck and strut, proud of their fat, of their market value, and of the brazen lustre of their fiery and emeraldine plumage—no great things at a poulterer's door, but here, in the living sunshine, flashing past us exquisitely. The wind has been blowing the dust along the glaring white roads in smoking simooms, the swallows have been glimmering and crescenting about the water meadows, like so many wild horses, and now I am standing on the dewy lawn of my little country inn—the Three Crows—in the evening, watching the stars light up their little diamond illumination lamps in honour of a young May moon, that is just at the full.

"Now, the moon," says the landlord, coming out with his white yard of clay and a burning Waterloo charge of bird's-eye, to be sociable with his guest, "seems to me to-night like a bit of butter that is beginning to melt on a hot toastess."

CHAPTER III.

A DAY WITH A WILTSHIRE GAMEKEEPER.

It is my fervent belief that the natural history of England will never be written properly till it is taken in hand by the English gamekeepers: given to those sinewy, stalwart men addicted to velveteen shooting jackets and leather splatterdashes, and taken from the ink-stained hands of those pale, weak-legged, purblind men in spectacles, who review everything second hand.

I maintain that old Targett, the gamekeeper at my friend Colonel Hanger's, who spends all day waiting for vermin, trapping, and shooting, and all night watching for poachers, in Redland Woods, must know more about the habits and customs of the fox, the badger, the marten, the rat, and the rabbit, than Professor Mole of St. John's Wood, who never goes into a field, never rode after a fox in his life, was never present at the "drawing" of a badger, never fired off a gun, never dug out a dog-rat, and never bit the tip of a bull-dog's tail to make him stop fighting; who does not know how pheasants roost, could not catch a weasel asleep, or otherwise, is, in fact, a poor, respectable, over-civilized, rheumatic, narrow-chested Professor; very great with his books and lamps, but a mere ignoramus down beside our tough friend Targett, who cannot write (who, in fact, I caught the other day tearing up an old volume of Cuvier to make wadding of the covers), but who has spent his life, not in reading other men's thoughts, but in observing living things, and studying their ways. He has never heard the word Mammalia, but he knows the individuals of the class, knows how to feed 'em, snare 'em, and generally circumvent 'em. Yet in fact, all he knows is merely how they live, eat, drink, and sleep; what they feed on, to what extent their instinct goes; how far they can be tamed; their times of breeding, and haunts—things which Professor Mole merely writes about.

It is a sad thing, as I often observe to my friend Mr. Fox, of Great St. Andrew Street, who stuffs birds and sells them, that men who know a subject generally, cannot write, and those who know nothing about it, but only think they do, can. Here, down in Wiltshire, we have Targett, who knows more about English natural history than all the F.Z.S.s and presidents of societies in the world, yet he cannot sign his name, and always puts a cross to his sharp son's weekly register of game killed that is sent in to Colonel Hanger. Professor Mole, who does not know a polecat from a ferret when it flashes across a country road, yet compiles his "naturalist's library," &c. &c., the only books where an Englishman can learn anything about the animals of his own country, though he may go to the Regent's Park and make faces at the lion, or throw a bun to the bear with impunity. In fact, the more I read Cuvier, and Jardine, and "the whole bilin' of 'm," the more I feel that English natural history is yet unwritten, and is to be compiled from the half-century wisdom of earth-stoppers and gamekeepers. O woe be to the infant science if we stop till these old men go to earth, or death makes game of our gamekeepers. As the Dodo and the Mammoth have perished; as the Great Sea Serpent of the Indian Seas, and gigantic Kraken of the Northern Ocean, have passed into myths, so will pass the English badger, the wild deer, and the cornerake. The wild cat is almost gone, the fox in time will follow, and where will be their histories?

Our children of the year two thousand and fifty, dressed in crimson silk breeches and satin and cloth-of-gold night-gowns, going out to dinner in steam balloons, and using electric telegraphs to ring the bell with, will, perhaps, some day, want to know what the fox people hunted in one thousand nine hundred on steam-engine horses, was like. This student goes to his cupboard of thirty thousand books, and running round the tramroad lined with shelves on a velocipede, he takes down a dusty French book, Dictionnaire Classique, or l'Histoire Naturelle, and finds to his delight that "the Renard is a Canis Vulpes of the order man." He is also overjoyed—this enthusiast for antiquarian knowledge—to find that "Renarde is the female of Renard." The food of the almost forgotten animal and its habits was too trifling a fact for scientific men to give. But still he is gratified and comforted to learn, on the conjoint testimony of MM. Bourdon, Pierrot, De Candolle, Delafosse, and others, that the fox is a species of the genus dog, and that it is a cunning and greedy animal, that its odour is unpleasant, and its fur of a reddish brown colour.

Stop! the historian gluts our enthusiast with information. Here is more news: "The tail of the Renard is bushy and of considerable magnitude." O these valuable and laborious French writers; what years of watching beside damp fox earths, under ash roots and behind tight-rinded oaks they must have spent in accumulating all this information, in addition to what Adam observed, as the great procession of birds, beasts, and fishes passed to the baptism. If Adam had written natural history, then we should have known if we have yet classified half the existing creatures, or have settled the question of that troublesome sea-serpent who keeps putting in alibis in different degrees of latitude, and whose existence (you need not go and mention it) I fervently and persistently believe in.

It is my fervent belief also—and I love heterodoxy, because it keeps one moving—that no one can paint a thing which is not before him as he paints; that no man can describe a place but on the spot; that no one can write on animals till he has chased, and shot, and petted, and watched them. Natural history is not to be written by professors in spectacles—timid, twittering, unsophisticated men—from stuffed animals and bleached skeletons. What we want is open-air natural history, such as Audubon, and White of Selbourne, and Gould wrote; more of it and deeper of it. What we want is gamekeepers' societies, and discussions duly reported: Leatherstockings president, Shotpouch corresponding secretary (if he could only write)—but no Monocluses and Moles, thank you. Then we might have something like natural history, and know where we were, and what to beat. When fish are bred and brought up in aquariums, and butterflies and reptiles in vivariums, then we shall know something about them. Till then, under the head English Natural History, write Chaos; which, being interpreted, means blackness and old night, for it is the land of Boshen and of fog.

Let me turn to the word "fox," and see what these dull, unadvancing pedants say—men who ought to discuss and chronicle every newspaper paragraph relating to wild or tame foxes, and examine the very length and breadth of their subject.

What does Professor Mole say? Here is his book, with a dauby, inaccurate, burnt sienna drawing of a fox, that a whipper-in would laugh at. The text occupies about two pages; it could be read in five minutes, yet it was only last November I had a burst of forty minutes after a fox that broke away from the Blackmoor Vale hounds, near Windwhistle Inn, and every minute of that time, I can assure you, furnished some

c

fresh instance of this incomparable animal's instinct. Riding home, the old whip told me enough stories about the fox's habits to fill a large volume of the Professor's works. And this is history! Shall I be ever driven to bring out that great exposure of mine, called "The History of Historians?"

Well! let us get to Mole's book. Here it is : "Fox—vulpis vulgaris—supposed to be indigenous to England—tradition says it was taken over to America by the Pilgrim Fathers— measures two feet five inches (I have known some hundred exceptions) ; tail cylindrical, one foot three inches ; head broad, snout sharp, eyes oblique, nose and forehead rectilinear." On the colour of this little known animal the Professor is very minute, stating the fur to be yellowish red, shading off to a paler yellow (few naturalists can describe colours, never using similes, the only way to express clearly and vividly subtle distinctions) ; this malt colour, or ripe corn colour, is mixed, it appears, with grisly white and black hairs ; or ash colour breaks out on the forehead, rump, and hams ; the lips, cheeks, and throat are white, and there are white lines on the inner surface of the legs ; the breast and belly are whitish ; the ears and feet black ; the tail is tipped with white, and sometimes ringed with black. The Welsh foxes, wishing for heraldic difference, and being probably of old Pendagon blood, and of a richer and stronger smell, leave out the black ring.

The Professor having here exhausted his limited palette of colours, branches off to the Syrian fox, that Samson caught and tied firebrands to, to the silver fox, &c. The Professor's mode of writing, however, is sometimes rather confused, for he describes an Indian fox that is so agile that it can turn nine times within the space of its own length—agility that even our English M.P.s could scarcely rival. More wonderful still, it feeds on "field mice and white ants, with tails like squirrels." What a terrible thing an ant with a squirrel's tail must be?

The great delusion of historians seems to be that they must write about nothing but the crimes of kings. The delusion of Professor Moles seems to be that their special mission is to describe in conventional language (generally second-hand) the colours of animals. This done, their task is over. Give me an old poacher; you take Jardine. Give me Targett then, you take Mole. I believe in few things, but the one thing I do believe in is the value of personal observation. All second-hand things are bad; for second-hand information is generally first-hand ignorance.

As for fish, I give up all hope of ever knowing anything about them. The turtle, turbot, cod, and sole I have dissected, and I think know pretty well; but who is to spend months off the Doggerbank, the Knock, or the Silver Pit sands, to study the habits of the tabbied mackerel and the pearl-coated whiting? who will go and live in a diving-bell, and see them play and dance, and feed and fight, and make love and go to war.

But the fox. Is it not dreadful to a progressive mind to hear that stagnant old Mole, surrounded by his glass-cases and stuffed deaths, potter on in this vein:

"Upper shades of the body red fulvous; muzzle dark rufous; on the back waves of whitish; chest grey; anterior line of the fore-legs deep black; tail mixed fulvous and black."

What is fulvous and rufous? Why, Mole, do you not go to the colour-seller and learn the names of colours, for are not maroon and burnt sienna more intelligible than your gabble of fulvouses and rufouses? And perhaps all this time, thou one-eyed writer for blind people, thou art only describing an exceptional fox, no more like the average foxes than an Albino is like an ordinary man, or a Yankee like an Englishman:

"Foxes have the lateral crests of the skull, which serve to attach the chrotaphite muscles in the shape of an angle, but slightly prolonged before they unite on the frontal suture."

Is not this throwing a stone at us when we ask for bread? Is not this pelting us with barbarous Latin and dog-Greek when we ask to know something about foxes?

Another quarrel of ours with Mole is that he is the dog in the manger—he does not write natural history himself, and he barks at any one else who wants to. And singular, although half his science seems to consist in the mere classification of animals, he always gives us careless daubs of them—rude, raw,

and impossible in colour. Here, for instance, is the tri-coloured
fox of Virginia, in an expensive work on natural history,
coloured as barbarously as if it was a Cupid holding a pin-
cushion heart in a penny valentine. "Silver-grey" is represented by a wash of lead-colour, and "rufous" by raw sienna,
which also daubs up the eyes. Surely no colour is better than
wrong colour, any day in the week.

But Mole has not yet exhausted his handbook to the fox.
Under the head Canidæ he kindly tells us—Sub-Genus 3,
Vulpes—the foxes—that "the pupils of their eyes are ellip-
tical, or contractile into a vertical slit—tail long, bushy—lower
on the legs in proportion to the body—fur finer—habit noc-
turnal."

And, wonderful to relate, I also find, under the head "Important to Fox-hunters," the following interesting bit of al-
gebra :

$$\text{"Incis. } \frac{6}{6}; \text{ carn. } \frac{1\text{-}1}{1\text{-}1}; \text{ check, } \frac{6\text{-}6}{7\text{-}7} = 12."$$

Which looks more like a calculation in arithmetical cypher of
the Professor's income than anything else; but at last I get on
dry ground, and read, as an alchemist's boy might read his
absent master's secret : "Muzzle elongated—nostrils naked,
binular, and open at the sides—tongue soft—ears erect—feet
anterior pentadactylus, posterior tetrodactylus, walk on the
toes—mammæ both pectoral and ventral." This is, indeed,
knowledge—something like knowledge!

Why is not this printed in a cheap form, placed between an
orange-tawny cover, illustrated with a Flying Dutchman fox-
hunt, and sold on railway stalls for the use of young fox-lovers
who run about England after a bad smell when they might get
it in full perfection in the Thames without running at all?
What a fine sight it would be to see a band of scarlet youths,
while waiting at the covert side some biting January morning,
instead of idle smoking, and scandal and gossip, improving
their minds by studying Professor Mole's (un)natural History
of the British Fox.

And fancy, too, in that golden age, when all fancies become

true, and all good men's wishes are fulfilled, fancy the Professor roaming about by moonlight with sanguinary Jem the poacher, studying with the zeal of a Columbus the natural history of the British rabbit; or mounted on a thorough-bred, trying to learn the habits and tempers of that " noble quadruped" the horse. True, the gallant professor might catch cold sitting down in the wet fern, and he might be pitched into the thorn cage of a bullfinch. But what of that? Has not science also its martyrs? Was there not once a Park, once a Perouse, once a Cook? Why then should there not be a Mole?

"Now for your own history of the fox, the rat, the dog, the badger, and all kinds of creatures," says Mole, spitefully.

No, Professor, it does not follow that because I see a shot-hole in the side of the vessel of science that I am necessarily sea-carpenter enough to at once plug it. I see the howling barrenness of your book, but I can only hint at the flowers that might turn it to a garden of Eden. I have certainly a few gamekeepers' notes that I keep as proofs and evidence. More I have had and lost; but still, what I have are a good specimen of the vein I have struck.

It was only last week I was down in a Wiltshire village; and, having studied the church—where on Sundays you hear the blackbirds in the rector's garden laurels making their blithe responses between the pauses of the Psalms, and where the arrow-fleet swallows often zigzag in and out the aisles between the lessons—and, having watched the reapers, with their steel crescents, busy in the gold rows of the sloping cornfields, and having read all the red and blue handbills on the folding-doors of the only empty barn in the place, I began to grow a little weary of lying down in the clover-field, and watching the bee excisemen, so I determined to follow the dark green line of path that led through the meadow where the young pheasants were dusting and sunning themselves round their coops, and go and have half an hour's quiet "crack" with old Targett, the head gamekeeper.

Off I went, rousing the dozing larks to their chorister duties, whipping the purple cushion heads off the thistles, taking the way to the hanging wood, in the heart of which our Wiltshire Leatherstocking lives. I love the deep greenness of the old plantations, where the ferns are high enough for a stag to pass under, without his antlers touching the keystone of the arch, and the honeysuckles wind so close together that they seem like chains twined with flowers. Here were glades, too, quite dry, and coated with the red brown aromatic dead needles of the fir; and, up in the tall beeches, whose grey trunks threw quite a light around me, I could see the bush of the squirrel's nest.

At last I got to the break looking down on the stubble-field where the keeper's cottage was. It was bosomed in woods, and down below, and before it, was a stile grown round with docks, and a blue Gainsborough glimpse of a church tower with the weathercock on it glittering in the sun like a burning diamond. A great white setter lay at the door; it had been too much with gentlemen to bark at seeing me. I entered. There was the old gun on the rack over the fireplace, and a stuffed white owl staring at you with glassy unblinking eyes from above the American clock. There was Targett busy chopping up rabbits for the young pheasants, while a nice old woman, with all the blandness and ease of a duchess, wiped a chair clean for me, and then smiling welcome, went on stirring the oatmeal over the fire. As for the younger Targett, he was stuffing a hawk to nail up over the window.

We first discussed the wonderful skill and readiness of poachers; how they bewitch trout with quick lime, and so send the three-pounders floating down the stream from under the weeds; how they use cherries with the stones out, and young grasshoppers and wasp-grubs, and salmon-roe, and all sorts of unlikely things for trout that the fish could never have tasted or heard of, yet always bring the poacher's creel home heavy. On moonlight nights, when they could see the hares, "these gentry" were sure to be about. He told me, too, that the herons had an oil in their legs that attracted the fish round those meditative birds as they stood in the shallows, and that poachers, it was said, about the Trent, extracted this oil, and used it with great advantage to dip their bait in; this was one of those things, he thought, that "gents as wrote on natyral 'istory" and were wide awake, should inquire into. He had no time to do it; it was quite enough for him to see the dogs were fed, and the vermin killed, and the rabbits snared to feed the pheasants with. As for all those bright varnished rods and expensive reels gents brought down with them, and wonderful flies with "mouse's bodies and peacock's wings," he would wager any night to catch a basket of perch with one gudgeon's eye on the hook—ay, even with mere line and no rod at all.

Then about foxes—they were cunning surely. Many a night watching he had seen them in the hare runs, practising how far they could leap from a certain bush so as to be sure of their prey, to the very inch, and off before the best of shots could get his gun up. Didn't they eat too, and spoil more than they eat? He had known a dog-fox, when it had cubs in an earth hard by, kill thirty ducks one night; and, a week after, thirty pheasants. Couldn't eat half of them, of course, but dug holes in ditches and buried the overplus. It often happened Fox forgot where he buried them, or at least never dug them up again. Why, he had seen them down in the water-meadows try a plank that crossed a brook, try it a dozen times, before they would go over; and he had marked them dip their tails in urine, and then drag a trail from a stone-heap in a field to where they lay hid. Presently, out ran the mice, followed the trail, and were instantly pounced upon. He had met them, too, with geese thrown over their backs, and the gooses' necks in their mouths. As for trapping them, it was difficult. Why, if you put a gin at the mouth of the earth, they would scratch out above it, or scratch out backwards, and so make the thrown-out earth spring the trap. Even when caught, they would sometimes bite off their broken leg and escape.

"Did they really read the newspapers to see where the hounds met next morning?"

"Well, that was a woundy good 'un!" (Here Targett beat his thigh jovially.) No, but he thought the varmint did everything but that. They had been known to breed on the top of a church, getting up every day by the ivy boughs, and had been at last killed by the hounds on the very church roof. They had been found with their cubs in the hollow top of pollard

trees, they had been known, when chased, to take to the
water and hang on by their teeth among the osiers to a willow
bough, their body being invisible. As for their cubs, the vixens
will carry them any distance; any disturbance or noise near a
hole will make the vixen and cubs change their hole. As for
the mange, that scourge of dogs, they "have it dreadful," and
have been found as bare as an old trunk, and without a hair
in their tails. Foxes would run twenty miles straight without
turning; even foxes hid in sea cliff that seldom ramble far,
perhaps living on fish; and I must remember, too, the fox was
always taken at a disadvantage, generally full in stomach and
tired with the night's prowl; an evening fox fresh from the
day's sleep few dogs could catch.

Here Targett, junior, who had been burning to put in his
oar, and was dancing round me with a half-stuffed hawk in his
hand, broke in to tell me how last night, outside the warren,
he had heard a dreadful shriek, as of a woman being murdered,
round the corner of a wall. He looked and saw a hare, its
head sopped wet crimson with blood, tearing along, and a stoat
riding on its neck, sucking like a demon at the spine. As he
got up the hare fell dead, and the stoat slid away.

I don't know what I might not have heard to enrich our
meagre natural history, had not at this moment the squire's
dinner gong boomed out an imperious summons for me, which
even my zeal for science was not strong enough to induce me
to disobey.

CHAPTER IV.

THE BUCKINGHAMSHIRE MAN.

A BULLET that "had really killed a man" at Waterloo, was one
of my playthings when a boy.

That bullet was as terrible in my eyes, and as much a fetish,
as the spotted snake that "had really killed a man" in India,
that we kept in spirits in a long bottle on the top of a book-
case. As that snake represented in mine eyes the whole India

of snakes, cane brakes, jungle clumps, plain and mountain, Deccan and Punjab, from Cashmere to Cape Comorin, so was that dull little battered leaden bullet a sort of a little sphere which became transparent as I looked at it, and disclosed embattled nations, in all the shock and grapple of mortal contest, or pouring along in headlong rout, with torn colours, broken weapons, and shattered gun-carriages.

My next step, after a personal taste of single combat at school, was to discover a man who had really been in a battle. I found him in no less a person than our old gardener, who did not seem to be especially proud of it, and took it very much as a matter of course. There was nothing specially divine about the man as he leant on his spade, cleaned it with a wooden scraper, and put a fresh plug of tobacco in his cheek; no special lustre lit his eye: yet he had been "baptised in fire," as Napoleon called it. I saw no special result produced by such a ceremony, but it is all in him, I thought, full of my Thermopylæs and Marathons, Bannockburns and Zutphens, and my shocks of spears and clouds of arrows—it is all in him. He is as a cask of very precious liquor, and I am the spigot that is to let it out. I shall now know what I have long thirsted to know—the feelings of one's first battle, and the details of what is actually done.

"Ranger," said I, with all the earnestness of fourteen, talking to him as if he was on oath, "did you ever shoot a man in battle?"

This I thought was quietly breaking the ground, and laying it open for innumerable tales of bloodshed. He spoke, after a minute, during which he looked down at the fresh mould, then up at the blue sky.

"Well," said he, "Master Joe, not as I exactly knows on; but I've fired into the thick on 'em a score of times."

I was disappointed at the time, and began to suspect there was no poetry in life if it was not to be found in a battle; yet when I began to turn it over, I think the answer was not so bad.

Yes, into the thick on 'em. I can see 'em now—rows of broad-topped shakos and red side-plumes, fiery eyes and mouths

fierce, black with biting the cartridges. Twist and ram the
grape. Fire! one man falls on his knees—another staggers;
two more hide their eyes; for, they are shot in the face.
Closing up to the front, fresh men step in their places. Charge!
away goes the level line of bayonet with three cheers. The
French reel—they break. The colours are taken—they fly—
victory—VICTORY!

True, I have ludicrous images of the Finsbury volunteers,
of their ramshackled march, their intermittent fire, the ravages
they made of poultry in their marches, of their general
cumbrous and inefficient look. No wonder the local militia
used to be called "The Locusts," for they cleared the country.
Then the Yeomanry, and their dusty triumphal entrance once
a year into Diddleton, shall I ever forget? No charge of
Cromwell's could have emptied more saddles than a wheeling
manœuvre used to on field-days; and as for the fat major, how
his hat used to blow off, and how the colonel's horse, if he ever
dismounted, used always to break away! How hot and dusty
they always were, how they seemed bursting through their
dragoon bob-tail jackets, how those huge swords used to
chink about the streets, how the gallant men used to brag
and drink! The city, while the Yeomanry were there, seemed
always as if it had just been sacked in a most comfortable
way.

A good old country gentleman I once knew used to tell three
times a day for forty years his adventures when he served in the
City Light Horse Volunteers, a gallant corps, indeed, of City men,
light perhaps on horseback, but I should think unsurpassably
heavy in conversation, to judge by my friend. He lived in his
early heroism, left his sword and sabretasche hung up in his
study to provoke remarks, had regular traps and means to lead
on to his stories, and always began them by swelling out his
chest, perking up his chin, and saying, "I once drew my
sword in defence of my country." His forced march to Ealing
(like Major Sturgeon's) surpassed Napoleon's attack of Lodi,
and the return to Hackney was something like the retreat
from Moscow, only shorter, and in the summer. If that gallant corps—and I say it advisedly—had had the opportunities

the regulars had, they would have done gallant things—but they hadn't.

The other day I chanced to meet an old militiaman who was great about the old days, and in the bygone glories of Stowe and the Dukes of Buckingham. I met him in a railway carriage thus:

I was on my way to Ireland, to establish a company for " Draining the Bogs of Allan in search of a Danish Treasure," which had been recommended to me as a good thing to invest money in.

I had refused to buy an " Illustrious Noose;" I had been driven at " by your leave" by ploughing perambulating trucks full of luggage; I had had my ticket nipped by something between a dentist's key and a cork-presser; I had at last taken my seat in a second-class carriage, arranged my plaid, laid my Times in a sort of Freemason's apron over my knees, and was getting all ataut. The day was burning and golden, the sky blue and spotless, except where the white clouds billowed and toppled about like poised avalanches. The bell rang, the guard waved his red flag, we were off with a hiss and trample, and a pulsation as of some angry giant's heart.

I settle myself down in the spare box of a carriage, I establish a treaty and alliance of legs with the Buckinghamshire man, who I find has been a militiaman, which is a tie between us. Lady's-maid, sallow and waxy with sitting up late at night, cheerless, for ladies coming home from gay parties, subsides into a stupor of rest, in the corner. The drummer—such a drummer!—a little pink-faced boy, say about fourteen, frank, and at his ease, with his great white buff belt, with brass scutcheoned buckle, lying before him on a vacant seat, beside his knapsack, only numbered with name, No. of company, and detachment. How firm and disciplined, and almost gentlemanlike, he looks with his black trousers lined with red cord, and his little scarlet frock, fringed white at the shoulders, and striped and epauletted with white lace, and studded with blue fleur-de-lis reminiscences of Cressy and Agincourt, and our old French claim.

The Buckinghamshire man, in an energetic and robust way,

announced himself to me as having been for thirty-five years watchman of Olney parish, sheep-shearer, brewer, and guide to Cowper's cottage, where the poet kept his tame hares and wrote the hymns, and other curiosities. He was a cheery, ruddy, large-made man, with eyes of washed-out blue, big, round, and staring; in his gestures demonstrative, stamping, and redundantly energetic.

But I must go back to the starting. Ching, clang! ching, clang! ching, clang! went the Euston-square bell. Whew! whew! whew! went the guard's whistle. Another drummer-boy, with two medals at the breast of his scarlet coat, and who had come to see his younger comrade off, thrust his hand in at the window to give him a last shake.

"Good-by, Tom," said the rough, kind stripling, "take care when you get to the station to go straight home, and don't let any blackguard wheedle your money out of you; get to your father and mother, then you are all right. Think of the regiment. Mind and write to the drum-major."

A demon-thirsting scream gave the signal.

"Good-by, Tom," said the lad.

"Good-by, Jack," said the boy.

The little fellow would have liked to cry, but he was a sol-dier, and a soldier's son, and he didn't, but he gave a rather rueful look at the blank, square window—no kind, sturdy face there now—and to hide his faint heart set to work buckling up and arranging the great, square, black knapsack, on which his name, "Thomas Wilson, Scots Fusiliers, 27, 3rd Company," was inscribed in great white letters. Then he shifted his linen bag, or haversack, which was slung at his side by a linen belt passing over his shoulder; he adjusted his smart foraging-cap, with the strap on his lip, and loosened, just to feel he was out of Trafalgar-square barracks, his white buckskin belt with the brass badge of a buckle. He was not going to compromise the character of the army among civilians.

We passed out of the great shadow of the station tunnel that fell on the white page of the book I was reading like the broad shadow of some evil angel's hand. Champ, champ! rattle, rattle! like the roar of a million of Parthian cavalry chafing at our heels—a battling, angry din that deafens and excites—and we break out into the free light.

Now, no noise but the gentle puff of the engine far away, and the white cloud at the window, as of the pipe of the great Manitou of the *Waim a nomen*, breathing sleepily on this pleasant autumn day; high in heaven all sapphire. Now, no brooding, noisy darkness, but a broad column of light like that of a sudden resurrection, or as the sunshine coming to us out of the grave of an eclipse. We settled ourselves to our places for the next forty miles' rush and roll, and the great white clouds of steam floated round us as if we were being borne on the Hindoo car of Paradise to the gardens of Indra.

We began to settle; the lady's-maid took out a limp, ill-used novel; the drummer began, with true boy's hunger, to pinch suspiciously certain projections in his haversack that seemed edible; the Buckinghamshire man's eyes fixed intently on him with mingled admiration, sympathy, wonder, and sagacity. He was eminently sociable, and began the conversation at once by aiming a playful blow at the drummer's chest, and asking a question so abruptly, and in such a deep chest voice, that it sounded like a blow too:

"Isn't a volunteer better than two pressed men, youngster?" said the Bucksman, as if contradicted and put out.

Tom laughed, and said he rather thought so. "This is a queer card," thought he, and looked so.

"I say," said Bucks (let us call him Bucks for shortness), with a sorrowful shake of his rusty hat and grizzled hair, at the same time wetting his lips to show that he was going to begin, "those were nice ones at that public-house with your comrade there and the other soldiers. Oh! they were bad ones, bad lot."

"Yes, they were," said Tom, in a neat, disciplined voice, recognising Bucks as having been with him at the "ale-us" before starting.

"Very bad lot; I should be sorry to see sons of mine like those gentlemen with the pack of cards. Did you see one of them pull the sergeant's sword and make a slash in fun at him. Oh! they were bad ones. I was sorry to see it. Bad ones, bad ones."

Bucks relapsed into silence after this simple homily on virtue, and proceeded with his staring blue eyes to take a careful inventory of the drummer's fantastic dress from top to toe: his scarlet coat, a little purple and faded in places, its long stripes of dull white lace worked with blue fleur-de-lis (strange tradition of the old Agincourt quarrel), his stiff collar, with its ruff of blue and white lace, his neat belt and shining brass, and his soldierly trousers of black, corded down the seams with red. Bucks never seemed to have enough of it.

" This is the stuff to make a soldier," said he suddenly, with intense enthusiasm, such as men who remember the old French wars and volunteering days can only feel now it is the fashion to be so philosophic and cosmopolitan. " Wert in the Crimear, lad, eh? Did'st box the Rooshians, lad?"

" No," said Tom, stoutly and honestly, " but that comrade of mine, who you saw shake hands with me, was, and was wounded, too. The band, you know, have to carry off the wounded."

" Look at this lad now !" said Bucks, addressing every one, and proudly, as if he were his father, with stentorian voice, hitting his corduroyed thigh violently with his clenched fist, " I saw, last week as ever was, a regiment pass through Tring with a drummer-boy no bigger than him, and they stopped at the public-house the Malt Shovel, in Tring, where I was brewing. Lor' bless you ! what a stir the farmers made with t' lad. I do believe if he could have eaten gold they'd have given it the little lad." (All this our honest friend spoke as if he was chewing every word, forte e molto staccato.) " Bread and cheese, good Lord ! I should think so ; good strong ale (six bushels to the barrel), and rattling good double Gloucester till he could not eat any more. I thought they'd have made him dead drunk, but the brave boy (he was the bugler) pushed back the glass at last, and said, as stout as a lion,

" 'Thankee, gentlemen, all the same, but I'll take no more, or I shall not be able to do my duty to-morrow—thank *you* all the same.' And HE DID NOT, for all the pressing. Ah ! 'twas a brave bugler lad, *that* was."

The drummer was intensely interested, and unconsciously, as

Bucks spoke, kept unbuckling his knapsack by a nervous restlessness of fingers.

"Well, next day," went on Bucks, "I saw this bugler go up to the sergeant, who had stopped his week's money to prevent his spending it. It was all kindness of the sergeant, but still he had no business to do it."

"No sergeant had no business," said Tom, determinedly; "a sergeant can't interfere with the boy's pay unless he has behaved bad."

"Well," continued Bucks, encouraged, "the bugler boy went up to him, BRAVE AS A LION" (roars so that the lady's-maid drops the limp novel, thinking there is a collision, and henceforward listens like a wise woman), "'Why have you stopped my pay, sergeant?' said he.

"The sergeant said, 'Never you mind, boy.'

"But he said, 'I *will* mind. I'll have my fair money.'

"Then the sergeant said, 'I'll report you.'

"But the drummer went on saying, 'If you don't give me the money, I'll report *you*, sergeant.'

"Then the sergeant, in his burning rage and furious spite, called out to another boy to sound the bugle, and he did it— sounded a sound, but rather weak and poor like, and the men who were by, laughed, and tapped their muskets on the floor. Then the boy stood up again as bold as a hero, and said, 'Is that the way you sound a sound? Give it me!' And he took the bugle, and blew such a sound, so clear and true, it was good indeed to hear. He said, 'That is the way, sergeant, to blow the bugle-call!'" Imagine this story told in a jovial, unflinching crescendo of voice, ending with a complete burst of laughter that stunned us.

We all laughed, which encouraged Bucks, and made him ten times noisier and redder. His face now was a burning coal— he must have been drinking. He now amused himself by going over all the boy's accoutrements. "This," says he, "is where you put your clean shirts in for home, your pipeclay, and your brushes; this is for your prog;" and so on, touching each article like a showman as he went on.

"Did you ever put your head in a beehive?" said Bucks, turning sharp round on me.

"No," said I, smiling, and watching his light blue Saxon eyes and inflammatory face.

"Well, then, that's just the feeling I have in my ears after being a bit in London—dang'd, dirty, noisy place! How glad I shall be to get back to Olney! I've worn this," said he, touching the boy's red uniform, "though you wouldn't think it."

"You have?" said I, with an expectant surprise, which was as good as saying, "Let us hear, then, all about it."

Bucks began by clenching both his red fists, and placing them firmly on his two knees; then, putting his head on one side, he opened fire thus:

"I was in the Bucks Militia myself when I wor eighteen —yes, I wor—eighteen as never comes agin, when one doesn't care for the king on his throne, not us!' (Violently, though no one interrupted him, but his nature was combative.) " I remember when the old Dook of Buckingham, father of the present dook (he's not worth a bad farthing now), reviewed eight hundred of us in the great park at Stowe. He was a big man, he was, a rattling good waggon-load of stuff, he was." (Laugh.) "Seventeen stone, if he weighed a hounce, gentlemen. He used to come in his open yellow barouche every parade day, and have his two greys (he always drove greys) drawn up with their two noses exactly opposite the two big drums" (digs his two hands into two typical places on his two thighs), "so as to accustom 'em to the noise, so as they shouldn't never shy. Yes, I remember as well as if it was yesterday the speech he made to us the last review day—ah, as well as if it was yesterday! I was only eighteen then." (Tone of manly regret not incommendable.) " This is what he said, said the dook: 'Officers and men of the regiment of the Royal Bucks militia, I thank you heartily for the admirable manner you have conducted yourselves under arms' (so we had —we had all presented arms when the dook came on the ground), "and I invite you all to dinner this afternoon in a tent in my park; and all those who have fathers, mothers, sisters, or sweethearts, let them bring them with them. Officers and men of the Royal Bucks Militia, I wish you farewell and good appetite!'"

"Bravo!" said I.

"Ah, bravo, indeed!" said Bucks. "That was acting like a king—ay, he was a king!—and we all went. Every man jack of us had as much roast-beef and plum-pudding as he could eat: good streaky beef, too, jolly good pudding, plenty of plums, and a quart of strong ale—Burton—that would stand by itself; and every one had a pound and a half of it to his own cheek, besides a large three-corner cocked-hat slice to take home for one's friend or sweetheart. I took mine home to a sick brother."

"Good," said I, "that showed the heart in the right place, that did." Drummer's eyes kindle at the memory of pudding, —pudding being a sort of divinity with boys. Then, ashamed of being caught worshipping pudding, he looked at his red corded trousers, and arranged his belt.

Bucks continued stormier than ever. "Well, and every five of us militia had a sort of flower-pot thing to put his grub in, and a cup—a new tin cup—to each one for his malt liquor."

"Much speaking?" I threw in.

"Lor' bless you!" said Bucks, "I should think so—toastesses and cheering and stamping. How I got home to Bucks I don't know, but I did it in time, by zigzagging all through Stowe Park and the long avenue.

"Lor'! to hear the speech-making in the red-striped tent and in the house, both at the same time, two or three rising at once. It *was* darned good fun, I can tell ye. (Slaps his knee, the nap of which many thousand previous slaps have altogether removed, and doubling up with a colicky chuckle that was almost too much for him, at which the limp, pale lady's maid smiled dolefully, and in a way that implied smiles were irreligious, unbeseeming, and ungenteel). "Speech-making! *I* should rather think there was, plenty of it, all under the flags in the marquis, as they called the tent set up on purpose for us to dine in, near the Flaying House, as it was called, where the deer killed in the park used to be prepared; and every time a toast was drunk the yeomanry guns fired three times" (shakes his head)—"yes they did. Then the dook gave the best men prizes for running in sacks, grinning through a collar, shooting at a target, dipping for sixpences in treacle, and all sorts of pastime, for the gentry likes to see the tenantry busy about in these gala days."

"That was doing it like a king," said I.

"What fun!" cried Drummer Tom.

"It *was* doing it like a king," said Bucks; "and he wor a king: more than another dook I know of was; he who was pelted with what I should not like to mention" (dreadfully mysterious), "in the streets of Buckingham, and who then swore he would do for the place, and make the grass grow in the streets."

"And so it did," said I, "when I last saw it; it was fast asleep was Buckingham, and snoring."

"Yes, the dook he moved the 'sizes," said Bucks, fiercely, "and all that, to Aylesbury, to pay them out. Dear me, what a grand place Stowe was in the old days! It was a reg'lar little kingdom, was Stowe, shut in with a ring fence—south front nine hundred and sixteen feet from east to west—I've paced it a thousand times—massy stone lions, and Corinthian statuaries, and all that, picters, and hundreds of weight of books, and water, and green turf, and bushes, and a flight of thirty-one steps from the entrance to the lawn. It wor beautiful. You never clapped eyes on—no, that you didn't——"

"I suppose you know Bucks well?" said I.

"Ah! that I do," said Bucks, "and enough, too, Risborough, and Leighton Buzzard, and Berkhampstead, and Wendover, and High Wycombe (good ale there), and Beaconsfield, and Woburn, and Newport Pagnell. Bucks, too! You should see the gilt swan in the Town-hall how it used to shine on market days."

"What, after the fall of Stowe?" I inquired.

"No," said Bucks, "no, no, sur, long ago; and I knows Olney, too, well, that I do. I've been watchman there, man and boy, thirty years. You've heard of Muster Cowper, the poet?"

"Of course I have, and his Olney Hymns, too," said I.

Bucks (enraptured) cried, "Yes, yes, and Mrs. Unwin, and the pet hares, and all on 'em! Well, I show gentlemen and ladies the house and summer-house where he used to write, and the garden, and where the Throckmortons, who were his friends, used to live. The Ouse, you know, runs through Olney."

"It was a melancholy, dull place, for a melancholy man to go to," said I.

Bucks took no notice of this remark, but broke fresh ground. "We have had a powerful lot of fires lately," said he—"incendiary fires—in Olney: a dozen cottages or more burnt down in a year or two."

"That's a bad job," said Drummer Tom.

"It *is* a bad job," said Bucks. "How they goes and breaks out I don't know, and nobody knows; but we must try and get at the bottom of it, we must. There is no ill-will between master and men, not as I know of"—(stops a moment and slaps his knee) "the whole thing is a mystary, a perfect mystary. P'r'aps it's the gipsies."

"You've seen hard work, I should say, to judge by your face," said I.

"Ay! that I have, sir. I tell you what, sir, I have stood at sheep-washing every day for three weeks, from six in the morning till eight at night, and hardly taken bit or sup from week's end to week's end—hadn't taste for it—nothing but drink for me then."

"Well, but one farmer's sheep would never last three weeks?" I inquired innocently, knowing no better.

"One farmer!" said Bucks, contemptuously; "why, I washed for half the county, so much the score. Tell you how I did it. I stood up to my lines in water, ready to take the ship; then my mate passes me the ship, I takes him head and tail, rubs him well all over, back and belly; then ducks him, and passes out to the mill tail. All the wool as comes off in my hands goes to me for parquisites—it does, true as I sit here, gen'lemen. Terrible hard work, cramping work too, worse than salmon-fishing. Of course you come out now and then for a drop to mix with all the water you've sopped up," he said, sympathisingly. Bucks winked, clenched his teeth, and rubbed his eyes, like the maddened gambler in Hogarth : " I tell you what, muster, I've drunk as much as nine or ten quarts of strong ale a day, besides spirits, and it had no more effect on me at the time than mere water, believe me ; but afterwards I had a raging, burning fever, as they called the deliddleum trimmings, orful bad it was—no that worn't the name, it was something like delcerium screamens, I know there was rum in it. But now, thank God (God be thanked !), I have not touched ale or spirits for these six months ; and look here" (tremendous energy ; invites me to pinch him ; and pinches the frosty healthy reds and purples of his cheek)—" you'd think I'd been just flushed with gin, wouldn't you ? Didn't you ?"

" I confess I thought you had been taking a farewell glass," said I.

" No, not a drop," said Bucks, evidently exhilarated. " Feel this arm : this colour is all nateral colour, and if it wasn't for a little ailment and sourment occasionally, I don't know now, at seventy, whether I was ever better in my life."

" So you have been up, I suppose, to have a day's holiday in London—to see St. Paul's, the British Museum, and Madame Tussaud's wax-works ?" said I.

Bucks whispered, putting his face close to mine, " I'll tell you all about it, for you and I put our horses together very well, and I feel quite neighbourly towards you, though you're a gentleman and I a poor working man."

Guard cries, " Stafford ! Stafford !" Bing, bang, goes the bell.

" Here's how it is : George—my son George—is in London, his going came about thus : he had been a long time without work, and he and his wife were living on me, and that preyed on George, so he got silent and moody like, and sat alone and said nothing, and mumped so that one would have thought he had fallen out with me (my missus, poor dear old 'oman, you must know, has been dead these five year). Well, one morning, a year ago, long afore it was light, I was awoke by something pulling the bed clothes, and I says, says I, 'Who's there? what's up?' and somebody says, 'It's I father.' 'Who's I?' 'Why George; I am going up to London to try and get work, for it breaks my heart to prey upon your little means like this. Good-by, father.' Then I sat up, and tried to reason with the lad; but lor', it wor no use. No. 'So,' said George, 'don't waken my wife, but make it up for me when I'm gone; and pawn this watch of mine for her; and as soon as I can hear of anything I will return, but not a moment before. Don't say anything, father; there's the watch. Good by!' And George went. We never heard of him for nearly a long twelvemonth arter, till last Monday was six weeks, when down comes a letter, sealed with a brave man's thumb—no bad seal neither—telling us as George was doing well, had got regular work in a London brickyard, and was very much respected by all as knew him, and specially by his employer. Says he in the letter, 'Come up, father, directly, and come and arrange about bringing up Mary, and letting us live altogether, comfortable like; and here's money to get my silver watch out of pawn,' says he, in the letter. Well, we were glad, I believe you, and so off I went. I didn't know George at first, with his Crimean beard. 'That isn't George,' said I, to the woman of the house. 'It is George,' said he himself, with his own voice. And so it was.

"Well, the next morning when I awoke, I looks around and wondered where I was. 'What's up,' says I, 'where am I?' 'With George, your own son George,' says he, from the other bed; and so I was. And now I'm going down to Olney, to have a sale, give away and sell all my things, send up my bedding by waggon—because George has got only one bed—and am going to settle in London, convenient to the brick-yard, seeing as how I'm getting a trifle old, and don't like living all alone. Olney is not what it was."

"I see how it is," said I; "all your old friends have died off, and you feel in the way among the young folks who jostle for the new paths."

Bucks replied approvingly, "Yes. Well, I suppose that's about the size of it. But here's my station, Little-Buzzard;

so good morning to you, sur! I wish you a pleasant journey and every excess."

Thus the Buckinghamshire man and I parted.

CHAPTER V.

OPENING A WILTSHIRE BARROW.

WHEN a friendly letter came to me one bright day last spring, from Oldbuck, a country squire down in Ramshire, that great sheep-breeding country, begging me to come and assist at the opening of one of the great Ramshire tumuli, I lost no time in at once packing up my portmanteau and setting off by the S. W. R. to visit my old antiquarian friend, my chum at Eton, and my comrade in the hunting field.

There is a charm in opening anything, whether it be a parcel from the country, or a box of books. I like the first analytic cut at a Stilton, the first ride over a new line of country, the first dip of the line in a new stream. There is a hope and expectancy about it, coupled with a mystery in the unsounded depths of the untried, which I suppose produces the pleasure.

But here the mystery sets one's antiquarian imagination indeed on the burn and on the boil. We might find a skeleton in armour, one of Death's sentinels, with spear and sword laid ready besides its fleshless hands. We might for all I knew, dig up Caractacus himself, or Boadicea's first cousin, or some silent Briton who had seen Cæsar, and drawn a bow at the legionaries. We might see through the fresh, dark earth a great gold torque, one of those collars of twisted bullion that the ancient British kings wore, or one of those tiaras of gold plate that the arch-Druids donned on great mistletoe-cutting festivals, when the men with the white and blue robes and the golden sickles rehearsed Norma on the most tremendous scale in the oak forest, or round the sacred circles of grey stones.

A dog-cart, steered swiftly by Oldbuck, bore me from the

station to the pretty Ramshire cottage, where my antiquarian bachelor friend hoards his flint-axes, elk-horns, torques, old coins, and bronze spear-heads. All I remember that night was a drive under a mile or two of black-boughed elms, among which the stars seemed to hang like fruit, or like the little tapers that twinkle in a Christmas-tree, a door opening into a glowing room, a supper, some seething grog, and a plunge into a feathery ocean of best bed. I dreamed of Caradoc and Vortigern, of Boadicea in Bloomer dress and pink parasol, on a velocipede leading a charge of perambulators on the X Legion, Colonel Bibo commander. I remember a large modern dinner party, with Oldbuck waving a knife and fork at one end of the table, and swearing because the servants did not bring the saddle of mountain; and, when the joint did appear, lo! it was a great tumulus that covered all the table, and at which we all began digging and scratching as if we were so many rabbits.

When I awoke next morning, I thought at first I was in a cathedral, and was staring through a great crimson stained window, but it proved only to be the sun-light shining through the red curtains. They were not angels as I had dreamed in the choir, but the thrushes and blackbirds singing in the laurels outside, boasting of their blue eggs, and their thriving families, and running off such roulades and fiorituras for all the world like a set of angelic music-masters practising, or a little choir of cherubim out for a holiday. When I wrenched myself from bed and looked out at the sky, the colour of a forget-me-not, and saw the sun actually blazing on the glossy laurel leaves, and the swallows studying entomology like so many transmigrated Kirbys and Spences and Rev. Mr. White's of Selborne, I felt quite ashamed of myself in not having been up to watch the pyrotechnics of a Ramshire sunrise, the only thing which Oldbuck acknowledges to be as good as it was in the thirteenth century.

I was busy down stairs watching a monster of a speckled thrush pulling a worm out of the lawn, which he did with a give and take, pull-baker pull-devil principle, like a sailor boy at a rope a little too heavy for him, when the breakfast gong went off and Oldbuck appeared instantly, like Zadkiel at the same summons, in high spirits—with Colt Hoare's Wiltshire under his arm. It lay on the side table beside the frilled ham, and was occasionally referred to during our meal by my enthusiastic friend.

Breakfast done, the dogs loosed, in case of a rabbit, off we set to Peterwood, a fir plantation about a mile away on the downs, where the resting-place of the ancient Briton we were going to wake up, lay. The keepers were to meet us on the upland with pickaxes, spades, and other resurrectionary apparatus.

Oldbuck was great upon the pugnacious, illogical Celt, on the boat-headed Pict, on the long-headed Scot, on the Belgæ, and the Allobrogæ, and the Cangi, on the slow struggle that the Romans had for Ramshire, winning it red-inch by inch, and dyking back the blue-painted deer-slayers with trenched camp and palisade and mound: for the eagle was no dunghill cock, and never turned back to its eyrie till it had driven its beak clean into the brain and heart of its enemy.

It was such a day of soft burning blue, with now and then a triumphal arch of rainbow for Queen April to pass under, weeping like a bride in mingled joy and pleasure. The roadside banks were starred with cowslips, weighed down by tax-collecting bees, and under the tasselled hazels the royal purple of the violets formed a carpet fit for the foot of Venus. As for the bosoming white clouds, their edges were so round and sharp cut that, had they been so much white paper cut out and stuck against the sky, they could not have looked harder edged; but they perpetually changed shape so often, and folded, and lifted, and scattered so much like snow turned into vapour, that they relieved the inquisitive and unsatisfied mind. In the farm-yards that we passed, the pigs were, as usual, wallowing in the straw jungle, or lying on their sides in the sun, in sleeping ecstacy; while the cock, his crest transparent crimson, Sultanised on the sunny side of the rick, where the elder boughs were budding fresh and free as Aaron's rod.

Now we reached the grizzled down, speckled with furze,

churlishly blossoming yellow amidst its thorns, and striking up
an old Roman road, called the Ox Drove, we made straight for a
white board, with its legend warning off trespassers who could
not read, just on the skirts of the fir plantation, where the
barrow was. A long line of tumuli, the labours of that modern barrow-maker, the mole, pointed our way. A shout from
the interior of the wood showed us we were right, as Oldbuck,
quoting Chaucer, a sure sign of his being in the highest spirits,
made a plunge among the firs, and I followed him.

Here was the Briton's burying-place—a low mound, covered
with scanty grass, and brown fir needles, and resinous scaly
fir cones, and just a violet or two, such as sprang from the
tears of the children in the wood. It had been nibbled away
by time, and rains, and heat, and the friction of winds, and
rabbits' feet, and foxes' scratching, till it was now a mere small
wen of earth, half hidden among the coppery fir-trees; it was
very many centuries since that mound was soft, fresh earth,
and since the warm tears fell fast upon its surface. He has slept
long enough. "Very ancient Briton, it is time for you to rise.
It is a fine morning. You will find the country improved.
Steam, sir, that wonderful invention, has revolutionised the
world. I will lend you Pinnock's Catechism, and you shall
read the History of the Norman Conquest, my good man.
These late habits never led to good."

The two keepers, who look like the sextons in Hamlet, are
of a coppery, winter-apple colour, and are of a strong build,
well adapted for grappling with poachers. They both wear
velveteen jackets, stained with hare's blood, and smeared with
fish slime, and their legs are cased in hard leather gaiters, that
look like greaves of rusty iron. To it they go, as if they
were digging for treasure, paring off the pads of turf, chopping
at the clawing roots of the firs, and picking out the broken
bones of mother earth, that men call flints, and geologists
sponges.

Oldbuck advised strongly at once cutting to the centre of
the mound on the Colt Hoare principle, in order to reach the
central burial chamber, which is generally found constructed
of four square stones. We opened, therefore, two trenches, one

in a perpendicular, and the other in a horizontal direction, so as to meet in the centre.

Oldbuck took a shovel, I a spade, and we worked as well as the best; no navigators ever earned their wages more satisfactorily than we did. The elder keeper, with the white moth trout-flies round his rusty hat, toiled after us in vain. We soon came upon the remains of bodies, at first merely small finger bones, brown, and not unlike the mouthpieces of pipes, then the ends of ribs, protruding like roots from the slabs of clay, then empty boxes of skulls, men's and women's, then puzzle-pieces of disjointed vertebræ. Oldbuck was in raptures.

Some bits of rude, black, unglazed pottery were next thrown up, and the brown bones, piled up at the foot of a fir-tree, began now to grow-into a heap that, when put together, would have been sufficient to build up six or seven human beings. But bronze spear head, or brooch, or Celt axe, we found not, much to Oldbuck's mortification.

I could not help thinking that as for the glazed pottery it looked wonderfully like the fragment of a modern Briton's black teapot; but I dared not say so to Oldbuck, who was hanging over it as Romeo might have done over Juliet's glove. It was certainly the base of some culinary vessel, rudely fashioned into a round shape, and totally without ornament, not even that toothed edge, which so resembles the decoration round the edge of a beef-steak pie, and which the modern cook's knife so readily executes.

As for the leg-bones, which had left moulds of themselves in the clay they had so long been imbedded in, they were sadly crumbly and porous, white thread-like roots of bent grass had crept into their sockets, the blue poisonous fibres of couch-grass had grown through their tubes, and matted round the caps of the thigh bones. But the skulls, some male and some female, sent Oldbuck into paroxysms of theories and into prophetical utterances of new ethnological systems.

They were certainly curious, and adapted to set one thinking about the dwellers in the wattled houses, and the blue-stained men who had trod the pleasant downs of Ramshire so many centuries ago. Oldbuck declared violently that they served to establish ingenious Mr. Wright's theory about the deformed skulls found at Uriconium where the Roman swords had operated upon them.

They were of a mean ape-like character, low, flat, and with scarcely an inch of forehead, though the bones over the eyes (where the perceptive faculties are situated) were coarsely prominent. They might have belonged to a sort of aboriginal race, scarcely of greater mental capacity than the Bushman, that had been destroyed by the Celt. The bones of the male skulls were of enormous thickness, twice the thickness of skulls of our own day; so thick that a bronze axe could hardly have split them; while the female skulls were thin as terra-cotta, and fragile as delicate pie-crust. Oldbuck suggested that the men, bareheaded, were out all day in the fen and forest; while the women remained in their huts, so that their bones remained finer and softer. I reminded him of the old story in Herodotus of the battle-field, when it was easy to tell the Persian's from the Egyptian's skull, because the one that had always been kept coddled in a turban was soft, and could be cracked by a stone, while the other, that had been ever exposed to the sun and wind, resisted the utmost degree of violence. Oldbuck kneading some clay out of the cavity of a Briton's skull with his finger and thumb, said the story was "very well indeed," and he would make a note of it for his paper on the subject of this barrow.

Some teeth, too, that we found set Oldbuck off again. They were of a curious, low, animal kind, very narrow and long, more like the front incisor teeth of a beaver than a man's. They had belonged to a young man in the age before dentists; they were still covered with beautiful white enamel, and their edges were not the least worn—only just a little deer's flesh the owner had gnawed; then, the struggle of swords, the blazing huts, the glare of the advancing eagle—then darkness, and this long sleep under the mound.

All this while that we mused and ravelled out our dim theories, the fir wood was pulsing with the brooding, motherly note of the innumerable wood pigeons, the leaping squirrels eyed us from above, the little birds, perpetually thanking God, sang their secrets to each other among the bristling fir-apples, and over the golden floor of moss and the last year's leaves raced the rabbits, frightened, yet purposely and unrestrainably inquisitive.

"And here, then," cried Oldbuck, putting himself in a Hamlet position, with a skull of the low barbaric type in the palm of his thin, pale, intellectual hand, "under these draughty trees, with the surf sounding ever through their prophesying branches, must this Bushman tribe of hunters and fishermen have dwelt, long centuries ago. Here their women must have cooked the deer's flesh, and plaited the wattled huts, and spread the fern leaves for the beds, and prepared the arrows, and nursed the children; here the sinewy men, with the low brows and blue-stained limbs, must have wielded the flint-axe, darted the spear, and raced with naked feet over the springy down, with no thought of Rome, or of the swift-winged eagle, till one brooding day came the legionaries in close phalanx, with a blaze of gold and purple, with a cloud of stones from the slings heralding their approach, and stinging showers of arrows from the light armed. They circle the wood, there is a crash of axes, a jar of swords, a burst of groans and curses, keen flames start up in a sudden volcano of vengeance; then a great silence, and through the twilight I see grassy mounds rising on the skirts of the wood, looking towards the lower country."

Here the keeper wiped his forehead, and threw out some more bones, with a reflection that they were "mortal old," which seemed to cover all he thought upon the subject, though he did go on to tell us that the barrow we were opening was in a line with two others, some distance off, and that the trench from which the earth was taken for the barrow then specially under consideration, was still to be seen a few hundred yards off. It was his "kippur's" opinion that the large flints found immediately over the bones were trod in upon them for security, and with malice aforethought. The "kippur" also was of opinion that the black particles here and there among the earth were wood ashes, whether placed there on purpose or not he could not tell, not he.

Oldbuck here remarked that it became me to observe that

the six or seven bodies had evidently been buried in a hurry, as after a battle or massacre, and had certainly not been interred with decency, or with care, or affectionate consideration. Had this tumulus been that of a chieftain's in time of peace, it would have contained amber beads, or gold torque, or spear head, or flint axe.

Here the "kippur," who had been examining the barbaric skull, put his enormous dirty notched thumb on a dent in it, and asked Oldbuck, sharply, "What that was?" Oldbuck at once—with an antiquarian's usual daring imaginativeness—boldly said, "An evident contusion from the blow of a blunt instrument, probably an axe;" which seemed to satisfy the keeper, and set him digging more savagely than ever. Oldbuck bade me observe that the bones lay all near the centre of the mound, and towards either side beyond the centre they ceased altogether.

Oldbuck was very entertaining on his way with me to the station. He told me how the finest gold collar ever found in Britain had been discovered in the loose earth that a fox had scratched out; how in Scotland a curious helmet of the Bruce period was found jammed between two rocks; and how in Ireland the relic case of a bell of great antiquity was discovered on the top of a mountain, where, if not placed by some rebels for safety, it must have remained for centuries.

What a walk back we had over those Ramshire downs, where the young winds seem to be put out to nurse. What mists of liquid opal and pearl veiled the grassy slopes, what white fans of sunbeams pointed me out my way to Chalkton, whose grey steeple I could see in the distance with the gilt weathercock on its apex, blazing as if it were melting in the sunshine. How beautiful are the different cloudy blues of the distances getting more radiant and spectral as they receded from you.

The awkward hares limped before us on the dark chocolate-coloured fallows, or over the broad dim sward of the down, speckled black with furze-bushes, or round by the dark battalions of firs that seemed filing down to meet some invisible commander-in-chief at some special spot of concentration. The rabbits cantered over the road as if running perpetual errands, and the blackbirds chinked and shot to and fro like pall-maker's black shuttles.

The shadows raced before us along the broad white road, putting out the sunshine with fitful extinguishment, having the effect of an opening and closing eye perpetually on us as we walked. Even the old battered milestones, grey with lichen and spotted orange here and there, cheered us by their lessening numbers, and soon the brown thatched roofs and white walls of Chalkton appeared before us in a vision of sunlight.

Hearty red faces were on the platform, and round hats and pleasant eyes under them ; and just as the train came champing and snorting up, slewing round its vertebrated back and tail, Oldbuck shook my hand warmly, and slipped into it the brain-pan of an ancient Briton, as a remembrance of the opening of a Ramshire barrow.

CHAPTER VI.

MY FIRST AND LAST RAILWAY COLLISION.

IF you mount the steps leading to No. 3, Upas-tree Court, Inner Temple (third floor, left hand), you will find on the outer door, in white letters, black rimmed, on an oak ground, my name.

On a foggy morning on the twenty-second November, that gentleman (myself) had resolved to go down on important legal business (first brief) to Wiltshire, my native county.

I was deep in a legal dream, and wandering through a cloudy Westminster, where difficulties entangled me, and getting into a sort of Castle-in-the-Air Chancery, when I was knocked back into life by Mrs. Dustall, my laundress, calling out,

"Seven o'clock, sir, and such a nasty morning."

(She needn't have said that.) Thump went my boots. In a moment I was splashing in my bath like a tame merman learning swimming. But something troubled me, and hung about me, like a damp shirt. What was it ?

IT WAS A PRESENTIMENT.

A foreboding of evil it was, and I will say it to the day my death, and would have said so even if nothing had happened. It was as a nail in my boot, as a whitlow on my hand; as an invisible millstone it hung about my neck; and I could not find the string that tied it on, so that I might cut it.

Breakfast. Butter in pats, clean-stamped as Greek cameos, bread floury white, toast warm and absorbent, tea balmy and fragrant as Nepenthe—which some suppose it was—mutton-chop juicy as a peach.

"Mrs. Dustall, tie on that direction. See if that barrel of oysters has come. There! bless me! I've forgotten my boot-jack! Strap up that portmanteau. Thank you, Mrs. Dustall. Now call a cab." The laundress runs to St. Clement's cab-stand, soured at being driven out in curling papers into the cold and wide, wide world. She calls the seven-caped cabman reading aloft, upon his aerial seat, his reeking Daily Telegraph. But I take five minutes more to glance at the Times.

French Invasion. Leader on Thames Drainage. Another leader—Abolition of the Lord Mayor's Show, &c. A bottom paragraph, at the bottom of the third column of the fifth page:

"TERRIBLE RAILWAY ACCIDENT."

Let me skim it. "Carelessness of pointsman—red signal mistaken for blue. Old story—foggy weather. Only three men killed—stoker mortally injured." Cambridge line, of course. Old story—Why not hang a director? Who cares to read railway accidents?

"Oh, cab! Thank you, Mrs. Dustall. Call the Cabby up for my trunk and hat-box. Mind and send my letters on. Keep my door safe shut. Good-by!"

I longed to breathe on the Wiltshire downs, where the strong-limbed hares enjoy a vacation uninterrupted by the opening of law courts, and where rabbits are regardless of Westminster. Tidd is on my hat-box, a neat little book on Real Property in my great-coat pocket. I was off. I passed through the black jaws of Temple Bar, but for one trifling regret, a free and happy man. I knew that in less than an hour I should pass, as out of a cave, from the tawny city fog into the bright autumn air, with just a dash of ice in it, so that the streams which bi-

seet our partridge stubble-fields down in Wiltshire will look
like iced sherry and water.

But "there's always a somethink," as my laundress, Mrs.
Dustall, who is given to forming proverbial lozenges from her
life experiences, says; and there was "somethink" now. We
all of us have Damocles' swords hanging over our turtle-soup
dishes. There is always (if I may use the homely but most
powerful simile) a button off the shirt of our temper. There
is always a corn twitching upon the mental foot; so that our
perfect balance of health, temper, and wealth is not very long
together maintained.

A fretful presentiment of a key lost, or a desk left unlocked,
buzzed about me like a little mosquito demon. In and out it
went, almost visible, through this cab window and out at the
other. What was it? I locked my dressing-case, my studs
are all right in my shirt-front, my desk I put away in a fire-
proof cupboard. What was it? "There's indeed always a
somethink," philosophical Mrs. Dustall!

I crane out of window: yes, trunk with the red star all right,
parchment label fluttering prettily in the wind; hamper, "Glass
with care;" all chained to the rail on the roof of the cab; hat-
box, plaid, umbrella in oilskin case all right. Yet still that mosquito of evil. Still the demon gnat flying over my nerves.
What can it be that pinches me like a tight boot, and yet has
no name? *I have it. It was that railway accident I was
reading*, falling upon that previous presentiment; it was that
which, finding some unguarded loophole of my nerves, had got
in, disagreed with me, and done the mischief. Strange that I,
who have skimmed over hundreds of railway accidents, to get
quickly to the end and see the total deaths, should be moved
by the loss of three men on the *famous* Eastern Counties!

I arrive at the station. A slamming of doors, the wave of a
red hand-flag, a smother of white steam under the station roof,
and we are off: shot out into the fog, that wraps us at once
in its dingy arms: rattle, battle—that is the brick walling by
the engine sheds; clamp, champ—that is the great fire-horse,
striking out its brave limbs; jolt, rattle! jolt, battle!—that is
crossing the turn-tables: that fellow in the green corduroy

jacket, bending on the low crank-handle, is, I believe, the pointsman.

"Pointsman:"—something bit me, as if a flea had got into my mind. Why, that is what they called the fellow killed yesterday at Splashread Bridge, on the Eastern Counties line. What malicious demon is it puts these things into a nervous man's head just as he is settling himself comfortably in the corner of a railway carriage, with Tidd on the seat before him, and a neat little book on Real Property fastened to it by a strap? I suppose it is that special small demon whose peculiar province it is to disturb men's equilibrium, and generally unchristianise one by blunting one's penknife, spoiling one's pen, ironing off one's shirt-buttons, mislaying one's studs, making one's boots pinch, and rendering it impossible to arrange one's white tie with the bow anywhere but at the back of the neck. The fog thins; it is getting positively bright, though we are not at Kingston yet; fields widen, trees and hedges flow by us as if an inundation was bearing them away, or as if we were in the ark, and were drifting on fast past them.

Three stations soon distanced. Whiz, faster!—whiz, faster! slide like a bullet through a gun barrel. Whiz!—that's a viaduct arch. Whish!—click!—clack! that's another station and some shunting rails.

Flight of white telegraph washing-lines, miles of signal posts, and split red and white targets, and dull red and green lamps, like prize jewels. Faster, till it takes the breath away. Out with the repeater and time it. Fast as the pulse—one, two, three!—fifty miles an hour if it is a yard.

Slower! slower! now we slacken! I thought we could not hold the pace. Slower! My opposite friend gets anxious and looks out of window. We can't be going to stop at Farnborough station? . . .

CRASH! SMASH! BASH!

Here imagine the end of the world. Fancy yourselves animalcule, shut up by accident inside a huge Brobdignag farmer's watch with a hizz, whiz, and centrifugal railway rush, when snap goes the mainspring. Imagine those small creatures' feelings of horror, surprise, and astonishment, and you

E

have ours, minus the fear. I felt no nerve shaken, though my head was giddy and my spine was numbed. Imagine a solitary man in a factory when a boiler bursts in the room above, and the mill falls to pieces like a card house suddenly round his ears. Imagine a quiet man looking out of his bed-room window, accidentally, as he is shaving, and seeing the deluge coming up to the front door for a morning visit. Imagine a Pompeian just home from Athens, and awoke by the red lava stealing under his bedroom door.   *   *   *

Bang! shiver! smash! bash! then an awful lull and death-stop as of a mainspring run out. It was as if the train had been struck full butt by a successful Armstrong shot. It was as if we had been riding inside a battering ram, and had at last come full smash on a wall which had been too much for us. I never rode on a cannon-ball, and don't want to do so; but an eighty-pounder when it beats in a French ship's bulwarks could scarcely, I think, hit harder than this.

Open fly the doors, some dozen white-faced men sprang through the windows like harlequins in a practising class, out poured the frightened people, lately so red and jolly; but a minute ago flirting, dogmatising, sneering, scandalising, frowning, disputing, now all full of one thought of terror, all become, in that one terrible moment, as brothers and sisters: so levelling is misfortune. We were lately in a good ship, all sail set, flags flying, no danger aft or fore or on the lee. Suddenly we had struck on a reef; we were leaking—we were sinking—we were a total wreck. Heaven knew only what still was left for us. It might be but a moment to live for some of us. Perhaps already bleeding men were groaning their last under that pile of ruin where the red flame rose from.

The guards, white as wood ashes, were running about, flags in hand, like the fuglemen of a scattered regiment. Far away to the left, at the end where the charge had been, the engine, a heap of broken metal, was roaring like a lion taken in the toils, and sending up waving pillars of flames; its wood-work had taken fire, and was spreading to the fragments of the next carriage.

As for the passengers embracing, or silent in staggered

groups, they were unanimously white in the face. One strong-
faced man was being helped from a carriage, his face seeming
to ooze everywhere with blood. A lady was carried away,
cut, bruised, and nearly insensible, to the little shed of a station.
A young farmer, seated on his striped carpet bag, was covering
his face with his hands to squeeze out a jarring brainache, produced by his being driven against a man opposite. Others
stunned, shaken, and bruised, were consoling, or being con-
soled, or running to see what damage had been done to the
train, and what danger still existed. There were messengers
racing to Farnborough, three miles off, to telegraph to
London for help; there were guards and porters running up
and down the line to put up danger signals, and keep trains
nearly due from heaping more ruin on us.

My presentiment had then come true.

My first business, on seeing no help was needed, was to wrap
up my plaid and books, and run to the ruin of the engine and
the actual spot of the smash. I found that we had driven, at
almost express speed, into a ponderous goods train, laden with
timber and blocks of asphalte, massive and unyielding as stone.
This we had partly driven back and stove in, pounding the
guard carriage behind to rags and pulp. On this bulwark our
own engine had beaten itself to pieces, by a series of leans,
jolts, and charges: it lay a wreck, the funnel torn to pieces
and scattered about the platform, the iron plates jammed in, as
if they were deal wainscoting; the buffers broken to morsels;
the giant wheels dismounted and buried in the earth; the
whole crushed and powerless as a silenced battery.

Beyond, and some yards further, lay the timber-truck, its
roof torn off; at a distance lay the planks splintered; as for
the guard-carriage, it was torn to pieces as a band-box might
be when a drunken man has stamped on it and trod it
to bits. It lay in pulpy shreds and fragments as of rotten
wood, without shape and void, and out of the pounded mass—
reduced as in a pestle and mortar, in a desperate attempt of
some starving apothecary to make deal soup—we picked a torn
rag with a fragment of the stoker's bread-and-cheese, and two

E 2

jammed and squeezed red books of by-laws, which looked as
if they had been disinterred at Pompeii.

But the torn planks and broken iron, and snapped-off wheels
and rods, were as nothing to us—though they rose, like the ruins
of a cottage destroyed by a hurricane, on the rails—when the
fire of the engine began roaring up in a smoky red and yellow
pyramid, with a bellow and troubled roar as if howling for victims. There, busy amid the ruins, the scared fireman and black-
faced stoker were shovelling in gravel to prevent the boiler
bursting or the flame spreading. Before the great leaping-out
violence we all fell back like the Babylonians in the old prints
when the furnace doors were opened to swallow up the children
of Israel, and the furnace was heated " seven times hotter than
it was wont to be heated :" we were all then, I suppose, in
that unconscious state of excitement, that if the earth had suddenly opened and swallowed us all up, train, wreck, passengers,
we should hardly have made a remark.

Having once seen the pile of débris, carriage roofs, iron bars,
planks, and wheels, I employed myself, in accordance with old
habits, in beating slowly over the whole scene of the disaster,
determined by graphic observations, fresh as I was to such
scenes, to realise fully the horror and danger of such accidents.
As I walked along the line of carriages, here and there crushed
or sprung, the first thing I stepped on was a round bar of iron
or steel, thicker than my wrist when my two coats are on ; it
had been, I imagine, part of the under work of the engine, and
was snapped short in two. The next thing I picked up was a
jagged piece of the funnel, still black and smoking : it now
stands on my mantelpiece, a lively record of my escape. I also
found and handled a huge screw made of iron, bound with
brass, which, perhaps, had formed the inner socket of one of
the buffers. It was cleft in two, as a sharp knife would chop
an apple at one stroke.

Under the carriages, blocks of iron, like the fastenings of
sleepers, were strewn for thirty or forty yards ; and in one of
the carriages ten or twelve from the engine, the floor planks
were torn up in great jags, protruding three or four feet, showing beneath them (between them and the ground) broken

wood, iron hooping, and huge gutta-percha circular slabs—
probably breaks or springs—torn violently in two. On one seat
lay a crumpled Times, with holes rent in it; and on another a
tumbled shawl, the fringe of which was entangled in the teeth
of the splintered and started planks. When I remembered an
old tradition about railway accidents, recommending you in
such cases to lie down flat on the floor, I trembled to think of
the paralysed victims of such a theoretical folly.

Now we were all safe, some of us began to grow cheerful,
wishing to remove the ladies' fear. A young barrister who
was near me, proposed, if we were kept many hours waiting,
to attack the luggage-van, and distribute the barrels of oysters
among the hungry passengers. Others asked the guards at
what o'clock the next collision would take place. I believe we
were all grateful to God for our escape. We must have been
scarcely human if we had not been; but the mind, when over-
strained, finds comfort in such relief, and so, to the end of the
world, droll witnesses at murder trials and odd events at the
reading of wills must produce an irresistible laugh.

While we were waiting for the express engine laden with
navvies from London, and for help from Farnborough, I strolled
away from the reassured passengers through a side gate, to
which a farmer's gig was tied, and walked along the quiet
country road, enjoying the calm fresh sunlight and the bright
chill November blue air.

It was humiliating to man, the monarch of the universe, to
see what little effect the all but death of some three hundred
human beings had caused the animal and vegetable kingdom of
Fleetpond, near Farnborough. The white and dun cows were
feeding leisurely and untroubled in the meadows, the rooks were
tossing about over the heath, the sparrows were visiting from
tree to tree, and the dead leaves were rustling in troops down
the lanes as if returning gay, in companies, from the funeral of
Summer. And there, where the beech shone red, and the few
birch leaves, dry, and yellow, and wrinkled, were wet and
golden with the morning dew, I could hear a farmer pulling
up his gig on the crown of the red-brick railway arch, just
above where the trains' smoke had blackened it, discoursing as

an eye-witness of the late collision or duel of the trains. Thus he put it to the friend he met, pointing with a shake of his fat head at the wreck. I was a long way from him, but I have the keen, practised ears of a hunter, and the air was clear and resonant, so, putting my head on one side, I caught it all as in a net:

"Lookum here, Friend Jackson, I was just crossing this bridge when th' express passed, and by the time I got up to yon, where the lady and children are coming, I sees the other train on the same line. I knew there would be something happen, so I push the old mare to a gallop and got up just as ur run into un."

He was not a graphic man, and seemed to have no further thought of the accident.

One thing was quite apparent, and formed my moral of the affair:—that it is the universal custom in railway collisions to hush up everything as much and as soon as possible. The broken iron was spirited away, the doors of the carriages where the floors were crushed were closed, the bruised persons led away, the ruins patched up, and the earth smoothed over the might-have-been grave as craftily and quickly as possible. Every moment the memory of the guards became more and more indifferent. A fog every moment opaquer rose between us and the accident. No one was hurt, nothing was injured. The engine, worth two thousand pounds, was a trifle, and might be repaired. The stoker was unharmed. The line would soon be cleared. We should be sent on to Basingstoke, where the Salisbury train was waiting us. It was no one's fault; no guard present had ever been in more than two collisions before. The head porter at Farnborough thought it better not to speak; it was "not his place, you know," and the company did not like speaking. You never, from anybody, could have gathered that we, the express train, had run into a goods train that ought not to have been on the line, that they were shunting to get out of our way a bad ten minutes too late; and lastly, that danger signals, both at station and on train, if up, had been utterly useless, and had been disregarded. One would really never have thought that three hundred Englishmen had just been driven over a place of graves and escaped by a miracle.

The next morning, as I sat at a quiet rectory window in Wiltshire, I opened the Times and read the following:

"FRIGHTFUL ACCIDENT ON THE LONDON AND SOUTH-WESTERN RAILWAY.—An accident of a very alarming character, and which might have been attended by a most fearful sacrifice of human life, occurred on Tuesday at mid-day at the Fleet-pond station of the London and South-Western Railway. It appears that the 11 A.M. express train left the Waterloo terminus at the fixed time, and proceeded with safety, notwithstanding the density of the fog which prevailed, until within a few miles of its first stoppage, Basingstoke, where it was due at 12.15. The Fleetpond station is a very small place, and the officials there having a goods train in charge, proceeded to shunt it, in order to allow the express train to pass. To prevent any accident the usual signals were displayed at the station and by the goods train, but it would appear that, owing to the fog or some other cause, the driver of the express train could not see them; nor were the men at the station aware of the approach of that train, for without any warning the express rushed through past the station at a rapid rate, and crushed the back portion of the goods train. The collision was most fearful, and it is nothing short of a miracle that the lives of a large number of people were not sacrificed. The locomotive belonging to the express train—a very magnificent engine, worth upwards of £2000—was almost broken to pieces; the tender and guard's van of the express train were also destroyed, as were likewise a number of the trucks belonging to the goods train. The shrieks of the passengers were awful, and it was feared at first that several were killed; as soon, however, as the first shock was over, an investigation was made, and it was found that, although the passengers had received a terrible shaking, and several were more or less bruised, yet no loss of life had occurred. It may be a matter of surprise how the driver and stoker of the train escaped with their lives, considering that the engine was destroyed; but we are informed that these two men, on seeing the imminent danger they were in, threw themselves down, and thus escaped injury. Information of the catastrophe was at once forwarded to the Waterloo station, and a number of men were immediately despatched to render what assistance they could, and to clear the line, but, fortunately, the line had been cleared before their arrival, so that the traffic on the railway was not impeded."

All the evening of the day of the collision I felt like a man who has been thrown heavily out hunting, not bone-broken, but jarred from top to heel, with brow headache and general sense of disturbance. Now I began to understand why timid men shut the carriage window when a black tunnel swallows them: why, when a train slackens speed or stops, a dozen staring, anxious heads emerge like tortoises from carriage windows. Now I know why fretful men thrust the reeking Times into your hands just as you leave a station, and with fore-fingers jammed on a small paragraph about a collision, ask you angrily if "it isn't shameful, sir?"

CHAPTER VII.

A RIDE TO STONEHENGE.

WE were lapped in a rose-coloured cloud the last five miles from Salisbury to Wilton, as the train that bore me towards the breezy Wiltshire downs drove through the sunset which tinged red the white vapours that drifted on either side of us from the wide black cannon-mouth of the engine funnel. I imagined myself in that "ship of the gods," or divine balloon, so famous in Hindoo mythology. I was rushing through the clouds at the rate of forty miles an hour: did the old Pagan divinity travel faster than our modern Christian mortality?—I trow not.

Need I say what I noted down as interesting from the square window of my padded carriage? Fancies not worth the noting,

the reader may perhaps think : " stubbles bristling like yellow
hair-brushes;" "green weeds wavering on the brook like drowned
Ophelia's hair, or a mermaid's emerald tresses;" "the shy
slant, shunting off the rooks as they cross the train's double-
columned path ;"—verse-notes, such as " a crow song :"

> " With a flapping, flap, flap, flap."

At length I, a knight-errant of literature free for a day from
the smoky riot and the swampy mud of Babylon, shut up my
note-book, pocket my pencil, and lie back to hear the gossip of
the carriage ; a second-class carriage, full of damask-checked
country people, hearty, honest, and untroubled by fears and
suspicions.   There is a large farmer, whose broad stomach is
tapestried by a huge flowered waistcoat, whose seals are as big
as a child's fist ; and some young country " chaps " out for a
holiday.   Their eyes converse in kindly exchange, but their
tongues are not fluent.   Listen to them for a moment, just as
if you put your ear to a counting-house speaking tube.   " Well,
Jim, how *was* you?"   " Well, I be nicely.   How's mother ?"
" Thankee, she be purely.   And how's Harry ?"   " Fust rate."
" That's right.   Where be you going ?"   " T' old folks."
" That's bravely."

Here I cork up the tube.   After some discussion on wool, a
sharp little man in the corner, with staring blood-shot eyes and
a droll mouth, informs us generally that there was a capital
card in the carriage with him from Warminster—" a good'un,
sure-*ly :*" he had a bottle of port and a bottle of brandy, had
the good'un.   It appeared he had distributed the fluid largely,
particularly to the little tailor with the tell-tale eye-balls ; he
was volubly enraptured with the wit and vivacity of the
" good'un," who seemed to have been a returned digger ; for at
the stations where he got out for beer to wash down the port
and brandy, he had always called to them to make haste, for
" the big smoke " (the train) was just going off.   The little
tailor was (episodically) severe against the modern bankruptcy
laws, and advised any one who was going to fail to do it for a
large sum while he was about it.   He was also satirical on the
severity of rich men on poor men's delinquencies, particularly

drunkenness (here he innocently smiled). If poor So-and-So got drunk at his club-feast and missed work next morning, Mr. So-and-So was astonished, and stopped the day out of his wages; but if Mr. So-and-So was the worse for liquor, lord he was at his own house, and could get from under the table without being seen, steal off to bed, and tell every one next day he had been confined with a cold. "Oh, I know all their tricks," said he, and his eyes grew redder and funnier than ever.

"Ashcliff," cries the guard, and the little tailor, rolling out a small avalanche tied up in a blue handkerchief from under the seat, wishes all the gentlemen a very good morning. The door slams—the whistle sounds—and we are away.

Then, to break the silence, a muffled-up man with a weak voice, and a wrapper round his mouth to give him still more of a conspirator effect, begins about America. He was on board the "Arab," going to America, when Mrs. Trollope was writing her impressions of a country she had not yet seen. He wondered where Catlin was gone to?—Catlin, whom he had travelled with down the Yellow Stone River, when the Black-feet were on the banks looking for buffalo. He had complaints of the arrogance of John Fenimore Cooper. He had laughed with Sam Slick at his Novia Scotia stories. He had seen Irving at Astor House. He chatted about Barnum's ploughing with elephants, and starting an exhibition of photographs of all the unmarried beauties in America. He had been in the theatre the night when the papers were to be read, in competition for the prize of one hundred guineas, offered by the Editor of the *New Orleans Picayune* for the greatest lie that could be invented. The hotel dinners in America, were they good? He should rather think so. Once, at Cincinnati, a man cried to him 'cross the table, "Why, stranger, we began together, yet you've got down to prairie turkey, and I am only at my roast meat. I guess, if you carry on business half as smart as you do eating, you'll lick every tarnation soul in this darned great city." The fact was, the poor fellow had thought it necessary to eat his way right through the bill of fare. The Indian element in the Yankee blood, the effect of a subtle climate on the Saxon brain, and the result of the junction of

Irish and American fun, kept us talking till the guard cried "Wilton," and I had to shake Mystery by the hand, and wish him good-bye.

I was soon in the Wiltshire Inn, where the landlady, a portly dame with the softest bloom of rose possible upon her cheek, received me with due formula. In sheets well blanched and lavendered I rehearsed my burial, and lowered myself down into a temporary grave of sleep. Next morning, directly after breakfast, I had my horse saddled, to start for Stonehenge.

While the horse is preparing, and his stable toilette is completing, I go into the inn-yard. The stable-door was a sort of Family Bible to the ostler. It was a genealogical tree, a bundle of Fasti, a Ragman's Roll, a Doomsday Book, all in one, to the sporting landlord. It was nailed on the inside with four or five tiers of racers' shoes, inside each of which semicircles was a narrow slip of parchment, inscribed with the horse's name and deeds. Such names, and such deeds! suggestive of glossy, satin-coated chestnuts; flea-bitten greys; pepper-speckled blacks; white-nosed jet mares; strong-chested and sure-limbed fiery roans, to whom rails were mole-hills, and seventeen-feet-wide brooks petty obstacles to snort and fly over; all duly recorded in broad, clumsy, or fairy shoes.

The inn was a pleasant little Wiltshire cottage, with a pendant bird's nest of an oriel window hanging over the porch; just such a one as you might expect Benedict, in slashed blue hose and carnation-coloured cloak, to serenade with theorbos in the dead of night. The grey thatch looks neat and grave as the combed-down hair of a rustic on Sunday. There is a sort of Sabbath peace in the air; a truce of God is in the sky, those larks going up through the blue are its heralds. God bless them! The laurels glitter in the sun like so many little emerald mirrors; the standard roses struggle with the bass bandages that imprison their young beauties to the old dead sticks, their withered husbands. I can read the titles on their curled and sodden parchment labels, as they flutter with gay promises in the January sun,—"La Reine Margot," "La belle Duchesse." The crisp sharp grass glitters with a rainbow blossom of dew that, out of the sun, lies on it in a grey plush

gloss, like the nap on new cloth of silver. I can see the foot-
prints, duller and deeper in colour, where the landlord has
passed this morning, to go and pick Brussels sprouts. They
trend round by that empty pond, where the dimple which is
the spring is candied over with ice, just as you would spread
candied silver paper, not less thin, crystalline, and transparent,
over a pot of new-made jam. Winter would pot us all if he
could, like this spring; but we will not remain potted, though
he does paint our windows with ice-flowers, and fur our palings
with crystal ermine fur. I observe with a painter's relish the
little white trench the drippings have made under the eaves,
the little net of blood-drops that dark-leaved creeper is spreading
over the wall, and especially the stars of white and yellow
lichen black and savage Time is writing his ciphers in, in his
own difficult language, over the stones. I remark with new
delight that burning-bush of the holly-tree, that burns but does
not consume, its berries red and glossy as sealing-wax kisses
on February love-letters; I marvel now to see it with leaves
as of gilt transparent to the sun, so that a sanctity and con-
secrating halo seem to surround the tree which old legend-
makers, marking its thorny leaves and blood-drop berries,
declared was the bush that furnished the crown of thorns for
our Saviour's suffering head. As for the windows, they shine
and sparkle like so much gold plate, so that the meanest cottage seems now to be the residence of some ostentatious gold-
smith, lavish in his display.

With a largesse to the ostler and the boots, and cheered by
their ostentatious blessing as they give a last pull at my horse's
belly-band, so that now no lady in the land is laced one half so
consumptively tight, I push forth, humming over my scraps of
rhyme; hammering at this one's rivets, soldering up that one's
leaky joint, or welding together two stray but congruous verses,
like any wandering troubadour of the good old times, when
nobody grumbled, and everybody insisted, from sheer good
nature, on paying double taxes. I ride by navvies with brick-
red cheeks, heavy, clay-clogged boots, tucked-up trousers, and
smocks knotted across their bull-chests. I think of the Berse-
ker Norsemen striding to their ships, and almost expect to see

the Black Raven banner leaning against the wall of the "Swan's Nest Inn" I have just left. The very first person I met as I left the old house behind me where Sir Philip Sydney once wrote his life and his heroics, and Spenser his *Faery Queen ;* where Ben Jonson walked, and Shakspere perhaps acted; was the village blacksmith, sturdy in his leather apron, carrying in his arms a heavy trayful of blue-grey horseshoes ready for the stable, calcined and fresh from the fire ; he carried them, good man, as gingerly as though they had been new caps going home from the milliner's ; and behind him came that cheerful sight, an old English labourer going to his daily toil, followed by his warning shadow nodding along the road-side wall.

> " Old Humphrey plods to his daily toil,
>   His shadow lags after, high on the wall ;
> Both are bowed, and crooked, and bent,
>   For the workhouse still is the end for us all."

So, thought I, not unjustly will sing the Chartist poet, who sees the cruel end of our labouring poor.

On I rode, now breaking from the walled-in lanes, glittering with wet, where the sun shone on the water-channelled ruts, driving clouds of frightened birds before me from the hedges or the loaf-shaped wheat-ricks, as I pushed my mare, Red Nancy, over the low fence, where the poplars nodded in stately company; I toiled up over the white stubble to the higher down, skirting the young wheat-fields that, like bucklers of emerald, spread themselves against the sunny horizon that was serrated with files and squadrons of lancer firs, that seemed marching and gathering for miles over the slopes. As for the downs, they stretched their dun-hued and crop-eared banks, spotted dark with furze, far as I could see. I looked out on the horizon as on a prairie of rolling bluffs, or on a great chart, with its squares and triangles of various shades of brown, yellow, and green. You could see where larger masses of the furze, dark and thorny, had sent out skirmishers and outposts of seedling bushes, which stretched beyond the main body in dots and specks as far as the chalky cups that the shepherds dig to catch the rain-water in.

Now as I feel my horse like a proud sea under me, a per-

petually advancing billow leaping and moving, with me riding
on its crown, and hear the pad, pad, of the hollow turf under her
ringing hoofs, I troll out a care-defying song, half-memory,
half improvise :—

> O tinkle went the bridle rings,
>   O pad, pad, went the hoof,
>   The merry sound made the heart of me glad,
>   And the blue devils keep aloof ;
> They'd hounded me long, but I left them behind
> As I tracked the sun and hunted the wind.
>
>   Chink went the stirrup-steel and spur,
>   Chink went the gold in my purse ;
>   I galloped on with no thought in the world,
>   Happy as child at nurse.
> After me flew the bullying blast,
> Before me the white cloud flew fast, fast.
>
>   Ting, ting, chorused the bridle chains,
>   Talking to one another ;
>   As I galloped over the down and moor ;
>   The blue sky, like a mother,
> Watching me still with unswerving eye,
> Chided me because I tried to fly.
>
>   Tink, tinkle went the chattering bit,
>   And pad, pad, went the shoes ;
>   Both striving strong with an equal song
>   In time to my carolling muse.
> The blue-devils raced, and galloped, and ran,
> But they could not catch the laughing man.

I dash past numberless fir plantations, where the thick green
crystals of the firs contrast with the silver stripings of the
birch, and the tight dull silver of the beech-bark. What is
that white board on a pole that stands out sharp and keen
against the dark wood?—a knightly challenge to all comers
from some golden statue of an elfin who is living in the green
darkness of this dim wood ? No! the usual game-laws'
churlish threat :

> " ALL PERSONS FOUND TRESPASSING
> WILL BE PROSECUTED WITH THE UTMOST "——

" rigour of the law," probably : but here some sturdy poacher's
knife had split off the rest, and left it as a laughing-stock.

Away I go past water-meadows, through villages, through Winterbourne Stoke, where I bent to the long up-and-down Amesbury road, that leads to the higher down, where is the Giants' Dance, as Stonehenge is called by Geoffrey of Monmouth, who, lying with his usual dignity, declares that all the stones were brought from Kildare by the enchanter Merlin; the Emperor Ambrosius, who had put Hengist the Saxon to death, wishing to commemorate his victory, and celebrate the great massacre of King Vortigern and the 460 Britons, by a suitable monument.

That side of the sun shone only that shone the way to Stonehenge, whither the long gold-ruled lines of sunbeam pointed me as with golden rods; in the distance I could look back and see the weathercock of Winterbourne Stoke church shining like a burning diamond in the sunshine, wherein the tower seemed to float like a great ark, for then the morning's fog had all burnt into blue of a liquid sapphire colour, and the white clouds were swollen out like the sails of angel-manned vessels. Flying clouds, would I could mount you, and so get quicker to the old Druid's temple! But as this, I suppose, is hardly possible, I dig my spurs into Red Nancy, who answers the appeal with a leap like a deer, and away we go at a pace that is a caution to livery-stable keepers, printing the dry, dun hide of the down turf with Greek omegas, and spurning out the blunt parallel lines that the wheels of the turf-waggons have made; soon rising over the left-hand bank of down, I see the huge wide stones which form the old Temple of the Sun, that Diodorus Siculus mentions: that is to say, he mentions that there was a sacred temple of Apollo in Britain, which is quite enough for your imaginatively hot though grey-headed antiquarian.

This is that ring of vast pillars of hewn-out sandstone, brought from somewhere near Marlborough, that wrong-headed Inigo Jones would have it was a Roman temple, about which there has been more ink than enough shed. This is the Stone-edge, or rather Stone-hang, the Saxon hanging-stones, that, according to those twaddling fairy-book old chroniclers, came first from Africa to Ireland, and then from Ireland to Wiltshire; which, considering that Pickford and his vans were then in chaos, must have been rather an expensive transportation than otherwise. Old Caxton wrote about them, and that addle-pated gossip, Aubrey, too, who compares them to the celebrated Grey-wethers near Marlborough. They look very wild and grey as I ride up to them on Red Nancy, who paws and snorts as if I were spurring her to do battle with a ring of giants. I draw up under one of the great Egyptian doorways, my head coming but half way up the grey shaft, which, as it is twenty feet high, is no wonder. As I stand chipping at one of the plinths, which, though tufted with a grey hair of moss, and much starred and crusted with dusky grey and orange lichens, breaks red and fine in the grain, as if just from the quarry, a buzz as of a tremendous organ-pipe strikes up a hymn of peace and Christian civilisation from the little trim farm on the neighbour-ing slope, where those new barns and gates stand. Christian men dwell now within hail of the old Pagan-work. Twenty of the forty stones of the outer circle remain, and some eleven of the inner nineteen. The outer still stand in threes, or door-ways, two stones supporting the joining one that lies across the top; under which great slab you can, by changing your point of view, get all sorts of strange combinations,—fallen pil-lars, glimpses of down and intersecting lines of sloping turf, while you look either towards the Amesbury and Wiley road, or the Heytesbury and Warminster way. This great Druidical temple lies stranded on a small turf triangle on the open down, between these two roads, and though once a lonely place enough for the winds to whistle round, and the plovers to dip and circle over, is now almost frayed by the wheels of passing carts, and is not a greyhound's breathings from the park-palings of the old Duke of Queensbury's property (now Sir Edmund An-trobus's), not a gunshot from a new farm, and within two miles of the village of Amesbury.

As for Camden, he notices the great mortised stones hang-ing on each other, twenty-eight feet high, and seven feet broad; but he half supposes they were made of some cement, exaggerates the height, and reduces the four circles, of which traces exist, to three. So much for Camden! Inigo Jones,

whom that slobbering schoolmaster, James I., set writing upon
these wonders, runs quite astray: he calls it a Roman-Tuscan
temple, built about the time of Vespasian, who conquered the
Belgic tribes of Wiltshire, and threw up enormous ramparts
and earthworks—those huge rude hills, overgrown with grass,
at Amesbury and Yarebury adjoining. Indeed he falls into all
sorts of blunders (all the worse for being learned): calls the
inner circle a hexagon, falsely describes the entrances as three,
and missupposes that the ring is built on higher ground than
the neighbouring down. A few years later, Mr. Charleton, a
physician, refutes Inigo's theory, and plunges himself ten times
deeper into the ink-pot. He attributes it to the Danes during
Alfred's retirement in the Somersetshire marshes. The next
champion of these never very clear writers is Mr. Sammes (1676),
who hands it over scot and lot to the Phœnicians. He is followed by Mr. Keysler, a Hanoverian, who equally resolutely
passes it to the Anglo-Saxons. In 1754, however, arose
Mr. Wood, a Bath architect, who finally all but ended the
contest by agreeing with the eloquent and erudite Dr. Dummel
that the whole work was palpably Druidic and British, and
probably erected about a hundred years before the Christian
era. Since that, the Welsh, fierce in their charge upon Celtic
remains, have laid violent hands on these ruins, and have spun
all sorts of astronomical theories about these stone circles. It
is certain that the Welsh triads do allude to whole tribes
toiling at piling up mounts, lifting stones, and building works;
and the Egyptian antiquities prove to us, that at a very early
time, by means of earth-propping, rollers, and the use of the
lever, the carriage of such stones was not impossible. As for
the Druids' doctrines, I am not going to bewilder my readers
with telling them how the old logans are types of the ark, or
how their night sacrifices were telegraphed across the country
by waved torches and fiery signals.

So I will get back to Stonehenge, with its circles of grey
gateways gapped out here and there, and especially levelled on
the Wiley side, as if destruction had come specially from
that corner. As for the great outer circle and rampart, single
entrance, and walled avenue, all that the purblind unantiqua-

rian eye can see now is but an irregular rising and falling of the ground till you come to the *Friar's Heel*, a single leaning stone, sixteen feet high, grey like the rest, except where hollowed out by the rain-drops of centuries, or scooped in notched ladders for the shepherd boys to watch their flocks from. No flowers ever grow from their chinks.

The stones are not, as might be imagined, Colt Hoare says, of the same strata and character. The fallen "slaughtering stone," the outer circle, and the five trilithons of the grand oval, are *Sarsen* stones, that is, silicious sandstone, drawn from the quarry in their rude state; probably from near Abury, where three such stones, perhaps dropped *in transitu*, are to be seen, two in the fields and one in a river. The modern geological theory is, that in some great water-change the strata of sand containing these stones was washed away, leaving them stranded on the lower chalk, now tufted over with downs. The altar-stone is fifteen feet high, of a micaceous fine-grained sandstone. Others are of hornstone, or silicious schist,—"most probably from Cornwall or Devon," says one antiquarian.

And now to turn surveyor for distances. I was told that the inside diameter of the circle is one hundred feet; the width of the entrance into the inner cell from the trilithons, forty-three feet. Industrious men, digging for treasure, have at various times found in the grassy area,—where uninvestigating, but still antiquarian-looking, thoughtful sheep nibble about— heads of oxen, pieces of our British and Roman pottery, charred wood, and an iron arrow-head. They say that in the old ox-road and Roman bridle-paths and waggon-roads round Stonehenge you still find chippings of the temple stones.

So much for the blind leaders of the blind, whom we can only follow, as we do moles, by the heaps of dirt they throw up from their sunless subterranean workings and dull books. There are the great stones bearded with moss, still clinging together, doing their long, patient, juggling tricks, and supporting each other in derision of poor weak mortals, and for the untiring amusement of the sun and moon. Here is that great disjointed stone puzzle that no man can again put together, but only stares, eats his sandwiches round, makes notes on, and rides away from, wondering.

Is that an old British MS. blowing about in and out the stone doorways, where the white-robed Druids, crowned with oak, once paced? No; it is only a *Times* supplement, the relic of a yesterday's picnic—for we, poor mortals, are here to-day and gone to-morrow; but these stones are like the sure-set mountains, and remain. Is that a war-car of the ancient Britons, with scythes tied to the wheels? No; that is a yellow postchaise, with a party of wandering German travellers from the "White Hart" at Salisbury. Is that Boadicea? No; that is Mrs. Alderman Rogers, of Portsoken Within, with her pretty daughter sketching. Is that one of the ancient Belgæ turning up the soil yonder? No: Lord bless ye! that is John Giles, who works for Farmer Smith, of the Down Farm, with his master's new patent plough—Mechi's patent—very good, only it won't work quite well at first, and that's why it creaks so, and why Giles uses so many loud adjectives, wishing Mechi would stick to his brown-paper tea-caddies.

So I bow to the great stone ring, and the Egyptian doorways, the fallen altars and blood cups, and the little stone posts, and the circles that want so much humouring in ground plans before—even to an imaginative antiquarian eye—they assume any reasonable and harmonious shape; I take a last look at the German travellers and the ladies in the blue "uglies," and the watchful, cackling hen of a mamma, who wonders why the ancient Britons painted themselves with Prussian blue, in patterns like the corazza fancy shirts, dig my spurs into Red Nancy, and am off.

CHAPTER VIII.

A BATHING-PLACE ON THE SOUTH COAST.

WHO invented sea-bathing? Chaucer's wife, of Bath, says A 1. A 2 says it is a sham, a fancy not fifty years old, and means only idleness, exercise, pure air, and unlimited washing. Men, before nerves were invented, never bathed; men who did not use umbrellas for the sun—who, in fact, did not use umbrellas at all—never bathed. A 2 goes on to say that half of those who do bathe, bathe injudiciously, and do themselves harm; and he asks, with a wicked Wilkes-and-45 look, do the inhabitants of Dippington, where we are now, bathe? I trow not. I never saw them. What first sent all of us, when the dog-days set in, rushing down steep places into the sea? I don't know, yet here I am, somebody telling me, "You want bracing." It takes a good many guineas to "brace" me, I can tell you, and guineas rhyme to "ninnies." I came down by railway, was sucked into dark pea-shooters of tunnels, spat out again into the sunshine, and was first aware of my propinquity to the sea by finding the trees diminish, and the fields get larger and wilder. Suddenly the great grey shield of the sea displayed itself.

A philanthropic grocer, who afterwards touted for my custom, showed me lodgings. I contracted finally for rooms with two old maids—one deaf, the other with a wax nose. I looked out on the sea.

The first thing Dippington mothers seem to tell their children about the sea is to learn to get something out of it. They are at it all day, dipping into it as if it were a lucky-bag, and had never swallowed their fathers or brothers. There they are now, hooking out star-fish, jellies, crabs, shrimps, parchmenty ribbons of seaweed, purple strips, pink roots, yellow shells, rubbed-down pebbles, cuttle-fish, shreds of liquid glue, green slimy weed, round bits of slate, and other scraps and trifles from the great marine store shop and lottery. They never leave the beach, those **Dippington** children, never, for the chalky walks on the cliffs, where the poppies picked to pieces show where lovers have been walking. No, they like better to see the boats building, or the signal-staff painting. The wetter they get, the happier they are.

THE SEA AT DIPPINGTON.

The sea at Dippington is, as far as I can discover at present from my window at the Marine Crescent, much the same as it is at Shrimpington, Whitecliff, or any other fashionable bathing-place. This rippling gown of Amphitrite has always a white frill round the skirt of it. In the morning, when you go to bathe, there is a silver tinsel shimmer on it, and at dusk a soft blue grey haze seems to join it to heaven. It can never make up its mind whether to come in or go out, and the great object of existence here at Dippington seems to be to sit exactly opposite it all day, and stare yourself stupid, by looking at its broad, vacant face. The result of this is extreme sleepiness and a tremendous appetite. Wiggle, the great art-critic, is great down here with his telescope under his arm, his dust coat, his buff slippers, and his boating-hat. He asks the diving-machine men what such a' vessel is " in the offing," and puts on a maratine air, though I know he begins to get sick when he passes Gravesend. Excuse the transition, but that charming Miss Trippet, the belle of Dippington, has just passed down the Parade with such a little pink cockleshell of a bonnet on, and a little blue parasol, like a grown-up air-bell. I wish you could see the pretty fits of abstraction she throws herself into on that seat under the flagstaff. Three youngsters have just passed—all three sputtering—a certain sign, if their dank hair did not prove it, that they have been bathing. Indeed, it is surprising how every small thing cries aloud to one in a watering-place and says, " You are at Dippington, behave as sich." I look out of window now, and lo! on the green, crackling roof of the verandah below I see a white shell, and a dry, crimpy star-fish, dead and colourless, that have been, I suppose, thrown there by the last children who occupied this room—this Dippington tabernacle—that has known so many occupants, but which a sanguine imagination might think had been tossed up there some stormy night by the sea down below there, for there is only a road, a railing, a grass-plot, an esplanade, and a cliff and the sands between my balcony and the Poluphlosboyo.

Besides staring yourself into idiotcy, walking your legs to pieces, and getting your feet wet, I see nothing to be done at Dippington. A little flirting, a great deal of tea and shrimps, billiards, novels, and talking to the sailors, that is our life—that is the creed and constitution of Dippington. Do anything else, and you become a Crusoe on a deserted isle.

"I assure you that last night," said Wiggle to me, as we were on our way to the billiard-table for a game of pyramids—"that last night, as I stood by the brink of that mighty ocean, and looked out over its changeless immensity—its great burial-ground of fleets and navies—its miser hoards of treasure that shall never see the sun—its millions of unrecorded and forgotten dead—I felt——"

"Like a shrimp, a stale whiting, a dried haddock?" I suggested.

"—I felt a mere insect—a transitory creature of less value than the spray that rolled white at my feet. I returned to my hotel——"

"And called for sherry and soda?"

"Be quiet! for my bed-candle; and retired to my couch a better and a wiser man."

More wrecked-looking men going home from bathing. Then a great lull—that is breakfast. Breakfast at Dippington is a solemn thing, so is dinner, so is tea.

The sirens still haunt the sea-side, I think, only they have taken to a more respectable dress, and no longer sit rasping their fingers sore on Erard's harps. The sirens now are fascinating widows, with becoming grief in their beautiful eyes; and bewitching maidens, just budding into womanhood, with round hats and azure "uglies." The siren widow passed just now, looking down, thinking either of the last wedding breakfast or the one that is to come, with violet ribbons fluttering about her black shawl—poetical grief-shroud, with a touch of hope trimming it. Violet, or was it mauve?—beautiful compromise with despair!

Wonderful air of Dippington, that, smelling of nothing, is yet so odorous of that nothing; so fresh, yet never cold; so balmy, so summerful, so flower-kissing, so health-giving! Blessed air, unpolluted by the fetor of cities! air that numberless interjections can alone describe, and then only by showing a redundant sense of pleasure—a freer pulse, a fuller heart, a brighter eye! Let the old writers say what they will of the unsuccessful voyages in the time of Columbus to discover the miraculous "Fountain of Youth," here it is:

THE BATHING-MACHINE.

The first thing, of course, I did when I got settled at Dippington was to inquire about the baths. In the true spirit of a discoverer, the very night I arrived I found my way by sloping paths to the beach, attracted by the ship lights, the red signal at the pier-head, and the sharp clear sound of the ship bells. I saw nothing before me but the boundless, the illimitable, the delight of the hardy Norseman, the terror of the squeamish, the silent highway, the green bank whose lock no burglar can pick, the unfillable graveyard, &c. The waves raced in, white-maned, many-trampling, and swift. They rolled in, twenty thousand abreast, and faded away like a charge of fairy Norsemen. I looked round: there stood the machines, solemn in the twilight, hooded-like sibyls, mysterious as the Pythonesses or the Fates, looking like the gigantic ghosts of the Titan bathing-women of the earlier ages.

" Do you want a machine to-morrow?" said a voice.

It was the disgusting voice of materialism and common sense, whose brutal foot (excuse the transition of metaphor) will trample on the fairest spots, and dissolve the spell of all the enchantments of even the strongest imagination.

" No," said I, with all the severity, but less of the truth than the occasion demanded.

I write at a window, so you must pardon side-notes of digression. A moving tulip bed, or rather a flower bed of parasols, is floating by to take an airing. It is just meridian—

ought I not to say so many bells? Last night, sleep wrestled with, and threw me at an early hour. With the crescendo of the surge in my ears I went to bed (O divine snowiness of country beds!), desiring to be called at half-past six for bathing; the consequence of which, of course, was, that I woke at six, and lay grumbling till a quarter to seven, when a voice dropped my boots with a double clump at the door. Getting up for a first bath is, to a nervous, imaginative man, like Twitter, the epic poet, a dreadful thing.

Podgers, the cheesemonger in Fetter Lane, has just passed with his six children, who all seem to have been born on the same day. Query: Can you call six children twins? ought not three to be called trines, and so on? Podgers wears a high, brown, flower-pot hat, and, of course, black trousers. His crafty hole-and-corner face jars on the broad, frank, impatient sea. N.B. He has brought his day-book down to amuse himself with to-morrow (Sunday) while the Sextines are gone in procession to church, each with a large Common Prayer-Book folded in a clean white handkerchief.

To return: I got up, trying to think it was very delicious, which it wasn't. I roped on my necktie, sloughed on my oldest boots; and buttoned up like a spy, a crimp, or an escaped smuggler, walked down towards the sea, now a laughing glittering green in the early sunlight—the shining opal collar that nature placed round a dove's neck was nothing to it. At the corner of the jetty a band of half-sailors, half-fishermen, beleaguered me with pulls at their forelocks.

" Want a machine, sir ?" said one.

" Just look at this towel, fine white diaper," said another, with a white slab of a towel balanced on his hand.

No. 802 was already out. No. 910 was having the horse put to. Screams and laughter were pouring from 605, and from under the hood of 703 there was a splashing as if Kempenfelt and all his men were going down together in the Royal George with one consent. At the door of 320 a respectable City tradesman, well known on the Corn Exchange, was combing his hair inside the machine, and looking wet and bedraggled into the glass.

No. 450 was mine.   A man they call something like "Loller" hands me three dirty-white tickets to frank me for three mornings' admission to the ocean—as yet unallotted or park-paled—one shilling.   Then he asks me for one of the three, and takes it just as a man does who is teaching you a game of cards, and is playing both sides.   I am introduced as a victim to a brother in red-plush breeches and jack waterproof boots, who is the driver.   I am handed two towels—sent up the steps of the "cairywan," and shut in.   I am shouted to that when I have had enough of it I am to open the door and call.

I am scarcely in it before the machine begins to jolt.   I feel like Jonah inside the whale.   We go out to sea.   There is a chink of chains—a crack of a whip—a shout—lower—lower. I try to keep my footing, I feel myself in a cart and yet in a ship.   I undress and hook up everything to the nails round the wall.   I don't know how it is, but I never in my life went down to the sea in a bathing-machine but I compared myself to Pharaoh entering the Red Sea in his chariot in hot pursuit after the Israelites.   "Suppose," I say to myself, "there was a leak in this crazy hut? suppose it broke away from the wheel, and drifted out to sea, to be nosed and bumped by whales, and sniffed at by sharks?   Suppose——"

Here a tremendous wave thumped at the door, as much as to say, "Come out and let us look at you, miserable creature of clay!"   I am now without the cloak that shadowed Borgia —in Adam's livery—a poor forked, pale creature, shivering as if for charity; trembling like Andromeda when the great sea-serpent approached.   The floor is gritty, the small slab of carpet is sodden and briny.   I undo the door and look out, kicking down the tilted hood, and clinging to the rope that is fastened to the outside of the machine, and which, like every-thing else belonging to it, is crisp and salt.   With crippled, crumpled feet, I descend the steps; a wave lashes up, and all but washes me off—surfing me up against the hood, and all but whipping the rope from me.   A singular creeping feeling of the blood as I step in waist high—a pull at my heart, as if the blood were driven back to the citadel, then rallied, and spread victoriously through my veins—a taste of salt surf in my mouth—now a duck under. I emerge, blinded and dripping, and wade out beyond the hood. I come out as from a cave, and am in the wide, wide sea. The horizon towards the North Foreland is a line of trembling silver—the junction of sky and sea—the welding line—the tenderest grey blue, which is neither opaque nor transparent—a soft apricot-coloured bloom in the eastward, Dover way—is here and there a sail catches the sun, and shines the colour of a light wall-flower. The chalk cliffs, cleft in horizontal lines, and bushed with wild mignionette and wild geranium, look blocks of opaque silver.

But I don't come here to study landscape, but to tear health from the jaws of the sea: and health I will have—so here goes! How soft the sand feels under my naked feet! I wade out to meet the waves—one, two, three. Here comes a huge one, cresting and combing over with a metallic shine, but without foam: it laps over me and lifts me off my feet. I stagger on defiant. Here comes one twice as high—the froth already out there rises high above my head. Nearer, firm, prepare to receive cavalry! form square! bang! wash! splash! It beats me over, it foams over my head, and passes on to lash and rage up the steps of my machine, as if it were looking for me. I am cuffed and slapped warm, I am in high spirits—braced and nerved. Now I understand what Dr. Bleadon meant by always saying to my wife, " He (meaning me) wants bracing— he must have bracing." Here I am bracing—hard at it! Here comes another rolling monster. Hurrah! Brace away! I leap at it, but it has me down, and tramples on me in a moment.

I am back under the hood. I got into the wrong machine first—they are so very much alike—and found myself in the presence of the Rev. Mr. Bellow, rector of the celebrated church of St. Barabbas. But then did I not see swimming near me just now, like a Ceylon diver going all naked to the shark, fast young Latitat, of the Middle Temple, swimming as if he were flying from the bailiffs, or as if Grinder and Crusher, the great attorneys, had sent for him to their chambers?

As I waded up the steps I met Bellow coming down. I

bowed and he bowed—he laughed; I laughed, and splashed
off, like a merman who has been paying a morning visit.   I
emerge from the wave and climb my steps.   Delicious glow—
warmth of health and life, enough to revive a dying man—rosy
glow of invigorated and purified blood!   I begin a Norse hymn
to the sea, such as "Harold of the Blue Eyes" might have addressed to his sword, "the Land-giver:"

> Health-giver, I hail thee!
> Man-slayer, I fear thee!
> Hope-bringer, I greet thee!
> Dirge-singer, I fear thee!

I gave the signal for being restored to land.   The horse is
put to.

"Right you are!" cries a voice, and a jerk nearly sends me off
my legs.   I leap down into the soft ancle-deep sand, wished
"good morning" by the "two noble kinsmen," and depart
to punish my breakfast; my chest expanded, my heart larger,
my eyes brighter, my moral nature improved, my physical nature padded out and developed.

NIGHT AT DIPPINGTON.

Night at Dippington is "mighty pretty to behold," as Pepys
would have said.   You can see the red light on the pier casting
a quivering column of liquid ruby, like so much burning sea,
below it in the harbour.   Far away in the distance, starlike
over the waters, twinkles the North Foreland light, answered
right and left by corresponding guardians of the coast.   Through
the dusk you hear from your open window the buzz of a beetle,
telling by association of the thundery warmth of the summer
night, and of the hush that must be away there in the fields
that lead down to the cliff, in the dense dark clumps of elms, and
in the light feathering ashes.   The ship's bells tell the hour with
their monotonous but clear and decisive cling-clang, in the harbour where they are moored near the red light, and everywhere
—whether in the high streets, between the rows of lamps by
the market-place where the fisherboys stand, in the sea-side
billiard-room, on the cliffs by the white lighthouse, or by the
platform (as like a quarter deck as possible) where the coast-

guard man in white trousers, and the eternal battered telescope under his arm, paces—you hear the roll, and surge, and lash, and chafe, and splashing drag, and tumble of the breakers, that spread white through the night. Now, one by one, on Terrace, and Parade, and Esplanade, and Side-street, and Cliff-crescent, the pleasure-seekers put out their lamps, and as they close like so many closing eyes, I turn in, and put out mine likewise.

MORNING AT DIPPINGTON.

One hour ago, by this repeater, and I was up to my chin in the green sparkling waves, feeling a little anxious as the sand seemed suddenly to recede from the extended half of the great toe on my left foot, and I looked back, and I saw I was fifty yards from No. 68 machine, and seemed bearing out every moment imperceptibly a little further from the white cliffs, and that man who, shining white through the waves, is floating on his back, calmly, some twenty feet off. Now, I am here, calm as Cato, at my tea and prawns, divesting those mollusca of their pink armour, and looking out, delighted at the diamond sparkle of the morning sea, the mile-long bars of purple cloud-shadows, the broad green field of opaque emerald, and the long dim blue line of land, that seems but consolidated cloud, yesterday cloud turned solid, yet barely solid. It is a sight to make an old man young again. The line of foam that breaks along the shore glitters like quicksilver; a dancing diamond twinkle and restless glimmer is on the sea; and the brown sands, where the sea washes, are transparent and luminous as if they were covered with a thin glazing of ice. Children laugh on the balconies and on the terraces—they hop up and down in the water like so many chickens round the old mother hen of the machine. Bathing-women, witch-like and hideous, in sodden blue flannel bathing-gowns, float about like stale mermaids or water ogresses seeking their prey. The sands are one immense laundress's drying ground, with strings of coloured bathing-dresses, towels, and other apparatus of sanitary ablutions. The machines in the water remind one of a French village during the inundations; those on shore, of the first encampment of a fair. The machines echo with screams and laughter. The proprietor of the bathing-machines, a lame man, who swims like a frog, walks about the sands with a contemplative, benevolent air, with his hands behind him. There are ships in the distance at all degrees of obscurity, from the palpable black boat that seems made of sticking-plaister, like the profile likenesses, to that brig out there, grey and dim as the Flying Dutchman. Truly, Dippington, of a bright morning, when the very air laughs, is a pleasant and cheering place. A little time, and it will be a desolate Sahara of fishermen, moping lodging-house keepers complaining of taxes: no children, no laughing, no nothing. The wooden spades will gather dust at the shop door—the buff slippers hang purposeless in the window.

CHARACTERS AT DIPPINGTON.

I am just home from a burning walk along the top of the chalk cliff, where the pink valerian bushes over into the blue air, some giddy eighty feet, where the wild geranium lures the bees into its veined honey-cups, and where the wild mignionette spires up, crisp and perfumeless. Here I have been lying down on the scorched, half-burnt-up, wild barley, by the side of the chalky path, where the wheat shoulders and billows ; I especially enjoy the quiet cliff walks outside Dippington, where the park palings, as you pass, wake into a hot stingbuzz of flies, and where the great orange and black bumblebee, bullying robber of the summer flowers, rifles the poppy that lies hid among the guardian spears of the wheat-field—a second Jason seeking his Medea. Am I to be called an idler, because I lie down on my rough bed of half-burnt-up white clover, and listen to the lark rising, through vistas of blue, to the inner heaven where the angels call him ?

"There ain't no thoroughfare this way, leastways there is no public road, but if you like to climb up, as I'm going off duty, and will come up through this gallery cliff, you're welcome." So said a coast-guard to me, as I find myself blocked up at a corner of the sands, and want to get back to Dippington.

I accept his proposal, and follow the sunburnt Neptune up

a dark gallery cut in the chalk, with loopholes here and there, letting in the clear daylight.

"Dull life this, isn't it?"

"Yes." So he was on board a man-of-war—petty officer, too—thirteen years, and wouldn't be here now but for an accident four months ago. He had been on the coast of Africa, passed Gibraltar a dozen times; didn't care for any sort of weather purwided there was plenty of sea room, which there was not when he once was in a sou'-wester in the Mozambique Channel. No, a tornado was not sudden; contrairy, it always gave you three quarters of an hour to take down sail, and get all square. No captain, if he was really captain in his own ship, and not a sort of foster-child of the first lieutenant, had any right to let any of his men get wet in a tornado; there was time enough to put all under cover afore the tornado broke. Some of them white squalls was twice as bad. A captain as really was a captain in his own ship, such a man as Captain Rood as the Amphitrite buried when she was taking in money at Chili, was the captain as he liked to serve under. Did he carry pistols? Yes, one by day and two by night, for signals; rockets too. Dippington was a troublesome station, because they wanted watches on the pier night and day to see everything as came in, right or wrong, rigler or unrigler. He wished me a very good night. That was eight o'clock; he was off duty now, and came on again at four in the morning. He wished me a very good night—"Good night, sir."

A gorgeous flame tableau was in the sky, wrangling with a pile of electric ash-grey clouds. The sea was rose-coloured —the sky deepened to purple—it was dark before all the stars lit their lighthouse lamps, and so did the North Foreland, which shone out like a small sun among them. Here my friend Mac-Hanno, who prides himself on his Carthaginian descent, would quote Horace, but I will not, on any account; a truism not seeming to me anything wiser because it is in Latin.

I had need of a barber. I found one who kept the circulating library. He requested my name. He told me it gave him the greatest trouble to get distinguished visitors' names correctly. Would I believe it, only that morning a Mr. De Frieze had come and complained he was put down De Sneeze. Names were always getting into knots.

My friend was a perfect specimen of the poor watering-place barber. The weather was very catching (short or long, sir?); always observed it was so after a long prevalence of the east wind (hair very dry, sir; do you use any pomade?) Now it was first the wind, then the weather, got the upper hand—weather and wind, wind and weather (short over the ear? Yes, sir); glad to see I wore beard and moustaches, advised every gent to do so; acted as respirator, protected the tonsils, kept out the dust; had a brother, a fine tenor, yes, sir, who could get up to A and B with the greatest ease; he held out against beard for a long time, very long time; left for three months, came back with a swingeing pair of moustaches (look in the glass, and see if that is short enough); had a dread now of their being sandy; advised him a certain wash that tinged without dyeing; it was a secret, but he did not care mentioning it; he told him—it was the very thing; he ordered a five-and-sixpenny bottle from London, and the effect was astonishing. Had I ever had excavation of blood on the head? Sometimes the effect of injudicious bathing. Could he recommend me any wash for the head? Certainly he could. Had I never heard of his celebrated Golden Oil? Agents all over London —cases sent away every day—surprised! Desk full of letters —sent off that morning a case of six to Hon. Mr. Foozle, Whitewash Villa, Worcester. A letter yesterday from Captain O'Toole, some castle near Dublin, couldn't remember the name of the castle; letter from Dr. Hardbox, mentioning astonishing effect of oil on Mrs. Blackline, who had evinced symptoms of baldness in lateral regions of the scalp—at once tonic, cleanser, and strengthener. The miserable London pomades left a deposit, and turned acid—that was the end of it— turned acid. This was what he lived by, making the Golden Oil. Dippington season only three months; couldn't live without patent for Golden Oil. Did I see that transparent bottle? that was the beautiful and nutritious Golden Oil. Did I see that dark liquid? that was the Royal Odoriferous Fluid expressly made to be used with it, and which, shaken together, formed a mellow and invaluable cream.

My personal friend Coxen, who calls his boat by the aphonistic name of "Help me, and I'll help you," is a good type of the Dippington boatmen. He has not a quick imagination, nor is he lightning-quick at repartee, but he is a brave, honest, stolid, unflinching, faithful, crafty old sailor, and I respect him, though he does hammer for half an hour at the same idea, and leave it at the end of this time rather bruised, distorted, and misshapen. His craft (I don't refer to the "Friend in Need" sailing-boat) consists in simply trying to charge you twice as much per hour as any one else, and in scudding you out to such a distance from any known land, that no canvas wing, or flying jib, or any shaking out of canvas, will get you in at the time you expected and intended to pay for; otherwise he is a rare old Neptune, and his stories of diving, smuggling, and wrecking, throw great light on the manners, customs, and moral standard of Dippington, which, with its golden and emeraldine sea, and its chalky ramparts of cliff, I take to be quite a type of Cockney sea-side places.

It is a sight to see him with the massy red braces, a foot wide each, crossing his indigo-coloured Jersey, that fits his brawny chest and arms like a Norse body-suit of mail, his enormous full-bodied breeches, reaching up almost to his arm-pits, his alert, nimble feet (sailors' feet are generally small), cased in canvas shoes, his strong brown hands, white at the knuckles, grasping lightly, yet surely the familiar oar, whose broad blades force the boat on with such quick, strong, and equal pulse. My young friend Parkins sits gravely holding the tiller-ropes and nodding at us (me and Coxen), as we bend, like two portions of the same body, simultaneous at the oars.

Coxen, like Dogberry, prides himself on "having had losses." If right was right, and all things was as they should be, which they ain't, Coxen would be, by his own account, the lord of half Dippington. If you ask him how all these enormous territories passed from the family of Coxen, he will tell you, with a grave shake of the head, "that it was the want of larning" that got it all "signed away." There cannot be the smallest doubt that Coxen's (let me see) uncle's father—no, aunt's sister—no—yes—father's uncle's mother—was descended from two East Indian captens, Capten Mover and Capten Redwood, which came to Dippington to moor quietly, and left their property tied up by the most solemn oaths and specific directions to the Coxen family to descend lineally and inalienably. There can be no doubt about this, because Coxen knows where to lay his hand on the house in Dippington whose best room contains a portrait of Captain Redwood in an oval gilt frame, and laying his fist on a terrestrial globe ; and, moreover, the captains lie together under a flat black stone just as you enter to the right of St. Lawrence's church ; and not only that, sir, there is, or was, in the same church a glass case, through which you see the worthy captain's will, leaving so much bread and meat to certain inhabitants of St. Lawrence's parish. And if anything else was wanted, there was a pilot as died last June was a twelvemonth, as told him (John Coxen) over a glass of rum and a pipe in the parlour of the Tartar Frigate Inn, that there was parties who could speak about that 'ere pier property if they had a mind ; and, what was more, he (Coxen) had seen maps of the property which covered the site of the present Exmouth Crescent, and all the ground where the pier now stood. How the alienation occurred, no one could see, but all he knew was, that there was an uncle of his who always knew what lawyer to go to for a pound, and I suppose he was told that the site of certain property could not be secured without him, and that it was of no consequence, and " sichlike," and so it went, all through "a want of larning," in a certain drunken branch of the Coxen family, who, if " right was right," ought to be gen'lemen.

On a morning misty with intense heat, I and Parkins stroll down to the Pier-gate by appointment, to meet Coxen, and take a row and sail up the Stour river towards Shinglewich. The machines are all down on the beach, like an encampment of Tartar gipsies in an inundated steppe—a cutter with sunburnt sail is passing, dark in shadow. The bathers are bobbing up and down like floats fidgeting under a nibble. The delicious emerald water is lapping in, and frothing and

splashing about the scarlet wheels of the machines, and rolling
in froth on the shore, as if white soapsuds were being swilled
out. Redgauntlet sort of amphibia, in flaming plush breeches
and bare feet, are riding on draggle-tailed horses at a merry
trot knee-deep into the sea, to link to the machines, whose
open doors announce their ripeness for return to land. A fop
in a Tweed suit has just loafed by with an umbrella up—frightful example of a nervous and debilitated age. Children are
grubbing about in buff slippers and with wooden spades, as if
to be a "navvy" or a gold-digger were the natural object of
every man. The shore, rolled brown, level, and hard by the
sea-mangle, is strewn with little green films and scarlet roots
and purple shreds of sea-weed, and here and there is piled
with strips of parchment-looking fucus and the bladdered tea-
leaves-looking refuse of the waves. The green light on the
pier, that looked last night so spectral in the gloom, is invisible; the distant Knock Sand and the North Foreland have
no star lit. There is a fretted sparkle on the waves, and on
the rolling crest of the surf there is a glow as of gold plate.
The bathing-women are floating out like Norse witches wading
off to curse a departing vessel and fling a foul wind on its
track, as the falconer whistles his Peregrine after a flying
heron out on the cliff. The upper flowers sway and nod, and
mock at the danger, and the lark sings above the barley that
rolls in glosses, like the wind over an animal's fur.

Now we walk down the pier, passing the shipwrights busy
with their heavy hammers, boiling tar, and caulking, piecing
the ship's skeleton in the dry dock; the old boatmen with
red button-holes of eyes and worn-out telescopes; the boys
playing in boats; the life-boat, with its padded-looking sides;
the floating shells of boats, like empty green pea-cods; the
huge buoys of the Trinity House, looking like floats used
by giants, or enormous iron fungi—and we are in Coxen's boat,
stepping by a ship-boy of dandy habits, who is washing his
shoes and bare legs with a stray cabbage-leaf.

We are in, past the keen-edged steamers, the yachts and
pleasure-boats, past the dense wedging sound of the shipwrights' hammers; past the cranes, clicking capstans, and water-

steps ; past the dredging-machines, and sluices, and great black and white diamond buoys that tell strange vessels silent tidings of the depth of water in the harbour.

We are off. There has been a scrambling out of oars, a hauling of ropes, an unbending of sails. We skim round the fort-like angle of the pier, with its massy stone-work and its green-slimed and barnacle-crusted bulwarks, and are out at sea. The nor'-west catches the sail and strains it forth ; we leap and dance over the luminous water, which seems like so much opaque sunshine—yesterday's sunshine in fact—faster than even those white-tipped, omega-shaped gulls that float questioning round our little red thread of a flag. The boat drives like a steam-plough through a trough of the waves, or dips down on one side till the gunwale nearly lips the tide. A boat lagging along slowly in the opposite direction, looks at us admiringly, and one of the sailors in it hums something. " What did he say, Coxen ?"

" Only a werse of a hold song," smiles Coxen—" ' Oh, scudding under easy sail,'—and we was scudding just then, sir, like flying Isaac, as they say. Now, it's a curious thing"— on these reflective occasions Coxen always stopped rowing, tucked one oar under his knee, took off his cap, wiped the " prespiration" from his forehead, and leant forward with appropriate gesture, laying the chopped forefinger of one hand in the woody palm of the other—" now, it's a curious thing, sir, that a man in a boat always thinks that the boat he see is going faster than he is. Many's the time as we've been going like glory, and the gentleman I've been a rowing of seen another boat not half as fast as we was, and, says he, ' Lord, Coxen, how that boat is walking along ! what a lively boat!' says he, ' Coxen ;' but it ain't my place, you know, to say anything ; so, on I pulls.

" There," said he, " that's the Belly View (Belle Vue(Tavern, and now we steer straight across for the buoy there, at the mouth of the river out by Shellness ; but to return," said he, " about that there crinkle on the water. People often says to me, ' Why, dear me, Coxen, how could you tell the wind was coming ?' Ignorant them Londoners as the dirt you

tread on, and worse too. Pull home, sir; keep time, not too
quick; capital stroke, sir; keep your oar a little more in.
I've been out once before to the Goodwin Sands this morning,
with a young gentleman and lady. I think as they was a
courting—I thinks they was."

Coxen here rambled on to a long and intricate statement of
his ill-luck during the last year. This was an inexhaustible
subject with him. He had a little house to let just up by the
Subscription Billiard-room on the South Parade; he had not
let it yet—such a thing had never happened before for twenty
years. As for his old woman, she never went out for fear of
anybody coming, but " yesterday a young fellar in the town
who had been in the Lancers, came back from India, and was
brought in from the pier with a band, and in comes Mrs.
Jones from next door, and says, ' Come along, Mrs. Coxen,
put on your bonnet,' says she, ' and come down and hear the
band.' Away went my wife. Why, will you believe it, sir,
in that very hour comes a lady and gentleman to see the
house, drat it! Then there was him and the boats, when he
ought to have been painting and doing 'em up for the season,
he was out in a lugger off the Goodwin Sands, looking out for
salvage—(pull left-hand tiller rope, sir; leave that buoy to the
right)—and now, when he ought to be looking out for gentlemen and sailing parties, he had to snatch a moment or two to
paint and do up the Smiling Sally and the Friend in Need."

Coxen's notions about the morality of the salvage were peculiar, and would not, perhaps, be thought orthodox out of
Dippington, as you will see. I asked him about the wrecks in
general, and he again tucked his oar under his leg, and
volunteered a yarn.

" It's hard life, sir, out there by them sands, when a heavy
sou'-sou'-west is blowing, and there's no rum or baccy aboard.
Hard work beating round the nine miles of Goodwin Sands,
and the sea washing over you so that you can't look to windward, and it pours off your back in bucketfuls. Sooner be off
the Knock Sand, or the Galloper, or plain out in the Gull
Way than that. There we lay four nights, running, maybe,
half asleep on the boards; no room for beds in a hoveller; half

on watch, ten of us altogether, and maybe rousted out twice a night, and frightened out of your wits."

I asked if they gave warning to vessels that they saw likely to get on that burial-pit of sailors.

"No," said Coxen, with a sarcastic shake of the head, "not we; we don't rough it for that. Captains wouldn't give us anything for giving them notice. We are there to get 'em off, not to prevent 'em getting on. It was only last week we were there getting up pig-iron, with the nipping tongs as we use, from a wreck, and we were rousted out by the watch, because a French brig was going between us and the sand. Another moment, by the Lord, and she'd have been safe on, when one of our mates cries out, 'Helm a starboard!' and she was off it. We asked him afterwards, but he couldn't tell why he cried out—he couldn't help it."

I thought to myself of the old story of the dumb boy speaking, and of the natural outcry of the heart; but I said nothing.

"When the Goodwin lighthouse sends up a rocket we know it is time to go off, for some ship is in distress, and off we bundles. Often and often the men in the Goodwin light-ship, who mayn't, whatever happens, leave to help any wreck, hear the drownding men a singing out, though they are two miles off. Sometimes when we get out we finds the ship a bumping and bumping, and a driving and a tearing, and the sand all in a boil round them, and the waves ripping off their copper."

"Great moment," says Parkins, leaning forward with the strained tiller-ropes in his hands, his nautical straw hat and blue ribbon on one side, his spectacles in a glassy stare of expectation, his cigar going out in his hand; "the joy of saving a human life, the transport and tears of gratitude!"

"Not they," says Coxen, winking at a passing gull; "not a bit of it. Last December twelvemonth as ever was, will you believe me, gentlemen, a vessel had gone down, and we was patrolling, as you or I might do, round the Goodwin, looking out for stray casks or an anker of brandy, or summut of that sort. Well, we heard a scream, and went up and found a man clinging to a spar. We went up and picked up a young

Frenchman, who had been clinging there nine hours, till his hands would scarcely come straight again. He had been washed off once, and made his way to it again. Well, we got him up, and then we picked up the captain. We nursed them up, and rubbed them, and gave 'em clothes and some rum, and I'll be hanged, next day, when we met them in High Street, if they would even speak to us; but, then, there is one thing, they was parley voos."

"Do you find them on their knees?" asked Parkins, timidly.

"We find them praying or shrieking, or anything; sometimes they have been a drinking, and, in that case, often they won't leave the wessel, say what you will, and swear and curse at you."

"And what do you do," said Parkins, "in these distressing circumstances?"

"Do," said Coxen, indignantly, as if all pity for anything but a family who had lost their property through want of learning was wasted—"do, young gentleman? why, leave 'em alone—leastwise if it is the master or capten; if it is only a common sailor, the rest force him into the boat—generally."

"Do they cheer," says Parkins the enthusiastic, "when they see the gallant fellows coming to their rescue?"

"Not they. What has ever put such things into your head?" said Coxen. "I never touches 'em either, till we have made a regular bargain what we're to get, or our salvage wouldn't be much. Generally the leak is coming in hot and fast on them, for a vessel gets above its mast-head in the Goodwins in three tides, and they want us at the pumps, and tremenjus hard they work us, and then sometimes won't give us even a Schnapps over. 'What for you English talk always so much about Schnapps? I no Schnapps for you.' They are of all sorts; some think nothing at all about it, others again cut it close and niggarly—there's where it is; and when the salvage money comes it has to be divided among a many hands. We saved a ship last year, a German emigrant vessel from Bremen, and got four hundred pound for it in the Salvage Court; the Admiralty don't allow money as isn't well-earned, and I got only thirty-five pound out of it. Unlucky vessel that was, too : dang if it didn't run against Dippington pier, trying to come in! Well, all her goods were taken out and reshipped for Bremen. Back they went, and came here again in another vessel, and dang if that didn't rasp the same place and all but go down, too! There is a luck about some things."

"Were these Germans grateful?" said I.

"They were that," said Coxen, bending Titanically to his oar; they "hidolized me, sure-ly. Wouldn't leave nohow; and if I went into a public-house they all came too, and stopped till I got up to go."

I pointed to some gulls, looking like specs of froth thrown from a wave, that were dipping and wheeling round the sole of an old shoe that was tied to a pole in the river to mark the practicable current. The "leather," as it is called, alternating with "twigs," placed here, probably, just as they were in King Canute's time.

Coxen looked at the wild birds with the tender eye of a farmer looking at his own poultry. "Yes," said he, "they don't come much here till the winter; in the summer they keep out at sea. Lord! you should see them stalking about the Goodwin Sands" (Coxen mostly spoke of them as the Goodlins) "at low water, as large as fowls, looking out for drownded men."

"Have you ever been to London, Coxen?"

"Yes," said Coxen. "When I goes I like to see Hashley's and the Monyment, and the theaytres. Lord!" (tucking the oar again chattily under his left leg) "how the gents as come down here do like to get out of that suffocating place! 'Coxen,' says they to me, 'how glad I am to get out of that filthy London!' What with the bugs and the rats, I think they has a hard time of it; and all I wonder is, with the jamming of houses and people, they escape being smothered."

From this our conversation turned to rats, about which I told Coxen the story of how, in George the First's time, the brown rat came from Norway, and, killing all the indigenous black rats, conquered the country. But Coxen, putting aside this story, would have it that London was the centre of all rats as well as of all evil. "There was a craft," said he, "the Simon Taylor, laden with sugar, as struck and was sinking just as me and my mates was a coming up in our lugger. One of us stuck his crowbar in the coating of the mast, and found the ship was choke-full of rats all under where the wedges of the mast was. I tell you what, sir, those rats will get so numerous that the sailors have to put victuals and drink for them reg'lar, or they eat the very planks through. They'll eat the horn buttons off the sailors' jackets, and the thick skin off the heels of the men as they lie in their hammocks."

A broad vein of dull purple here spreading through the light chrysolite green of the sea, arrested Coxen's weather eye, who declared, as it moved along, that it must be a "school" of mackerel. It proved to be only the flying shadow of a grey cloud, but it was sufficient to turn the conversation on fishing, for, just at that moment, row after row of floating corks, branded with the letters of their owners' names, and indicating sunk lobster-pots, brought us on to some busy boats of fishermen, who were drawing up the net cages, weighted with flints, inside which hung strings of dead plaice.

A word of mine about the fishing cormorants of China, and the chance of taming the fishing eagle, led Coxen to curious revelations of the fish world; about the devil-fish, the jelly-fish, the fiddle-fish (shaped like the butt of a fiddle), the stotter, and especially the dog-fish, the special enemy of the fishermen of Dippington and everywhere else.

" Lord !" said Coxen, " you should see how them dog-fish tear bits out of the net, and swallow the lobster-nets right down in their hurry to get at the fish. I don't mean the piggy-dogs, the fellows all over prickles like, but the spur-dogs, the largest ones. The fishermen know when they are coming, they can smell 'em a long way off, when the dogs are coming in packs after the whitings, they are so oily and ranky. Why, I saw one just now on the pier as we pushed off, that one could not bear one's nose near. They're as bad as the gannet, that the sailors declare lift up the net for each other to get the herrings out."

Here we sighted two Hastings fishing-luggers in which a crew of sturdy giants in orangy blouses, under their black, patched, and tawny sails, were uproariously shouting and rejoicing at having secured a boat and a half, fourteen thousand herrings in one night.

This event having passed, we returned to the dog-fish, just as our boat passed a ruined castle on a cliff, whose broken towers cut dark against the great shining disc of the setting sun.

I inquired if the whiting were a peculiarly timid fish.

"That's right," said Coxen, dipping his oar in the water to try the depth; "they run from them dog-fish like a rat from a dog, or a mouse from a cat. You see, sir, the herrings are too fast for them till the nets stop them, so that directly they come up to the nets, they gap at them; when they do catch these customers, the men take and cut them up piecemeal, or stretch them across with a spritsail-yard. Same with crabs. Don't you buy those red prawns they hawks about, they're only bastard shrimps. We have no prawns; they've left the coast these twenty year. I can remember when I used to go on the main head, and pass the net up the weeds off the pier, and hear them rustle in—a good basketful. The haddock, too, has left the coast. I don't know whether their food is gone, or how it is. I remember when they were a dozen for a shilling in these parts."

These parts meant Splashington beach, which was by this time scraping our keel.

ROWING AT DIPPINGTON.

The greatest jealousy exists between the people of Dippington and those of the adjoining watering-place of Splashington. "The Splashington people," according to Coxen, "are all bounce,—awful bounceable, they are, surely Their boats are allays the best and the fastest, and when a gentleman asks them to have a nip of grog, they allays mention a shilling's worth."

"Bragging fellows?"

"That's right. Splashington for pluck, is their cry, and Dippington for money." Coxen had never seen the like of them, he hadn't.

Indeed, there had once been a regatta at Dippington, and he (Coxen) had to pick his crew, and he chose two Splashington men who was good hands, they was; but they came after a boosing party of three days, during which they had eaten scarcely anything, and so lost. "Oh, they were a queer lot, they were, at Splashington—no account at all."

Now came Parkins's rowing lesson.

"Keep time, sir; no chopping, like a man-of-war's-man—hands closer together, sir—oar more aft, sir—now well home!"

The "well home" consisted in Parkins's missing the surface of the water, "catching a crab," and being nearly knocked off his seat.

More directions to Parkins's confused and troubled mind: "Dip your oar a little deeper in the water, sir—to the end of the blade! It is no exertion if you lean well back, and then pull the oar home—well home."

Coxen might be right, and rowing may be no exertion, but Parkins certainly at that moment looked as if it was. His coat was off, his braces undone, his face a vivid carmine.

"Steer straight, sir, for the Belly View Tavern—keep time, sir, or it's no use—the faster you go, you see, the worse you does. Now, one—two!"

And so we returned to Dippington, and that night I finished my Epic.

CHAPTER IX.

THE SQUIRE'S PEW.

(A DREAM THAT CARRIED ME BACK A HUNDRED YEARS.)

> "And other faces fresh and new
> Shall fill again the Squire's pew."

ONE day last summer, I went down into Wiltshire on a little antiquarian tour with my friend St. Ives.

His chief object was brasses—mine was tumuli and Roman camps. He cared nothing for camps, I for brasses—the day of which I speak, we had started from Hindon in a trap for Beaulieu, a little retired village on the Wiltshire Downs, ten miles from Warminster—the church there being celebrated for its

brasses—we reached it after a pleasant drive over breezy
downs, glorified with sunshine and dotted black with rooks—
we got the key from the sexton; to work on his knees went
St. Ives, with tracing papers and rubbers in due form. I soon
got tired of watching the enthusiast, and retired into the
Squire's pew, up in the gallery, to spend an hour over
Hobbes' Behemoth, which I happened to have brought with
me. But somehow or other, Hobbes' heavy dialogue and the
heat of the day soon sent me to sleep, and my dream (written
out that night at the Hindon Inn) took somewhat the sub-
joined form:

DREAM.

Methought it was a bright Sunday morning, in the year
1761, and I had strolled into Beaulieu church just in time to
see the worthy old Jacobite baronet, Sir Henry Cantelupe,
enter his pew—the one I had my dream in—it was an old
family prayer-book, embossed with fine old arms, and stamped
1760, that had set me off.

I looked, and behold, five minutes before the commencement
of divine service, the right hand door of the squire's gallery
opened, and Sir Henry entered; it did me good to see that
brave old gentleman hide his face for a moment in his gold-
laced cocked hat, as though acknowledging that he had entered
the Presence Chamber of the great Lord and Master of us all;
and this grave and sincere act of homage was all the more com-
mendable, because there was much in that old church to rouse
the pride and vanity of a Cantelupe.

In the first place the moment the brass handle of the gallery
door had begun even to move or jostle from the outside, that
moment it had been the custom in Beaulieu church, for a good
forty years, for the choir of Beaulieu parish to tune up. The
choir consisted of, imprimis, Robert Lightfoot, carpenter, first
fiddle; secondly, Tom Teddington, grocer, second fiddle;
thirdly, Jeptha Heavytree, blacksmith, bass viol; fourthly,
Obadiah Maybole, a farmer's son, who performed on the flute;
and lastly, but not least, that rival of the maddest wild goose
as to upper notes, and as to *chalumeau* no mean competitor

with the bull; Will Golightly, farmer, on the clarionet. The
choir began to strike up an appropriate anthem—such as
" *Lift up your heads, O ye gates,*" Blow; or " *Why hop ye so, ye
high hills?*" Pursell; or some other burst of exultant religious
music that might not appropriately be construed by a profane
stranger into a compliment to the squire on his entrance into
the church. Indeed, there can be little doubt that the Squire
so construed it, as he generally after his short prayer rose up,
hung his laced hat on a curved peg which jutted out from a
neighbouring mural monument, and taking the large quarto
silver-clasped red-edged common prayer from the velvet-lined
shelf, for a moment stood up, slightly inclined his manly head
to the congregation, many of whom rose too, and stroked
down their forelocks or nodded in the direction of the Squire's
pew. Then the Squire sat down and calmly looked round to
see who was present—or if anyone was away who ought not to
be; and just as Parson Greenoak sails in, worthy old vicar, in his
white clear-starched gown puffing as a swan's breast, and banded
by the crimson hood of Oxford, he looks up at the Squire, down
the chancel to the school-children, smooth-haired and red-
cheeked, then buries his face in his hands, and is absorbed for
a moment or two in prayer.

Hitherto the choir has been jubilant, but subdued; now the
members of it break out into extreme and enthusiastic violence
from the benches at the west end, which are their chosen seats.
Lightfoot's fiddle-bow balances and saws with dolorous excitement; Teddington, who is strong in his bow hand, rasps
the strings as if his sole purpose was to drown and oblivionize
his worthy colleague's instrument; Mayduke, who is a sturdy
young farmer's son, the buck of the village, cannot get his
lower lip quite comfortably on the aperture of the box-wood
flute, but Will Golightly comes to his rescue, and shrieks into
his clarionet loud enough to awake old Sir Walter Cantelupe,
who sleeps on his back in an alabaster suit of mail in the south
chapel: as for Heavytree, who has but one arm, and holds the
tremendous bass-viol with an iron hook (he lost his arm
thirty years ago, in one of Queen Anne's battles), he toils
away with the solemnity of a man in a saw-pit at the huge

instrument between his legs, that roars, and groans, and bellows in a way that is not merely praiseworthy, but tremendous.

Now as we do not intend to follow Sir Harry through all the grand liturgy or solemn prayers of the early saints, martyrs, confessors, and last, not least, reformers of our great English church; let us explain what we mean by saying that incitement for worldly pride existed within that church of Beaulieu on that pleasant autumn Sunday of the —— year of the Hanoverian Monarch King George; well, in the first place, the old church would seem to a sneering man, it must be confessed, to have somehow or other forgot its primary destination, and from a church erected by good men for God, to have grown by an almost unconscious progression into a church erected to the worship of the Cantelupe family, whose rich-coloured arms — per bend or and azure — three dexter hands couped and erect gules, with the crest a dragon's head cloven, and the proud motto, "TRY ME," shone and glistened in every part. Its luminous red and azure outshone the old quaint crucifixion in the east window, and quite hid the sun and the moon, which the artist had tried to represent as eclipsed. It was let into the centre oak panel of the squire's pew, amid a nest of long apples, and strings of flowers, and fruit, executed by the hand of some disciple of Grinling Gibbons, but who had not his great master's art of turning heavy wood into airy and pendant flowers. It came out in full force in the chancel, where the school-children huddled and chattered in under-breath, quite regardless of the rhythmical prayers that rose like perfume from a silver censer from the good vicar's lips. It blossomed on Sir Roger Cantelupe's tomb—Roger the courtier, who Elizabeth herself smiled at when out hunting one day at Hampton, and declared that "stout young Sir Cantelupe was a very tall man of his hands," and who eventually falling into disgrace for secretly marrying pretty Mistress Anne Beauflower, a maid of honour to the old-maid Queen, was disgraced, and retired to forget miserable court intrigues, and be happy in the Wiltshire Downs, eventually to come and lie here in stone-ruffs of countless quills, pease-cod doublet, Venetian hose, and stiffened shoes, sumptuous in alabaster, beside Dame Anne his wife, guarded by a little band of sons and daughters, who kneel round his tomb in relief, all with ruffs and fardingales like their good parents. Then opposite them broke out the or and azure again, on the cavalier General's tomb, brave Sir Peter, who fell for his king at Northamptonshire, bravely—there he was, not a bit more humble than the Crusader in the chapel or his Elizabethan ancestor opposite, in the chancel, resting on his left hip; a General's truncheon in his right hand, on which is a fringed cuff glove; while he wears a serene expression of loyal determination in his oval face, which is so like his foolish, unfortunate master's.

It is true there is no or and azure, and cloven dragon's head on the whitewashed ceiling, nor in the carved oak pulpit, nor on the font—but why go on cataloguing the church, for it is carved on the great blue flag-stones in the side aisle, it is on that scrolled marble shield slab, with its cherubs, skulls, hour-glasses, and thick dismal bordering—it is of various degrees of lustre in every window but one, and that was smashed by a Puritan clerk in a fit of drunkenness during the Sacheverell agitation, and never yet replaced. We do not mean to say that this elaborate emblazonment of the whole church, as if it were a family salver or punch ladle, has arisen from any irreverent or arrogant pride of any individual Cantelupe; but the race is a proud one, and it is the result of a long crescent pride here represented in aggregate. From the Crusades, when Sir Walter or Cantelupe took the Dragon Crest from some monster of unknown name and fabulous attributes he slew in Egypt, down to the time of the present warm-hearted, good old Sir Harry of the keen brown eye, and cheek of frosty red, every century has but added to these heraldic records: one knight has given a window, another has erected a tomb; one gave that carved goblet of a pulpit, with that strange stalk to the sounding-board that is meant for a palm tree, but looks hugely like a great gilt stick of celery, the sounding-board that mushrooms out above like the dial face of a compass being starred and lined with magnet-rays of light and dark woods. It is something solemn and reproving, though, to human pride to think how many gene-

rations of the name of Cantelupe have sat in that pew lined
with blood-red velvet, faded here and there to yellow brown, or
looked down on those green lined, high sleeping boxes that came
in with Queen Anne; one after the other doled out by Time,
and snatched up by Death in their great card match at which
the stakes are human lives. Cantelupes not only lie under the
pews, and at the door, and in the chancel, but in the niches of
the wall, where the builder himself slumbers. It is a short
time is man's life—not many clock beats, not many buddings
and leaf falls—not many ebbs and flows; a little longer than
the birds—a little shorter than the avenue trees, yet time enough
to be proud in, and time enough to earn Hell or win Heaven.

But we are getting too serious: now there was nothing dole-
ful or whining about that day's religion in Beaulieu church, in
the county of Wilts. Parson Greenoak stood up erect in his
hearty age in the high reading desk so bathed in the slant white
sunlight that fell darting through a near window, that to those
in front of him he appeared in his white robes like the spirit
of some departed prophet appearing in vision of glory to a
dying saint; but this effect was marred somewhat by the threads
of light which strung across like some angel weaver's woof,
shining here and there behind good Parson Greenoak, on the
crimson velvet of the pulpit cushions, which were stamped in
the centre with the arms of their donor, Sir Harry, who gave
them to the church on his marriage day, now thirty years ago.
Apart, however, from all spiritual resemblance, which a touch
of worldly pride thus profanely broke in upon, it was a pleasant
sight to see the October sunlight mottle the opposite wall of
the Squire's pew with a glowy, quivering, golden mottle, that
as the service progressed, slowly passed further eastward, as the
sun rose higher towards noon. No wonder that when these
errant lights and fragments of glory glowed around the semi-
bald head of Lightfoot, Heavytree, and their tuneful band, one
old woman, whom many people thought a witch because she
was presumptuous enough to say she saw visions, declared in a
whisper to a red-cloaked gossip as the strings of the fiddle-bow
shone gold and transparent, and the heavenly but rather nasal
music rose up in a thick and almost visible steam, that she

never beheld anything so like her idea of the Elders with their golden harps except once when she saw King George attending service in Salisbury Cathedral. "Poor Goodie," said this worthy vicar, when somebody told him this, "wiser people than you have had meaner ideas of Heaven; you had better think of God visibly up in Paradise than in no heaven and no hell, like that poor Atheist they make so much ado about in Paris." Good man, he had always an excuse even for bad people; and to hear him you would think that we were living in the golden age, and that gold-worship was generally becoming extinct.

True, that a man like Swift, at this time fast sinking into idiotey, (dreadful punishment of wasted and perverted intellect,) would have smiled cynically to have seen the way in which the excellent vicar seemed unconsciously to direct all the prayers to the Squire's pew, as if that was the first turnpike gate on the road to Heaven. He would have scoffed in the churchyard afterwards at the vicar's bowing that way in the creed, waiting to begin the gospel till the Squire's pew was well on its legs, and in the sermon abstaining from touching anything but poor men's ills. There was nothing about pride, but a good deal about poaching; no word about the rich man stuck in the needle's eye, but a good deal about laziness, sottish idleness; a severe logician might almost have gathered from the sermon that poverty was a sin, and that no one but a child of the devil was either poor or was wicked enough to remain so. The church of Beaulieu was, in fact, rather a dangerous place for a keen observer, unless he could chain up his eyes; for it was amusing to see the old clerk John Nightwork, village undertaker, who sat under the pulpit, folding his arms on his breast, and deliberately dozing with a set expression of serene and tranquil enjoyment on his wrinkled mask of a face. It was amusing to see at fervid moments of the discourse, when the vicar got excited about some perverted text of Polycarp's, and drove down his hand on the desk and cushion with half the bang and almost the dust and smoke of a cannon; to see how the clerk looked up and nodded his head approvingly, as much as to say, "I knew very well it would come to that, and here

I am sound awake to show I was listening." Sometimes it would disturb the squire, who was no great hand at theology, and he would start, open his eyes, look round rather astonished, half rise up, shift his legs, and subside again into a smiling doze of nodding approval. The clerk had been known to say "Amen" loudly in the midst of the sermon; but we believe he tried to prove that it was an uncontrollable token of admiration, and meant in the Greek "so be it," alluding to "the original Greek," of which he knew about as much as of Chaldee. It was, indeed, one infallible move Nightwork had of ending all theological disputes at the *Duke of Marlborough*, in which he was a distinguished disputant.

The poetical observer and listener in the church might almost, without losing the thread of the vicar's discourse upon the heroism of Judith, coupled with denunciations of the excessive use of ale by the poor, illustrated by the not very appropriate example of Holofernes, who never drank any, have had many pleasant sounds mingled with the divinity that found its way into his watchful ear. First, the deep roused tick of the clock, which came as regular as a giant's breathing, from the belfry upper chamber, with a drowsy and unceasing monotony that furnished some excuse for the Squire's attention, that seemed now gradually to have settled down into what men call sleep. Secondly, the pleasant, soft, soothing cooing of the Squire's doves as they perched themselves on the ledge of the said belfry window. Thirdly, the noisy, but innocent chattering chirrup of the pagan sparrows in the churchyard lime trees; and lastly, not to mention the delicious glimpse of a fading rainbow through a side window, there was the incessant low whisper of the village children, which came like an under-current athwart the parson's sermon, and stood for the voice of the world negating the voice of religion.

It was quite proof enough of the vicar's being a good Christian, that he never once looked angry over his silver spectacles at the incessant barking coughers that seemed trying to cough him down, and put an end to protesting Christianity. Now, certainly, it sank to almost a whisper, but no sooner had it done so than some bell-wether croaker broke out in a deep bass, followed by a dozen or so of light skirmishers, who answered each other with a dropping file fire that seemed really intended, as I have said, to put down Christianity altogether ; as far as the vicar, in that church at least, could expound it. Then a sleeping boy fell off a form, or a book dropped, or the clock struck ; and through such conflicting obstacles it was that the good man fought his way to Heaven.

But we must not be stopped by futile delays, but describe the soft, green wandering light that on summer afternoons strays about the white walls of the church at Beaulieu, and that now in this autumn time had changed to a pale orange glimmer; the lime-leaves now were all so much leaf-gold, among which the orange-breasted robin piped like a child tired, thoughtless of what it disturbed, at the church porch ; one would have thought it longed to come in and serve as a chorister, but not daring, sat like a fairy bird without, and sang its little old world, mournful, and unchanged hymn alone on the cold bough, over the graves, waiting a minim rest or two between each verse of the spontaneous little anthem, as if first to hear if anything was said about it ; but hearing only a bull-frog croak from Heavytree, the bass-viol player, half strangled by a rheum in his first sleep, beginning again, paying no heed, no, not a whit, to the admirable divinity of the sermon.

Now the sermon was a good one ; but I am inclined to think too learned and disputative by half for the rustic congregation, whose minds, unaccustomed to be focussed to attention, would have grown cataleptic with a forty minutes' strain of such compulsion, though the subject were Heaven and their own heavenly mansions. If Sir Harry, the Squire up at the hall, and the churchwarden slumbered, what could be said to the smaller fry ? in fact, who could have girded at them but the vicar ? and he was too rapt in his own earnestness and his heavenward flight to observe them, unless one snored himself awake, and then looked up at him guilty red, as the vicar swept the area of pews over his spectacles. An Indian brought for the first time into that big wigwam, would have thought that the seventy heads were nodding in approbation of what the man, up the tree was saying, or he might have thought the heads, if he knew our customs, nodding for bids round the man at an auction, or saluting each other at some silent feast with friendly noddings, certainly anything rather than——

But why am I to chide my weaker brother? have I not, too, slept when I meant to be attentive? have I not, when I should have listened, caught myself taking notes of the side twitches and noddings of sleeping men, who have jogged themselves awake, stared awhile at the preacher and smiled, as much as to say, "that last argument was a clencher," and drawn back again into the blank, dark land of sleep; besides, did not Sir Harry just now, nodding, open his eyes at the two-and-thirtieth minute, unfold his legs, look complacently at his shining shoe-buckles, blow his nose with watchful dignity, at which all the twenty sleepers awoke, as he looked at them with mild reproval, repeating to himself "*Homerus aliquando dormitat*," in a low voice, as if it was a text.

Who says that the sermon was a bad sermon? yet it consisted chiefly of angry replies to some imaginary subverter of the Christian faith about the time of Cyprian; still it was a vigorous attempt to refute the errors of Arianism, which, however, certainly did not prevail much in the parish, the very name of that illusion in fact, but for that forty minutes' sermon, having, after so many centuries, not yet reached the tranquil village.

The Latin quotations, which were numerous, struck awe to the minds of the rural congregation, who the sudden transition of sound generally awoke just as the angry clashing and trampling of your railway train suddenly diving into a tunnel awakes the railway sleeper. The clerk always stirred at the sound of Latin, and nodded angrily and with dignity at some playing boys in the school benches. Now the sermon begins to wane, there are symptoms of its conclusion. The vicar looks forward over the last leaf. His voice perceptibly sinks, the cough chorus, hitherto increasing in violence or fitfully breaking out in gusts, as if one incited the other, lulls as if the thought of getting free sympathetically does everyone good—now with a benediction the vicar dismisses the people. The instant the last word is uttered, the turbulent children rush out with a jostle and tumbling scuffle, impatient for play or dinner—a few red-cheeked village beaux wait at the door for their sweethearts— there, too, the old men rejoin their wives, and go tottering past the place where they will soon rest for ever, while the boys run in and out, careless, between the grassy mounds.

Gravely after the last lagging alms-woman emerges the good vicar, who sails home to dinner in his white robes, &c.

I was still simmering on in a cozy warm sleep, when a shout from St. Ives, about a new brass that he had found under the matting in the north aisle, awoke me—I now took a turn at rubbing, and in twenty minutes more our trap was bowling back again across the Wiltshire Downs.

That night I wrote down my dream of the Squire's Pew.

CHAPTER X.

CROMWELL'S HOUSE IN LONDON.

THE dark, massy ghost of Cromwell haunts more than one locality of London. It has been seen a pillar of mist in Long Acre and Brompton, at Bermondsey and Westminster, in all which places the great Protector alternately lived.

Of all the London ghosts, except Dr. Johnson's, Cromwell's is, perhaps, the most corporeal and sturdy. Black suit and cloak it wears, and long boots; the hat, such as he donned the day he was proclaimed Lord Protector, has a broad gold band, in fashion not unlike a crown, girding it round.

Where shall we follow the stately ghost first? To the far Bermondsey; to the old house now the Jamaica Tavern, that is embalmed by the horrible fumes of the glue-makers and the tanners, whose steeping pits, filled with a dark liquor the colour of spiced ale, has a dust floating on the top of them that (following the simile) looks very much like grated nutmeg. All green then, I daresay, with bushy elms, when Cromwell perhaps brought his bride here from St. Giles's,

Cripplegate, or mounted at the door for Naseby or Dunbar, where the godless cavaliers and rebellious plaids fled before the battle-psalms of Oliver's troopers. Only a slice of the old building now remains; the other half has gone to the winds years ago; but in the half still left there are staircase beams stamped with carved quatrefoils and flowers; and there are old bolts that the mighty Protector of England may have stopped and loosed; long and high tables, larger than those of these degenerate times, old black settles that the Ironsides may have slept or watched round; and oak wainscoting that Oliver's breast-plate may have shone upon and his sword have clashed against.

No wonder the ghost rarely visits Old Brompton, for Cromwell House is gone to the ground years ago, and the old green lanes are now streets. Besides, ghosts lead and point and shake their heads, but they will not enter into discussions with you; and I do not find much evidence that Cromwell ever did live at Hale House, Brompton, the seat of the Methwolds, though Henry Cromwell perhaps did so before he went the second time to Ireland, and not improbably even married from hence. As it is a bygone house, we will speak no evil of it; but we may just say that it was a mere square brick chest, with a room in it lined with Dutch tiles. Nor are we, indeed, lucky with our other Cromwell residences; for our next trip is to the present Privy Council Office in Whitehall, where once the Cock-pit stood, in which locality dwelt the great country gentleman who governed England so well, and made her the terror and admiration of the world. It was to his wife, living at the Cock-pit, that Cromwell wrote the news of "the crowning victory" at Dunbar. Thousands of omnibuses rolling past to and from Westminster have, however, long erased all footsteps of our great Cromwell.

But the greatest portion of Cromwell's career, before he became Protector, was spent in King Street, Westminster, in an old wooden house lying between the Blue Boar's Head Yard (to be exact) and Ram's Mews. The street then ran straight from Charing Cross, past Whitehall, to Westminster, and had a great arch standing across it. It was a well-to-do street; for though poor Spenser the poet had died of starvation in it, Queen Elizabeth's Lord High Admiral had held Privy Councils there—councils so disastrous to the Spaniard. Through this narrow street the halberdiers brought King Charles in a close chair to Whitehall, after his trial at Westminster, and from its latticed windows Cromwell himself may have looked with stern sorrow at the sedan that bore the faithless king.

But I never meet Cromwell so often, even a dim shadow, in the sunshine, (for it is all nonsense about your ghosts walking only by moonlight : the mind's eye, to which alone they are visible, can conjure them up by day or night,) as in Long Acre, that quiet street of coach-builders. I specially love to track my sober ghost hither, because I know, from a dull, industrious book-grubber of my acquaintance, that my friend Oliver lived here quietly from 1637 to 1643, (eventful years for him, as for others,) where he was rated for the large sum, in those days, of ten shillings and tenpence. My date-grubber is even kind enough to inform me that the same not unknown Captain Cromwell lived on the south side, the Strand side, two doors from one Nicholas Stone, a sculptor.

And here I shall refuse to go any further with my ghost, or he will keep me half the night leading me about—to the Star Tavern, in Coleman Street, where he used, before the king's fall, in the dangerous and troublous times, to meet his adherents ; or to the Blue Boar Inn, High Holborn, where he intercepted the treacherous letter of the king ; so here I must stop him, for even a ghost may be troublesome. It was not in Long Acre, in the quiet Captain's house, that Cromwell kept his seven tables spread, as he afterwards did at Whitehall, nor his twelve footmen in grey jackets laced with silver and black. It was not here he saw his famous "Coffin Mare," with his favourite groom Dick Pace on her back, fly over the green turf ; nor from this house did he ride to waken the echoes of Hampton Park, or to shake down the chestnut bloom of Bushy with the sounding feet of his Flemish hunters.

How often, as I walk in the sunshine through that busy coach-builders' street, do I fancy I see coming towards me a form of massive stature, with leonine head, which, by the wart

on the right eye-brow, which marks his frown so dreadfully, I
know to be Cromwell, whose early life was spent in this neighbourhood. I know well his heavy eyelids and his full aquiline
nose, his broad lower jaw, his strong chin, and the long, soft,
curlless hair streaming down over his plain doublet collar and
steel breastplate. There is a natural majesty about the Huntingdon country gentleman, indeed, such as kings rarely possess.

How unlike this Long Acre, with its black still houses, to
that great yellow brick mansion at Huntingdon, where Cromwell was born! that house, not far from the dark Ouse, that
passes on sullenly to the Fen country through rows of dull
alders and drooping willows; or the stately ancestral house where
Oliver's grandfather entertained James I. with almost regal
splendour. Nor can we here help stopping for a moment to remind our readers that Cromwell was of no mean family, if truly
to be of a mean family is a disgrace in the estimation of any but
a mean mind. Cromwell was sprung of noble Welsh blood,
especially from a certain Dick of the Diamond, whom Henry
VIII. knighted for his unrivalled prowess in a Court tour-
nament. On both father and mother's side, by descent as well
as by various intermarriages, Cromwell's family was deeply
connected with that brave middle class which has produced
England's best and bravest men. He was educated at Cambridge, and studied law at Lincoln's Inn.

He returned home to become a careless roysterer, fond of
cards, quarter-staff, and rough country sports, till a great
darkness fell on him, and slowly through that darkness broke
the light from heaven that brought joy and peace. In country
quiet and ease he lived, "nursing his great soul in silence," as
his friend Milton said afterwards of him. It was no adven-
turer of restless ambition who became really King of England,
but a brave, pious, industrious country gentleman, who, at the
mature age of forty-one—more than half life over—took his
seat in the Long Parliament as member for Cambridge, resolved to throw himself into the front rank as a buckler for his
suffering country.

Still, through the pallor of ghostliness, (it is a long way to
walk from Connaught Place, where, under Tyburn gallows,

base hands threw the great man's corpse,) I can still see the bluff Oliver's tanned dyspeptic face, that Hudibras and the other cavalier wits thought it not disgraceful to mock at; the heavy red nose, too, the result of fen agues, I am not insensible to. But I forget it all in that glance of blended love and majesty that Dryden mentions so beautifully. I bow, therefore, with reverence when I meet the ghost of that good and truly great man. The ribald cavaliers—such men as Rochester and Buckingham—talk of him as the moody Puritan; but I know that he loves music, and will listen for hours to voice and instrument, with Milton his friend dreaming at his elbow. They call him the red-handed murderer; I know that he loves children, and is the tenderest of fathers. They think him a melancholy madman; I know that he loves an honest jest, and roared with laughter at seeing a soldier jam his head inextricably in a Scotch churn. They call him niggard; I know that he feasted all the Parliament House, each Monday dined all his officers, and every day kept all but open table, though in his own diet truly he was spare and costless. They call him an ignorant brewer; but Milton tells me that, had he chosen, Cromwell's natural capacity was so great that he might have equalled the greatest masters. They call him a hypocrite; but I know that he begins and ends every work with prayer.

I see him in Long Acre—this great, good man—walking with that dear stripling son Oliver, the news of whose death went like a dagger to his father's heart, with lazy, careless Richard, or his dear Dorothy (his daughter-in-law). That hooded graceful old lady, with the pure simple pearl necklace, must be the dear mother he loved so much; she of whom he always wrote with such respect and love; she who, in parting from him, gave him her blessing in these fond but broken words: "The Lord cause his face to shine upon you, and bless you, and comfort you in all your adversities; and make you to do great things for the glory of your most high God, and to be a relief unto his people. My dear son, I leave my heart with thee; good night."

Surely, when we reckon up the mothers to whom great men

have been indebted for their greatness and their goodness, we must not forget Cromwell's. I love the dear old mother that never heard a gun shot off at Hampton or Whitehall, but she trembled for the life of her dear Oliver. When I meet her now, she wears a plain white satin hood, fastened with decent gravity under the chin; her broad lace handkerchief, drawn closely round her neck, is tied with a black string; and over all this there comes a green satin cardinal, fastened with one simple jewel. Indeed, I often meet all the fine Puritan family in Long Acre—for ghosts love the home of their youth. Here I overtake his favourite daughter, Mrs. Claypole, who had the unfortunate Royalist bias; the more austere Lady Ireton; and Frances, whom Oliver's chaplain courted, but a Gloucestershire gentleman married.

I often think, when I see the stalwart ghost, that I respect him more as the kind father and firm friend, than even as the conqueror of Dunbar or Naseby—more as the retiring country gentleman, who would have been glad to live under his "woodside shade and have kept a flock of sheep," than as the kingly Protector, trampling down the cavaliers at Marston Moor. I love and venerate the man who, amid the cares of state, found time to console a bereaved father, and to recommend a dead officer's children to the consideration of Parliament.

I remember him as the most tolerant of men. He protected our universities, and preserved the dead king's scattered works of art. Sectarians of all sorts, and even Roman Catholics, met at his table. To Ussher the prelate he gave a pension; Baxter he sought to make a military chaplain to the Ironsides; Milton, the ideal republican, was his secretary.

I venerate him as the armed apostle of reformation, as the sworded advocate of liberty of conscience, as the Gustavus of England, as the warrior of Protestantism. He saved the bleeding Vaudois, he encouraged the Swiss, he threatened Turin, he scared the Pope, he humbled the Spaniards, he defied France. In all treaties he stipulated for a toleration of Protestantism. He planned a great armed alliance of the Protestant powers. He protected a society that was to correspond with all parts of the world, to encourage, aid, and defend Protestantism. Universal toleration, evangelical alliance, and all our grandest missionary work, were foreshadowed by this great man. It was not in Parliament or in power that this ghost of ours spent the best part of his life; no, but in grass farming on the flat banks of the Ouse among dank willows, in prayer, in preaching, and in the tranquil pleasures of home.

I gaze at the aguish ghost of the Protector, which I follow afar off, as children do a street show, with respect, yet with awe, whether he go towards Drury House or towards Whitehall, where the bad king lost head and crown at one blow.

But I must part from thy great shadow, as I have had to part from so many others. Oliver Cromwell! I see thy stern eyes and grave large features melt into vague sunshine as I still address thee. Now thy sword is gone; now thy grey stockings; now half thy mirror of a breastplate; now thy falling bands; now a radiant brightness that enwraps thee. Blessed spirit, may thy doom be mine. Glorious shadow of immortality, may I one day be as thou art, though my life shall have been to thine but as that of a pigmy to a giant. Illustrious among the crowned angels, may I learn more and more to venerate thy memory—a true king among men, a true saint before God.

CHAPTER XI.

THE OLD MULBERRY GARDEN, NOW ST. JAMES'S PARK.

TIME, who is a harlequin, famous for his tricks and changes, seems to treat London as the scene of a pantomime that takes a great many centuries playing, but still must come to the green-curtain drop at last. Wonderful are the changes and tricks he effects, telling, too, all the gentlemen of the stage, whether clown or king, the proper time for their entrance and their exit. His scenes are on a large scale, and they flap and slide about just like the scenes of the pantomime of my simile—(this hot weather it is impossible to keep metaphors quite congruous). Now a king's London palace, at a slap of his wand, becomes a hospital; now a gallow's green becomes a fashionable street. Perharps Harlequin Time wills it that now a Niagara sausage-machine roar in the cellar where Mrs. Brownrigg murdered her apprentice, now that a coal-wharf shall take the place of the Norman castle that once frowned upon the banks of the crystal Thames, the "silver-footed Thamesis," whose *strand* the poet Herrick, exiled to his rough Devonshire vicarage, longed to repace, or "reiterate," as he somewhat fantastically calls it.

The harlequin Time, with his changeful wand ever vibrating over our dear black-faced, changeful, dirty, delightful city, has played, and is still playing, strange tricks. There was the little, swift, crystal streamlet, the Fleet—swallow-swift and fleet-chasing ripple after ripple, from its hilly source in some Hampstead meadow, it is now a vaulted-up, loathsome, poison-breathing sewer, full of rats and odours that are so strong they run about in visible shapes, and is no more fit to be seen than a charnel-house, or a plague-pit newly covered. The little fairy nymph of that Fleet stream has long since died an Ophelia death, and lies buried forty fathoms deep in this fat and stagnant Styx of subterranean London—a sad type of all the bright youth and childhood that has grown old, and wicked, and festering, bad, and has died, and corrupted away, in this our wicked old London. The Fleet seems to me—if I may be allowed to draw a simile from a book I love much—the unhappy *Little Nell* of rivers; the Babe in the Wood, killed by its naughty uncles, the nightmen of London. Shall I stay to trace its decline, as it thickened and darkened like a painter's glass, when he washes his Indian-ink brush? Shall I tell how it flowed under the cruel thieves' haunts of the bad cocked-hat time—the heartless, false, artificial time—when, through bloody trap-doors and secret apertures, often by moon glimpses at the dead of night, stabbed and battered bodies were splashed into its waters by masked highwaymen and blaspheming wretches, with pistols still smoking, sticking from their huge flapped pockets. This is *Change No. 1.*

Change No. 2.—Lincoln's Inn Fields, where the Duke of Ancaster and other of Horace Walpole's grand, patched, and perriwigged, false, fribbly friends lived, with sprinkle of judges and great men (brain great, not pocket great)—fading to the stony row of silent chambers of 1861—where the grimy laundress sweeps the foot-marked door-steps, and where sparse grass grows between the bald white stones of the courtyards.

Change No. 3 of my sample changes; taken at random. The site of the National Gallery, in the middle Ages the King's Mews; where, in grassy plots, the dandelion balanced its hollow globe of down, like a floral acrobat, with only one trick, or spread its yellow shield flower, while the white falcons of Norway fluttered and whistled on the gloved hand of some lucky accident that wore the regal coronet, and strutted like a deity got down from its pedestal.

Change 4.—The silent and blocked-up warehouses, where chains dangle, and custom-house cats collect revenues of mice, where hops smell sweet, and hay spreads about—dry memorial of summer fields—and bales of spices tell stories to each other at night of Ceylon cinnamon-groves and Malabar jungles—stand now where once the Globe Theatre stood, where for the first time the great Elizabethan men sat and wondered at the magic world unrolled before them by that short prick-bearded Shakspere, who sat on the stage among the smoking gallants and their pages.

But I might go on all day, showing the pantomimic changes of harlequin Time; showing how London has eaten up all the green fields round it, and spread like a gangrene, killing and deadening as it spread. I could show how the rich citizens' houses of middle-age London are now chandlers' shops in small alleys, and that where Jane Shore, with her jewelled hair, sat and waited for the king, is now——but I must get at once to my special change—the change of the old Mulberry Garden of Charles into the modern Buckingham Palace; the change of St. James's Park from the swampy meadow walled in by Henry VIII., to the trim modern triangle where the children play, the ducks strut, the swans pout, and the cows stand so patiently to be milked; where once fat Prior and black-browed Swift

walked together, to better, not the English constitution, but
their own.

It is delightful even now going down the tumultuous Strand
—to pace which Dr. Johnson thought the glory of existence,
and the whole *Duty of Man*; to pass the pert statue of Charles
I., with the honeycombed pedestal; and to thread through
those iron Horse Guard gates, under the infallible clock; and
between those mirrors of knighthood, the two horse-guards,
who seem always so bran new, so veneered, so brushed, so
Windsor-soaped, so killing, so fatal, if not to their enemies—
whom they never meet—certainly to the Carlton Terrace nurse-
maids, who regard them as demigods and Achilleses—as probably they are, if Paris were to be again troublesome. I still
like to pace the hard clean walks that border the lipping water,
where the yellow puffs of ducklings scull about, and where the
frowning swans spread all their canvass to the blue June air—
just as some chiding monitor of time—some dull mechanic
sexton of the day—knells for the bygone hour over Westminster
way, and announces, with the indifference of a herald, the
coronation of a new king of sixty minutes. I like the barrack
sidewalk, where you hear the drum noisily vibrant, reminiscent
of Waterloos, or of many Vittorias. I like the open breezier
palace-end, where the fountain sows rainbows, and the once
royal home, so unhealthy, as Leigh Hunt will have it, raises
its wealthy but unmeaning bulk. I like to look at the hideous
monster of Mr. John Nash, architect—the place that bluff old
William IV. would not inhabit, and that, tinkered up from
time to time, was originally nothing but a cheating enlargement
of the old Buckingham House, by that heartless, cunning fellow,
George IV., who thus intended to trick parliament into building
a new palace. I remember, without even the intelligent aid
of Mr. Peter Cunningham—whom so many old writers have
aided—that this was originally a house built for Dryden's
Duke of Buckingham; that it was again rebuilt and sold to
George II., when a " pouting" Absolom; that then George IV.
played his tricks with it; and so, with some modifications
and enlargements, it now stands scaring the sun and frightening
the moon—a very hideous modification of the wattled cabin of

the early British chief. I like, too, the centre walks, where
our little Benjamins of London play, and cry, and babble, where
seedy meditators, and out-of-doors and sometimes out-of-
elbow philosophers think and doze, then wake, and doze, and
think ; where the thin, nervous, fine-fibred grass struggles for
a living, and where the pampered swans steer past with their
orange feet. Here, too, sometimes seated between an oily
farmer up for the "show," who rubs his red face with a silk
mainsail, and a gentlemanly vagabond, who tells me he has
been in the "Rifles," and who looks rather like a rifler—I
sometimes, in a day-dream, find myself asking the farmer who
that swarthy man in the dove-coloured velvet and cloth-of-gold
sword-belt is, who stands just opposite, throwing showers of
dry hemp-seed to the ducks.

"I see now't—sartin I don't," says the farmer.

I appeal to the ex-officer of the Rifles.

"You haven't sixpence about you, honoured sir?" is all the
reply I can get from the subaltern with the packet of greasy
letters. But yet I do see him ; my retina takes the full image.
By the apple of my eye, I know now that grim dark face, that
heavy eye, and black wig, that strong sure walk, and that train
of little waddling spaniels. Charles II. is watching the three
hundred men at work, and talking with some French gardener
about throwing all the ponds but *Rosamond's* into one strip of
water, with islands for the ducks ; there is to be a rising fence
for deer, decoys for ducks, broad gravel walks instead of narrow winding field-paths; Italian ice-houses, avenues of trees,
and, above all, a mall. I suppose the king got his love for
ducks in Holland, where he brought the use of skates from.
No use now, decoys for wild fowl in the Park ; the wild fowl
that Charles saw on their own nests are gone far from the roaring city, gone like the "fat and sweet salmons" that the historian Harison saw daily taken in the Thames—gone where
the woodcocks of the West End squares are gone, and where
the whitebait of Greenwich will follow, if the Thames goes on
still getting worse as it gets older.

St. James's Palace was once an hospital for fourteen leprous
sisters, and dedicated to the Spanish Saint who gave a name to

so long a line of Scotch kings, the dregs of which line we had the blessings of in England till we tossed them on to a foreign dunghill, where they ceased to trouble us, death shutting them all up, the lost drunkard, with the other bigots and *mauvais sujets*, in a certain quiet mortuary chapel of the Vatican that I have often visited with much thankfulness. Henry VIII., hateful to God and man, laid his fat hand on this charity, as the English Rehoboam did, wherever he could on church or manor-house.

The site of Buckingham Palace was once, as I have said before, a suburban mulberry garden, or Cremorne, that existed when Cromwell shut up Spring Gardens and they were built upon, and before Vauxhall was opened. It was a fashionable botanical-garden sort of place, where you ate tarts, and had wine and cheesecakes. Lord Goring lived close by, at the house that the Earl of Arlington and the Duke of Buckingham successively inhabited; and there was good air there and good company, and here, at a glass-smashing banquet, Charles II. himself violated his own decree against pledging and the drinking of healths. Ever since Cromwell shut up Spring Garden, the Mulberry Garden flourished.

But of that anon. This garden originated in a planting of mulberries near Westminster Palace, by that erudite and most wise simpleton, James I.,—the man born for a village school-master, or a country Shallow. It consisted of about four acres twenty-two perches of land, and stood on the north-west side of the present palace; it was intended to set an example, borrowed from some Italian traveller, of the cultivation of the Eastern tree, the poor witch-frightened pedant having some gleam of an idea that such culture would promote the manufacture of English silks. At that time, even in Scotland, the first principles of political economy were unknown, or the murderer of Raleigh would have known that new trades may be grown, but cannot be forced by the hotbed of royal decrees. The mulberry-garden silk—the due time of decomposition having come—like Chelsea china and other artificialities, " exhaled and went to "—limbo. Charles I., that melancholy and wife-ruled bigot, before its complete decease, granting it, mulberries, swaddled silk-worms and all, to the care of Lord Aston for "own and son's life," as laborious but dull Mr. Peter Cunningham has discovered, after much dusty grubbing, and dry diving into registers.

I will not stop to restore the old mulberry garden even in imagination; let the old haunt of folly be buried under the kitchen paving stones of the unhaunted palace. Let us picture only for a moment, if we like, and then dismiss for ever, the great shrubby unnaturalised tree of Palestine, with the thick sappy boughs, and large green toothed leaves,—what time the ground under their dark shadow during Charles I.'s anguish were purple, blood-stained with fruit, as if some Cavalier and Puritan had indeed been struggling for life or death under the fruit-laden branches; we may picture the Vandyke men, in suits of white silk or carnation velvet, pacing on the turfen bowling-greens, roses in their shoes, swords by their side, their hats plumed with blue or crimson, their bearing stately and grave, as befitted the gentlemen of whom Falkland and Hampden are the two contrasting types. Here, perhaps, too, grave-faced Puritan divines—Hugh Peters and his brother preachers —in sad-coloured raiment, short cropped hair, and black skull-caps on their heads, paced up and down, between the fountains, the silver columns; the flower beds—that seemed to rebuke melancholy as sinful,—and the large-leaved mulberry trees. Here, with heavy folio volumes of Prynne, and other faithful men, under their sinewy arms, they repeated the story of how King David once waited for the Philistines in the valley of Rephaim, and went forth to battle to smite them utterly by God's direction, when he heard a sound as of a rushing wind in the tops of the mulberries. It is true, says Brother Hew-Agag-in-Pieces, afterwards trooper in Cromwell's Ironsides, that the Douay version for "mulberry trees" substitutes "pear trees," ["but what is the Douay version?"—Drawer, bring three stoups of wine,—and again in the Psalms lxxxiv. 6, we hear of him 'who passing through the valley of mulberries;' —"and, Drawer, some pasty, if you have it."]

Here, without stopping to sketch that good and virtuous Surrey gentleman, Mr. Evelyn, who loved gardens so much that he expressed a wish to be buried in one, and who was treated to wine and cakes at this spot we speak of, on a certain afternoon in Cromwell's time, just after that iron-handed man had shut up Spring Gardens, and left the Mulberry Gardens as the only place of refreshment where "persons of the best quality could be exceedingly cheated at,"—we can but wonder, in a blind sort of way, at the quiet decorum with which so good a man must have moved stoically among the ladies and gallants who selected this place as one for special, and too often guilty rendezvous. He must have been a little reproving and chilling, and sad in face, for that loud-laughing, many-tongued place, where wanton satins swept the sward, and wanton fans beat the blue air, keeping time to amorous lutes, and satin shoes measured out the minuet, and much dangerous smiling and mischief were wrought on the primrose edge of the abyss of ruin.

But though Milton may have strolled here, thinking of Comus, and his revelling rout, and Cromwell have strode up and down thinking of how he should best bruise the foul fiend's head, trusting much in Providence, yet taking care to buckle his secret breastplate firm and tight; and Selden have mused on rabbinical lore, and Newton have looked at the stars, and Wren have traced out St. Paul's on the orange gravel,— we pass to a far more congenial figure, and one more befitting the wanton pleasure garden and the silken Circes of the lamp-lit arbours, than grave Mr. Evelyn, the sober and wise country gentleman.

Need we say we allude to Mr. Pepys—Mr. Samuel Pepys of the Admiralty, that fat-faced, rather pompous looking, fussy official,—not too moral, and an arrant time-server; a Puritan once, which he does not wish known,—a tailor's son, which he wishes forgotten,—in a word, a selfish gossip; but, nevertheless, a useful, hard-working, tolerably conscientious man, particular with his wig, expensive and showy in his dress; fond of amusement, and not unknown at the Duke's Theatre.

It is a May day, also, but long after Evelyn's visit, that we find Mr. Pepys here for the first time, eight years after the Restoration,—about five years before the place was finally closed, and its enchantment broken up. Mr. Pepys found it a silly place, worse than Spring Garden, but thought the "wilderness" somewhat pretty; and April next year he was here again, treated by some one with an olio made by a cook of the place, who had been to Spain with Pepys' great patron, Lord Sandwich; he found the podrida "a very noble dish, such as I never saw before,"—and let us hope digested it; then he took a walk, and eventually returned again, to sup on what he had left from the dinner at noon.

And who dare call us to task if we choose to presume that in the next arbour might have been seated a certain, not unknown, poet—one Mr. John Dryden; not in his old bookseller's hack uniform suit of Norwich drugget, but rather freshcoloured and grand, in his sword and Chedreux wig, drinking Rhenish and nipping cheesecakes with a lady in a mask—one Madame Reeve, the fair actress. Perhaps he is reading to her, under breath, his Ode to Charles II., which is poor compared with that he wrote to Cromwell, because, as the poet wittily says, in his quiet way, " Poets succeed better in fiction than in truth." "Well come off," laughs Madame Reeve, putting down her slender wine glass, and flashing out so bewitchingly with her sparkling white teeth.

It was to this bygone Circe land, Sedley, Etherege, and Wycherley, better poets than men, came to glean from life. Here they sat, and watched their Modishes, and Wildishes, and Snappems, their musicians and dancers, their 'prentices and sedan men, their young-old beaux and their old-young prigs, their citizens, servants, and children. Here (to Colby's) came gallants full of French oaths, and their new perriwigs and sword-belts, fresh from " dozens of champagne," and riding races round Hyde Park. Here, tired of Ombre, or of presenting oranges at the theatre, came the sparks to see the country ladies, whose great resort the gardens were, after the play had closed and the park had been visited. Here men came fresh from their dish of coffee or tea, to spill some Burgundy, and to drink toasts in brimming glasses. Here ruffians, fresh from the filthy dens of the Fleet, came to brag, and bully, cheat, and pick quarrels.

To judge by Shadwell, this garden must have been a place not always undisturbed by the clash of swords and the trample and scrunch of broken glass; for spirits were high in England then, and swords were ever ready for sudden murder or duelling, which is analogous to it. Fat Shadwell, whom Dryden attacked as a fool as unjustly as Pope did Dennis, talks of the "pleasant divertissement" in the Mulberry Garden—and one of his Frenchified humourists says: "Ay, I was there, and the garden was very full of gentlemen and ladies, that made love to each other till twelve o'clock at night—the prettyest; I vow 'twould do one's heart good to see them."

And here a word or two about that unknown vice of the present original day—plagiarism. I should be sorry "to rob Peter to pay Paul;" that is to say, to quote Mr. Peter Cunningham's useful if not brilliant book on London, when I had his authorities myself to go to, and some knowledge how to use them.

For in these times of literary filching it highly becomes a man of honour,—if he have any generous fire in him,—to sit down and settle this question of "plagiarism" with himself—how far honest quotations can be used without becoming dishonest thieving, and how far, when practised on oneself, stealing is to be resented, posted, and exposed. Now, Mr. Peter Cunningham, being a busy, not always accurate, compiler from all good books in London—such as Leigh Hunt, Smith's Rainy Day, &c.—must needs be used seemingly, though one go first hand for everything, and even set right, and fill up his numerous short-comings—the sin, not of error but of omission, being his most special one.

This settled, and feeling easier now having nailed the colours of a principle to my mast, I go back to the garden that changed into a palace about the same time Spring Gardens became Lockett's tavern, the great resort of the Queen Anne wits; and from here, where mulberries no longer stain pretty crimson mouths, let us return to the St. James's Park and the quiet cows, that West, that most smooth and intolerable of all dull artists, once painted. We have already in an erratic way, as becomes the legendary stroller, described how that fat tyrant,

Henry VIII., turned St. James's Fields, that were probably the people's lands, into a small chase; and how, in his corrupt and vicious cruel old age—this favourite of Mr. Froude, the crotchety and the changeable—turned out the fourteen leper ladies and the eight monks who kept up daily prayers. Here this "soul of leprosy," as Leigh Hunt, generally rather mincing and affected, finally calls him, lodged his "swathed and corrupt body." The very year he married Anne Boleyn it was that this tyrant of so many flocks and herds took away the poor man's "little ewe lamb." He who had seized on good men's lands—who had revelled, Belshazzar-like, out of even sacramental cups—now spared no one; his thirst for lust and revenge grew like Nero's. He had dead Wolsey's Whitehall and Hampton Court, he had Royal Windsor, he had many palaces, but he must, too, have this little leper's hospital, this Naboth's vineyard, so he clutched it. The black red-brick gateway of it, dull and drear, still stands facing the steep street of clubs, and the initials of Henry and Anne still stand together in the "chimney-piece of the old presence-chamber."

It was the same royal murderer of More, Fisher, and Surrey, who made a tilt-yard and cock-pit where the Horse-Guards (equally useful) now stands. But now no blows are exchanged there, and military millinery is all that remains of the old brave buffeting that was the horse-play of Henry's time; that king who made up for a good youth by so wicked and corrupt an old age—Henry, the Vitellius of England.

History, as hitherto written, has been nothing but a record of the crimes and blunders of kings. The history of the English people I hope some day to enter the lists for, caring myself more for the species man than the genus king. Of king-history St. James's Park gives us plenty. We see that false king, Charles I., with his dull, sad face, pacing across it on his way to his execution outside the Whitehall window. There is Charles II., his hopeful son, talking to Nell Gwynne over the garden-wall of the Mall. There is James II., thinking of the bishops, and wishing they had but one neck. Then dull Queen Anne, nibbling her fan for want of a repartee. George I., short, snub, and pale, with his fat German mistress or burly Walpole by his side; George II., coarse and rough, with his aquiline nose ever pointing to Chatham; George III., scarce saved with Pitt, the lean; and George IV., the handsome and vile.

There are wonders too, hidden in this avenue of trees beyond the sooty Egyptian cannon. There grow sable descendants of that tree that King Charles pointed out, as he paced bravely to execution—soldiers before, soldiers behind—as the very tree planted by his unlucky brother, Prince Henry. Is that the one the Horse-guard sits with his back against, or was it that tree's grandfather? Might it not perhaps, too, have been that tree under which, on a certain fair November evening, the Lord-General Cromwell took aside that heavy man, Whitelocke, having first saluted him with more than ordinary civility, as he met him on horseback, or, worn with business and State papers, which are not light reading (as dull men call all reading which is amusing)—was it here, with saturnine face, dyspeptic red nose, and wart on the left temple, the great general put that very leading question to a cautious statesman—" Whitelocke, what if a man should take upon him to be king?"—to which answers Bulstrode, reasonably honest, "I think that the remedy were worse than the disease"?

Is it possible that the great saviour of England did plan this step, feeling no hope of doing permanent good without thus settling that question of Divine right for ever, and did this sounding satisfy him, and scare him for ever from the abyss? Or is it possible that Bulstrode — in the retirement of his Wiltshire house, and surrounded by those sixteen children to whose society Charles II., forgetful of friend and enemy, had dismissed him—invented this conversation in order to blacken Cromwell, as the manner of the age was? A man who serves first one party, then another, may be admired for his talent, but can never be respected. Like woman's virtue, political character is irretrievable. Perhaps some of those numerous State papers that Bulstrode's wife burnt after his death might have explained away or contradicted this momentary weakness of Cromwell—the true-hearted.

There must have been great walking in St. James's Park in the Queen Anne times, so dear to old students of the

"Spectator," of Pope, Prior, Swift, Arbuthnot, and Gay. The Boscobel oak acorns that Charles II. planted and laughed over with Rochester and Sedley, and Killigrew and Arlington, are gone, the very lines of the Green Walk and the Jacobite Walk (or Duke Humphrey's Walk, and the Close Walk), and the Long Lime Walk, are forgotten and scarcely traceable; but there is still Duck Island or its successor, that St. Evremond, the wit, was made governor of, as a joke, by that "Merry Monarch" who made so many of his subjects weep. One can still see the Parade where Le Sueur's bronze gladiator stood on its stone pedestal, but it is difficult to imagine the green ditches and mounds that Charles II. had levelled, and the trees he had cut down, and the avenues he made, and the fruit trees he planted, or the bridge that he removed.

But here Mr. Leigh Hunt's reminiscence of the "Music in the Park" recalls a fine chivalrous legend of the place, which interests us more than that measured tramp or that thrill of the drum. It refers to the stanch fidelity to a fallen cause of old Lord Craven, the supposed lover in early life of James the First's daughter, the exiled Queen of Bohemia, whose great house stood on the present site of the Olympic theatre. He it was who was on duty at the palace the day the Dutch troops were marching triumphantly and bloodlessly into the park. The blood of the old soldier of Gustavus—the Dalgetty of a corrupt court—fired up; he would have borne down with half-a-dozen men on these pickle herrings, and died fighting among their swords; but his master forbade him, and he strode away "with sullen dignity."

But here, too, as we look towards the forsaken palace-court of St. James's—never a lucky home for royalty since the poor leprous sisters were expelled—arise unhappy memories. Here George IV. was born to bless the nation; and here the unlucky Pretender—"a warming-pan" changeling, as the Whigs said; here Charles I. parted with his children—the swarthy boy who was born here, and his large-nosed brother of York; here Mary died, and Prince Henry, the lad of such promise, who pitied Raleigh. Like other London houses less celebrated, much good and evil has been done in that palace—

many heads and many hearts broken—much joy and much sorrow has entered there.

And now, before we leave the Park, we remember how otherwise it has altered. Being no longer a sanctuary from bailiffs, there are no hollow-cheeked men now gasping about on benches; and if a modern Lady Bradleigh had an enthusiasm to see a great novelist, such as Richardson, she would not ask him for an elaborate " Hue and Cry" description of himself, that she may know him when, on a certain day, the author of " Clarissa" walks in St. James's Park.

But now, with the clash of cymbals in our ears, mingled with the mild lowing of cows, and with a gleam of scarlet and flash of steel in our eyes, we must quit the park, the swamp of the ante-Norman days, the fields outside the lonely isolated leper-house of the fourteen sisters, the Duck Island of St. Evremond, and the walks the swarthy Charles paced, and hie to other legendary scenes, where we may again meet the reader.

The Horse-Guards' clock, with both hands for once united, points to twelve—I must away—I hear a 'bus conductor you cannot hear—I see his tin whistle which you cannot see—and his cry is, " Bank, Bank," which is my way to London Bridge.

CHAPTER XII.

IRISH FAIRIES.

I WAS, knapsack on my back, with occasional lifts on jaunting-cars, making a tour of Ireland, hearing shillelaghs rattle, seeing whisky drunk, and listening to rebellious songs all about pikes and the *Shan van vocht*, or the old prophetess who in '98 predicted the arrival of the French.

I was a tourist on my way through Connemara, determined to hear as much of the brogue, see as much of the big blue mountains called "the Twelve Pins," and pick up as many stories of banshees and Ribbonmen as I could in a dozen weeks. I had come from Killarney, where the spectre king, O'Donohue mailed in sunshine, rides over the lake every May morning, and I was going to Donegal, the country of rock dwarfs, smugglers, and mine spirits. I knew if there was a fairy to be found in Ireland I should hear of it from Dennis O'Flanagan, who was to drive me in the jaunting-car between Ballyrobin and Ballynabrig, and so it proved.

The day had turned out wet, the rain fell in long slanting cords, and beginning first by covering the window-panes of the inn at Ballyrobin (where I was detained) with silver scratches like so many feeble attempts at autographs by some traveller possessed of a diamond ring, had at last come to a wide, washing stream that flooded the glass, and kept it dripping, like a thatched roof on a wet day, the bright drops matching each other in races to the bottom, as if they had determined to be merry, and to get up small Derbys on their own account. The car waited till the cushions got wet, and Dennis then drove it back again under cover.

In my room there was not much to amuse a weather-bound traveller. The only books on the shelf over the illuminated tea-tray were a Catholic Testament in the Irish language, a dismembered volume of Tom Moore's Irish Melodies, and a History of the Irish Rebellion, black-greasy with thumbing. The mantelpiece was stuck with bagmen's cards. There was nothing in the room peculiarly national except the peat fire and the big peat basket, which in Ireland stands where the coal-scuttle does in England. There were the lumps of dried black turf, looking like small oblong cakes of chocolate, burning, or to be burnt. There is no blaze about a peat fire, but only a quick, earnest, white flame, that slowly burns the sods (where once the snipe and wild duck fed and nestled; where the moping, bankrupt heron brooded over his irremediable misfortune; where the hooded crow watched the lamb, and the endless magpies strutted and fluttered) to a blinding pure crimson, so pure and intense, that it gradually alchemises into a bloom of colourless radiance, and then, lowering and sinking, lapses into white stillness preparatory to fusing into the mortuary ashes of old age and repentance. There is something primitive and savage in the tall basketful of dry turf, and I like to throw it

on the fire, fancying myself Caractacus, or Phelim O'Toole, the
first King of Munster.

The Three Salmons at Ballyrobin is not an hotel like the
Hotel du Louvre at Paris. It more resembles an English village inn, with a dash of the English beer-shop. On the mantelpiece was the gresset (cresset), or rush wick in a pool of grease,
that flared for me last night while I chilled my blood with
stories of the Irish pikemen, and warmed it with sips of whisky-
toddy. Then there is the rude deal table, which appears to
serve the landlady's family for a sort of register or family
Bible ; for it is carved with hieroglyphic notches of past scores
and initials of great men of the Joyce (landlady's family name)
lineage now dead. O'Flanagan, when he came in to tell me
that he thought there was a bit of blue showing over Benabola,
and that the weather would hold up yet, was great in his com-
mentaries on these initials. He said what I took for J for
Joyce, was no J, bedad, at all, not a hap'orth of a J, but F for
Flanagan, flaming O'Flanagan, his great-great-grandfather, who
held the inn before the Joyces was born or thought of. He
was of the O'Flanagans—the flaming, combustible, mad, burning-
hot O'Flanagans—the ould Irish chiefs that the monks used to
mention in their litanies, and pray specially against, chanting,
as the candles twinkled, the incense smoked, and the bell
tinkled, " From the wrath of the O'Flanagans—the flaming
O'Flanagans—good Lord deliver us !" Well, but about the
initials : there was M. F., that was Murphy O'Flanagan (rest
his sowl !), that bet the big grazier at Ballinasloe, and was
killed at last by a foul blow on the back of the head of him
from a thundering stone in an old woman's stocking. There
was D. F.—that was Dennis O'Flanagan, who, at Donnybrook,
wopped Slippery Sam, the English drover, and was transported
for so getting the better of him. P. F.—that was Paddy
O'Flanagan (Dennis's father, rest his sowl !), who ended his
life bravely on the drop at Derry, for cutting the ears off of a
" dirty blackgaird " of a Dublin land agent.

While Dennis, really trusting it will hold up, goes to get
out the car, I turn over all my Irish stories, whether of banshees or ribbonmen, of leprechaun, crock of gold, changeling,

demon horse, croppy, fairy, or what not. I bethink me of how a Doolan once tamed the demon horse, and of how the famous O'Rourke went up to the moon, and was left there by the " big thafe " of an eagle. Tired at last of my rumination, and finding no one coming, I rouse myself and go out into the kitchen to see what delays Dennis and the car. I find Dennis, totally forgetful of me and the journey, intent on teazing Mistress Joyce's eldest daughter, a little wicked, black-eyed colleen, who has her back to me, and is arranging her long hair, which looks something like a horse's mane, by means of a cracked three-cornered bit of looking-glass stuck on the second row of plates on the dresser, and singing like a mermaid as she weaves her tresses :

> " Sweet Molly Carew,
> It wasn't for you
> That I gave in the banns to the parson,
> Yet for you I'd do murther,
> Yes, trayson, or further,
> Stale, felo de say, or rale arson."

On one side of the crystal triangle sacred to female vanity, was a truculent, black-browed, burglarious portrait of Dean Cahill; on the other, a fubsy caricature of Napoleon, who is still the idol of the Irish peasantry, though he never did anything for them; these impulsive, inconsequential Celts always like best those who serve them least. Three brown, smoky lumps of ham contributed by the deceased " gintleman who pays the rint," depended from a beam over my head, like swords of Damocles. In one corner of the earth floor rolled a heap of " pink eyes," mixed in brotherly union with the " baskets-full," the genus potato the Joyces especially affect. On the shelf near Dennis is a suspicious green bottle half uncorked, and as he hears my foot, Dennis drops his whip, cries " Whisht! in a moment, your honour!" and is off to the stables, while Kathleen looks round, colours, and brushes a stool clean with her apron for me to sit down on, then kneels down and puffs at the smouldering peat fire, which she had nearly let out while Dennis had been whispering soft nonsense in her little pink ear. I observe on the mud floor, which is scooped out in hollows, and is anything but level or clean, the shavings of an alpeen (shillelagh) which Dennis has been long seasoning in the dunghill, and which he has just now been shaping into a terrific mace, intended to thin the ranks of the base anti-Flanagan faction; a rope of onions, in their smiling, bronzed, red-yellow skins, dangle overhead, and a salmon rod, with a spear at the butt-end, rests in a corner of the room. Kathleen, her mermaid dressing over, is now sitting down at the back door, on a chair without any particular seat, with one eye on Dennis, who is putting-to the car, and flapping the blue cushions, and with the other on a she-goat, that feeds, tethered, near the stable, and is waiting for Mrs. Joyce to milk her. At Kathleen's feet rolls, not over-dressed, young Teddy Joyce, playing with his mother's beads (the rosy darlint!), the very beads she counted as she went last week on her pilgrimage up that holy mountain near Westport, Croagh Patrick, which is as conical and nearly as steep as an extinguisher.

Dennis gives a howl of delight—one of those howls that you may still hear even in a Dublin concert-room—as the last buckle of the harness is slipped into place. He reappears in a large blue great-coat that reaches down to his heels, and with a rusty hat with a flapping lid that goes up and down, twined round with white shiny lines of gut, and studded, not with brooches, but with gaudy "macaws" and "golden pheasants," as the best salmon-flies are called. Amongst these, like a gun from an embrasure, obtrudes the old Irish Adam, in the shape of a black dhudeen pipe, oily and odorous.

A truly Irish hubbub announces our departure. Mike Joyce emerges from some cellar, or secret distillery, red and rejoicing; men come out and shake hands with Dennis; Mrs. Joyce, with her white frilled cap and pleasant staring face, insists on mixing me a "stirrup cup," in the shape of a glass of whisky-toddy: the sight of the sugar distilling down in a silvery shower in which, gives me quite a new impression of the charms of chemistry.

I shake hands with everybody, as if I was one of the Allied Powers in a popular print. I balance myself sideways on the shelf of the jaunting-car, feeling as an Englishman at first always does in that wild, erratic vehicle, as if I was on a side-saddle, or rather on a chair which was being drawn from under me..

I felt slightly qualmish, and clutched at the back rail as we started with a spurt and jerk that nearly unseated me.

" Hurrah!" called out the Joyce family. " More power to ye!" said Mrs. J. " Good luck to the worst of ye!" said Kathleen, looking up with a smile at Dennis from her stocking.

Off we were—that is to say, off I nearly was—but I managed to keep my seat, which is more than some M.P.s can say, and away we went at that headlong, reckless, generous, pelting pace that Irish carmen, reckless of wear and tear, always do go in the south of Ireland. Ballyrobin faded behind us. Now, you who have laughed at the incomparable traveller who told you of coals being brought up on a china plate, guess what luggage we had in our car. Rats in a bottle? An elephant in a jam-pot? But you would never guess. A turkey in a bandbox—yes, positively, a turkey sent in an old bonnet-box to Ballynabrog market by Mrs. Joyce the prudent. I have seen a few droll things, but never anything odder than that. A swan in a basket at Basingstoke, with his neck out and a parchment direction round it, is droll ; but the turkey in Mrs. Joyce's bonnet-box was irresistible.

Dennis is a Connaught man, pale and whiskerless, but with straight black hair and good features, with a serious, earnest manner, changing rapidly to rollicking fun and drollery, and with a fine swelling low-toned voice, capable of much rise and fall, much in and out, and endless subtle gradations of feeling.

It is rather startling to a sober, cynical, sceptical English-man, who believes what he sees and can handle, and little else, to hear, for the first time, an Irishman telling you a fairy story with a quiet, almost sad, air of intense conviction and feeling ; it is startling to one accustomed to see sham ghosts brought up at police-courts and sentenced to the tread-mill, one accustomed to hear aerial voices and winking statues accounted for by spectacled men on scientific principles, to find a person soberly and calmly relating, with a voice thrilling with emotion, some narrative of a dumbly prophesying banshee, or a child stolen by the fairies. At once a great mist rolls away, and you see the centuries that roll between the Protestant and Catholic, the Saxon and the Celt. You feel that you are in a twilight country, where faith is still unreasoning and supreme; where miracles and relics, and ghosts, are still believed in; where ghost stories are matter of life and death to men; and where the beautiful monsters of our nurseries still walk, even in the daylight. Dennis has heard the banshee in the blue cloak, with the grey dishevelled hair, wailing under the peat heap; he has seen the phooka, or demon horse, tear past at night, with fiery mane and phosphorescent eyes; he has seen the fairies in green, garlanding the mushroom; he has beheld O'Donohue on his white horse rise from the tranquil morning lake; he has stolen up and heard the cluricaun, or little dwarf in the cocked-hat and scarlet Hogarth coat, tapping at a shoe on the sunny side of a haystack; and here am I, who love everything Irish, quite an outer barbarian, who has never been granted any of these privileges! The banshee I saw near Cork turned out to be old Mary Burke, drunk under a hedge, crooning a croppy song to herself; my phooka near Ballycastle was a tinker's Kerry pony; my leprechaun an itinerant cobbler, mending a shoe under a bramble hedge outside Blarney Tower.

I was interrupted in these mythological reveries, and was prevented from coming to my final conclusion that more of the old Paganism remained in Ireland than in any other European country, by a tremendous split and crack of some part of the car.

"Be aisy," said Dennis. "You get on the 'crow's-nest'" (the little nook for the driver in front of the car and between the two seats, where no Irish driver, if he can help it, ever sits). "I'll stand up by you, and it'll be all right. The car's not so young as it was, but it's——"

Here we gave a tremendous bump against a roadside post.

"Bedad! not many a car 'ud stand *that*, and be the better for it!"

Just then the rain began again—such rain! grape-shot and

razor-blades—as we tore on—"slipping through it," Dennis called it—between walls of mountains capped with cloud. For more than an hour, head down, we butted through this, our shining yellow waterproofs glistening like gold.

At last it cleared up, out came the laughing blue. The bedrenched horses struck out sprightlier than ever. Dennis began to sing, then to talk, and our talk fell on a certain mountain we were passing, called the Giant Mountain.

Now, Dennis was great in giants, being one of an old family who had numbered many giants in its ancestral roll.

"Did you ever hear of the giant who could hear the grass growing?" said I.

"No," said Dennis, "he couldn't have been a native of these parts. (Well, that's a good one too.) But I have seen a giant's grave there away in Ennis, your honour. They say that he had the biggest bones of any man in those parts, but that his wife, falling in love with an ould haythen King of Clare, with the big gold crown on him, so that he looked like a walking jeweller's shop, *snigged* off his head with his own sword, for no other had any power over him. Many's the time I've sat making salmon-flies on that giant's gravestone. It wasn't twenty years ago that a party of the Green Horse came by that way, and stopped there, at the very stone, to water their horses. 'What's this?' says the corporal to a countryman, who was digging praties fornent it. 'It was the work of a big Irish giant in the ould times,' says the countryman, civilly. 'Well,' says the other, 'then it will be the work of a young Scotch giant in these new times to remove it.' So he tries, and tugs, and tugs, and gives it a terrible howge, but he couldn't make anything of it. (Laughs.) Och! the giant was too much for them—for it's there now."

"I suppose," said I, "the baushee is seen sometimes hereabouts."

"'Deed they are, your honour," said Dennis, seriously; "we generally hear them in the evening, or at twilight-fall, and we know then it is no human voice keening, because it is so sweet and mournful, like a sorrowing angel in purgatory (rest their sowls!) for all the world, your honour. The noise is just as if it was some old woman was sitting down under the wall yonder, and beating her thighs at intervals with the flat of her two hands, then flinging them up over her head and clapping them together, as the country keeners do when you hire them at a funeral to chaunt out the Ologaun."

"She dresses, I have heard," I said, humouring his belief, "in an old blue cloak, with her long grey hair falling over her white staring face, which is generally wan and famished. At Dunluce Castle they showed me a round room at the base of a tower overlooking the sea. It was once the prison of the Earls of Antrim—some foul deed must have been done there in the black old times. The earthen floor of this banshee's tower is always kept clean and free from dust, and people say it is swept daily by the banshee."

"To think of that, now, your honour!" said Dennis, with intense interest, feeling his faith confirmed. "Well, a banshee was heard the night my mother died, and it was in an old Danish fort at the end of our praty ground; when my poor mother, and she in her death-struggles, heard that terrible wail that she knew was not human, and she down in the fever, she says to my father, says she, 'Dennis, I must go,' and sure enough she died that day week, at the very hour—and the same thing had happened to all her family, for she was of a good owld stock, your honour. A year or two after, what did she do but appear to Teddy, one of my little brothers. He come in one summer evening, and told us that as he was playing about with the yellow flowers that grow in the bog-holes, making them into necklaces and belts, and what not, he feels a sort of warning, looks up and sees mother sitting on the stile just as she used to do, but now very sad and pale. He ran to her, but just as he got near her, she melted away and disappeared. Then he got frightened, which he wasn't before, and run screaming home and towld us; and I remember it more, by token it was St. Dennis's day, and he is my patron saint, rest his sowl!"—crossing himself five times.

"Did you ever see a cluricaun, Dennis?" said I—"one of those little wizen fellows in red-heeled shoes, scarlet coats, and laced cocked-hats, who is seen hammering at a tiny brogue inside the ruins of a chapel, and who, if you gripe him, tells you where the crock of gold is?"

"No, your honour," said Dennis: "but I met a fairy man once when I was a boy. It was up a high mountain, where I went to cut a stick, for it was all shaking with hazel-nut bushes, and I didn't care then for the story of the old folks that it was slap full of fairies, and what not, being a devil-me-care gossoon. I got up the hill, scrambling through the stones and dry fern, frightening rabbits, and startling thrushes, treading the swate breath out of the dry purple thyme, thinking of my girleen, as I always did when I saw anything specially bright, sweet, or in any wise purty; up I went and up, now pushing through the thorn bushes, and now getting out of the green dark into the broad blue brightness and sunshine, till I got nearly to the top, and looking out clear over bog and river, thanked God for having made such a country as ould Ireland. Then, looking above, what do I see but, twenty yards off, as nate a stick as I ever saw in my life, and, by my sowl, I didn't forget to cut it, and just as I was stripping off the broad woolly leaves, singing 'Ould Ireland's native shamrock,' I looks up and sees a common-looking queer sort of ould man coming straight towards me along the path. 'What do you do, you spalpeen,' says he angrily, 'cutting my trees?' And he spoke as if they all belonged to him. Well, though it give me a little tremble, I wasn't to be put down, and thinks I, I'll walk nearer to you, and see what sort of a man you are—for I was ready then with my hands, your honour, and I walked straight on—straight on. But when I got to the place, tare an 'ouns, where he had stood, he was gone—gone. I looked everywhere, under the trees, behind the bushes, over the big stones, but no man. So, thinks I, it's a fairy, sure enough, and with that, as if I had been shot down, I ran like a fellow from a mad dog. Och! it was divil a time I run faster in my life but once. Sod, wall, stone heap, bramble-bush, water—gap, nothing stopped me, till I got home, three miles off, torn, wet, dirty, red-hot, and frightened."

"But did you keep the enchanter's stick?" said I.

"Och, faix did I," said Dennis, "for a year or two, and the

old man never claimed it ; still, I always felt rather quare with it in my hand, and thought it would get me a bating maybe at a fair, or bring me into some bad luck ; so I never took it to a faction fight, but one night, getting drunk, I lost it at Westport."

"Didn't you tell me," said I, "your father died for grief at a bating he got at a faction fight ?"

"True to you, your honour," said Dennis, clicking his whip, "or may I niver spake again. He was the champion of Knockmagee, your honour, he kept all the Joyces and the rest of them at bay, till one day twelve men of them got round him and bet him down when he was tired. I saw his shillelagh the other day over the chimney of a cousin of mine ; it was twice as big as any other shillelagh. Och! he was a powerful, strong big man, your honour (rest his sowl!), but they put him in gaol for the fight, where he was hurt, and it broke the heart of him not to be able to pay them out. That was a dreadful day to see the women with the stones in the stockings, and as for the loaded sticks clattering, you could have heard them two hundred yards off. Och! but I owe it to those Joyces, though Mike is my master. He had an extraordinary way of holding his stick, your honour, in the middle, and letting the end cover his arm and elbow, that has never been aqualled since. He had seen some ghost sights, too, had my fayther."

"What! more banshees ?" said I, anxiously.

"Oh, no, your honour, but fairy pipers—the fairy pipers, your honour. He was one day near the Danes fort, as we called it, at Ballyrobin, which is now little better than a grass hill with a hollow inside to it, when he heard, as he was driving the cows home, some sounds he thought was some neighbours staling his hay, which was making at the time, and lying about in dry heaps, your honour ; so he goes home quietly, and gets an old rusty bagonet, and what does he do but lies down to wait for them behind a large hay-cock outside the fort. Presently, what should he hear with his two ears, but a blessed sort of music oozing out of the fort, just like a thousand birds singing together on a May morning. Och! your honour, it was

K

nothing but the good people dancing and figuring inside the hill. Well, before my father could make out where it came from he fell in a sort of swound, and when he awoke he was outside the fort, two fields away ; it was quite dark, and as for the bagonet, where was it but stuck in some hay just behind him ! Well, never a word did he brathe of it till his dying day, when I leant over to catch his last gasp. But I'm tiring ye, your honour.'

" Not a bit, Dennis," said I. " It prevents me counting the milestones."

" Well, then, I'll be telling you how there was a young Scotchman who took the farm after we went, and who used to be always laughing at the humbug about the fairy piper. ' Pipe away,' says he, ' and be plagued to you ! So long as I don't have to pay, its chape music is that same.' Thim's the words, or very near, he made use of at the markets and patterns, till one evening he was coming through the snipe meadow, and what does he hear but a piping just as if it was underground, and underground was heaven, and these were the sowls of baptised children making merry and dancing for joy. As it was, as soon as he got home, ' Ma lanna vicht,' says his mother, who was half Irish, ' saints in paradise, what's turned your blood, jewel ?' Then they teazed him, especially the girleens his sisters, till he recovered a bit, and up and tould them he had heard the Macarthy's fairy pipers."

" Those Protestants are very slow of belief, Dennis," said I.

" Och ! and you're right, your honour," said Dennis. " Penance, pilgrimage, cross, mass, it's all one with them. Faix ! it puzzles me to say how the likes of 'em will ever find a back way to get into heaven without paying St. Peter's turnpike. But has your honour ever heard of how the fairies change the children in ould Ireland ?"

" Of course I have, Dennis," said I. " Don't we all know how they pine and pine and get wizen, and knowing, and say things any old men could say ; and then the mother, after much praying, rushes at them suddenly in the cradle with a red-hot poker, which she has been getting ready for the hour past, and then, with a scream, the change comes, and she finds, instead of the little knowing dwarf, her own fine rosy child again, crying for the breast."

"Bedad! Your honour," said Dennis, "has got it all by heart, like a schoolmaster gets Latin! Well, I heard a case of this kind the night of a birth only last Paschal. A friend of mine who drives a car was coming along the road, and sees something white at the window of his brother's house yonder, so what does he do but get out and creep up closer did Patsy, and what should it be but an old woman, wrapped up in grey, handing a child out of a lattice to another ould creatur in grey, who held up her arms for it down below. 'Have you got it?' says she. 'I have,' says the other. Well, he thought it was all witchery, and that, perhaps, it was a little owing to the whisky he had drunk at the fair; but, sure enough, next day, he found his brother's child had died at the birth. So he knew what had become of it, that what they buried was a mere trick of flesh, and that the real child was snug and safe in fairy-land —which was a comfort to him, though he kept it to himself. So, niver mention it, your honour, or it'll hurt the family."

"Why, Dennis," said I, "you are as full of old stories as an egg is full of meat."

"And fuller too, begging your honour's pardon," said Dennis. "I remember hearing a neighbour of ours at Kilmore tell me that the night of the last great storm she and some other women were sitting round a fire in a cottage, listening to the pelt and drive of the rain, and the fluster and worry of the wind outside the cabin—crossing themselves, I'll be bail, and thinking of the forrior ganogh (bitter sadness) of those who had gone to Ameriky, and might be then on the broad say (rest their sowls!). All of a sudden there came a bigger roar than ever, as if a wild baste and the divil on it was waiting hungry at the thrashal, and bang the door flew open! some of them saw nothing more but some windle straws (larsar lena) blowing round the floor, but she I spoke to saw distinctly troops of fairies riding round on horses no bigger than small birds. Then the door slammed again, and they heard a clash of swords outside, and a hurry as if there was a scrimmage going on in the air, which passed down the road, and gradually died away in the distance. The next morning, sure enough—and the woman who told me saw it with her own eyes—there come news to Galway of the battle of Salamanky, and there was drops of blood seen for a quarter of a mile down the causeway ; so no doubt but that was a fairy battle."

" Which clearly accounted, Dennis, for the big wind and the ships that went down," said I.

" Not a doubt else, and hear me now. The only way in such perplexities is to go to the fairy doctor, who knows all about the blast and the changes and the meal cure. Try a drop of Parlemint (legal whiskey), your honour ; it keeps the cold out of the stomach and the heat in it. Good luck to thim who invented it (rest their sowls !). Well, as your honour sames so fond of these old pishogues (God between you and harm !), I must tell you about the fairy cow that used to feed every third night inside the ruins of Castle Ballynock, till the naygur who kept it, who was a relation of ours (a third cousin) on my mother's side, kilt it, and laid the skin to soak on his dunghill. From that time everything went wrong with him : the cattle died, his sheep had the rot, and he got into a lawsuit (rest his sowl !). While he was puzzling his head to know what brought all this mischief on him—whether it was missing mass, or not going to St. Bridget's Well, or up Croagh Patrick and doing the stations, as his dacent father had done, or what—a fairy appears to him one night in a dream, and says she to him, ' Mr. Flanagan, that cow you killed was my grandfather, and that's my grandfather's skin, you spalpeen, you have got soaking in your dunghill. You blackgaird, if you have any manners, go take and lay it in the fort to-night, and when the cow comes to life and runs round the enclosure, turn your back, you villain, and take care not to cross yourself, Mr. Flanagan.' This he did, and glad enough, and out come the cow ; he heard a voice thanking him for returning the skin, and all went right with him ever afterwards."

After this, Dennis grew silent, and I fell musing. " The old superstitions of Ireland," thought I, " are dying out like the old language, still Munster has its cluricaun artisan, its Merrow and Duhallane, its O'Donohoe and its Macgillicuddy. The islanders of Shark and Baffin have their Terence O'Flaherty, as the Connaught man has his Daniel O'Rourke, who rode on the eagle all the way from the moon to Munster, while the May-day bonfires still redden the sky in remembrance of Baal.

The Irish philosophy of fairies is that they are fallen angels, who, being neutral beings not altogether lost, are sent to suffer a further probation on earth before they are raised again to heaven or sealed up for ever to perdition. The Ulster men think the "wee folk" live wherever they at first fell. The Irish fairies are generally old, ugly, lame, and wizen, but have a power of assuming shapes, as a witch can change to a hare or a cat. They use these shapes only to reveal themselves to men in. They haunt old ruins, where they dance and revel, and, if possible, they injure or allure men. Sudden deaths are generally attributed to their agency, merely from such deaths being unaccountable, and so, petitio principii, supernatural. The Derry and Antrim mountaineers have their brownie, who with Scotch industry labours for his "cream bowl" duly set; in other words, the brownie is a sly servant, working overtime. Still if on a summer's day, when the sky is burning blue and hot, the Irish labourer, going to the bog for turf, sees a whirl of dust twisting playfully in the air, he ceases to sing and laugh, holds his breath, looks down, repeats a prayer, and crosses himself, for he knows that that whirl of dust contains a flock of the "good" people.

These days of simple faith are, however, fast going for ever, even in Ireland. Fairies disappear before the red-whiskered bagman, with his tin boxes and bundles of pattern cards; before the snort and tramp of the steam-engine; before fashionable tourists and fashionable guide books. O'Donohoe no longer rises on his white horse from the lake on May-day morning. No longer the Antrim brownie, hairy and rude, sweats at his kindly task, more grateful than man; no longer fairies circle the mushroom, or minuet in and out between the rows of daisies.

The great granite mountains, scathed with thunder and furrowed by the lightning's stroke, no longer see the giants striding from peak to peak through the violet-coloured mist. No longer the banshee wails under the leafless thornbush; no

longer the tap of the cluricaun's hammer is heard by the gold-
seeker. The black bog pits have yielded almost their last gold
chain and brooch of the old Danish king, slain long since, and
buried amid gigantic elk bones blackened pine trunks, and
stone-axes, down far below the quaking surface, over which
the snipe zigzags or the bittern booms. The tumbling waggon
jolts by with its cargo of laughing revellers, where the croppy
piper was buried under the sign-post during the troubles; or
by the heap of stones, once a happy home till the red night
that the Shanavests, Carders, or Hearts of Steel, hemmed
round its burning roof. No bleeding nun or ghost of the blaspheming foxhunter, who chased the vermin to the very altar,
appears now to scare the English pedestrian; for even the
ghosts have emigrated out of Ireland since the Union. Catholic spirits, abhorring Repeal, will not take the trouble to scare
Protestant land agents sneaking about in disguise, for fear of
the flint-piece and the sight behind the wall. The good old
days of female hangmen, and processions of corpses in crimson
carts, are gone by; the ribbonmen no longer flaunt their ribbons
at night upon the Curragh or in the bawn; the gully, where
the foxes are, no longer has its black peat water stained with
the blood of Molly Maguire's children; the tullagh's slope is
untrodden by the insolent hoof of the butcher yeoman's chargers; the tubber (spring) is left by the barefooted pilgrim to the
snipe and the moor-hen; but still the sliebh is bluer than ever,
because a brighter sun shines on its mountains of piled sapphire; the old night stars shine cheerier over the scorched
headland where the gull screams and the great droves of silver
salmon still leap and swim; the Dane's rath grows greener, and
the Druid's ghost lies at rest on the grassy knoll by the sea,
listening to the old ocean hymn.

Tide of Lough Erne, let thy floods rise and hide the ruins
of dead men's graves, so that old wrongs be hidden away and
forgotten; let the Croagh's peak point to a new heaven and a
new earth, so that the crimes of the old blood-boltered Don
and Donagh be forgotten! Round towers, where the squall-
crow and starling only build, echo once more with the voice of
the prophecy of a happier future! Shall we never see the day

when the coast of Ireland shall be starry at dusk with the answering lustres of the warning light-houses; when her mountains shall be circled—not with black Phlegethous of bog, but with smiling fields and belts of cottages; when fleets of fishing boats shall fill her bays, and her roads shall be crowded with merchandise? May the blessed day soon come when her cities shall widen and her commerce increase; when her fisheries shall become as numerous as her manufactories, the north be white with bleaching-fields, and the south be yellow with flocks!

Dennis here became uneasy about a seat-cushion he had lost. "We are sure," he said, "to meet the masthur. He'll want to get up just because it's dropped somewhere on the road. Now, if I had them all right (bad luck and the devil) I shouldn't have seen the sole of his foot."

"What shall you do? The agent will be stopping your wages," said I.

"If I don't find it to-morrow, I'll just stale another," said Dennis in a low, quiet voice.

"Who is that thin man in front, Dennis?" said I.

"Oh, that's a schoolmaster," said Dennis. "I know by his cut, but I won't see him, or he'll be wanting me to take him to Clifden, and pay me with a writing lesson. Sorra a one that we meet but I know, yet they don't know me, that's the best of Here's the two Mr. Bradys. The top of the morning to you, Mr. Brady! They're brothers; yet you wouldn't think, your honour, there was a drop of blood between them, no more than there is between you and me" (abruptly, with true Irish discursiveness). "Do you see their oiled coats? It's better than any mackintosh; it's soaked three months in oil; it's better than all your mackintosh, or the soft soap and ingy-rubber."

We were now entering Ballynabrig, along whose suburban road was pouring a train of country people returning from the fair. Now, it was a primitive tumbling car, with its flat shelf and outrigger crowded with grey-stockinged farmers and laughing colleens; now, it was a cage-cart full of pigs, who looked out between the bars, with that calm, observing, friendly independence peculiar to the Irish pig; now, most amusing of all, it was a rough, conical-hatted, old, raw-boned schoolmaster riding a donkey, with his splay feet stuck in hay stirrups; now, we met rough graziers wrapped in frieze; countrymen of all ages in the constitutional tail coat, gilt buttons, and knee-breeches, and the slip of a stick stuck under the arm. Every eye was bright with good-humoured whisky—some sang, while all greeted us with a shout, a flourish of sticks, and a joke.

CHAPTER XIII.

DRIVER MIKE.

How can I find words to describe the barrenness of Connemara, except by comparing it to that of County Mayo? and how can I describe County Mayo except by comparing it to Connemara?

Here have I been riding on one of Bianconi's cars ten miles, from Clifden to Galway, and have not seen a soul yet, and scarcely a body, except the two half-naked children that were playing round a peat-heap at Ballyrag, and the old woman with the grey hair tied in a knot who put-to the horses at Croppy town. Not a house either but that one hut, beyond the old castle of the Martin in the lake, which was announced to us by two or three spindly trees full an hour beforehand.

Still bog, bog, bog, mountain, lake, like the enchanted, doomed country in a fairy story.

Two inns to-day—the first kept by a Church of England clergyman, the second by the parish doctor—do not indicate much traffic or commerce in this beautiful region of blue mist and brown, burnt-sienna-ish bog. It remains, I should think, much as it did when St. Patrick, in his white robe, tramped barefooted to seek audience of the savage Irish king, who was dressed in wolf-skins, and had a spiky mace for a walking-stick; much the same as when the black Danes carried their raven banner through it; quite the same as in the croppy times, or when cocked-hats and swords were seen in Galway streets.

A heron stands on one leg, in a meditative way, like a one-legged pensioner; waiting till the coach-wheel nearly touches him, as if he were stopping there to hand the coachman a parcel. Rushes, with their little green tubes, burnt red-brown tops, and little tufts of flowers, are pretty enough; but ten miles of rushes is too much of a good thing. If we do see any children, ragged and picturesque, in the scarlet frocks worn by the Connemara peasantry, they run from us frightened, like a parliament of rats disturbed by the appearance of a terrier.

There are two other depressing things about Connemara. One is, that the roads are so wild, and mournfully desolate, and unpeopled, that wild creatures have claimed joint possession, particularly the wild ducks and the magpies. They form a feature in all the wild parts of Ireland. Looking far ahead down the dry, blue, hard road, you see suddenly a flock of black spots in the centre of it, perhaps a hundred yards off. As you get nearer you find this is a batch of little, callow, half-fledged wild-ducks, brought here by the fussy mother to dust and sun themselves from some adjacent bog-hole or clump of friendly rushes. The young ones have never heard of coaches, and would not rise at all but for the pecks and bustle of their mother, who fluffs them up and scrambles them off just in time to be saved from our swift revolving wheels. Off they waddle, only disturbed for a moment; and, as you look back, you see them again just where they were before.

Then the magpies—those black and white clerical-looking birds you see in England, perhaps once in a long summer day's walk—here you put them up in couples, ten in a mile, with their long tails and their shy, mischievous manner, jerking about on the road-side trees (when there are any), or balancing awkwardly on the clumsy stone walls.

Then, as for weasels running across the road, and carrion crows looking out for lamb, they are seen constantly, and, in Connemara, eagles too, as you will hear. But let me get to my account of the energetic Italian Bianconi, who single handed has permeated all Ireland with cars, and done more good to poor Ireland in twenty years than——But I am getting treasonable. In the midst of these observations, my Bianconi driver

Mike Joyce, breaks out with a song, written by the schoolmaster at Derry Knowing, and, as it is not devoid of quaintness,
I give it:

Tune of the Nate Gould Ring.

"O gra machree,
  You don't love me,
  Or else you wouldn't linger,
  This little ring,
  Which now I bring,
  To slip upon your finger.

"Colleen asthore,
  My heart is sore,
  Too long I have been waiting;
  I've feed the priest, ·
  And cooked the feast,
  It is no lies I'm stating;
  It's truth, bedad, I'm stating.

"Mavourneen, then,
  Be one in ten,
  And do not look so tazing;
  The pig is bought,
  The fish are caught,
  The day and hour are plazing;
  O, Kitty, ain't they plazing.

"You smile at me,
  O, gra machree,
  Love, dear, you will not linger.
  'No blarney, Tom!'—
  I'm deaf and domb,
  The ring is *on* her finger;
  Whoop, boys, it's on her finger."

I had complimented him on his song, when who should get
up at a road-side whisky-shop where we changed horses, but
two bagmen? who, having hoisted in their tin boxes and
mackintosh-covered bundles of patterns till the car groaned
again, began at once, before the car moved off, playing at gambling games of cards, with an ardour worthy of a better cause.
We were still in sight of Benabola, king of the Twelve Pins (or

skittle mountains), and they were on the seat with their backs to me and Mike, who drove sideways, as carmen love to do.

Mike cast a malign glance at the bagmen, as they imperiously stowed away their tin boxes.

" One would think," he muttered to me, " it was the Juke of Wellington and Admiral Nelson out, arm in arm, for a holiday. I'd upset them in the next bog-hole for a tinpenny."

But the red-whiskered, fresh-coloured, pompous, slangy bagmen went on throwing down the red and black pipped cards on the car cushion between them quite unconcerned, the money lying between them in reasonable pools of silver. If we had been driving through Paradise they would not have looked up.

As a road-side dog broke out on us from a cabin, Mike began to talk.

"There's a power of agles," said Mike, suddenly, "up in Derryclare, there. I sometimes am getting them at three-and-sixpence the couple for gentlemen that keep menageries on their lawns. I'll tell you a story about them."

" Give that yelping dog a cut with your whip, Driver," said the gamesters.

Mike replied, seriously, bending down to them, " Perhaps one of you gents would be kind enough to fling half-a-crown at him. Well, as I was saying when the dog interrupted me, I had a man from Letterfrack on the box the other day, who was a powerful one on agle stories, but they're not worth telling. Hold up, Jinny !"

" Oh, the story, by all means, Mike," said I.

" A year or two ago," said Mike, " it may be more—there was a poor widdy had her slip of peaty ground not far from the foot of Benbaun, that big blue fellow there to the right. She had just her handful of goats, that nibbled about Bencullaghduff, and her slice of bog, and such parquisites as she had got given to her by one of the great Martins of Ballinahinch, before old Cruelty to Animals reigned in Connemara (rest his soul !). Convaynient to this widdy lived an eagle. ' Do you see that tree we're passing ?' said the Clare man to me. ' To be sure I do,' said I, ' how can I help it ?—did he live in that ?' ' No,' says he, as pat as could be, ' he didn't, but he built on that

wall just beyont it.' Well, one unlucky Friday, the widdy's
sons—two stout lads ready for any mischief, and more fond of
snapping at snipes and listening to the gentlemen's beagles
than work—climbed up that wall of a rock, pulling themselves up by the long green strings of ivy and the little
hollybushes that grew in the clefts, and, when up there,
what did they do but bring down two of the young birds.
Soon afterwards, the widdy's lambs began to decrease in
number (it was yearning season at the time), and so it went on,
till only forty out of seventy were left. The widdy, thinking
it had been the herd, had him watched, and then found out,
sure enough, it was devil a one but the ould thafe of the world,
the agle. So she goes to a wise gossip, and asks her what
was to be done. Says the gossip to her, 'Have you never
done any provocation to the agle?' And the widdy says to
her 'that her sons had taken two of the young birds to bring
up in the house as pets.' 'That's it,' says the ould woman,
'and there'll never be good blood between you, Widdy Grattan,
and the agle, till you give back them cubs, and the boys go up
again and put back the birds, and make all smooth.' The boys
then took back the eaglets, and from that day no more lambs
were taken out of the flock ; nor was that all, for the agle behaved like a jintleman to her, and because he couldn't give them
back—seeing as how they were picked to the bone—he flew
forty miles a day for thirty days running into county Clare,
and brought back every day a lamb, to make up the number
he and his family had eaten. And this is how it was found
out. The man that told me, and who lived near the widdy,
had lately married a Westport woman, he came out of Clare
into these very parts, and he declared the brand on the lambs
the agle brought back was the brand of a squireen from his
own neighbourhood. Now, isn't that mighty quare?"

"It is, indeed," I said, believingly.

Mike continued: "Well, this same Clare man told me
another story of an agle that beats Banagher. There was a
countryman near Bencore who used to cross a ford every day
to cut his little slip of turf to boil his wife's praties with. One
day, as he goes across with his spade over his shoulder and his

kippen at his back, balancing himself on the stones, that the water dips and tumbles over, what does he see but a big baste of an agle, with wings as big as a fishing-sail, sitting on a rock half-way across, ating a salmon with all the relish of a priest at a wedding? The man up's with a cleaver he has with him to cut a stick or two of bog-wood, lets fly at the agle, who drops the salmon down at his feet, and, without waiting for the change, flies off, as Rory thought, to his wife and family in Bencullaghduff. Pleased enough, the man goes into the bog, scoops out his kippeenful of the driest turf, ties the cords across, hoists the fish, shining like a new dish-cover, in between the fastenings, and hurries back to the cabin, glad to bring Biddy, who was ailing, so pretty a dinner without changing a one pound bill for it. But he hadn't got the pot that was to boil that fish; for, as he just got half across the water, flop comes his friend the agle down on the creel, pitches on his head, gives him a buffeting with his wings that half blinds him, and flies off with the salmon in his claws."

" Teaching him to do as he'd be done by," said I.

" Divil anything else," said Mike. " ' Bedad!' says the man to Biddy, ' I'm not the Christian to be made a fool of by an agle that has only two legs and no arms. No,' says he, and he loads a blunderbuss up to the muzzle with swan shot, and goes off to the ford the very next day, and hides under an alder bush to wait for the agle when he came to drink. In about half-an-hour he sees a dark spot over Derryclare that gradually gets larger as it gets nearer, and by-and-by turns out to be the agle. Now, I'll tache you manners,' says Murphy Joyce, but before he could pull the trigger, which was rather stiff—it hadn't been used much since the throubles in 'ninety-eight—the agle was down upon him again, and gave him such a dose of it as knocks his senses quite out of him. He could not see out of his eyes for a month afterwards, and I don't think would have ever seen again, if he hadn't made a pilgrimage to Croagh Patrick, and drank out of the Holy Well three mornings running, fasting."

The moral, thought I, of which is: Never take a salmon away from an eagle without remembering his bill.

"How can those fellows go on playing at cards instead of listening to your good stories?" I whispered to Mike.

"Oh, bad luck to them," said Mike, "they always make up their losses from the first fool they get hold of. Hear me now."

"The twelve Pins look well, gentlemen," said I, stooping down.

The gents, looking up in a desultory way, said, "Oh, very—wonderful! Fifteen-two and a pair are eight—that makes me three-and-sixpence."

"Oh, let them be, the nagurs," said Mike, with extreme contempt.

Just then, a pig-driver passed, trimly dressed, driving, with unnecessary noise and solemnity, four pigs, completely tattooed with red bars across the back.

"That's a young pig-jobber, I know," said Mike.

"How do you know he's only just begun business?" said I.

"Why, there's too much ruddle. He's more ruddle than pigs. As he gets older he'll put less."

Mike, the Connaught man, was a shrewd, good-humoured, sagacious madcap; with a man's body and a boy's heart, like half his countrymen; his voice stammering with fun, became, when he grew serious, deep, rhythmical, earnest, and pathetic. Having sounded him in legends, I waited till moon-rise for his ghost-stories.

After a short stare at the horses' ears, which passes with a car-driver for meditation, Mike said abruptly, "Did you like Sligo, your honour?"

In the course of my reminiscences of Sligo, I mentioned a one-eyed and left-handed waiter.

Mike laughed, and said, "I know that waiter. Ben and me have an old grudge; he's one of the ferocious O'Flaherties."

Here our recollections of Sligo were interrupted as we approached Letterfrack, the Quaker settlement, by a sinister-looking old man with bare feet, and a patched great coat, with a scrubby ram's-wool collar, who bore on his back an enormous round bundle of old clothes wrapped in a rug, that gave him the air of Atlas, learning the use of the globes. After much higgling he gets up to ride to Clifden, and ties his bundle to one of the jaunting-car rails.

" Is your portmanty safe, Tom ? Are you insured from fire, or won't they insure tinder ?" said Mike in a kindly voice.

" I'm all right, Thad, and thanks to you," cried grateful Tom.

" Very well, Tom. (Then chip, Jinny.) I thought you were off to Coleraine, Tom ?"

" No ; I've just been reprimanded " (he meant remanded).

The picking up of passengers makes a long day's ride, on an Irish jaunting-car, one of the merriest things in the world. Nowhere can you pick up stranger sayings or more pleasant bits of observation to chew the cud of in after and duller days. Now we drew up at a white-washed cabin, with its brown pool and dung-hill before it, the pigs nuzzling at the potatoes, that smoked straining in the basket-lid before the door. Facing the door, slops down a peat buttress, which feeds the fire ingeniously enough, and also keeps out all the pure air from the circle round the red-hot peat. Our friend Tom, the pedlar, was already snugly established as a balance to the commercial gentlemen, who, with antagonistic rows of half-crowns, were now absorbed in the mysteries of blind hookey, and were blind to everything else except an occasional tinted yellow glass of whisky, brought out from a shabeen by a bare-footed urchin who acted as pot-boy.

A turn of the road brought us to one of those cottage stations where Bianconi keeps his relays of horses. A thin, cheery old woman, with her dry grey hair blowing in wisps over her face, tripped out, and began to put to the horses. " Fergus and Kitty" were marked by Bianconi's royal decree upon the collars; so that Fergus should never wear Kitty's collar, nor Kitty Fergus's. She slipped in the buckles and whipped up the cheek-straps as deftly as a smart young ostler of sixteen. She even smeared some black ointment on Kitty's cracked hoof, and had the leather case on before the Connaught man could get round and help her. I rejoiced to see her slap the wet flank of Jinny, to send her into the stables, and pull Brian's mane as a token of recognition. Five minutes more and Mike was on the yellow box, tucking the oilskin apron over my legs, and hoping I had room.

" Now, your honour," said Mike, " for the next ten miles

you'll have as pretty a rocking as ever a rowler tourist had in his born days. You might as well be at sea in a gale of wind."

The next time we stopped, Mike exclaimed: "You see that nate little gurl that brought us the parcel at the gate?"

"Yes," I replied.

"Well," says Mike, "she's one of the *jumpers*."

"Jumper. What's that?"

"Why, one of the *soupers* that went over to the black faith in the famine times for soup. She is a nate little girl, and takes in millinery. I've seen fellows change their faith for a pair of breeches."

"No?" I said.

"Is it no you say; it's yes I say," cried Mike. "There was a young Brady, of Mollycullen. When the committee was giving away the clothes, he sees a pair of breeches as mightily takes his fancy. 'Give me them,' says he, 'and I kiss the Bible.' Well, next day when he went, they'd been given to somebody else, so what does Brady do but come back again to the ould faith, though divil of a haporth of credit he is to that same. Look there, your honour, at that field where the potatoes are lying out in clean rows. What young children for work, and how purty that handsome girl with the bare legs shows them how to use the long spade. That land was all bog four years ago, and all that track furnent. It belongs to a Scotch farmer, who turns out his children to work directly they begin to thrive, from six years old to sixteen, all the same. That girl is the beauty of the place. Now if he had been Irish she would have been working at her piany, and had her big lump of a novel, and have been merely looking out of the window for the purty young man."

"Yes," thought I, and fell into a reverie, "the Scotch are conquering Ireland. The old hard-drinking, open-house days are gone by for ever; witness the Martins, who ruled half Connemara and had the lands of a prince; witness—— and —— and all the old clans."

Before I could finish my apostrophe on the Middleman question, the Orange and Green question, the Absentee question, the tithe question, the Popery question, and some others,

I was interrupted by our stopping to take up one of the county constabulary, a force which few armies of Europe could match. The smart young fellow, in his light rifle green coatee, flat cap, and side bayonet, leaped up with a soldierly-like nod to the driver, bound for some session then sitting.

As he alighted a mile further on, Mike said, " Good luck go with him, it's some poor widdy's heart he'll make ache to-night, sorra guide him !"

" Have you been long in Bianconi's service, Mike ?"

" Ten years last Rogation."

" Have you ever seen him ?"

" Have I ever seen him !   Often and often, your honour. He's a little, smart man, with a quick eye, and have heard him tell his own story how he was shipwrecked, when he was quite a boy, on his way from Rome, and left with only three shillings in his pocket on a *desert island*.   With these he came and bought some pictures that he saw in a window in Dublin, and selling these got more, and so on, till he started a car, and then another, till now he employs ever so many hundred drivers, and the divil knows how many horses, and lives in a grand place near Clonmel.   They say if he gets a halfpenny a day from every horse it pays him."

" I suppose that B on the harness stands for his name," said I.

" An' be sure it does," said Mike.   " Every horse has its own name and its own harness.   He's mighty sharp.   He has travellers to look after us, who come about on the road and are taken up as regular fares, who note down the time they get on and off to compare it with our bills at the station.   Now in London, they tell me, they do it by getting into an omnibus with a right-hand pocket full of marbles.   For every one that gets in, they move a marble into the left-hand pocket ; isn't that cute ?"

" Very," said I ; "but is he kind to the poor ?"

" He is," said Mike, " and to his old drivers, if they do their duty, but if they ruin a horse he is out with them in a jiffy. His way of rewarding is by taking you off a wild, scanty road, and putting you on a good one ; or by changing you from night to day duty.   He tried me once, but I bet him.   I had

L

to take some horses for him down into Tipperary, and when I got near his house my money ran short, and I went up to his place, told him my case, and borrowed five shillings. 'Be sure you pay it again, my man,' says he, 'next time we meet.' I thanked him, drove off, and six months after this he met me somewhere about here, and got on my car to go as far as Clifden. Now I knew he had my five shilling down in his red pocket-book, and remembered it, so I went up to him and said, 'Here's the five shillings, Mr. Bianconi, that I borrowed at Clonmel, and thanks to you, sir.' 'Keep it, my good man,' said he, with a pretty smile that did me good. 'I like to see my drivers remember their debts.' I'd had as soon put my head into a menagerie of wild bastes as see him again if I hadn't."

Our next passengers were two decent country-women, with their gowns tucked up and their shawls drawn over their heads.

It was getting cold, and as it grew cold we grew silent, only now and then blurting out a sentence when we got down sullenly, with heads butting at the bullying wind, to walk slowly up a hill beside the car. But it was every moment with Mike some kind, encouraging, cheery words.

" Well, girls, how are you by this time ?" cried Mike.

A chorus of women replied, " Och ! dead entirely with the chill."

" And if I sat like that," said Mike, reprovingly, " all the time in the car wouldn't I be as dead as the fur that was under me ?" then added, under breath, " There's no worse driving than the women, 'cause they never get out to spare the horse, poor craytur."

With the exception of a dark avenue just as we entered Galway, which was rendered dangerous by a rush of cars coming home from the fair, filled with reckless, exhilarated country people, we had no risks to encounter on our way to the semi-Spanish city where Judge Lynch hung his own son.

We had traversed that day a wonderful panorama of Irish scenery, bog, coast town, arms of the sea, lakes, and mountains —a country wild as Siberia, ending in civilised city, with rich suburbs, packet station, and commerce. In the morning, a stone-built whisky-shop; in the evening, a civilised hotel, with conventional waiter, and all other sophistications. This morning, untrod mountains, miles of snipe track, and wild duck country; to-night, paved streets, neat shops, and starry rows of columned lamps. It was like coming from the thirteenth century into the nineteenth, and I felt grateful for the change, yet pleased with the experience.

CHAPTER XIV.

THE IRISH JAUNTING CAR.

I was on a Wicklow jaunting-car that was climbing one of those steep hills that lead into the mountain country, that you see blue and tempting, smiling to you with promises of fairyland, from the pleasant green deer-walks of Phœnix Park, Dublin. The car was the old Irish car, with the two hanging shelves back to back, and the little iron-bound crow's-nest in front, but where the carman never sat, preferring to sit sideways and drive, sharing in the gossip of the passengers, be they priest, labourer, or quarryman, or black-eyed girleen, we picked up by the way.

My temper clarified as we slanted up the blue billiard-board, dry, hard roads peculiar to the mountain districts of Ireland. Not an hour ago I had been in a dreadful state of rage and indignation. They had told me in Dublin, at my hotel opposite the College, that the Wicklow car started at two o'clock. At two o'clock, therefore, the vanguard of our army moved on O'Grady Street, where the car was reported to start, and was deposited there, with "the blessings of the Lord" upon it, by Tim, the incomparable boots. If I waited in that dirty street opposite that little spirit-shop—where they also sold herrings, biscuits, and candles—ten minutes, I waited two hours. I reconnoitred all the neighbouring streets, looking at prints of the last ill-favoured saint, Doctor Wiseman, Napoleon, and Daniel O'Connell. I became the scorn of the adjacent clothes-cellar, where the faded regimentals dangled in the wind, and the very red painted Gorgon masks over the doorways lolled out their tongues at me. I was the butt of a select clump of greasy beggars from the slums of the Liberty. The carmen leered at me as if I was the first invading Saxon that had set his foot on Erin's shore. The boys, striped with rags, walked round me suspiciously, as the street dogs at Constantinople do round a stranger, suspecting his creed. No signs of the car, in spite of all the anathemas I heaped on the inconsequential, hare-brained, reckless Celtic race.

All I got was ridicule. For instance, when I asked a woman who was driving about coals in a cart, with a bell jingling in front, if the car was not punctual,

" Punshill!" says she, showing all her yellow teeth, and flinging up her dirty hands with a laugh as she drove on— " punshill is it? What, Jack MacGan punshill! Away wid ye!"

" Did ye' ever hear the likes of him?" said a woman, passing with a square of brown cat's-meat on a skewer.

Some thought me cracked, others foolish, but the majority shrugged their shoulders and said, " Can't ye see, Biddy, he's an Englishman, the cratur!"

Then a horrid crowd of armless, eyeless objects surrounded me, baring their stumps and thrusting out their snuffy, lean hands. One said he had a "family of ten orfins to maintain, your honour;" another, turning up his pulpy, opaque eyes, said, " I've been dark these thirty years, your honour." It might have been so, but the dirty rascal looked scarcely nine-teen, which rendered the optical delusion a difficult feat.

At last, innocently, shambling, calm, and resigned, came Jack with the rickety car, which he proceeded to build up with parcels. Touching his brimless hat to me with an air of con-sequence, business, and authority, he drove off the beggars, as a village cur would have chased away a flock of geese. The man was one of those wild-eyed, reckless-looking fellows you seldom see among the dull-blooded Saxons. He caught up the reins more like Phaeton out for a mad holiday than one of those steady English coachmen who sit as if they had grown to the box, and are immovable till some operation has been performed with a head-stall or splinter-bar.

At last he got under way, first running into the spirit shop, to exchange half-a-dozen jokes, and to toss off a glass of some shining quicksilver, which I suppose was whisky, for he went in laughing and came out singing. We drove off from that squalid side street on our uneasy throne, with our feet on that swinging leather shelf which is at first so fickle, unstable, and unpleasant. We bumped against a post, which rather tickled Jack, tied up the harness, which subsequently gave way with a snap, and got into the more fashionable quarter, where, by dint of pounding along in defiance of everything, a screech on a battered horn, and a crack of Jack's whip, we produced rather a sensation among the fashionable and graceful loungers of Grafton Street.

Once between the whitewashed villa walls, and climbing the hard blue road of the suburb, Jack was happy and talkative. Now he gave each of his parcels an adjusting kick—leaped out and pulled up his horse's buckles tighter, tied a fresh knot in his short whip, caught up the lash in a knowing way, after flipping a fly off his horse's left ear ; then shuffled his coat easier, and rubbed his brimless hat round with a twirl of his elbow. Jack was anything but an hypochondriac ; in fact, his spirits, in comparison with those of any ordinary Englishman, were the spirits of inebriation.

But Jack had not a "hair turned" with the whisky. We soon began to pick up passengers, but from Jack's uneasy and sideward eye, I could see he still waited for some special addition to his load. Could it be some colleen bawn (fair-haired girl) he expected ? or was it some police sergeant, tithe proctor, or notice server whom he dreaded to meet ?

"Sir to you," said Jack, suddenly snapping round on me, ceasing to mechanically flog his horse, "it's the Doctor I'm waiting for ; we were to take him up at the Knockmadown four cross-roads, and we are within a ha'porth of them now. It's perhaps one of the pleasantest gentlemen you ever spoke to, the best shot, rider, and fly-fisher in all Wicklow, so quick with the tongue, and always his reply as pat——Och ! but

here he comes: and it's pretending I don't know him I'll be.
Saints above us, how he's running!" And Jack slapped his
thigh to express supreme delight, looking away from the coming
man, and driving slowly on.

However, to Jack's great vexation, the runner turned out to
be only Mr. Plunkett's man, with a parcel for Rathdrum. "I
wouldn't miss Mr. Saul for forty pounds," said Jack, pulling
up at the cross-roads; "it does me good, like medicine, seeing
him; besides, I want to see him about Crazy Jane——"

"Some poor insane relation," I thought.

"—for she can't take her grass."

"A vegetarian," I said to myself.

"Millia murder!" which means ten thousand murders in
English, cried a passenger, "will the Docthor never come?"
We were waiting at the cross-road for the take up.

"Here he comes!" cried a bagman, who was stamping at
the delay, "looking like a ha'porth of soap after a long day's
washing."

"Och! the mummy of a monkey. Look at him!" cried a
third passenger—"look how he pulls his legs after him, as if
they were only borrowed for the day!"

"If you don't make haste, sir, we can't be waiting," said
Jack; and Mr. Saul, with "Don't you know me, Jack?" tumbled up. "Cross about us! Don't you know me, Jack, ma
bouchal? Give us a light. Haven't I been running like a
madman to Bedlam to catch the bit of blood there you're driving three miles an hour to the knacker's! Give me the whip!"
He was at home with all of us in a moment.

"Och! is it you, Mr. Saul? And how's somebody's sweetheart, the black-eyed widdy's daughter at Rathdrum, Doctor?
When's the banns to be up?" said Jack with a bit of fine acting.

"Och! be asy, Mike, get out of that," said Saul, colouring
and flogging the horse.

"Who is this?" I said in a whisper to the man next me;
"he does not look like a doctor?"

Said Jack, sotto voce, "A cow-doctor, your honour, but we
call him 'the Doctor,' out of respect to his father, who is the
great farrier in Rathdrum; and sure hasn't he got the brass-

plate and the knocker, and the red and green bottles and the pounder for the salts, and what would a rale doctor want more? And a tidy bit of land, too, fornent us."

Jack, our driver, was a bugler in the Wicklow Rifle Militia, and he was now driving bare-headed and in an easy undress, consisting of a dirty, ragged, red militia jacket, much the worse for stable practice. In his military capacity, Jack was pugnacious and talkative, brusque and abrupt, but in his civil and Augean province, silent, stolid, quiet and social.

Our new passenger, Mr. Saul, the doctor, was a wiry young man of some five-and-twenty shooting-seasons, fonder of salmon-fishing than farriery, and of giving himself whisky than of giving invalid horses drenches. He wore a soiled green shooting-jacket, a loose, untidy velvet waistcoat, and a red rope of a handkerchief strangled round his neck, which gave him at first sight the appearance of having unsuccessfully attempted suicide. As for his face, it was thin, pale, and I must confess rather debauched-looking; his eyes were wild, excitable, and blood-shot; his cheek hollow and hectic; his mouth wide, wavering, and witty. He was always mercurially shifting his seat: now he was on this side, now on that; now driving, now leaping out to a walk; now singing, now shouting.

"Jack's a soldier; you should hear him on the bugle; bedad he's powerful," said Mr. Saul, patronisingly looking at Jack.

"Get out of that, doctor," said Jack, colouring.

"A purty regiment it is too," said Saul, becoming ironical suddenly. "Divil a one of 'em could hit a tree at twenty paces. They might rifle the inimy—bedad if they'd shoot 'em!"

"You ought to know, Mr. Saul," says Jack, reprovingly and hurt, "how many feet off we were when you saw us firing with the rifle at the butt—was it twinty?"

"None of your brag, Jack," said Saul, laughing him down, "or I shall have to thrash it out of ye. Why don't you learn to box, Jack? The fist never misses fire."

"Last time as ever I went to Dublin, didn't I box a porter and two carmen before I got to the end of the first street, little as I am, say now, Mr. Saul?" said Jack.

"Weren't you rejected twice as a soldier? What did the old sergeant at Rathdrum say of you?" said Mr. Saul: "'I wish the Rifles luck!'"

'Oh, this sergeant's nothing!' said Jack, "or why does he take to black clothes?"

"Bedad," said Saul, "get out of that. He's a brave man, Jack; and I'll knock down any one who says he isn't. You know as well as I, Jack, the Sergeant was of the Seventy-eight formerly, who they stripped the colours of because they would beat to mass against government orders."

Here we came to a shibbeen, and for the third time the young doctor got down and called for whisky. Mr. Saul was not a teetotaller, no more was Jack. We all got down.

"I hope you won't care, Mr. Saul, but here's some of the crathur we haven't had time to get christened," said the widow landlady, evidently knowing her customer.

"All right, widdy; bring two dandies," said Saul, seizing a glass, "and some cordial. Faix! an' this is rale Innishowen" (smacks his lips), "divil a bit else to me! The beer's bad about here—all" (learnedly, and with chemical authority) "because of the sulphurous vapour, and having no elixir of oxygin in the centhre of the wather. Widdy, some soda-wather! I had too much stuff last night at the fair, and I'm still thirsty, though I drank four jugs of cold pump-wather this morning, besides two bottles of porther. Take a dandy, sir, there's no headache in Irish whisky. Well, then, I'll take it to prove to you. By all the Byrnes and O'Tooles in Wicklow—and that's saying something this side the Scalp—you're the best fellow I've seen for many a day!"

A scene more intensely Irish and more intensely un-English could scarcely be conceived. Here was a car reckless of delays, a consequential, drunken, sporting farrier passing for a real doctor, and a driver quite indifferent to punctuality, parcels, passengers, or nightfall, stopping at the bidding of a half-drunken cow-doctor at a roadside whisky-shop. I saw it was no use to lose my temper. There was nothing to do but to observe the humours of Saul, the cow-doctor, snipe-shooter, and salmon-fisherman.

As for Saul, when he was not bragging of the reputation he might have attained in medicine but for his fondness for snipe-shooting, he was tossing off burning thimblefuls of whisky, rallying Jack about his regiment, courting the landlady, singing snatches of songs, or enlightening me on Irish customs.

Mr. Saul was just one of those reckless, idle prodigals who, with much good-nature and many social companions, become, when squireens with a little money and a little land, the special curses of an improvident country—just the man who, in Ninety-eight, would have been beguiled into a secret club, and have headed a clump of 'pikes at Vinegar Hill; who, later, would have floated his friends in claret, ridden over his hall-table on his spanking mare, or got up, on true Lever principles, some wet day, a fox-hunt inside the old house at Tubbermore. Impulsive, quick blooded, he would be led about by cunning priests, and die of delirium tremens before thirty. At a fair dance, at a faction fight, or at a race, Saul was, I could see, the leader of the Wicklow hot-bloods.

As for Jack, who sat there perfectly merry and at his ease, with no trouble about his passengers, parcels, or horses, with his whiplash serpenting about the hard-trodden mud floor, and his dirty red jacket open, fluttering in the draught, he was quite a type of the southern Irishman, choleric, generous, thoughtless, impulsive, with all the materials for a soldier or a poet burning within him, a man who, now laughing from ear to ear at Saul's songs and local jokes, and telling stories of his Dublin fights, with the widdy's child dancing on his knee, might, years ago, under certain provocations, have been to-morrow night, pike in hand, lurking round some Protestant farmer's burning homestead, stabbing at a slashing English Dragoon in a rebel fight, or waiting with clenched teeth behind a stone wall, where the ferns grow, for the hard landlord quietly ambling home from the sessions meeting.

I got so tired of the noise and delay, at which I saw it was no use grumbling, that I suppose I fell asleep over the red peat fire, for when I awoke after many nods and uneasy twitches, I found Mr. Saul, Jack MacGan, and three other passengers, joining hands round the whisky bottle, and singing

a croppy song from the Nation newspaper, evidently not un-
pleasing to them. The only bit of it I remember is:

> Croppies, arise! Croppies, arise!
> Let the old angry light burn in your eyes;
> Rig the old scarlet drum; banner of green,
> Now shall thy dusty folds once more be seen.
>
> Croppies, arise! Croppies, arise!
> Once more the green flag of Liberty flies;
> Now by the stone walls, and long level dikes
> Shall glitter bright ranks of our bayonet and pikes.
>
> Dragoons may rush down, with their sabres abroad,
> Tory statesmen may come with their prating and fraud,
> But we'll scourge them away, with their tricks and their lies,
> When the brave croppies shall once more arise.

"Now thin, jintlemen all," says Jack, with an air of a
punctilious man of business, "I think it is time to be moving."

"Glasses round!" roars Saul, "d'ye hear, widdy? not for-
gitting the Saxon jintleman who has this day honoured us with
his company amongst us. Glasses round, and we'll be off."

And off after that we went, Saul driving like a madman to
make up for lost time, but no accident happening. Indeed, a
jaunting-car is a very safe vehicle, for if it upsets it only dis-
perses its passengers into roadside bogs, dikes, or rush bushes,
with now and then a concussion against a stone wall or the
roadside post, that foolishly and unluckily does not get out of
the way.

Saul, elated with whisky, grew laudatory of himself, and
said: "If it hadn't been for the cock-shooting I should have
stood as high, I think, in docthoring as the best man in
Dublin; but some time ago I had a fever from checked per-
spiration and the bile—biling over!—and ever since that I've
lost my retention of memory. Before that I used to be a great
dab at Pope:

> Order is Heaven's last law, and this redressed,
> Some are, and must be fatter than the rest.

Do you remember that? You see I'm down upon ye." (A

whisper.)—" I've got a remedy for jaundice, bedad, in my resate-
books that will cure it in any stage"—pauses solemnly—"except the stage of *daycomposition*." (Abruptly breaking off.)
" The man who isn't sociable is a fool, and if he likes I'll box
him."

" Give us a song, Mr. Saul," cried Jack, looking round.
" The cup of O'Hara, or the Black-haired Rose."

" Why not leading the Calves, Jack? or The twisting of
the Rope? But now, come, I'll give you a snap of my own,
written under whisky on a frosty morning to the old tune of
Cormac Oge. You've seen Nelly :

> O little Nelly Connellin,
> Gra machree, my soul, my beauty !
> Loving ye is just a duty.
> Don't say kissing is a sin,
> Little Nelly Connellin,
> > Begin.

> Little Nelly Connellin,
> Gra machree, colleen asthore !
> But one kiss ? Ye're plenty more.
> Kissing never was a sin,
> Little Nelly Connellin,
> > Begin.

Widdy, give us another dandy, and put it down to me—that
makes three. Och! there's no widdy! we're driving, I see.
Hurrah! we're driving. Larrup 'em, Jack !"

" Is there much snipe about here ?"

" Is it snipe ?" said Mr. Saul, angrily. " I believe you, and
salmon too. If you'll come and stay with us next year, we'll
show you as pretty shooting and fishing——It's that takes me
away from medicine, or I should soon be a match with those
fellows in Dublin ; but och ! I'm always on the blue gravel, or
up to my armpits wading after the heavy twenty-pounders
for hours without coming to land. Then there's the races
——Stay awhile, Jack, how often can you load in a minute ?"
(Abruptly, as usual.)

" Three times," said Jack ; " but the buglers don't have gun
exercise."

"Why, heart of faith!" said Mr. Saul, fervidly, "what use is bugling, when a man should be——I've a good mind to go on with you and have a wake's diversion in Dublin. What I do is drink, and eat, and sing — that's what I call real happiness. The man who is not sociable is a fool, I say. Put me on a horse, and I'll go anywhere and over anything. This isn't my best hat, this is a disabil beaver" (rubbing it round with his sleeve). "I'm a nice young fellow, I've got a little property, and I want to see the world. Sit forard, Jack." (Takes the pipe out of the coachman's mouth and puts it calmly in his own.)

At the next stage Mr. Saul got down.

"Good-by, Mr. Saul; mind you remember me," said I.

"Remember ye!" said Mr. Saul; "yes, till the day of my death; 'While memory,' &c."

What a look his wild whisky-and-water, religious, poetical, random eye gave me as he squeezed my hand blue.

Here, too, I parted with the Wicklow bugler, and Darby Doolan, a quiet, buttoned-up, moody man, now taking the reins, our conversation fell on dress, upon which subject Darby had very serious and esoteric opinions.

"Gentlemen," said Darby, gravely, "don't wear stays now as they used to do. Och! it was dreadful! Sure if I was a lord's son I shouldn't like to wear any more than my own bones about me, let alone a big baste of a whale's. Did you ever see those dolly pegs they use in washing in England?"

Somewhat confused, I asked what a dolly peg was. "No—yes—no. I think not."

"To see how my wife slaves," said Doolan, "while them ladies sits at home all day curling their hair, not thinking of the dirt in their yesterday's gown-tails, nor caring for all the grinding and the elbow-grease it takes to clean them."

"What does that mean over the grocer's shop, there?" said I, pointing to a shop we were passing. "Top Tay? What's top tay?"

"Top tay," Doolan said, with a long look of pity at me, "why it means topping tay, of course—our tay as tops all other tays."

A drunken sailor, who had got in at a turn of the road, now, by various marine eccentricities, amused me, but disgusted Doolan.

"Skipper," (that was Doolan) said the sailor, "let me get in the head (that was in front). What is that woman dancing bare-legged in the tub, there?"

"Oh, she's treading flannel," said Doolan. "Bedad, if she had but a partner in a tub opposite, there would be a pair of 'em."

"Have you been always on the road, Doolan?" said I.

"No, your honour," said Doolan, "I was ten years at Barbadoes with the Ninety-first. I used to mind the colonel's horses, and ride them to exercise. Many's the thing I've seen there among the niggurs, particularly the Johnny Canoe riots, when they used to take to the bush and slap at us from behind the trees. I remember once, your honour," Doolan went on, "I went out in the bush to cut supple jacks, and before I had gone half a mile, what should I see on a flat rock under a sand box-tree, but a great brown snake with his flat head up ready for me. So I makes no more to do, but raps at him with my stick, and never stops wopping till he's dead as Pilate. Then I puts a bamboo in his jaws, and carries him home on my back, eight foot of him."

Here the sailor became troublesome.

"Drunken baste, where's his manners?" muttered Doolan.

Now Doolan bit his lip and swore inwardly, talking it out of the horse, which he flogged viciously—now our maritime friend and brother would stand up to see if the tackling was all safe—but how he wanted to drop anchor at every whisky-shop—how he cried out alternately, with the voice of a boatswain in a storm, "Belay!" and "Reef!"—how he rolled and sang—how he wanted to cry "Starboard!" at every turnpike, and to board every rival car that passed us—I leave for other chapters. At the next change of horses he got down, and I left him fast asleep at the shebbeen fire. My Barbadoes friend now resigned his throne to a brisk dare-devil Connaught lad, with a slight squint and a weak chin, warping an otherwise handsome face. Tom Reilly's peculiar hobby was a fondness for practical jokes, and an admiration for O'Connor, a famed barber at Wicklow.

"Och! he has such a tongue," said Reilly; "you should hear him. I do like a turn with that barber; it bates cock-fighting, and there's sport in that, too. I'll just tell you a thing he did only the other day. Bedad! it bangs Banagher, and Banagher banged the divil, your honour. I'm ready to burst when I think of the fun of that barber. There were two countrymen, with their sickles wrapped round in haybands, comes into his shop, on their way home from the harvest with those nasty foul people the English, and says they, 'Barber, we want a shave for a halfpenny.' 'I don't shave for less than a penny,' says he, 'my bouchals.' But at last, after a dale of higgling, he agrees, and both of them sits down. The barber froths both the chins and the two months' beards, and says he to me, 'Tom, run for my Ballysader razor,' for he keeps this for tough jobs, and when he gets it he shaves half the chin of one and half the chin of the other. 'I fear I'll never level it now,' says he. 'I fear it was not a man of business cut your hair the last time.' Then, after dancing round them and figuring about for some time, he washes off the lather, whips off the cloth from under their chins, and gives them the handglass to see themselves in. 'Why, you've notched us like forks; we're only half shaved,' cried both of the reapers. 'That,' says the barber, 'is what I do for a halfpenny.' Well, you'd have killed yourself with laughing to have seen the two Munster men look at the glass, and then at each other, turning the pence over in their pocket, then rubbing their chins, till at last they out with twopence each (twice the usual sum) and sat down and were shaved like Christians.

"And this reminds me of the trick I played a Dublin bag-man at Galway once. There was a lot of us at the Malt Sho-vel Inn, where the Clifden coach, which I then drove for Bian-coni, stopped, and the loudest talker was a tailor bagman, who you'd think was made on the eighth day; all by himself he was, so swelling with his pudding-bag sleeves and peg-top breeches. We fell a talking, and at last he bet me a quart of ale that I could not smoke a pipe of tobacco while he walked once round the green. Well, I took care to pack it very loose, and away he went; but I beat him, and brought it all to ashes before he returned. Then I must let him do the thing again, to give him his revenge, for he swore he had been so sure of beating me he had taken no trouble to walk fast. I was determined to play him a trick, so I challenged him again, and away he went. In the mean time I sent out and got a rapping dose of tartar emetic, and slipped it in his quart of ale, that was ready frothing for the winner on the bar. Presently in comes my gentleman as proud as ninepence, puffing and blowing. 'Well,' says he, 'have I won?—have I won?' 'Yes,' says I, 'you have; there's your ale: drink it. I am dead bet this time, anyhow,' he says, and off he drinks the whole pot, without resting his elbow. Wasn't he sick; faix! his worst enemy wouldn't have wished a better sight than to have seen him holding his sides, as blue as the devil when St. Patrick took him by the nose with the red-hot pincers."

"Are you fond of driving, Reilly?" said I, lighting a cigar, and giving him one.

"Not over and above, your honour," said Reilly. "Put me on top of a hot chesnut and I'm at home; but this rolling on a rickety coach-box spiles the digestion. Och! there's no greater divarsion now to my mind than to sit on a hill and hear the music of the beagles down in the valleys. Och! the echoes talk and jangle to each other; it's mighty divarting, and the purtiest thing in life of a bright blue Autumn morning. I had two beagles when I was a young man; I called one Fly and the other Bird. I should say, in all Ireland there was no two better dogs to turn and wind a hare; for faix, they played into each other's hands just like two players at whist."

"And what became of your beauties?" said I.

Reilly sighed. "Why, Bird was killed leaping over a cliff, and Fly ate a poisoned lamb they'd set for these carrion-crows that kill the game on the hills. He swelled up as big as a barrel, and died while I was carrying him home."

"Poor Fly," said I, lighting a sweet-scented fusee.

"By the powers, your honour," said Reilly, "as a boy, I should have got down from a gibbet, I think, if I'd heard the dogs' tongues and seen the scarlet topping the stone walls in little lines of red, till they all joined into one great red sea at the blackthorn covert side. Blood-and-ouns, that makes my blood bile and the pulse go like a steam-ingine. One day, when I was a boy, I and five other lads were going to school with two sods each under the arm for the master (that's how we paid him in the poor parts of county Mayo), and presently we saw the hounds coming up in full cry after the bushy tail. Now mother had said, ' Patsy, whatever you do, don't go after the hounds.' But she said nothing about going before them, so away we went, hedge and ditch, barefoot, splash through the black bog-holes, tip tap over the hard blue roads, and hop-and-hop over the plough, and skim and drop over the stone croppers, till the fox was run into. May I never hear mass again if we weren't some ten miles from home then, and we with-out our dinner. Well, just as we were looking about for berries, mushrooms, or anything, what should we see but a dish of smoking maly potatoes, laughing themselves out of elbows, at a cabin door. Sorra guide me, but before I knew what I was about, I had it under my arm, and was a mile off under a bush counting them out, and trying if the sort could be spoken well of. At the next turn of a road, what should the great tempter show us but a large flat-head cake cooling in a window, and that one of the fellows took and ran off with too. So that's the way we made out our dinner. Do you see that house yon-der, sir?"

" Yes; you mean the white one, with the slate roof," said I.

" Yes," said Reilly ; " that belonged to a magistrate that they tell a good story of. He was always in debt and being watched, but he kept himself so close, that divil a *fy far* or a *car sar* could the bailiffs serve, till one day a Bray man, one Phil O'Shanghnessy, determined to be up to him, so what does he do but sham drunkenness outside the magistrate's door, for he thought he saw the man he wanted peeping through the window-blind; out rush two policemen, and take him to the station-house, and presently before the magistrate. ' Who are you?' says the magistrate. ' Read this,' said the bailiff, handing in the latitat, 'and you'll see.' And so he grabbed him. Mighty nate it was, anyhow."

" Whose is this cottage, Reilly ?" said I.

" Oh, that's," said Reilly, " the priest's, Father O'Dwyer; and there he comes, in his Hessian boots, on his little cob. He's not so poor as Father M'Guire, in the next village, who lives in a little *boreen*, in a cabin with only two whitewashed rooms. It's as much as he can do to live, though he's the *sogarth aroon*, the darling of everybody; and just over agin him is the Protestant clergyman's, with his snug glebe and lawn, and the divil knows what not."

" What a crop of grass there is on that cottage roof," said I.

" Sure," said Reilly, strongly agreeing, " the man might keep a cow there, and no hurt to the crop."

It was, indeed, such a sluggard's roof as one only sees in Ireland; a century old thatch, long, brown, and jagged, sunk into deep clefts, and hollows, and furrows, covered moreover with clumps of nettles and tufts of long shaking grasses, tall enough to hide a man in. There was here the antiquity of decay, the pride of sluggardness, the triumph of corruption. When we got nearer, I saw that the gable end had fallen, and that one window was a blind heap of stones.

" Why it's a ruin, Reilly ?" I said, inquiringly.

Reilly, looking away, said, in a low voice, " That's the house of the degraded priest; and about this priest I have a terrible story, but too long for to-day, your honour."

CHAPTER XV.

PADDY AND I.

When I heard a grave gentleman-like man, at the Ballybrogue Station of the Great Punster Railway, say to a friend, who asked him how he should spend the half-hour he would have to wait, that he should spend it thinking of all the kind things he (the friend) had been saying to him, I said, " *The Irish are a polite people.*"

When I saw, at a Dublin theatre, the whole house to a man get on their legs, and howl at the manager because he wouldn't introduce a national jig in the middle of *La Sonnambula*, I said, "*The Irish are an excitable people.*"

When a Killarney guide swore to me on the tomb of his grandmother that there was a small lake up in Mullacap, county Kerry, which contained a giant eel, that swam twice round the enclosure every day at two o'clock, with a pan of ould gold tied to his tail, I said, "*The Irish are a superstitious people.*"

When a Tipperary landlord, in a Galway railway carriage, told me he was surnamed "the Woodcock," because he had been shot at so often by the "noblest tinantry" and missed, I said, "*The Irish are a revengeful people.*

When I saw my friend Mike Rooney's best blue breeches stuffed into his cabin window to keep out the rain, I said, "*The Irish are a thoughtless people.*"

And lastly, when I refused the beggar-woman at Castlebar a half-penny, and she ironically hoped "the Lord would make my bed that night in heaven," I said, "*The Irish are a witty people.*"

But this is nothing to do with my story; for what I want to say is, that I got into Westport on the fair-day and the sessions-day, and found the coffee-room full of bagmen and sessions people, just hot from a case in which an action had been brought against the owners of a steamer for putting a cargo of eggs with which they had been intrusted too near the funnel, in consequence of which half the eggs had been hatched and half addled. I first threw myself heart and soul among the bagmen; those whom I chiefly valued were a big-headed elephantine Smith, in the hardware way, and Fitzgibbons, an invalid—a neat-featured, droll Dublin man,—very full of anecdote. Thus they began:

"Why, what's the matter, Smith!" said Fitzgibbons the Dublin bagman to the big-headed gentleman in the hardware line.

Smith had thrust his hands in his pocket, shut up with a bang the order-book, in which he was making memoranda of the day's work, stretched out his shapely legs, and seemed entirely intent on staring with a quaker-like concentration at the tips of his boots.

" I tell you what is," said Smith moodily; " I can't get on without my claret."

" The house is going to rack and ruin since Proger's death," said a neat band-box man in the floor-cloth line.

" O, you shouldn't be hard on the house. They do their best," said the full-whiskered, neat-featured Fitzgibbons. " Have you ever heard, Smith, that story of Dwyer, the Dublin ' beak ?' "

" No," said Smith, not yet rallying from the effect of the absence of his favourite wine, but wishing to be amused.

I was somewhat tired of the endless ceremonial of " Mr. President, may I be permitted," " Mr. Vice, I am intruding, I fear, on your province," and bridled up to hear the story which the eccentric dispenser of justice had himself told Fitzgibbons.

" Fill your tumbler, old fellow, before you begin," said Smith.

" Thank you, old boy," said Fitz, twisting his mouth into an elongated tube adapted for probationship in " screeching" hot whisky and aqua.

" I'll tell you the story, boys, as the ould jintleman himself told it me. 'The other day,' said he, in his own mealy brogue, ' as I was sitting for the administration of justice on my judgment-sate in Ormond Street, a little boy was brought up before me charged with robbing an orchard out somewhere by Donnybrook. The case was clearly proved; and the keeper of the nursery-garden deposed that the boy was an old offender, and that he had visited the place so often that he had cleared it of every sort of fruit. Having no pity on such villainous young marauders found guilty upon the clearest possible evidence, I sentenced him to three months' imprisonment, not forgetting to add the usual whipping,—the peculiar prerogative of juvenile offenders. Just as I had delivered this sentence with a solemn air, I looked in a dignified way round the court, and to my surprise observed the old gardener, who lingered in the witness-box, standing there still, pulling down his forelock as if he wanted to speak to me, and had something on his mind. " If you plase—" he said. " What are you wanting,

M 2

fellow ?" said I. " If you plase," said the man, " I've got a peculiar favour to ask." " What is it ?" said I. " Why," said he, " if it plase your honour's worship, that I may see the little boy receive his sentence." " What, be whipped ?" said I. " Yes ; be whipped," said he. Well, as soon as the business of the day was over, I went down into the back-court, feeling anxious to know what sort of morbid curiosity impelled the man. When I got there, the little boy was receiving his first lash, and I saw him, all in a shivering heap, cramming his dirty knuckle into the extreme corner of his left eye ; and there, in the corner, stood the prosecutor looking on and rubbing his hands as if it was, 'pon my sowl, the Royal Theatre he had got a dress-box in. Well, I watched him ; and before the whip could come down again on the poor little devil's dirty hide, he goes up to the urchin, and giving him a dig in his very small ribs, cries out, " There's a Mogul plum for ye ;" and the next time the whip came down, he goes up on the other side, and cries, " There's a jargonelle for ye ;" and the third time it was, " There's a Kerry pippen for ye ;" and so the cruel villain went on, till, I'll be bail, there wasn't a fruit or vegetable known in Paradise, much more in Ireland, that he did not mention to the poor boy." (Loud laughter, &c.)

Smith. It's a good story now, ain't it ?

Fitzgibbons. Why, you never heard it before.

Smith. Och, haven't I! Weren't we all half kilt with it the other week at Derry ?

Fitzgibbons. Bad luck to the big head of ye, so I did. Well, it's a good story, ain't it ? Yet, hang it, I towld it the other day to to a man who couldn't for the life see the point of it. " Why did he say, ' There's a Mogul plum for ye ?' " he kept repeating ; " ' Ah, there's a jargonelle.' Now, why did he say 'jargonelle ?' " I could have laid hold of the boiled leg of mutton, and beaten him into capers with it.

After this, the neat little man in the floor-cloth way volunteered a long and pointless story, all about " *a clock* " running up a wall. Now, I could imagine a clock on a wall, or a man running away over a wall with a clock ; but what was this ?

It was a new hotel, and he had just gone to bed, when he

heard a mysterious noise, and presently saw "a clock" run up the wall.

"A clock?" said I, unable to contain my amazement.

Smith. O, they call them in England beetles.

Well, the clock did not end the story; for the small neat man went on to say, that in all his circuit he had never seen such a place. All night he was kept awake with the gnawings of something sharper than even conscience. Day broke, and yet no sleep. He really could not stand it; he leaped out of bed, and rang a yawning peal that made night hideous and roused the whole house. Soon at his door came the half-dressed indignant landlord. Our friend grew tranquil; he asked if they'd any toast-and-water ready made. The landlord was furious. "Look here," said I, drawing him to the bedside; and flinging back the clothes, I showed him the white sheets spotted with black. "Lord!" says the landlord, with an expression of mingled astonishment, pity, and indignation, "*why it's only a parcel of bed-bugs;*" and he went shuffling off, and grumbling at being rung up at such an hour about so mere a trifle.

Fitzgibbons. That's a neat little mare you drive in your trap, Grady; but where's the cob gone?

Grady. Gone? why, where the good niggers go,—to the knacker's.

Fitzgibbons. Well, I hope you sent him to our ingenious friend at Sandymount. You have heard his way of doing business, haven't you? No? Well, I'll tell you. When a man takes his horse there, he generally leaves him in the yard, panting and wheezing, while he goes into Geoghean, in the little box of a counting-house, where he finds him, pen behind his ear, running his finger down a ledger, and sharper than a Tipperary fox. They cannot come to terms at all. Our friend asks 3*l*.; Geoghean won't give more than 2*l*. 2*s*., and wants the harness in besides. At last, in a tiff, off goes the owner to get up in his cart and whip home again. In the mean time, however, Geoghean has slyly sent out one of his men to knock the beast on the head, and there he lies stone-dead between the shafts. The owner does not know what to do. He won't take the price; but he cannot get the carcass home, an if he does, it won't keep. While he is trying to flog his brains for a plan, out comes Geoghean in a burning, storming rage, threatens him with prosecution, orders him directly with his own hand to remove that carrion from his yard, or he will charge five shillings for every hour it is kept there. In despair, the mortified owner re-opens the negociation ; but Geoghean, stern and obdurate, will not now give more than 1*l.* 15*s.*, and at that miserable and insufficient price the bargain is closed.

Smith. And mighty ingenious too. The *coup-de-grace* most judiciously applied. (Seriously.) This house isn't as it used to be in Rooney's time : there was no talk of a gentleman wanting claret then——

Fitzgibbons. Och, man, never mind the claret ; tell us the story how you took in the Dublin carman.

Smith. Oh, it's not worth the telling. It was last year, I was coming home from my circuit, and I arrived by the seven-o'clock train at the Drogheda station in Dublin. I thought I would have some fun,—for I had a white hat on at the time, and looked mighty like a tracker (pedestrian) ; so I went staring about the station, and called for a jaunting-car. Three men ran up, whip in hand : one would drive me for nothing, and give me a dram besides ; another had a horse that would make the tay-kettle's steam-boiler burst ; a third would go bail that his horse could drive all the rest before him. I hired one, clung on the side-seat like a stranger, and told him to drive to the Gresham. "The Gresham, is it ?" Away he went,—such a drive!—round by the Quays, and the Phœnix, and Grafton Street, and the Liberty, and back to Sackville Street. Then he pulls up at the lamp with a start, leaps off as if he had done the thing well, and waits for his fare, expecting a crown or so. I handed him the statute sixpence. "What's this ?" said he, looking at it as if it was a bad one. "Is it bad ?" said I. "No," said he ; "but I want four-and-tinpence." "For one set down within the municipalities," said I, "fare sixpence." "O, by Jabers," said he, "the mealy-mouthed rascal ! To the ould Harry with your municipalities ! Sorra to your big head, if I didn't take ye for a *rowler* (tourist) !" (Laughter.)

I. They tell a story in Dublin of a magistrate there who has a peculiar mission for putting down carmen. His object in life is to check extortion; he lives to suppress carmen. One day he sent his little girls to school in a car, putting them in at the turnpike to save over-fare, and directing them with many precautions to get out this side the municipal boundary. When they get out, they hand the carman, who had prepared himself to pluck his young fare, sixpence. The carman looked at it first, and then at them. "What's this dirtying my hands?" says he. "It's your sixpence." "Is it sixpence?" says he. "It's your proper fare," they said, "and we shall not give any more." "You'll not give any more?" "No; it's what papaw told us to give." "And who is your papaw?" (with a voice of drawling disgust). "Mr. Flannigan, the police magistrate." "Mr. Flannigan!" (with a look of discomfiture rising to terror, regaining his seat, and whipping off). "Och! then good morning to ye, my little darlints, and remember me to your papaw."

Smith. There are two magistrates, Flannigan and Flaherty, of whom many good stories are told. One is peculiarly hard on people who are found incapable of taking care of themselves or of anyone else, and who, because they have been generally already robbed, are also fined. The other is equally forgiving. I heard a drunken fellow once, lying in the gutter and talking with his wife, who was swearing at him for not coming home. "Where's your manners, ye dirty baste," she said, pushing him with her foot, "bringing disgrace on the ould name and the ould blood? Och! you big baste, to leave your poor neglected wife and childer;—get up with you." "Biddy," said the drunken vagabond from the kennel, "for the love of the Virgin and St. Patrick, just rowl me over to Flannigan's side of the street, and I'll be all right in the morning."

Fitzgibbons. He's the magistrate who examined the man of straw as to the value of his property. "Will you swear," he said, "that your holdings are worth twenty pounds?" "Bedad," said the bail, who was holding his nose as if he was rubbing it, "I swear that I wouldn't part with my holdings for twice twenty pounds." So he was admitted.

As a change from the bagmen, I turned to the sessions-table, where the chief speakers seemed to be a Mr. Joyce, a low attorney and parasite, a fat Falstaff, with a wavering cunning eye; Mr. O'Donnel, a barrister; and Mr. Muffington, the owner of the steamer in fault in the egg-question. He had a swollen-looking red face, and a punchy, vulgar little body; but Joyce spoke of him as the prop of the town, and the glory of county Mayo. Joyce was not a peace-maker, as we see when he gives tongue.

Joyce. I go on the broad principle. I say, put a six-barrelled revolver to their jaw, and blow them to everlasting blazes.

I. Gently, gently, Mr. Joyce; the law will see us righted.

Joyce. (squeezing a lemon viciously). What I told them was, when you're all dead and rotten the steamer will go ahead. Westport for ever! What I want is a revolver—a legal revolver. Revolver is legal; who says it isn't? I should like to see any one say it isn't. Where is he? I'm not too old yet to fight; and I can hit a gnat at forty paces without telescope-glasses.

Muffington. We shall win our action; there's no doubt about it: Counsellor Brady says we shall.

Joyce. Snaffle him, that's what I want; just as I did for Captain House. Is the country to be destroyed, that's what I ask. Is it to be ruined? Och! rascal; och, the murthering villains! Take it patiently; yes, I will. Let me purpose as a toast, "Muffington and the steamer." Hurrah! GIVE IT STAMPING.

Toast drunk with dance and jingling acclamations.

Mr. Muffington, the little podgy, red-faced, swollen sort of man, got up and proposed the health of the counsel for the defendant—Mr. O'Donnel.

Drunk with fresh glass, dancing.

Joyce. That's what I like. I hate all your finical dirty talk. Grapple with 'em; drag them to blazes; throw rotten eggs at 'em; pillory them. Och! that's the way; give 'em Lynch law!

Mr. O'Donnel, a spare, care-worn, pale, clever-looking man, his thin face working with excitement, got up and made a speech to return thanks. He had striven to do his duty, as he always tried to do, without acrimony or personal feeling, as he always tried to do it. His name was, he hoped, a respected name in the county—

Joyce. Bravo for the O'Donnels!

O'Donnel. It has been known in Mayo for centuries.

Joyce. The Tyrconnels!!

O'Donnel. But he could not sit down without saying, that he thought he never, in his small experience, had conducted a case which reflected more discredit on the plaintiffs.

Joyce. Mat, get a six-barrelled revolver, and blow them to ould Nick.

A quiet farming-man in frieze rose to propose the health of a gentleman well known in Westport,—a gentleman respected, he believed, by all who had the pleasure of knowing him,—he meant Mr. Muffington.

Tremendous cheers; old Joyce beating on the table with both fists, and continuing two minutes after every one else had finished.

Joyce. Shoot them all, like d—d rapparees, as they are; nothing less. I say it emphatically, be gad, shoot them all! I go upon the broad principle.

I (aside). Good heavens, what a man for an attorney!

Bystander (in a whisper). He used to keep his carriage and four; but he drove through all his property, and is now known only for his chicanery and trickery: as an attorney, sir, he is sunk to the lowest depths.

Joyce. Play up, Larry,—"Mike Rooney's Ganther." Put 'em in the pillory, that's my way; give 'em good musical and pistol law. Every one knows Phil Joyce. He has a fine constitootion (slaps his stomach), and never goes beyond his nointh tumbler! Shoot 'em all, I say! Send round the hat for poor dark Larry.

Larry. More power to ye, Mr. Joyce.

Joyce. There's an ould proverb about the transplanted tree. Now Mr. Muffington is a transplanted tree, whose roots have taken great and deep hold in this Irish soil; and all I wish to do is to end my days under the shadow of the Muffington tree,—

may it live for ever, I say, and a day longer. The chairman is
the man who knocks down any one that disagrees with him, and
so will I any one who says the word against "Muffington and
the steamer." I'm for morality and all that sort of thing.
Now, then, we must remember Larry. No one will grudge
sixpence for poor Larry. Mr. Muffington, I respect ye ; the
Muffington tree is what I hope to die under, when this last—
John, some hot water,—quick, you divil,—and more spirit on
the top of it, you blackguard.

Tired of this scene of blarney, confusion, and noise, I broke
from the turbulent coffee-room, crowded with witnesses and
attorneys, and got out into the pure air of the street. It was
fair-day, and the town was alive with moving wheels, bellowing
oxen, and expostulating pigs. There, in a snug corner, was
the indefatigable brogue-seller, with one hand in a shoe and
the other rubbing it, as he spit upon the leather. "If it does
this with a spit, what will it be with a black ?" is his argument.
There, safe under the church-tower, were the women with their
stalls of clean printed calicoes, running their fabrics between
their fingers and thumbs, to the intense admiration of the
dark-eyed Colleens, the young sisters that clung to their skirts,
and the boy who stopped the slip of the "peg" with the long
hayband tied to his left hind-leg as a sort of rein. There
was the bowl-seller, with his nest of bowls, cogs and noggins,
at whose store stood the sturdy farmers with buttoned-up
frieze and stout blackthorns under the arm. There were gin-
gerbread-stalls, and men selling halters and whips, all ranged
in rows on either side of the High Street, round the chief inn,
through whose door worked in and out a jostling crowd of
graziers and drovers, from the mere cotter, who had brought
his single pig—the hope of the family—as a great venture, to
the lordly grazier, with his five dozen bulls of Bashan, and his
big pocket-book, swollen with greasy one-pound notes. And
through all this chatting, laughing, excitable, cheerful, eager,
good-natured crowd, with variegated colours flying, came the
band of the Galway militia,—the non-commissioned officers,
four abreast, as large as life, with drawn swords ; the drum in
a painful state of apoplectic excitement and inflammatorily red

in the face; and last, four abreast, arm-in-arm, the newly-caught recruits, shouting their sanguine and sanguinary anticipations of endless booty and tremendous glory. Raw Irish lads, just caught from the bog, they looked as green as the laurels that a phantom without a head waved above their as yet unbroken skulls.

"Militia is doing better than the line," I said half-maliciously to a grizzled recruiting sergeant of the 52nd leaning against a chemist's door-post, his stained scarlet matching very well with the adjacent blue bottles.

"Och," said he, with a professional and crafty smile, "they're only decoy-ducks, sir." And away they went, ruffling the fair with their parchment-thunder to the Spartan-like bray of the

> "Tow, row, row
> Of the British grenadiers."

Pushing through the crowd of hot rosy girls, uncomfortably fine farmers' sons, and sagacious old women, and farmers with hay stirrups, narrowly escaping a violent Juggernautic death from cage-carts of anxious-looking and self-conscious pigs, wondering empty-headed calves, and mischievous-looking runts, driven with yells in the Irish language, and thwacks not needing translation, I worked slowly through the gossiping, busy, chaffering crowd, till I got to the low stony hill with the turf trodden off it, where the cattle market was held: it was a bovine Witenagemote, an Æsop parliament. The money-market I saw was tight, by the buttoned-up look of the old farmers, and the reserved and cynical manner of the splashed graziers, who eyed the cows with contemptuous criticism, nudged their stomachs with Abernethy-like roughness, and then walked off, beating their muddy boots with their ground-ash sticks. Between the countless horns of leathery dry-looking kine, country girls and farmers' sons with meteor-like neck-handkerchiefs exchanged meaning nods, in spite of watchful mothers heedful of bargains, and Fardorougha-like fathers. The busiest men were the small higglers and jobbers, with only two dirty pound notes or so to invest, and determined to speculate desperately in some moribund cow or spavined horse. I saw one of them leading about anything but the fatted calf; its hide a vamped old shoe, its hair like an old school trunk's, its eye fishy, its gait feeble. A jolly Rory O'More offered him a pound-bill for it, and said it didn't look likely. "Never judge a book by the cover," says Jim, down upon him with an old saying. "Don't be wiser than wise," says another O'Rourke to a well-to-do farmer, who is sticking out for a high price. Talk of co-quetting! these graziers know every trick of the art. Look at that fellow with the frieze-blanket coat, how much he longs for these tight-skinned active pigs—pure Connaught; but he fights, and scolds, and beats his hands, and buttons his coat, and scares the pig-jobber, and now that all is nearly over, he actually claps on his hat tighter, puts his shillalah under his arm, and walks coolly off to one of the long waggon-tilt booths for a "half-one" of whisky. That bold act is a fine stroke of generalship; it is the *coup-de-grace;* it wins the day. The pig-jobber, almost tearing his hair, runs after him, claps the earnest-money in his expectant palm, and cries, "Mike, the pigs is yours." Then with stentorian violence to the boy, he roars "CALL 'EM BACK! You've got them dirt-cheap." Out comes the pocket-book, out come the notes; and observe the dry smile of the satisfied pur-chaser, and the feigned discomfiture of the diamond-cut-diamond jobber. The long low booths—so low that you cannot stand upright in them,—are worth a visit. See the little peat-fire at the door, with its pleasant whiff of curling blue smoke; that's for the hot water, and the hot water is for the whisky. Within, facing each other, on long low benches, sit the drovers and farmers, scraping their boots with switches, with hands on knees, they laugh and chaff with thorough Irish lightness of heart. They do love pleasure, these Celts. French or Irish, they work at play, and play at work; they dance themselves to death, but they dig with the listlessness of convicts.

Between the rows, smoking jug in hand, passes the widdy Grattan, with always some story to tell you of what M'Cor-mac's pig said to King O'Toole. O the pleasant bustle and flurry of those simple-hearted, happy, wretched-papists, who should be miserable with pigs, priests, mud-floors, and dung-hills, yet are so obstinately jolly while Paddy's rich morbid brother John is hipped in spite of mahogany, port-wine, and roast-beef! Shall I ever forget, dear Ireland, the fun and witty bantering on that grassless hill, where shock-headed boys ran about madly after mountainous short-horns ten times their size, where pigs nuzzled in straw, where horses trotted in and out, where everybody shouted, sang, bellowed, and brayed in noisy competition? How the farmers' wives culled the fairest pigs with the proud air of experience; how the jobbers rushed into butting knots of oxen, and picked out their own special brand; how everybody escaped goring, and made a bargain, and finally went home, driving like drunken goblins, singing and racing,—I still remember well! In a little green field of my mind, that grassy hill, stands up the Acropolis of my Erin, the echo of a perpetual laugh always round it, and the smell of the peat-fire dew ever filling its soft nimble air.

CHAPTER XVI.

BOATING IN KILLARNEY.

HERE we are, then, in the boat that rocks at the little stone jetty fronting the Lake Hotel, Killarney. A morning of a bright October; the water clear,—as water should be that is the crystal roof and skylight of the " ouldest fairies in Ireland." The trees are all a-flutter with leaf-gold, the thin blue air is busy and alive with thousands of winged clouds.

The oars poise in the rowlocks, when Phil O'Donohue, the head-boatman, shakes his head, pauses, deliberately takes out his short, black, oily *dudheen*, places it in the obedient and grateful mouth of Will Macarthy, his subordinate,—a silent and imperturbable man, except on the subject of fees and finance,—girds up his loins, gives a cheering yell after the manner of his country, then leaps out of the boat, and runs towards the hotel-door with the speed of a startled buck.

" Decided dementia; disturbance of the cerebral functions."

said one of my companions, a Dublin medical student, with a pleased manner, at the same time scraping out his pipe. "Is it colouring?" he said, rubbing it and holding it up to our third friend,—a little pragmatic, wizen, bow-legged Welsh commercial traveller from the coal-districts,—just as a mother would show her firstborn to her gossip. The Tore mountain might hold up its bragging arms to catch the clouds of Kerry, but he (Brady) was only solicitous about his eldest meerschaum, ornamented with the playful skull and cross-bones.

"What is the matter with Phil?" said I to the stolid boatman. "Is he gone for the salmon-rod? It's a pretty day for fishing."

"Is it Phil? (with a puzzled and inquiring air). Sure he's gone for the whisky,—the *cruiskeen-lawn,*—your honour."

"Lawn, lawn, lawn!" shouted Brady, still screwing at his pipe with a sculptor's care. "Bad-luck to him, am I never to get a patient? Then it's not dementia."

We looked, and sure enough we saw afar off our favourite waiter Tim—the horseman, the fisher, the fiddler—handing with religious care a deliciously green transparent bottle of the best Bush Mills—potent, fragrant—to Phil, who received it as a proselyte would the viaticum. He wrapped it in the breast of his jacket as a father might a frost-bitten lamb in a snow-storm among the hills. He came back at a bound over the pier, with a cheer from Tim, and a "good-luck to us" from the bugler and a dozen hangers-on, who were waiting about the door with a score of ragged ponies, ready for Mangerton and its stony clamber.

"Is it right?" said I.

"It's right, your honour," said Phil with a look of sagacious approval. "There's the rod by the jintleman that's nursing the big pipe: and the bugle, ready for Paddy Blake, by the jintleman with the spy-glass on him. Now then, give way, Macarthy, and remimber that I'm an O'Donohue; and don't let me do all the pulling, you *bodagh.*"

"Be asy, Phil, be asy; the day's before us."

Away we went, cutting the water like a ploughshare does

the clay furrow, straight for Ross Island, and the ould castle that big thief Cromwell pounded to smithereens, "or at laste his son-in-law; so that it was all in the family." Probert, the little Welsh bagman, gave a spasmodic bob forward as we throbbed on; Brady lit his meerschaum with a red sod, brought for the purpose, and declared the scenery would be d—d fine if the mountains had only been taller and the lake wider.

"Will your honour tell me how to put the say in a whisky-bottle?" said Phil, brushing his mouth with his sleeve, and readjusting his feet against the holdfast.

"None of your impertinence, sir," said the bagman.

Phil only pulled viciously, and asked me if I had ever heard of what the piper of Killaloe said to Macgillicuddy of the Reeks when he gave him a bit of his mind, and called him an infernal spalpeen.

"No," said I.

"Faix, then I'll tell your honour some day when the wind's favourable and the company selecter," with a wink at the irascible bagman, who was inquiring of Brady the price of coal in Dublin.

"If it was tobacco, now," said Brady, "I'm your man."

"Impertinent pody!" said Probert, still sore at Phil. "T—d poatman, t—d poat!"

"Will it be fine, Phil?" says Brady, looking up at Mangerton with pipe sideways in his mouth. "I fear it'll be soft."

"It will not," said Phil.

"How do you know, poatman?" said the bagman pertly, as little men generally speak, and looking as if he had caught Phil in a dilemma.

"Well, God Almighty didn't tell me," said Phil.

"I was up doosed early, bedad," said Brady, "and I don't like the look of things."

"But God Almighty," said Phil triumphantly, winking to me, "was up before you; and it will be fine. I know by the look of the Purple Mountain, by the flies on the water, by the leaves of the arbutus on the little rock there, and by—"

"Now then, men," I said. "Pull away for Ross Island. Brady, chorus." I sing improvising:

"To Dinas, to Dinas, we pull, we pull,
  With the leap of a stag and the rush of a bull,
  With our gurgling bottle and hamper full.
                    Hurrah!

Where the green holly dips its berries of red
  Over the fairies' fern-leaf bed,
  Where the drowned monk sings a mass for the dead.
                    Hurrah!

Over the silent reefs we sail,
  The boatman telling a banshee tale,
  The fresh night wind is her mourning wail.
                    Hurrah!

Then a health to the King O'Donohue,
  Who dwells far up in the mountain blue,
  Macgillicuddy, with you, with you.
                    Hurrah!"

" Long life to you," says Phil ; "and may we have many more such jintlemen with the tongue well hung, and the heart in the right place. (Looks on the bagman.) Isn't it beautiful?" (to Macarthy, who had been eyeing Brady's pipe attentively for some minutes, to that enthusiastic gentleman's almost coquettish delight).

" Och, beautiful entirely" (waking up).

Probert thinks, as it is a little cold, he will take a pull, and lays his hand on O'Donohue's oar.

" Now get out of that (' you *leprecaun*,' under breath); sure, and an't I Phil O'Donohue, boatman and guide of Killarney Lakes, descended from the great O'Donohue of the Glins,— and am I to give up my trust, and sit like a fat priest doing nothing?"

" Nonsense, pother! Didn't you let this gentleman pull but half an hour ago? I will pull ; pody and soul, I will pull —by St. Tafid, I will!"

" Mr. Probert, keep your temper. Phil, be decent. Here's a big lump of a rock : what's this called, Phil?"

" That's O'Donohue's dining-table, your honour, where's he's seen dining on the turtle-soup and the pig's trotters, and all the dainties mortal man can think of."

" It is ferry pig," said the Welshman, forgetting his anger

and staring at the huge slab of rock,—square, flat, and vast as the key-stone of the ruined gate of Eden, which Irishmen say was undoubtedly hereabouts,—with the little playful waves kissing its rough cheeks, and racing round its giant angles.

"It is not a pig at all, your honour," said the wilful Phil; "but a table—O'Donohue's table. You've maybe heard the old story,—how, on the 1st of May, once in every seven years, O'Donohue of Ross, an ould king of these parts, rises out of the lake, and takes possession of his ancient demesne."

"And collicts the rints," said Brady.

"Exactly, your honour; that's it."

"Has any pody seen him, then?"

"Dozens upon dozens, your honour; and my father among 'em."

"And how does the old buffer look?" said Brady with philosophical anxiety.

"Well, then, (rests on his oars at Ross-Castle landing-place, where the blind piper with the pretty daughter is blowing himself to pieces for the small sum of one halfpenny)—Larry, you ould Trojan, play the Fox-hunter's jig,—and look alive; that *ologaun* gives me the stomach-ache."

Phil continues seriously: "Well, your honour, my father described him as a bould-looking man, in scarlet, on a white horse, with a three-cocked hat and a rijimintal band playing behind him." (Roars of laughter, which almost capsize the boat. When we stop, he continues with unbroken gravity.)

"A what on his head?" says Brady.

Phil (sternly). A three-cocked hat! (Fresh roars.)

"A what behind him?" said I.

"A rijimintal band. (Increased laughter.) They went marching along in the early morning close to my father's boat; but when he followed them, they disappeared. You see, jintlemen, there was two of 'em—O'Donohue of Ross, and O'Donohue of the Glins. The great O'Donohue was just and honourable; but the O'Donohue of the Glins, who I come from, was bloody and tyrannous; then there was Macarthy Moore and Macgillicuddy,—all great men about these lakes. Tore and Glena were their hunting-mountains."

N

"I shouldn't like to have gone to their meets," said Brady contemplatively.

"O'Sullivan, too, had bloody wars with the O'Donohues in ould times—But the whisky is getting quite mouldy, your honour, for want of drinking."

"It's a long pull, your honour," said Macarthy, wiping his forehead. (The spirituous essence of smoke is handed round.)

Phil. You mane the pull you took at the bottle. (Larry, play up "O'Sullivan's Joy;" and handle the keys as if you smelt the rale stuff, and a glass of it was pouring out for you. Well done, Larry; play up! Och, nivir spare the bags!) If there's no one here of the wrong way of thinking, maybe I'll give you a Croppy song.

"He has a beautiful pipe of his own," said Macarthy, critically, putting his head on one side ready to listen.

Phil spits and looks hard at the bottom of the boat.

"Now then, Phil, no nonsense."

Phil sings.

"Och for the day we marched into Athlone!
 Didn't the aldermen give us a groan;
 Seeing the sogers race out of the town.
  Major, the bodagh, went off in a swoun.
        Down, down, Orange lie down!

Thunderin' thick were the crowds of the pikes,
A musket a piece for whoever that likes,
And a drum sure as big as e'er butt in the town,
With, och, such a beautiful musical soun'!
        Down, down, Orange, lie down!

There was O'Brady, the top of 'em all,
Cheering the boys from the ledge of a wall;
If but a Croppy gave even a frown,
For mercy men fell on their marrow-bones down.
        Down, down, Orange, lie down!

The Green flew above and the Orange below;
A rush at the guns, they were ours at a blow.
Then blast all the bugles to frighten the town
For Liberty's up, and the Protestants down.
        Down, down, Orange, lie down!"
                Chorus, &c.

Omnes. Well done, Phil.

Brady. Infernal good song. I must learn that. **Try a pipe** of Canaster, old fellow. Smokes doosed well.

Phil. Thankee, your honour. More power to ye, Mr. Brady.

Probert. It's a fery coot song; but I prefer "Of noble race was Shenkin" (that *is* a coot tune); or "Codiad yr Hedyd," or "Codiad yr Hyllion."

I. But now, Phil, something more about the jintleman with the three-cocked hat and the rijimental band.

Phil. Well, your honour, there was a Scotch gardener, who worked for Mr. Herbert on the Muckross demesne, who always used to make his jeers at my father when he talked of the O'Donohue (rest his sowl). Play up, Larry, you villain! That is "The Fox-hunter's Schame" he's playing, your honour. Play up, Larry. Well; and it went so far that they had words between them about it; the Scotchman saying, that upon his sowl he was ashamed to see so sinsible a man talking such trumpery. My father was but a gorsoon then, or maybe he'd have up with his shillalah and knocked the impudence out of him.

Brady. Go it, Phil; I like your pluck.

Phil. Well, my father and he were up early one morning in the autumn, cutting down some young birch-trees that hid the view from the sketching jintleman that came to the Tore water-fall to look for something they call "the picturest." The fog in a silvery stream was smoking up from the blackberry bushes; and the broom, and the fern, and the blessed sham-rock, lay with a silver beading all over them as if, bedad, the last night's fairies had shed their jewels as they ran away frightened at the first beam of the peeping curious sun. The rabbits were hopping over the dead leaves that lay about like great heaps of bullion-gould; and if you listened carefully, you could hear now and then the belling of a buck on Glena (and a purty sound it is in the fresh morning). Well, my father and the Scotchman were busy as pipers at a wedding with the bill-hook and axe, when the Scotchman, who had been looking for a long time at the lake, and the island showing through the fog, suddenly gripes my father by the arm, and asks him, for God's sake, if he didn't hear anything. "No," says my father. "Why, you must be deaf," says he. "There," says he, "for all the world like a flock of floating angels passing low over the lake." "I hear nothing but a squall-crow on the firs yonder," says my father. "You must be a fool, then," says the Scotchman, quite scared; "for there it is again."

"It was the rijimintal band of angels," says Brady.

Phil. Whatever it was, it was too much for the Scotchman; for he went home, sickened with a fever, lay at the gasp for three weeks, and never laughed at the stories of the O'Donohue again.

Brady. Why, you omadhaun, the thing is as clear as the nose on your face,—and an ugly one it is. Sandy was delirious with a fever; the blood was heated in the vessels of his upper gastric region.

I. Excuse me, Mr. Brady, but we must land.

And we did land, and dined and sang and rambled all over the blessed old ruin, that was the last hold in Munster to yield to Cromwell, that is, Ludlow. We saw the great gun with the big Irish name that burst in exultation when it almost knocked down Killalea tower, that was brimful of sour Puritans, with their great clasped Bibles, buff suits, Andrea Ferrara swords, and endless sermons. There the cannon grin at you with hard silent mouths from ivied loops and crumbling ramparts, where "bog-oak girls" teaze you in the prettiest brogue to buy arbutus-wood card-cases.

Brady. What a jolly old place!

Probert. A fery prave place, but not so prave as some of ours in Wales.

Brady. When I walked the hospitals—

Phil. (who had followed us up the stairs to the O'Donohue dining-room). Begging your pardon, jintlemen, this is the O'Donohue's dining-parlour. (How the bees are humming on the ivy-blossom, the craturs!) That window looking on the lake is the one which O'Donohue leaped out of.

Omnes. The story, the story, Phil. Here, wet your lips with whisky.

Phil. Well, you see, this O'Donohue was a mighty grate enchanter, and had dalings surely with the ould jintleman that bit a bit out of the mountain forenent the Punch-bowl there. Now his wife got curious about these tricks of his, and one day tazed him till he would show her some proof of his power; "For," says she, "O'Donohue, I belave it's all sham, so I do." "Well," says he, "go up in the tower, and look out of the window, and you'll see what I can do, devil a doubt of it." So she goes and looks; and presently comes O'Donohue like an elephant, and roars till every stone of Ross Castle shakes again. But the wife wasn't a bit troubled; and so he turns into a leaping fire and a whale, and a red deer with a salmon's head, and then into a lion in a cocked-hat—and she wasn't troubled,—till at last he comes climbing up to this window like a big, rolling, fiery serpent; and when the lady sees that, she out with a prayer, and O'Donohue leaps from the window and disappears for ever in the lake.

Brady. Verdict, "*Felo de se.*" I should like to have sat on his body, Phil.

Phil. There's no end to thim stories, jintlemen. Come up a little higher to the top of the tower, where we can see all the island below, and you shall hear some more.

Brady. Take a pull at my pipe, Phil; it doesn't draw quite right. Pull harder. That's it.

Probert. It's fery peautiful; but not so peautiful as Peth-gelert.

Brady (looking critically on the scenery as he pinches a pipeful of Canaster out of his seal-skin pouch). O, not so peautiful! Get out with ye! Wasn't civilisation in Ireland before Wales was aven invinted? I ask you that now.

Probert. What does the pody mean? Wasn't Cadwal-lader—?

I. Take some whisky, Mr. Probert; we really musn't lose our time in discussions. Now, Phil, tell us the story about O'Donohue and the countryman.

Phil. More power to your honour, sure and I will. Well, it happened thus. It was just a pig-jobber, jintlemen, who was coming home round by Brickeen Bridge in the dusk, driving a little pet *bonoveen*,—a slip of a pig,—by a garter tied to his left leg. Pat was sad enough; for he had not been able to sell the pig in that day's market at Killarney. He was going along, head downwards, like a mare that has lost her foal; for his landlord was a cruel ould hunks, and had swore a week before, that if his rent wasn't paid by that Friday night, he'd sell Pat's very bed from under him, and seize his two milk-cows. Well, at the turning of a road, Pat hears a step behind him, and looks up and sees it is the O'Donohue riding, with his three-cocked hat, on his white horse, grand as a jineral. "Good evening, sir," says he. "Good evening, Pat," says O'Donohue; "you look but sadly." Then Pat out and tells him all his troubles. "Pat," says he, "you're an honest sort of a man; and I'm sorry that you are fallen into the hands of such an ould rip of a tyrant as that landlord of yours. Give him this for a quittance;" and he poured a heap of gould into Pat's hand, and then, before Pat could turn round thank him, or make his bow, he had gone. Next morning early, down comes the landlord. "Pat," says he, "I'm come for the rent; and as you haven't got it I shall take your cattle; so let's go to the stable." "Stop a bit," says Pat, "here's your rent;" and he asks for a recate. "What's all this?" said he, as Pat whips out O'Donohue's bag of money and puts it in his hand. "Take that," says he; "and, by the holy poker, it's me is the boy that would like to see you putting a finger on the cattle." So away went the landlord with Pat's rent, grumbling and swearing like a Tom-cat at dinner-time. And, faix, he didn't make much of the money either; for when he came to look in his greasy ould drawer next morning, what had it all turned to but a parcel of dry leaves; but he never could come down upon Pat, who had got his big recate as snug and sure as the Pope's Bull.

Brady. Verdict, "Sarved him right." I say, Phil, is this a crack coming in my pipe?

A pleasant hour it was we spent in old Ross Castle, the fallen stronghold of the enchanted chieftain of the Lake, the magician of Kerry, the sworn enemy of the O'Donohue of the Glens, the Macarthy More, Macgillicuddy of the Reeks, and that big thafe Cromwell, whose red nose local legend duly chronicles. We groped up the winding staircase, and walked

cautiously along the defaced battlements; and every where—
by embrasure, loop, old fireplace, door, and window—sang the
bees on the ivy-blossoms their half-angry purposeless melody,
as our eyes glanced from island to mountain, where the cloud
poised above the coloured shadow, its spirit sister, that watched
below.

Now a tumble into the boat; and with a merry tune of
Larry's ("Couldn't you lave the rose-bloom alone, Katty, and
not stale it all for those checks?") we pulled for Innisfallen,
the island of the ruined abbey, with the fat lawn-pastures and
the patriarchial holly-trees.

Phil. Play up, Larry. (He's been dark, your honour, ever
since his mother knew him; but a purtier finger for the silver
keys isn't in all Kerry.) Try the line, your honour; there's a
nice curl on the water now. Did you ever hear of O'Donohue,
and the challenge he sent?

Omnes. No: out with it.

Brady. I like the old buffer with the three-cocked hat,
(Whispers to me)—This Phil is of *grate* value.

Phil. Well, your honour, if you must hear it, this is how it
was: Once upon a time, there was a cowherd, and as he was
driving his cows one morning to the field, who should he meet
on a grand white horse but the O'Donohue; and says O'Donohue
to Mike, "Mike, I've got a letter here which I want you to
take to the other side of the lake, and give to the first jintleman
you meet riding on a bang-tailed chestnut," says he. Well,
without more boderation, Mike takes the letter; and sure
enough, just over, not a mile from Killaloe, who should he
meet but three jintlemen horsemen, and the first of the
three was on a bang-tailed chestnut. So Mike out with the
letter, and gives it him bould. "It's fighting he manes," said
the man on the chestnut, curling up his nose as fierce as a
boar-pig when he read the letter, naming the place and hour
that the O'Donohue had fixed on. Now, Mike, who was ready
with the stick, determined to see the fun, and goes at the time
appointed, and gets up in a willy tree, snug and safe out of
sight. In half a minute both the armies come into the field,
and such a scrimmage begins as I make bould to say even

Donnybrook couldn't match. Heads and arms flew about like sods at a hedge-school when the masther's away—"

There is no knowing where Phil's eloquence and power of invention would not have carried him, had not the boat-head been half an hour since turned homeward, and a cry from Brady now announced that the lights of the hotel began to be visible. There they shone, low on the water, now dark, now lurid, guiding us to our desired haven.

I. What a night for the O'Donohue to be abroad, with the banshee of the family riding pillion!

Brady. O boderation with the banshee! what I want is a good rump-steak and some bitter.

Probert. What *I* want is peer.

Twenty minutes' strong pulling brought us again to the jetty; two minutes more brought us to a white-hot peat fire, with a darling kettle singing all to itself. What a breach we made in the *peef*, as Probert called it! That night we had pleasant dreams of monks praying on lonely islands; of O'Donohue in his "three-cocked hat;" of Cadwallader boxing with Macgillicuddy of the Reeks, and getting the worst of it; of hospitals, pipers, and pipes. The first thing I heard when I awoke the next morning was Brady in 32—I was 31—calling faintly to Tim the waiter for another glass of bitter.

CHAPTER XVII.

A NIGHT AT KILLARNEY.

I. BRING another matarial, Tim, for Mr. Brady.

"*Matarial* means, in Irish, whisky-and-water," said I to a tall, thin, soured, wondering-looking man, who I found to be a London land-surveyor, with a very bad opinion of the Celtic race as his predominant peculiarity. He generally spoke in spasmodic short sentences, and uttered them with a snap as if he had stung you. His name was Dabble.

Dabble. O, "matarial" is whisky-and-water. Why can't they speak proper English?

We had just finished dinner at the Lake Hotel; the salmon was our own catching, the snipes our own shooting. We ate like creatures who had pouches rather than stomachs; and now, the table pushed back, the red cloth brushed, the tumblers waiting, the little trays set ready for the white cigar-ashes, the volcanic fire heaped up with slabs of chocolate-looking peat, we drew round our chairs like true fire-worshippers, and sat hungry for talk. Tim entered; and with the knowing smile with which waiters always bring in whisky, deposited on the table four little cruises of the brown smoke-spirit.

Tim. There's the cratur, jintlemen. You won't cry out perhaps if I tell you it wasn't christened, that same.

Brady. More power to ye, Tim, that's the sort. And, Tim, more spoons, and some small glasses to sip the dear thing in.

Probert. It's such a devil of a place for bad seeze; I never tasted such seeze, indeed. In Wales they would throw such tammed seeze out of window.

Dabble. Why, Lord bless you, these fellows are beyond all improvement. As long as they can save stooping with their twelve-feet-long toy-spades, and pick and play at work, what do they care. I never was in such a country before, and God keep me from coming to such a country—

Brady. Keep a civil tongue in your head, sir. I am an Irishman; and I won't have the gem of the sea run down. When I was at the hospitals, if a man—

1. No words, gentlemen. Hot water, Tim—boiling.

Tim. Is it biling ye want?

Dabble. Look at this (holding up his tumbler)! why, the very whisky's made of bog, I may say puddle-water. Ugh!

Brady. It's a pity to poison you before your time: don't drink it.

Dabble. O, I don't mean to say the spirit is in itself bad (sipping it).

Brady. I hate to see a man fall out with his drink. It's not right, Tim, is it?

Tim. It is *not*, your honour.

Brady. Have you had many tourists this year, Tim?

Tim. Divil a year more, your honour, bad luck to 'em! There they go out in the cars of a morning, and some of 'em sure have their maps as big as the thrawing-room table; and when I drive they sit as still as a poker, and never ask the name of nothing, but say to their wives, "This *must* be Ballyswilly," or "This must be Killaloe;" and by the holy jabers (slapping his knee and doubling up in a choking laugh), ten to one but it's Stranorlar or Killygordan. But I'm not going to interrupt them, or it would be, "What an impertinent fellow that driver is!" and there'd be the bright sixpence less to take home to the wife.

Dabble (to Probert, apart). What an ignorant fellow this is!

Probert (to Dabble). Fery, fery! (shaking his head).

Tim. May I go on, your honour; or am I stopping the avening?

I. No, no, Tim; let's hear more about our friends the tourists.

Tim. Then the wife, with the rosebud of a mouth, God bless her! says, "Dear me, James, how picturest!"—always "*picturest.*" Divil if I know what it manes; and bedad, Father Reilly couldn't tell me, for I asked him the last blessed Sunday as ever was after mass. Well, then, there are the five sisters all in a row, just like so many goslings,—with always half an eye, and more nor that, for any dacent young fellow who is on the car,—who all open their mouths together, that you'd think they'd swallow the lake, mountains, and all, like so many red herrings; and they all call out, especially when the dacent young man looks their way, "How picturest!"

Brady. The little hypocrites, how I should like to stop their mouths! Och, the craturs!—I say, my dear fellow (to me), just look how this meerschaum's colouring. You don't think that is a crack, eh?

Tim. And why do the darlints call out "picturest?" when the place is not plisant game-feeding land, but just the mere scrapings and rakings of the world.

Brady (to Tim, maliciously, to vex Probert). And have

you many of the bagmen, Tim, with the great tin-boxes and the mackintosh bundles ?

Tim. Bedad, sir, we have ; and as much fuss with their dirty tin boxes as if they was Lord Lucan or Lord Ragland, bad luck to the big heads of 'em ; and every third word they utter is, " He's not a *business*-man, sir." (Bell rings.) But there's the masther ringing like a Bengal tiger. I'll be in upon you in a brace of shakes ; od, if the tin toes isn't all but off my feet with this running up and down.

Probert. What a tammed trouplesome chattering fellow ! Why, a Wels waiter would no more dare to talk to his pet-ters—

Dabble. O, they're all alike ; quite hopeless, quite hopeless !

Brady. More water, sir ? (Burns Dabble's finger.) Och ! it's sorry I am, because these sort of kettle-burns lead often to the cusaneous erasypilitis and the grand scurvy. (Winks to me.)

I. Well, what did you think of Muckross Abbey, Mr. Brady ?

Brady. Infernal dull, and infernal dear.

Probert. A shilling a head was plackguard cheating.

Dabble. Nasty, lazy, lying set. Ugh ! Pigs under the bed, pigs everywhere.

Brady. No, no ; bacon in some places.

Dabble. Dunghills at the door, and the wretched people sitting as if dunghills were always intended to be at doors. Ugh ! Drinking and fighting. Ugh !

I. The happiest people in the world.

Dabble. Yes ; thoughtless, that's the worst of it : dancing at funerals. Ugh !

I. But about Muckross. Isn't it solemn ? with that yew in the courtyard, spreading over its dark banshee arms as if pronouncing an eternal malediction, keeping out the sunshine and starshine of centuries from the humble unknown graves they have tried so long to visit.

Brady. Sarve the old buffers right ; they were always eating and drinking, and playing the divil's own mischief.

Dabble. Popery, Popery, gentlemen, is the curse of Ireland.

I. So I have heard; but England got on very well with it once, and the whole world too. Some good men have been Papists, I suppose. Under the darkness of that yew thirty monks met daily for some three centuries, parting, after prayer and praise, to climb higher than the eagle, to ford torrents, to wade through swamps, to carry God's message to the dying, and to lift the cross before their glazing eyes.

Probert. But don't forget the putcher's pill.

I. Well, suppose they were fat, and did enjoy the spotted trout and the wild deer's haunch, what then? Are good men to starve? Can good works never be wrought but by skeletons? Must all fat men be sent to hunt whales and live on blubber? No, we must not think of such a thing.—It must be a solemn sight to see a funeral in the old burying-place of the O'Sullivans and the M'Carthys.

Brady. Yes. Shillibeer's cheap funeral—£3 3*s.*

I. The country girls with the shawls over their heads, the old crones raising the *keene* or *ulagaun*, flinging up their skinny arms and clapping their hands.

Brady. Telling such thundering lies of all the O'Gradys the dead rascal had wollopped, and not a word about the times he had been in gaol or before the beaks.

I. Leave some poetry in the world, Brady. Think of the neat gate and the sloping shaven lawns, with old thorns bushy red with berries, among which the blackbird pipes his solitary matins over the monks quiet under the turf beneath; of the black funeral yews dull and grand, like stupid rich people; and the blossoming ivy round the clean cut gray stone, fresh as if quarried yesterday from Tore mountain yonder—

Brady. And Mr. Herbert's gate-keeper,—the old buffer, with the frosty red face, gray whiskers, and baggy black velvet shooting-jacket is of grate value. Bedad, there wasn't a word I told him about the hospitals that he didn't say, "O my!" with his Kerry brogue on him, the *omadhaun.*

I. And did you hear, Brady, about his once visiting England, and meeting the great stage-actor Mr. John Kemble; and how astonished he was at the civilization of England, and especially the *warm plates:* only to think of that, above all things,—not steam-engines, Income Tax, Thames Tunnel, or St. Paul's,—but —warm plates. (General laughter.)

Voice at the door, which opens. O my! (in shrill voice).

Brady. Hush, you spalpeens! here's the old codger himself. No; it's Tim. Tim, if you come here again with your tricks, I'll break the head of you.

Tim. Be asy, Mr. Brady. Is it more hot wather ye rang for?

Brady. We didn't ring, and you know it: it's whisky we want, and plenty of it.

Tim. By jabers, it isn't fair on the gauger.

Brady. And to return to the old buffer. Did you observe how he kept bowing and pointing to the board I longed to knock his ould head against, saying: "The attendants are forbidden to *ask* for gratuities?" What a confounded careful emphasis he laid on that same word!—Well, go on and tell us about Muckross; for I wasted my time writing nonsense in the visitors' book.

I. I love the old abbey of the lake, with its little porch, belfry and windows, where no stained glass now stops the sun, with the great square fireplace in the refectory; and the niche, where, doubled uncomfortably, the wistful unheeded novice once read to the revelling monks; with the old dim cloister, with glimpses of sun scattered about here and there just to light up a hood, or cast a shadow on the sallow, hollow face of some ascetic father; and, most of all, I loved to watch the specks of sunshine move about the wall, like scraps of faded gilding on a niched-surface tomb. O for some chant of Palestrina to have risen like incense then from the vaults below our feet!

Probert. Tidn't I sing, "Ap Shenkin," eh? Look you now, that's a coot tune.

I. You may climb Glena to hear the wild buck bell above the Eagle's Nest; you may feast on salmon broiled on arbutus-sticks at Dinis—

Probert. Ah, salmon on arbutus is fery coot eating.

I. Yes, pretty picking; but you needn't have spoiled my apostrophe by bringing in Soyer's cookery-book. You may listen to Tore spilling its silver treasures over its rocky brim;

you may thread the gorges of Dunloe; you may rise into heaven by way of Mangerton; you may storm Glenacuppal, Coom-a-Duv, and Stoompa; brush through the green glossy arbutuses with the crimson sorbs, or press the yellow moss on Caran Tuill—

Brady. Well, what then, when you have done all this?

I. Why (have a bit of patience), you will find nothing to surpass the placid beauty of the Monk's Island, Innisfallen.

Brady. Killarney is very well; but I like it best on a regatta day; or when the wild deer of Glena are being driven down into the lake. O, it's beautiful then, entirely, to see the boatmen breaking each other's heads with the oars, to try which shall secure the bit of venison first! Every rock then has a tongue of its own, and every echo begins babbling and calling to the dogs, as if Paddy Blake and his big brother, who lives up in the Eagle's Nest, were all out after the dogs; and then a horn wakes up in a rale Irish yell, which is sweeter—

Tim (looking in). Thrue to you, Mr. Brady; that's no lie.

Brady. Tim, you villain, more sugar; and send for the piper, that we may have a jig in the kitchen when all the boatmen have come in. That pretty girl in blue in the bar can take her part in a reel, I know, as well as any lass in Kerry.

Tim. She can, your honour (with tremendous energy). Larry will be here in half an hour.

Brady. I suppose you have been through the Gap?

I. Of course, or what was I born for? Didn't I enter in triumphal procession, driven by a bugler of the Kerry militia, in a red jacket, singing "Brian O'Lynn," and "Leslie Foster," to the tune of "Lesbia has a beaming eye;" and telling me stories of his father, who died broken-hearted because he was *bet* by the O'Sullivans in a faction-fight? Didn't I go through the *Pike* like a Cæsar, attended by a retinue of bog-oak girls and goat's-milk and potheen sellers, all with their red bare feet, dusty hair, and wild looks,—not to mention the two canneneers, ready for the echo, running by my angry side, with the long slips of peat blowing red in the wind?

Brady. What struck you most in Killarney town?

I. Not the Bishop's-chair Tower, nor the Round Fort,

where the gold-seekers grub and burrow, nor its suburbs Aghadoe and Killalee; but what always does strike you as most
costly and grand in every Irish town—the union work-house
and the lunatic asylum.

Dabble. They're all poor or mad. Ugh!

Brady. Be civil, you spalpeen, or, by the holy poker, I'll—

I. Mr. Brady, Mr. Brady! Well, we got out of the car at
the hut of the granddaughter of Kate Kearney (O, Lady Morgan,—such a hag!—with her yellow whisky and her snowy
milk!); and as we entered the pass between the Ricks (Ricks)
and the purple mountain, which is just a long shoulder of the
Toomies, and prepared for our four-mile mountain-plod, past
the Fathomless Lake, and the stream of Loe, and the Cumi-
neen Thorneen pools, our five senses were driven out of our
head, and sixpence out of our pocket, by the blast of Ted
Rafferty's cannon, with which he calls to the echoes. Then,
followed by old women with strings of stockings, who run
about and talk Irish, who curse your long legs in Celtic, and then
bless the beautiful face of you in English; arbutus-wood girls—

Brady. With divil a thing that is not yew in their boxes.

I. And urchins praying, "long life to your honour, and may
the merry dancing sixpences you give them be put down
in big letters to your account in heaven."

Brady. Before you got to the Cave of Dunloe, where the
Ogham letters are on the stones, did you mark the iligant detached villa residence of the great Dan's brother?

I. Not I, Brady; nor the beautiful demesne of the great
O'Sullivan More. I don't come to Ireland to see nate villas,
with the fir-trees all in a row, like the teeth of a comb. This
beautiful county—

Dabble. Beautiful! Ugh!

I. Well, we won't dispute. Oh, on I went through the Gap
with that sort of uneasy delight with which one always pene-
trates such gorges, made to be manned and kept.

Brady (quite abruptly, but thoughtfully stooping down his
head). Just feel that lump; that's one of Flynn's tumblers.
Flynn's tumblers are so cursed thick: by the powers, I'll wager
they're a good half inch at the bottom of solid glass. Excuse
the interruption.

I. Don't mention it, Brady. The Gap is quite an Irish Thermopylæ—sea, bog, and all perfect; and I half expected to meet there the red Earl of Ulster, Brian Boru, or the Desmond, at the head of their kerns and gallowglasses, with their jingling mail—

Probert (who has been asleep). It's a pad place for the mail.

I. The gray, bare, beetling walls are black with the silvery spills of water that splash and trickle down them; here and there, in cleft and chink, the ivy-bushes or the heather-tufts nestle in. It is fairy-land; and every moment, from bridge or the lake, where St. Patrick flung the last serpents, I look for the castle of the giant. Then comes the Black Valley, which we see as the Gap opens into slopes of rock and heather, stretching like a by-way to the right, lone and desolate,—the Valley of the Shadow of Death; with the lake of the red trout, black as Acheron; the rocks blasted and calcined; the cascades here and there jerking down like fairies' silver ladders.

Brady. I like the lake islands,—the Lamb, the Elephant, the Horse, the Crow, the Heron, the Gannet, the Books, the prison-islands, and Darby's Garden, that Lord Kenmare gave the old fisherman who made him a present of a salmon. How loaded they are with the arbutus with the crimson drops, like deer's blood, and those broken rocks, where the herons sit and think!

I. Yes; Killarney is never so beautiful as now, when the red rain of autumn comes streaming down into the lake, and the leaves come swirling from Glena, as if the ghost of O'Donohue were throwing his treasure down to an awaiting crowd below; when the blue of the mountain grows opaque, and the cloud hangs heavy, moored to the peaks, or at sunset blows from it in a long thin sail, like a crimson flag half shot away.

Tim (looking in). Now, that's what I call beautiful!

Brady. Bring a sod, Tim.

I. You seem rather dull to-night, Brady. Perhaps I bore you with my poetising in this region of perpetual honeymoon.

Brady. Not at all, not at all, Mr. Edithor. It's myself that wishes I had a hundred ears to listen night and day.—To tell you the truth, I'm expecting to hear every post whether I have passed the college. I'm rather afraid I shall go a mucker.

Probert (to me apart). Why doesn't he speak coot English, like me. What's a "mucker," Brady?

Brady. Why, I'm afraid I shall come to grief. Now, I'm perfectly sure if I only got my diploma, and gave up the whisky and the cock-shooting, I should very soon chaw up the best men in Dublin, not to be the laste concaited. Why, I've got a pill for jaundice that'll—more glasses, d'ye hear, Tim, you blackguard, and——Tim, another matarial. (Sings)

"THE WHISKY CASCADE.

O have you ever heard, my boys, of the holy man of Ennis,
Who asked O'Sullivan for alms in the name of good St. Dennis?
The chieftain gave him ring and robe, and a kicking chestnut filly,—
A purty thing for jaunting-car, for market-cart, or dilly.

The saint he touched Tore mountain-side, and looked up to the ceiling;
He groped about, for he was blind, and found his way by feeling.
'My blessing on O'Sullivan, his wife and son and daughter;
Accept a poor man's benison upon this holy water.'—

He would have added twice as much, but lashing out behind,
The chestnut, hot as gunpowder, flew off before the wind.
Stone walls to her were lumps of sod, the hermit gave her head:
Her mother was the 'Colleen Og,' and almost thorough-bred.

The chieftain cried, 'Good luck to him! I hope he'll not be silly,
And use the spur, or throw her down: I'm sorry—for the filly.'
Then stooping down, he drank a sup, and leapt up mad and frisky:
'More power to him! By jabers, sir, he's turned the stream to whisky!'

Ah, sure enough, by my ten toes, it was enough to scare one;
He'd gone and done what Moses did before the nose of Aaron.
Through woods of oak and alder gray, and birch the silver twinkled,
The whisky ran, a mad cascade, and fern and foxglove sprinkled.

O'er giant slab of level rock, green with the nodding bramble,
The whisky broke in froth and foam, then stole away to ramble
In silver pool and inky deep, far, far from human folly,
Deep hidden by the branching broom and the red-berried holly.

Bedad, if man and boy and girl, down to the oldest cripple,
Did not soon come to drink and sip, to sot and soak and tipple
The priest he brought his shovel-hat to dip in as a ladle;
Begor the gauger's second wife came with her largest cradle.

Such bottling and barrelling, and broken heads and cursing,
Such maudling, and shaking hands, and gossiping and nursing!
Till all at once, one April day,—it must have been the first, sir,—
The whisky changed to water back! the change was for the worse, sir.

Och! one by one they stole away—the priest unto his village;
The farmer to his yellow ricks, his cart and horse and tillage;
The gossip, making faces sour, ran scolding back her daughter;
'Rheumatics, spasms, colic, gout, all come of mountain water.'

It's Tore Cascade they call the place; you still may see it splashing
O'er broken rock and ledge and shelf, like crockery that's smashing.
It's only sixpence at the gate, to Mr. Herbert's porter;
It is requested on a board you do not stay to court her."

(Laughter.)

Dabble. No hope for Ireland till they all turn teetotalers.

Brady. Fill your tumbler, sir, and don't quarrel with your liquor.

Dabble. Your sociability, my good sir, will be your ruin; but our thanks for your song. Is not the Tore Cascade a good place, sir, for the *Lichomanes speciosum* and the *Hymenophillum Tunbridgense?*

Brady. Divil if I know. It's a rale good place for a veal pie, champagne, and a Colleen Og, with the nate blue eyes to smile on you, and to talk love to as you pop off the cork.

I. Capital, Brady, quite Irish. Now that's a miracle worth working. I can fancy the nation getting extremely pious, and extremely drunk, as the holy water came running and tumbling and jerking and frothing through the silver birches that feather over the mossy rocks.

Dabble. Those waterfalls are always such confounded places for catching colds. Ugh!

Brady. To the divil with your colds!

Probert. A colt is pad.

Brady. So is a spavined horse.

Tim (rushes in breathless, executing a double-shuffle step).

The piper's come, jintlemen, and the kitchen's swept and da-cent.

Brady. Famous! Now, Dabble.

Dabble. I shall go to bed. I hate dancing—it's foolery. Ugh!

Brady. So it is when fools dance; but then fools may go to bed. Whoop! (Gives a war-yell, and runs out.) Now for " Planxty Drury" and the " Tatthering of the Quilt!"

Tim. And " Jim O'Halloran's Ganther." Whoop!

Scene changes to the kitchen. Boots seated meditatively on a pile of peat; chamber-maid in buff, chamber-maid in pink, man-cook in white jacket, charwoman in bare feet, drawn up in rows, and in high spirits. In the back-ground, relays of more chamber-maids, fat black-eyed landlady, cheery landlord, and nimble clerk of the establishment. Larry, the blind piper, is seated on a barrel turned upside down.

Brady. Now then, Larry, " The Fox-hunter's Schame." (Larry plays a wild sporting tune, which he ekes out by verbal remarks and comments: as, " Here the huntsmen come up; that's the whipper-in's horn; this is them laping a sod-ditch; that's a fall; here's the death—of the fox." Every one cheers.) Now then, sixpence each in my hat for Larry.

Larry. More power to ye, Mr. Brady. Gintlemen, take your places, pigeon's-wing, and cut the buckle.

Then the jig began, fast and furious. Brady's partner was the bare-legged, girded-up charwoman, an old body who danced with ten-horse power. How we twisted round, and unwound, and advanced to partners, and toed and heeled and shook the toes, till the kitchen-roof rang again with the fun! Hands across; and when the dance flagged for a moment, there came such a yell from the man-cook to hearten us on to ten times more intrepid exertions in the most pleasant of all dances!

To use Brady's expression, the fat landlady's performance was of " grate value," the boots was serious and misanthropic, the buff chamber-maid was vigorous, the pink chamber-maid agile; but as for the thin clerk, he was at once stupendous and surprising. He performed all sorts of Irish feats with his feet; he danced down everybody, and was the incontestable champion of the evening. Tim was glorious and gorgeous; Brady could only be compared to a demoniac dancing-master. As for Probert, he was pragmatic, bow-legged, and sententious. Dabble twice rang for hot water merely to interrupt us, and then was heard of no more.

*　　*　　*　　*　　*

As we were going up to bed, Brady suddenly stopped, gave a twitch at his pocket, and pulled out a letter.

"Bedad," said he, "if this letter didn't come for me just as we went into the kitchen, and I forgot to open it. It's the college seal." He read it.

"Have you passed?" said I.

"No! By jabers," said he, "if I haven't gone a *cropper again!*"

CHAPTER XVIII.

THE BANSHEE'S CASTLE.

THERE was, we heard, a Banshee-haunted Castle, on the Antrim coast, and I and my friend Vaughan, the artist, were on our way to find it out.

Our campaign had been planned, we were to start that morning, when the shrimps were cleared away and the loaf and eggs had melted into air, thin air. When we had seen the ghost castle we were to take the car, and go on to the wonderful Salmon Bridge, near Ballycastle, and the next morning to the great promontory of Fairhead, and that wonderful legendary passage through the cliff called by Antrim fishermen and smugglers "The Grey Man's Walk."

"Our work was cut out for us," as Vaughan said, and we were ready to do it.

It was a grand day. The sea ran on the side of us in a dancing sparkle of glimmering emerald, we were intoxicated with air and sunshine. We were fresh from the rugged west of Donegal, and the warning tone of the sea in that blow-pipe cavern called "M'Swine's Gun," was still in our ears. We had fished together in the salmon-haunted river Bawn, and we had stared together at the Skerry rocks, lying like dead whales out in the broad blue of the Antrim sea.

Few vessels come this side of Ireland, and none were in sight, but here and there a brown fishing sail tossed and rocked over the dancing tumult of the waves, that rolled and tossed like a tumultuous multitude round the tall giant cliff on which the Banshee Castle stood, spectral and forlorn, and apparently insulated and inaccessible. At last we had neared the Banshee Castle of the M'Quillens, of the conquering M'Donels, and, lastly, of the Earls of Antrim, now haunted by the wailing Banshee, who lodges there in permanence. We only passed one man on the road, and he was a little bandy-legged, pragmatic Welshman, with light plaid trousers and shooting jacket. He carried a large carpet bag slung to the end of a crab stick, and by his side, attached to a cross-belt, hung a padlocked fishing-basket, that seemed full of books. We challenged him at walking, but the wiry little Celt beat us off bravely, and when we were dead tired, set to and actually ran a mile. I am inclined to think he was "no canny," and some third Welsh cousin of the Banshee, sent to lure us to destruction.

I had on my old macintosh soiled, serviceable knapsack, with the handle of a refractory hair-brush sticking out of a side compartment. Vaughan had his portfolio and fly rod, and his paint-box of moist colours. Vaughan was an open-hearted, cheery fellow, full of humour, and with a lynx eye for the picturesque. We were all bent on mischief, being hard of flesh and pliant of limb. Hope and merriment danced in our eyes. We sniffed the sea-air like the horse in Job, who said ha! ha! to the sound of the trumpet. The sea was our trumpet, the merry wind our herald. We tightened each other's straps, we arranged buckles, we shifted loads, we jerked up knapsacks, we tossed off some Dublin porter, whose brown froth was pleasant to the sense, and then started on the sea-side road, stepping out like Banshees bound on pleasure, determined to go down and up everything, to see every cave, ruin, foreland, or cliff in Antrim. Glory be to it. Our first lion was the wonderful eagle's nest of Dunluce, where the Earls of Ulster and Antrim once looked down on the sea, almost ever since there was a sea; for, indeed, so grand were these M'Quillens, that they seem to have looked down on every one and everything.

To see the wild blue sea after the trim white-washed inn was a pleasant contrast. As those fretted arches and chasms in the limestone cliff are to the dreary bogland grave of MacPhelim, MacBryan, MacNeill, of Clandeboy, so those white gulls are to the dark, heavy ploughland they flap over, thinking it some dark, dismal, frozen sea. Not ten miles, and we have seen twenty caverns at least—mere rat-holes from here, but really great bays for the northern waves. How fluctuating and restless the sea is compared with those steadfast towers of Dunluce, on their hundred feet of perpendicular rock, now bannerless, rent, and smitten.

Vaughan had been on this coast often with Stanfield, who sometimes comes here for new sensations when he begins to lose his sea legs by stopping too long on London Turkey-carpeted floors. That next gate to the left leads us down to Dunluce and the Banshee's Tower.

We entered the gate, passed a sloping meadow bound in with stone walls, and saw before us a great pile of ruins, battered ramparts, crumbling turrets and enclosures, now scarcely definable as either square, round, or oblong. Here was the hall, there the lady's chamber; here the kitchen, there the chapel— one of the wildest places to live in surely, man for safety or defence ever built. Yet this, for centuries, was the night-star for mariners, a beacon rock for the sailor to shun and yet to steer by. The outer walls were but continuations of the rock. A seagull could not rest on any intervening ledge there is visible. From this rampart dizzy workmen fell headlong, and slain knight fell plump down into the greedy waves that opened for their prey and closed the mailed corpse in the living tomb, so that till the judgment the white bones locked in steel might stare through sunless day and moonless night at the bulwarks of its mortal home, so regardless of its fate. Here the Banshee wails over the grey night sea for the dead Earls of Antrim. Here the—

"We never take less than a shilling," said the guide, "and it's little of that goes to us."

"Perhaps, my dear fellow," said Vaughan, "when you have told us all that ever was here, you will go on in a second volume to all that never was here, so that your reader can take his chance."

"The causeways is a poor thing after this," said the guide. "Don't listen to all the stuff the carman crams you with. Dunluce is generally reckoned the first thing of the kind in Ireland, and bedad, I wish I had all the fees: but of course they always give apples to the man with an orchard, so I get only the paltry pence, and me with the flenzy on me, and the lumbago in the lines."

"The carman," said Vaughan, "would have it that you keep all his journeyers staying about here, and that there is nothing to see."

"Hear him!" said the rival showman; "what, not the big, tall Castle, and the cave under it, and the Banshees, and the narrow bridge that the lady with nerves fell over and was saved by the balloonness of her petticoats, which landed her clean and safe at the bottom of the rock? The ignorant craturs, to talk of the causeway. To tell you sober truth, as I wish I may be hung—I don't see much in the causeway, with the holes they call caves, and the lies about Fin-maccoul—it's a good deal boderashun."

Threading our way through ruined court-yards, past defaced chapels, dining-halls, guard-rooms and prisons, we began to see the plan of the whole. The outlying grey walls and enclosures were mere barracks and outposts. The castle itself lay before us on an island of rock, moated by the sea; the only approach to it was a plain wall of earth, over which a portcullis, now destroyed, once ran.

"Come along, Vaughan," said I, "follow me, and we will storm this Banshee's Castle. Here, come over, don't look down, it makes the eyes dizzy."

"It's all very well to talk," said Vaughan; "why, it's worse than the top of a garden wall, and sixty feet drop. My feet stick as if I were chained to the ground. I could not move if a man with a sword were pricking me on. It is a dreadful nightmare feeling. I feel giddy and sick. I shall be like that old gentleman at Snowdon, you remember, that the guide had to carry on his back over Crib Coch, or he would have actually crawled over on his belly like a big turtle, as he was."

"Come along, Vaughan; why I've seen you break through a hundred twirling oak sticks at Donnybrook, as easily as if you were elbowing your way through an illumination mob."

"But it is no joke really for me, my dear fellow," said Vaughan. "Come and lend us a hand, and don't stand preaching there like a second-rate Spurgeon. And I say, you Banshee keeper, lay hold of my coat-tails behind, for, by heaven, that yawning pit seems to me to be the very mouth of Gehenna."

He crossed, trembling.

"Well, now we are over," said I, "my brave man, mix a little vermilion for your lily-livered cheeks, and take courage. The castle is our own—the men-at-arms have all been stabbed and thrown over the walls to feed the gulls. A pocket handkerchief with my initials and cognizance waves upon the highest chimney-pot. The bastard king gnaws his flesh in the dungeon, the ladies wring their hands in their barred-up chambers—Lord of Dunluce, welcome to the castle of the chasm. I will have the corpses all cleared, the king put in chains, and the prisoners fettered. And when the smell of powder is gone off, bring up my dinner. To leave the mock-heroic, victorious De Courcy, what a scene this must have been for a scrimmage. Fancy the fight below in the underground cavern—the grapple of mailed men in the boat—the battle of bloody and broken oars—the push of spear—the clash of axe—   *   *   *   *   *
See the lichen stones, and the hanging turret, where the dry grass nods and blows. Fancy the rush over this hanging chasm, piled up with red smeared men, groaning and screaming in a knotted heap. Then the fight up the narrow tower stairs, and the slow retreat backwards to the edge of the sea-wall, where death hung in air waiting for his prey with black and outspread arms."

" Lend us your whisky flask."

" Of course, said Vaughan, "you know *the* legend of this castle."

" Not I."

" Well then, here goes. On a stormy night in November, 1580, as Newby's novels would begin, a vessel, bearing Colonel M'Donald coming to Ireland to assist the Turconnell against the O'Neil, saw the lights of Dunluce, and bore into Portrush, not knowing that M'Quillen, the lord of Dunluce, was an adherent of the race he came to exterminate. M'Quillen, concealing his name, feasted him on his fatted beeves and strongest ale. It is not impossible that whisky above all proof was produced, L.L. whisky, strong enough to draw its own cork—stuff that would bring a dead buffalo to life. The name disclosed, the itinerant colonel's generosity was aroused, he became the friend of M'Quillen, and to prove it spent the winter in the small castle, his men being quartered on M'Quillen's vassals. He eventually ran away with Nora, his pretty daughter, in order to avoid a conspiracy of the Irish, to murder the Scotch intruders —when the faithless stranger returned, he returned to make himself, by fire and sword, lord of these poor ruins you now see. The M'Donnels have passed away, the M'Quillens are now become serfs."

" Nor to forget," said the guide, "your honours, gentlemen, the story of the kitchen wall falling into the sea, just as the countess, in Elizabeth's time, was about to return from London to the castle, which had been rebuilt after a fire. I don't know how many cooks or workmen did not fall in the say."

" True," said I, " but be quiet, M'Cormac, while I relate the sins and sorrows of the old castle. In this very room, the stately Earl of Antrim, with his black velvet suit, peaked beard, and point lace collar, received as guest the Parliamentary General Munro, who suddenly, as the third course came up, stamped his foot ; instantly the muskets, halberds, and pikes flocked in, and arrested the struggling earl, the brave gentleman, the gallant cavalier, and dragged him to Carrick by the sea, from whence he broke away soon after, and got himself to England, then streaming with cavaliers' blood."

"Very well, then, give me the whisky bottle," said Vaughan.

"We had better be off," said I.

So away we went along the bold road, through the North of Ireland fields, where the white birds flew about over the chocolate-coloured fallows, skimming after the trailing plough, drawn by the black and white horses with ponderous broad chests; a deserted and unoccupied country, except for two or three of the soldier-like police, in their green rifle uniform, and a young girl or two with the neat shawl over her head—dangerous as a mantilla, and wonderful target for black eyes watching for hearts. Leaving the causeway with the angel's building stones, the unfinished sea pandemonium or Irish rostrum, dedicated to the forgotten and discrowned Neptune, we walked away merry past scattered tracts of white-washed stone cottages, where strings of dried herrings waved over the door.

"Do you see the line of land yonder?" said Vaughan.

Well, that was Islay, *the nearest of the Orknies*. The boatmen offered to take us there for four-and-twenty shillings, but I was afraid of being locked up by contrary winds, or of a rough night coming on. I said, "Will there be wind?" They said, "God willing," and I would not trust myself. Fancy such a boat and every man drunk. M'Namara pulling at wrong ropes, fighting about the helm, swearing at the sea, some drawing knives about the way to steer. Horrible! it makes me sea-sick to think of it.

It is pleasant to feel near Robert Bruce's Scotland and Burns' Scotland. Presently we come in sight of the Mull of Cantire, only fourteen miles off, then the great lump of Ailsa Craig looms in sight like a great stranded whale—such a monster as heaves its emerald mountain of a back through the green waves of northern seas. That line of rock away there is the island where Bruce flew with his three hundred men to escape Baliol, the angry rebel that hounded him over moss and moor. There he could look at Scotland, and think of fresh Bannockburns, red with Norman blood. There is eight miles of it, and its cliffs are fronted with basalt columns, which, at a distance, look like the walls of some sea Carthage. Here is Dunsverick. Yes, here was Dunsverick, ancient nest of the O'Kanes, on the

bare island of rock; its fragment of yellow tower, with as
sharp and clear an angle as if it was pulled down yesterday, so
gently time visits the old place. There the O'Kanes of the
saffron mantles and matted hair looked out on Ruthlin, or right
away to Islay, with the green, glassy sea stretching between,
as safe from the English of the pale as the eagle on the top of
his purple mountain. There is still the basalt rock, flattened
at the top for the mangonel and the watchman, and down on the
south side is the great gap of a bay, where the boats look as
small as walnut shells.

Now as it gets towards twilight, between the fishermen's
houses, and just over the grey stone walls, down the dark bay,
and between the bleak heap of rocks, the twin-lights of the
distant island move and twinkle like two lone stars, the first
blossoms of the evening heavens.

We pass through a wild bit just in the dusk, a dark tract of
a bog—glistening here and there, where the setting light glances
in the rain-pools—the brown pared walls, where peat has been
cut, still showing the trenching marks of the spade. Just as we
approach the stone stile leading to it, Nora trips over, showing as pretty an ankle and as trim a leg as ever trod Irish
earth. She colours a little on seeing us, and with a gentle
" save you," tells us the way to Ballycastle, speaking even more
broad Scotch than the Antrim people are prone to do.

" Just push up my knapsack," says Vaughan.

" Just buckle my chest-strap, Vaughan," say I; we had
reached a stage of feeling familiar to knapsack tourists.

The knapsack has grown heavier, the two straps slightly gall
the collar-bone, the fastening across the chest pinches; we
require frequent jerks up to change the bearing of the load.
There is a slight straining sensation down the front of the shin,
a slight ache in the calf of the leg, a slight soreness from the
hard limestone about the soles of the feet. Now we get
silent, and disposed to stop at those parts of the road particularly near a wall, where you can lean your knapsack against.
Wonder how we could have been fool enough now not to come
by car; resolve never to walk with a knapsack again; a light
shines out in the distance — another — then half-a-dozen—

hope revives—the heart jumps for joy—the brain clears and quickens—the pulse enlivens—we step out—give one stare—then on we push, determined by the last spark of daylight. "Blind man's holiday," indeed, to look down the winding road that branches from our due road to Ballycastle, to *Carrick a Rede, the rock in the road,* where we know the salmon bridge was. A winding terrace brought us into a field, and the rock lay before us. The bridge had been taken up for the winter—the rock stood alone some sixty feet from the shore; the top looks so thin, it seems as if no one could keep on it; unless he clung with his hands and feet, be blown off, or topple off, he must be it, seems. Half way down the side of a rock you see a rude cottage, where the fishermen dwell during the summer, (by day only, as a boy told me,) but in the winter the bridge is taken up and the cottage deserted. We saw the place where the fishermen fasten the bridge-ropes—and even to look at that made me giddy.

A rough fisherman's son, with rough red cheeks, and fell of black hair blowing about his eyes, told us he had often been over the bridge with a load of silver salmon on his head. It was rather springy and planky like under your feet, you had to trot it, it wasn't safe to walk, and seventy feet was no joke to fall, otherwise there was no danger.   *   *   *

"I liked Connemara," said Vaughan, placing both feet on the hob, and trying to roast himself simmeringly. "I liked the red petticoats and the bare feet."

O Lord, how it poured next day in streams. We were accoutred in tremendous oil-skin, covering us from chin to toe—not flexible water-proofs, but good, stiff sail-cloth, such as the captain of a whaler might put on when a sou'-wester was blowing—the rain poured down in heavy black drenches. It was no summer rain skirting sunshine, it was no short spring shower, but a day of ill-tempered, sullen wind and rain we were going to encounter; so we hitched on our oil-skin hats, pulled down the flannel-lined flaps, and took our seats sullenly to bear the storm. Our two umbrellas bent down deprecatingly before the wind, and arched over our heads like bronze tents.

Vaughan regarded rain as an indifferent thing, and disdained to do more than button his coat, with a sort of spiteful twist, as if he was trying to dislocate himself, or alter the arrangement of his spine.

"Have you been to Wicklow?" said Vaughan.

"All over it" said I, "especially the ancient Churches."

"That's brag," said Vaughan. "Have you seen much of the emigrators? There is a power of them ready to leave the old country."

"Yes!" replied I, "much; at Dublin the country people, in their frieze coats and grey stockings, were sitting on their bundles outside the emigrant offices on the quays—father, son, mother, daughter, waiting with frightened, listless, torpid expectancy for the steamer's starting—the same by the water's edge, and by the ferries. At the Kilkenny station, too, the whole place was crammed with peasants, strange, eccentric, hard-featured fellows, in bob-tail blue coats and knee breeches, lagging about two and two, huge clothes chests—hurrying them into wrong carriages, and getting in everybody's way—then came the old father, or the pretty daughter, with her handkerchief round her head; and wandering, anxious matrons, too excited to cry, though the children were bursting into tears.

"'Take your places,' cries the guard in his mechanical monotone, the confusion grows hopeless; more boxes—more goods crushed—more crying—more rapid interchange of Irish farewells. Quick goes the engine—the wheel moves—then arises such a yell of grief and sorrow—of passionate heart-breaking at this farewell, such as I have heard at the grave-side, and nowhere else. I love to see them too reading an American letter in some lone part of the county Mayo, under a peat stack, the father leaning on his long six-fork spade, as the little sister spells out the good news from the joyful letter from America."

The next morning early we started for Fairhead, the great promontory of Antrim. "What are you suicidally thrusting your head out of the umbrella for? you'll be wet to the skin in two minutes." "Why," said Vaughan, "I think I see just a-head that drunken villain who drove me to Portrush the other night from the half-way house. I told him that I should give him a return this morning, if he waited till ten o'clock. He agreed, but the first thing I heard when I got up this morning, was that he had gone off at seven."

"Hark to him," said I, he is just within reach—jogging on with his side to the horse, as if no guilt were in his soul."

"Hallo! you fellow," cried Vaughan, standing up like Caractacus in his war chariot, one hand gracefully waving an umbrella for a sceptre. "What do you mean by leaving us this morning, and putting us to the expense of another car? What do you mean? I shall be representing the matter to your master at Westport. Take my word for it."

The fellow turned round, and, to my amazement, instead of merely confessing his fault, drove full in our way, and commenced a volley of abuse, in the voice of a stage bandit, which was caused by a cold he had lately caught, as he lyingly said, from having been kept locked out of his hotel all night, and made to wait at the gate in the rain, without food for himself or horse.

"Go on yourself," said the bellicose Mike, "you murdering divil, with your gentleman-jacks, and your winning manners— go on, ye Irish Sepoys—go on, you spalpeens, and the Devil's blessing go with ye for laving a poor man in the bitter winding could all night; and he with a wife and family. Too much is it, your dirty blackguard—you sink of iniquity—you dishonest Philistine—you miserable nagur, with your too much."

"If you won't go on," said I, "let us pass you."

"You shan't pass—you shall keep behind me for thirty miles. You big imposthumes—you bad half-pence—you—you miserable hypotheses."

"Let me get at him," said Vaughan, trying to get down.

"The man is drunk," said I, "and he is old—let him alone."

"Get out of that!" said the rogue, gaining courage, seeing we were for peace, "clear the way there!—get behind, will ye?"

"Make room for your betters, sir."

"I must get down," said the fiery driver.

"Be quiet," said I, "his mare is dead beat; she has had no food or rest all night—see how her hind legs totter, and come down shaking—she cannot keep up for two miles more, whip past him, and when he races us he will soon founder."

Whoop away we went, whipping at him as we passed, for he had now cursed himself hoarse, and letting the reins hang about the horse's legs, was walking by the side of his car, threshing his horse in a mad-drunk, torpid way.

In a moment he was up on his side seat, and off after us; but then his greasy hat blew off, and he had to zigzag after that, and by the time he had got up again, we were some distance off. His cries of "och, you murdering craturs! villains! Och, you thundering thaves!" came to us on the wind as we passed on.

When we got to the next town, Vaughan went instantly to complain to the car-proprietors, who promised to punish the insolent fellow, whose misdeeds and neglects were not for the first time chronicled.

We had set out to see the green promontory of Fairhead. The sky was an overgrown forget-me-not; the sand downs by the sea were alive with a thousand rabbits, trotting in and out, as if they were playing at hide and seek. The low, quick wave washed on the pebbles, and turned them into carnelians and garnets by the moment's transparency—fragments of rainbows frittered away on the beach, where dull sheaves of brown, bladdery sea-weed lay like old clothes drying on the walls, ready for the kelp burners, who, wet and eager, scrambled it up. The nets were drying on the cottage roof—on every stone, the yellow oil-skin-wrapper dreadnoughts of the fishermen were spread, sure sign of the last night having been rough, yet there was the guilty cannibal sea, as gentle now as if it had never done harm to any one—as clear and level as if it never could rise into great hollow hills, capped with foam, wrathful and terrible. As we clamber past the hollows the cross beam engines, and tramroad slack heaps, every minute came a cracking burst of blasting powder, like the sound of a cannonade at sea, with thundering thumps, and shocks of sound that seemed to bellow to the distant sailor.

A guide took me over slopes of bare land, and past vast blocks of green stones stubbed with heather; past the Black Cape, and the lake of the Druid's Island to the Grey Man's Path—the extraordinary scene of one of Antrim's interesting legends. It is a fearful rent some nine feet wide in the edge of the cliff, down which a strong dangerous scramble—a goat's path unchristianly dangerous, leads to the shore, which, lonely as a churchyard, is covered with innumerable monumental-looking stones, gray with moss. Across this gap rests, high up, a pillar of green stone, firmly wedged in, under which you descend to the shore. This is the path of the Grey Man—a sort of kingly mysterious phantom that in great storms and troubles is seen here through the sea fog, standing and waving his hands —in fact, telegraphing in an imperfect and vague way to the viewless spirits of sea and air.

" Do you see that large stone on the beach—the white one ?" said our guide.

We did.

" Well, I found a man's skull there on Tuesday week, and the foxes had been fighting for it."

My bed that night, at Ballyna, was a dreadful phenomenon of upholstery. It resembled a turtle's back; it was high and round, and unless you nailed yourself on the apex, you might as well have tried to sleep on the top of a crocodile. It was, I believe, firmly stuffed with tin-tacks or tenpenny nails. I kept firm awake all night, and at three in the morning found myself still restless and worn out, staring at a truculent portrait of Dr. Wiseman, on the opposite wall. If this dreadful lump of a bed had allowed me to sleep, two other monsters of evil were waiting to hinder it. My door would not shut, and it opened by steps into the smoking-parlour, so that it was just convenient for the tap-boy to have cut my throat and gone off with my watch. This, and several other stories of inn murders, arose in my memory as I rolled out of bed for the eleventh time. A lively story, too, of a Tyrolese landlord, who to murder his guests and throw them down a precipice behind his house, would not let me alone.

I dozed and saw the sanguinary landlord. He wore a red waist-coat and chamois leather smalls. Another grievance was the fact of my being over the inn stable; the floor was chinky, flat, and unplastered. All through that dreadful night I heard the car horses drag their manger chains to and fro, and stamp and move their hoofs, and snort in that restless and sleepless way that horses do. Every now and then a heavy turn announced the awaking of some steed who had dreamed he was over-driven. To my excited fancy it seemed that one particular animal was trying to gnaw through the ceiling, and tear a mouthful of hay off my troubled bed.

Three o'clock!—One—two—three! I am drowsy—two sounds fainter than one, three softer than two. I am going at last—low music rises; to that opiate serenade I am sinking a million fathoms down through the blue yielding Hellespont. I am lost—I have fallen from the ram with the golden fleece, three days through the air, and three nights through the sea—going, going, going; but not gone.—Millions of demons bear him to torture, fiery whips and sulphur whirlwinds—it is the stable-boy come to begin work. Shall I fire down at him between the chinks? No, that will not do. Shall I call and deprecate? No, he speaks only Irish. Dreadful wretch, with what insolent alacrity he begins his daily toil; with what gratuitous and unnecessary clatter he hurries about the iron-rimmed buckets, knocks down the horn, smashes back the door, splashes and mixes the water. The fool is a cheat—he cannot be a stable-boy—he must be and is a Corporal Starlight trying to destroy and fire the premises. Fire—ha! save me!—yes, it gets hot—I'm warm—warmer—help! engines! murder! I am roasting, every plank under me is a red-hot bar. Help! I won't be another St. Lawrence—wasn't one enough? Here, some-body—landlord! I'm a Protestant, and no saint—help! No—no—it's all right—he is only doing the horses. I can hear the rap, rap of the currycomb on the stone. I hear him hiss. I am pleased with that hiss. Bravo! he's a good fellow after all. I am going again, sinking, sinking—going, going, *gone*—firm as a church.

This was four o'clock; at six an importunate and officious rap at the open bed-room door awoke me. I start up, and, as a necessary consequence of any movement on the turtle back, roll out of bed.

"Good morning, sir," said the waiter, eyeing me through the door with admiration and surprise, believing that I usually

P

got up in that gymnastic way, and with the military promptness of a Wellington. "What will you take for breakfast, sir?"

"A roll and an egg. Shut the door," said I, rubbing my shin vexatiously.

"Bedad, and you have had the roll already, I think," I heard the impertinently witty fellow say as he shuffled off; "well, if ever I saw the like of that same."

"Waiter!" I cried, rushing to the door, "bring me more water."

"Would you be wanting a tumbler?" he said, holding his mouth with his hand, and then blowing off the steam with a burst of horse laughter.

"Waiter (it would not do to appear annoyed)! have you any mutton chops in the house?"

"Well, your honour, we have a *shin* of beef."

Drat him! why did he look at the leg that I was holding, and lay such an emphasis on the word *shin*.

In half-an-hour I was down. Mary—fie on ye, Mary—the affianced of Tim the waiter, was heaping sods on the fire that already covered both hobs, and rose in a roaring pyramid of flame, which would in England have been thought extravagant in the house of a man with ten thousand a-year. The broiled ham, red and unctuous, came in—the porcelain-shelled egg, the fragrant coffee, the home-made bread, so brown and savoury. I forgot my bed and my martyrdom. I arose and went to the window with that sort of dreaminess and quietude that a bad night produces. The chapel bell was going. The pretty neat country girls were passing to church—all was calmness and quiet. Opposite me, under a dead wall, on which was a torn bill announcing the sale of a farmer's effects, including the usual "*Bay mare and piano*"—sat Kitty, the old beggar woman, who had been "dark these thirteen years." She was crouched up, telling her beads, and mumbling some prayers in a low voice, looking up when she heard a footstep, praying the rich for alms, and giving the poor her blessing gratis, for she knew them both by their voices as they accosted her. I saw no one who did not bestow some mark of recognition.

That next night we got to Belfast, and the next afternoon started for Dublin, Vaughan and I.

Belfast Quay.—Three o'clock.—Grey October day, with a dancing, breaking froth to windward, that is ominous. Anxious, buttoned-up men, ask busying sailors nautical questions difficult to answer. It was *rather* rough last night, but on the *whole* a very good passage—men run about with briny ropes, race up and down the brazen-bound engine-room stairs, or toil about like small Arrowsmith's atlases, with swollen portmanteaus, and strange packages, containing everything, from periwinkles to air pumps. I look down on the great monster engine, whose lungs seem chronically out of order, and whose throbbing mouth the pale, perspiring stoker feeds and crams so pertinaciously with shovelfuls of carbon. I go below, and find experimental men knotting themselves up in various recumbent attitudes, or trying the smiling steward's bottled porter—I admire the daring men who, till the vessel gets into trouble, turn down the flaps of their travelling caps—light their beaming cigars and pace up and down with the determined air of Sebastian Cabots. But my attention was at once riveted on a horse-box, a sort of square wooden crate, in which, fastened securely up, stood a race horse, whose frightened eye—of which the reddened-white only shows—indicates great alarm. Its guardian was a tight-legged, broad-shouldered, middle-aged groom, in a green shooting jacket, fastened knowingly by only one button at the throat—neck-handkerchief stamped with white wafers—cheeks, a dull purple, with cold and anxiety; small, wrinkled, winking eyes, artful, but anxious. Such was my Linnæan definition of the two animals I saw before me. The man left feeding the horse, who taking the hay, mechanically champed it up, fast and voraciously, and then beat with its front hoofs against the wooden box for more.

The Yorkshireman with the tight-skinned legs had a regular programme, which he repeated, with petulant indifference, to every questioner. It ran thus :—" Yes, sir, good morning, sir,—quietly, old 'os, quietly.—This is the well-known stallion, Ilderim, sir—almost thorough bred—by Barley Bree out of Cherry Pie. Father won the St. Leger—mother won the Oaks.—

Quietly, old boy!—don't be frightened—Bother this small box —he'll hurt his knees—I only wish we was safe on shore; that's all I wish.—Try a mouthful of hay—the swell frets him so—there, gently, old fellow—I've taken him safely all over Ireland, and now we shall come to grief at last. Drat this old horse-box!—There's the wind rising, too,—gently, lad—How long more shall we be, cap'en?"

"Why, all the week if the north-west and east-west goes on blowing as it have done, and we have to reef the main jib-boom, and set the mizzen halliards."

The Yorkshireman patted the horse and looked dejected.

But we did at last, after some "sea changes," duly reach Dublin—the fast-asleep city—but whether Ilderim and the insufficient horse-box got safe on shore I never heard.

CHAPTER XIX.

THE SEVEN CHURCHES.

Not of Asia—but of County Wicklow. More power to ye! Where am I now but in the heart of those mountains that look so blue from Phœnix Park, Dublin.

A lazy, wild Irish lad brought me to the snug inn, and from there I, with Mike Doolan the guide, had begun my tour of the valley and the mournful lake that mirrors its ruins. There was the old round tower, like a vast factory chimney, and to make it more like, the conical roof was off, and crows were screaming in and out; then a little stone hut, which was once a church, with a little tower built into it so as to make it look like a kitchen; then a little ruined churchyard with many crosses; then another ruined chapel at the foot of a wood; and, lastly, up a rock hanging over the lake, the cell of the hermit, whose fame and sanctity led first to this early Christian settlement.

This is one of the most characteristic and interesting places in Ireland—not more than a day's journey from a large city, yet wild as the recesses of Horeb or of Sinai. The lake, inky dark, is girt by bare, stony mountains, that run down steep into it wild and grassless. Here, to the site of the old fire worship of the Druids, came the hermit, the friend of Columbkill, to burrow in the rock and pray and meditate far from man and man's sins; and here, to his grave, sprang up a seat of learning and religion that made an Eden of this lonely valley —that the Danes and English over and over again burnt and ravaged, and now time, more ruthless than Dane or Saxon, laid waste. As good men as ever knelt to God rest under these seven churches, under the light shadow of these ash trees, and under the rude stones in the churchyards, where the beggars now sit and count their beads.

The vales of Laragh, Clara, and Glendalough meet here in a lone wilderness, where, hundreds of years ago, the hermit Kevin came to seek God and shun man. It is a place for mountain goblins and witches' dances; Great Britain has not a sterner place. Elijah, when fed by the ravens, had never a stonier, drearier home than this, with its dark, deep sullen lake, walled in by its barren rainy mountains. On these peaks of Derrybawn, Lugduff, and Mullacup, the saint's eyes rested in the intervals of prayer. This strange round tower he ascended; in this lake he fished or swam; in this hut of a church he prayed and mused; in this scooped-out hole in the rock he read the gospels and thought of the blessed apostle at Patmos. Here wild men in wolf skins came to hear him. Here met kings with yellow mantles and war axes, and knelt before the cross he upraised, for this was one of the starting-places of Irish Christianity.

That night, in the Glendalough Inn, by a white hot, fierce fire, and with our whisky tumblers smoking before us, I and Darcy, the reporter of a Dublin paper, who had been attending an inquest on a murdered landlord in the neighbourhood of ——, had a warm discussion upon the traits of difference in the English and Irish character.

"Well," said I, throwing on a lump of peat, "Mr. Darcy, I suppose Ireland is now prosperous—at least, so your papers say."

"Pretty well for that," said Darcy, and looking at his face as it elongated itself in the bowl of his spoon.

"Pretty well!" said I; "why, you have drenched your green island with landlords' blood, and the only proprietors you have spared have been the absentees. You have had a healthy, hungry famine; a hearty fever has thinned down your redundant population, according to strict political economist principles; and having been further bled and sapped by the departure of so many thousands of your strongest, richest, and happiest peasantry, Ireland is now, according to smirking diplomatists, declared to be 'most flourishing.' God help England from that sort of flourishing."

"You're right, sure," said Darcy, filling his glass; "you might as well congratulate an apoplectic man on the fine colour in his cheeks, or a dropsical man on his stoutness—unfeeling spalpeens. So you found us hospitable?"

"Indeed I have," said I, "almost carelessly generous, and, without any cold-blooded class pride; we English do a kindness, as you put out money to interest, not throwing it away on pleasant strangers, or for mere caprices of good humour; but you are an excitable people; I will give you three instances of it. The first night I arrived in Dublin, having admired and walked round the great black Bank, and the old houses of Parliament, and the stately domed customhouse, having passed by its river moat, and its thicket of lance-pointed masts, flags, and brown banners of weather-coloured sails, having circumnavigated Merrion Square, admired the curious coal-carts, with their waggling bells, and the rakish-looking, disreputable cheap hearses, with the dirty white plumes; having waded through the Liberty, visited Swift's monument, and performed other religious ceremonies of the Saxon, I went at night for a recreation to a grand concert at the Rotunda. Found the same full of black eyes—natural ones I mean, those who entered contrasting favourably with the selfish, boorish English crowds, who too often jostle for places.

"The concert began; Miss Elvina somebody, in white muslin, sang something in Italian, all about 'Crudel, perfido.' She finished, and curtsied as she retired. To my utter astonishment a row of thorough gentlemen behind me gave a whoop of applause, more worthy of Donnybrook fair, I thought, than the stalls of a concert room. I attributed it to ill-regulated spirits, and forgot it. The next night I went to the Theatre Royal; to my utter surprise, when a favourite actor was called on the stage, after the success of the first piece, the whole house gave just the same sort of yell I had heard in the concert-room; and not only this, but in the farce, when one of the actors fell into the orchestra, as he did every night at the same hour, every one present not only gave a yell, but leaped upon the seats with an excitability that no real event could produce in the more stolid Saxon mind. I assure you that the Shoreditch Theatre, on Boxing night, could not equal the noise of the gallery boys in the Dublin Theatre any day in the week. An Irishman's blood is champagne and fire."

Darcy smoked and listened—I went on.

"I'll give you another instance of what struck me as a proof of your universal pugnacity. Last Monday I was on my way from Bray to Dublin by train, I amused myself by watching the green whale back of a headland melt into the blue of ob_livion, when a jerk of stopping aroused me from my musings. It was Ballybrag, a quiet little place as need be, with its little cottage of a station, and its level stone terraces; when I passed it two months before, it might have been a station for Drowsy-land; now, it was up in arms, crowded with eager faces, and pugilistic, combative-looking passengers, who had poured out of a train that stood alongside of ours, as if preparing to board us. Every eye flashed, every fist clenched, every arm worked as if the biceps could not rest, and was longing to set in action the flexors and extensors. From the guard, with the whistle round his neck like a child's coral, down to a clergyman—a rural dean, in snow-white neckcloth and spotless grave black clothes—every fist shook and moved, every eye glared.

"'What is the matter?' said I, to a porter.

"'Matter,' said he, 'the station master has just caught two Dublin men and a dog trespassing on the line, just squint by the tunnel, he's bringing them along by the collar, single-handed. Hurrah for him.'

"'Whoop for him,' said the rural dean, and we all gave a yell worthy of Brian Boru's days.

"'I saw their arms up as we passed,' said a lady next to me, as much interested in the fray as if she had been Mrs. Bellona."

Darcy laughed, and said, rocking himself in the chair, "It's true, it's true—we do like a scrimmage. it warms the blood, and prevents spiteful things rankling. I am always afraid of your professing Pharisee. I always notice he has some mean way of taking it out of you, if he wait even ten years for his chance. Forgive, but knock him down first, and forgive him afterwards, or else you'll have to be knocked down, and then have to forgive him, which is much harder on the ould Adam."

"The next day after Bray," said I, laughing, "I went to Howth, climbed the hill, and crossed to the Eye."

"Of course," said Darcy, "and went to see where the villain murdered his wife, a shilling a piece more for that. Nobody cared for the Eye before that."

"Well," said I, "and a rare tumbling, see-saw pull we had from the pier to the island. 'Is it going to the Eye you are?' had said a brown-faced, amphibious fellow, carrying wet strings and flakes of sea-weed to burn for kelp; 'it's too wild, and it will be rougher yet, if the Lord will.' But I am of the bull-dog breed, and always do a thing if I'm told it is difficult; so I went and talked to a disappointed-looking Peter who had been toiling all night and caught nothing but a small, ugly, large-headed, dog-fish, which he was going to cut down the back, trim and fry for dinner. We agreed for three shillings, and got a lame-footed fellow, who steered, while I took the heavy sixteen-foot oar we had borrowed from a smack in the harbour. 'That's a man to take a glass of grog without help,' said Peter, pointing to his mate approvingly. Peter's conversation was laconic and ejaculatory. He talked of increasing the fare, because the wind was so high and the pull so hard. I cut him in two with an angry negative, and bade him keep to his bargain. 'Sure,' said he, 'we're poor, but we're honest.' He pointed to a screaming, whirling gull over our head, and talked of his trade. He usually went out a mile to sea, and baited with whelks for cod and haddock. If they were blown out further there was no land to put into nearer than Holyhead. He showed me where George IV. landed. ' But that,' said he, ' was before you came to these countries,' (a metaphorical way of expressing a time before my Anno Dominis began). Fishing was an uncertain life ; sometimes days of dearth, then a great catch and plenty galore for a time. The great hauls were not great profits ; because too large a catch reduced the price, and with the price fell the fisherman's profit. Howth, they told me, was a great place till Kingstown sprang up, after George IV.'s visit. The Eye was where St. Frennan built his chapel ; the small, round bell tower still stands, and the bramble throws its strong arches about over the altar. I saw the Stags and the Rowan rock, scurried the deer over the slopes, and saw the waves beating the transformed Thulla. When I got out of the boat to land, Peter shouted after me, holding my umbrella, ' Here's your parasol, sir.' That was his joke at my being afraid of rain.

"Never believe an Irishman's feigned ignorance ; he was only laughing at me. What struck me most about Dublin was the provincial character ; its Mullingar canal, lined with trees ; its suburbs of cots, made of clay, whitewashed, and its black-peat stacks on the Drogheda road ; its transitions from Sackville Street to the Liberty, from its Grafton Street shops to the sheds, with fresh sprigs of heather stuck in the new dry peat loads ; its highly-coloured pictures of saints in the window ; its large Protestant churches and humble chapels : its lamplit apple-stalls, and its crowds of sea-gulls, foraging up the noisome, dark Liffey, that unarched sewer."

"Well, if it is a sewer, you needn't be too hard upon it ; even a sewer has feelings, I suppose," said Darcy, as he rose for bed. We arranged before we parted that night, my second visit to the churches on the morrow ; he himself had to be off by the first mail car. I arose the next morning an hour after he had knocked at my door, and wished me good by ; dressed— took a hasty breakfast, and started with Mike, the guide. We began with a short car trip.

" That mountain fornent you is the Three Crowns, and that bit of a hill to the left is Kit of Galloway ; she was either a

great queen or a great witch, and had that mountain all to herself for a kitchen garden."

That's what the Kingstown carman talked about, but here
on the Wicklow mountain roads the talk is all about the Sugar
Loaf, and the Scalp, and the Gap o'Crockan, and Derrybawn, to
say nothing of Loughnaquilla, Croughanmoira, and Blackmoore.

"He's as supple as a buck," said Mike the driver, as he
pointed out these great hills, referring to a stonemason from
Pembroke dockyard, who kept leaping off the car, and racing
up the hill in sheer wantonness of health and strength, much
to the annoyance of a quiet fellow, his companion, who sat beside me. The one was a stone-dresser, and the other a stone-
setter, though the first could also set, and the latter also dress,
stone when times were bad. The one was a wild, handsome
looking fellow, in a blue cotton-velvet cap, new black coat, and
showy waistcoat; while his friend wore the plain, honest fustian
shooting-coat and worn cord breeches of his every-day trade.
He was learned in hard and soft stone, and criticized every wall
we came to; he told me of the various diseases of the eye and
lungs that the soft-stone men experienced, and that the hard-
stone men escaped. He was prosy and diffuse on the black
eyes and decent behaviour of the Pembroke lasses; he told me
of the fights and jealousies of the Welsh and Irish, and harangued upon the old castle where "Henry I.," as he would have
it, was born. Behind him, in the car, was his bundle, tied up
in a red handkerchief, with his stone hammer tucked in the knot.

"I'm glad I've put down those women," said the ungallant
Mike; "I'd sooner have a load of wheat any day than a load
of women."

"It is not every one," said the buck in the blue cap, "that
can get rid of them as easily.'"

"Thrue to you," says Mike; "but here's your place—look
sharp. Thank you; good morning. Whist! That's a wild
one," said Mike, giving a valedictory look after blue-cap.

"Do you think they escape colds by going without stockings?" said I, as a quantity of bare-footed children passed by. "It
must kill the weak ones, and leave only the strong to grow up."

"Listen to me," said Mike, pointing to a steep mountain,

"*bare feet never slip*, that's our Irish saying; the bare foot wants no shoeing, and the same soles lasts us out."

The only persons now on the car were a land agent and a farmery-looking man fresh from Australia. The land agent was a nervous, muffled-up man, who seemed in a perpetual state of masquerade, with a comforter round his throat, and his hat drawn over his eyes. His views of Irish politics were practical, but not sympathising. He approved of emigration. "Draft off all your surplus population." "Get rid of all your superfluous mouths." "Enlarge your farms, and get more responsible tenants."

"But this dread of your life must be painful?"

"It was at first," said he, "but one gets accustomed to it. I have had my life attempted three times. When I began I used to think how dreadful it must be to watch every stone wall as you rode along for the spurt of fire and the pale face; but I think nothing of it now, for these crimes grow scarce."

"But there was a murder in Tipperary last week," said I. "A barricade was set across the road to stop the landlord's gig: and, when it stopped, a man ran up, blew out the driver's brains, and whipped the horse back to the house. The gig passed back through Templemore with the dead body lying on the seat, a dreadful sight."

"Don't talk about it," said the agent, "I am just going my Tipperary round: but still these crimes are now few; rents are higher, and are regularly paid. The famine made Ireland prosperous."

"The famine," said I, "was a dreadful cautery for a dreadful ulcer. Last week I was in Donegal. I drove on a cold Sunday morning right from Londonderry to Lough Swilly with a pleasant, witty fellow, and his trunk and fishing-rod. It was a long, cold drive; and when we got to the bare, wild, pebbly shores of the lake, we had to go up to a hill and burn a bundle of hay as a signal for a boat. We then hoisted a flag to tell the man on the opposite side to send for a car, and waited on the rough stone pier, where the little waves washed and rippled, till the big clumsy boat came tacking across and bore my friend out of sight."

"Well, who was he, your honour?" said Mike.

"Why, a land agent and attorney, from Cork—sent [for by a Scotch farmer just over Lough Swilly, who has just had a thousand sheep destroyed last year by the peasantry, who won't allow him to settle there; they kill his lambs, carry off his sheep, and no one is detected. If I had raised my hand then they'd have flung him in the Lough, for the sea birds to scream over; but I didn't, for I suppose even an attorney has claims as a man."

To my surprise the agent went on to take the popular side of the question, and recounted many stories of landlords and tenants, and their forgetfulness of the love of the Irish for the soil. His whole endeavour was now, he said, to induce men to emigrate. All this was uttered in a low voice, with frequent interruptions and looking round. The next time I saw my friend he was perched on the top of a coach, with a travelling cap's flaps drawn over his ears. He looked the very image of a suspicious spy, risking his life for small gains and mean purposes. Yet he talked of foreign tours, and seemed in dress to be a gentleman.

As for the returned Australian, he was a burly elderly man, with sorrowful eye and a compressed mouth. He was dressed well, and wore a thick, curly wool waistcoat of pure Australian make. He had been ten years away and seemed stunned by the changes he saw.

"I wouldn't live in Ireland now for five-hundred pounds a-year," he said. "The potatoes are grown smaller, everything is changed, (yes, may be better); but I want to get away."

Australian. Is Doolan of the Bawn dead?

Mike. Yes, and his son too.

Australian. What! Tim, the soldier?

Mike. The same.

Thus they went on till every recollection was demolished. This friend was bankrupt, that dead. He was eloquent about stringy bark trees, kangaroo soup, bush-rangers, 'possum-traps, gold cradles, &c. There was something sad and complaining about his eyes, which was strangely in contrast with his well-to-do dress and self-conscious air of prosperity. He wanted to get back: all he wanted was to get back—Ireland had nothing for him now; but he should take back a broad sod from the old country to cover him with in his grave in his new home. When I saw that agent, whose head looked always ducking from bullets, who seemed shrunk and thin, as if he had just been pumped on to cool him after a bating, and when I saw that rich Irishman in the Australian wool waistcoat, and with a pocket-full of the newest gold of our antipodes, and yet with a heart grown cold to the old mother country, I thought to myself here I see two types of the miseries of this dear land—the exile and the agent; the exile who has forgotten his native land, and the agent who never cared for it.

" But, good heavens, Mike," said I, " what's that ?" seeing what seemed like Cleopatra's needle rising before me.

" Why, bless your honour, that's the round tower of Glendalough, one of the wonders of Ireland. There's nothing now in it, you see, but the squall crows that come in and out, for a storm has blown off the top," (he assumes a look of awful deliberation, stops and points with his whip.) "There has been a great *dicision* about them round towers among the *rantiquarians*. Now I've seen eighteen of them towers, and never saw one that wasn't near a church. Some think they were belfries ; others that they were watch towers ; a few that they were for fireworks, and such like, in honour of Baal. But if they were for signals, what I say is, why wasn't they built on that hill yonder, and not here in a hollow, where nothing can be seen but the rocks ? If for sun worship, why not on the hills, where the sun is seen long before it touches the valley ? Now wait awhile, your honour."

" Then, Mike," said I, " as you doubt everything, what were they ?"

" Belfries, your honour, divil a thing else—begging St. Kevin's pardon. Look at St. Kevin's kitchen, and you'll see the belfry : for what the people, as ignorant as the childer, call the chimney, is nothing more than a round tower, with a little chapel built on to it. Now I've been up this one, and I can find no traces of stairs, or of beams for the bell ; so that it must have been only for defence for the women and valuables, when the Danes came up to the valley. [Sings.]

"And if you come on any day
'Twixt twelve and one o'clock,
Why, there you'll see the geese may be,
On the lake of Glendalough."

" Why, what's that song about, Mike ?" said I, much amused.

" About, your honour? why, about King O'Toole being changed into a gander, with his seven sons, because he didn't keep his promise to the blessed St. Kevin ; but here's the Glendalough guide."

The guide was waiting for me. The guide, Regan, was a lean, wild, hungry-looking fellow, scantily dressed, and with red, bare feet. I slided about the splashes of bog, but he made clean leaps, and effected a steady picked-out progress.

We got into some hillocky, greasy ground round the cathedral and St. Kevin's kitchen ; two small stone chapels, now ruins, about twenty feet long, the roofs formed of stone shingles.

" This is the ancientest of the seven churches," he said ; " there used to be service here even a few years ago ;" a few yards off is a large slab of stone, with a round scooped hole in it, as if it had been used by the monks for a font. There is a legend about a poor widow with a sick child, who met the saint here one day as he came from his cell up in the cliff over the lake, and begged him for milk. He instantly sent her down a milch hind, whose milk the widow poured into the stone cup.

" That was a great miracle, your honour," said Dan, winking, (cross about us). " This is the stone that's worn away with the elbow of the ould woman, as she sat waiting for the milk St. Kevin promised her, and here's where her fingers went " (pointing to five small indentures, with a cunning leer, seeing me incredulous, and wishing to show himself to a Protestant above superstition) ; " and sure I ought to know, for didn't I chisel them myself ?"

" It's only a quern," said I, to try him, " where the women used to bruise the corn before handmills became common."

" Thrue to you, your honour, but I never give it them so at all. They must have the fine stories, so I makes them fresh and fresh. I hope it won't rain, your honour, for when it rains here, it manes it. The round tower you see there is one hundred and ten feet tall, and fifty-one feet in circumbendibus; it's built all of granite, for the slate in it is not worth mentioning. There are two windows near the door, and four more near the top. The story is, that the Druid used to go up every morning, and when he saw the sun rise in the horizon, then he took off his hat and bawled out ' Baal!' north, south, east and west. It must have given him an appetite for his breakfast; but, the haythens, they had no tay, and what's breakfast without tay ? [Sings.]

"Saint Kevin says to King O'Toole,
    I do not want to wander ;
So give to me, for a little see,
    As far as flies the gandther."

" Do you like peat better than coal, Dan ?" said I.

" Well, it's no cheaper, and takes some trouble to light," said Dan ; " but there's no smoke, and we thinks it agrees better with us. Now, your honour, Trinity church and its high round tower, you passed at Laragh and St. Saviour's Abbey, makes the last of the seven churches."

Well, thought I, here I am in the centre of Irish tradition. Lough Dan, yesterday morning, where Holt used to lurk, and Anamoe, where Stern fell through the mill-race ; then Castle Kevin, on the green, once Pierce Gaveston's, and where afterwards the O'Tooles, the great clans of Wicklow, lived to fight and fought to live : now Glendalough—the treeless, grey, stony valley, where the dark Glencoloe feeds St. Kevin's lake ; tomorrow Avoca, where the sweet waters meet, and Rathdrum, where the chiefs used to assemble. Here I was, in the Irish Iona, where, in the dark, bloody times, St. Kevin the companion of Columbkill, came, between the two lakes, to lead a holy life. Here Kathleen tempted him, and here he pushed her into the lake.

"Ah ! you saints have cruel hearts,
    Sternly from his bed he starts,
And, with rude, repulsive shock,
    Hurls her from the beetling rock.
Glendalough, thy stormy wave
    Soon was gentle Kathleen's grave."

Round that hermit's grave sprang up a cathedral, a city, and a seminary of learning. Burnt down several times by the Danes, and rebuilt, it was then destroyed by a flood; and finally, when restored, fired by the invading English, who the Irish, then in vain, wished to become absentees. Here are stone crosses to be seen, and ruined chapels and abbeys, and burial grounds, and a round tower, and the lake where St. Patrick shut up the last serpent (not priestcraft), and the lake where Kathleen of the blue eyes and the honey breath perished; last of all, there is the hermit's bed and the outlaws' den.

True the seven churches are very poor, the crosses mere blocks of almost shapeless stone, the lake but a black pool; the round tower a factory chimney with no smoke coming out, and the saint's bed a mere crevice in the rock; but then, a glass or two of whisky fires the imagination, and what with a song, and a climb, and a row, and a little discussion, by the time you get to St. Kevin's Bed, you are ready to believe the yarns of Sinbad the Sailor, or anything else.

Dan (in the cathedral) said to me (his victim)—"This is very ancient and antique, but it has been pulled about by fellows mining for treasure. It was all built during the Pagan persecution and war. This cross was the monument of St. Laurence O'Toole." He and the saint were great friends.

"Did they take their tay together?"

"Sure they did; and their beer too, which is a trifle stronger, as you read in the old writers."

Leaving the grey turrets of the seven churches and their scattered burial-places, we got into a sort of plantation, through which we saw St. Saviour's Abbey, half hidden by mossy ash trees whose slight leaves flickered round the broken walls. To the left, a mountain stream poured down, sliding, slipping, trickling, and crushing past tree trunks, and over flat slabs of rock and giant stepping stones; "like running whisky," said Dan, as he tripped before me to show the way.

"And divil a lark," said Dan, " is ever seen over the blessed lake, more by token, your honour, there's a story about it. Some say that as they had no repaters in them days, St. Kevin taught the skylarks to wake the men who builded the churches.

Well, when the last nail was put in, says St. Kevin, 'As no birds will ever be your aquels, there shall be no more larks seen over Glendalough;' and the ha'porth of a one there has been since, so he spoke true, if no one else ever did."

"I have heard a different story, Dan," said I.

"The landlord told me the mason men swore to the saints to get up with the lark and lie down with the lamb; to be dacent people, as the O'Byrne's kith and kin always were; but the larks rose so unconscionably early, that the men didn't get their natural sleep, and so many died, that the saint, in sheer compassion, at last, issued a proclamation that no lark should sing again near the Seven Churches, and so he saved the men's oaths and their lives too."

"Now," said Dan, "I've shown you the sacristy, where all the clargy are buried, and where any one who is lucky enough to lie, secures a snug berth in heaven; and you've heard all about poor Kathleen with the blue eyes, who followed St. Kevin, praying to look at his shadow, or to hear if it was but the call of his voice. All she wanted was to be like a dog at his feet, to take penance for his sins as well as her own, and even in prayer to remember him before herself—everywhere she followed him till he took to that hole in the rock. Even here she followed him: and when he awoke on his hard bed, her blue eyes were always watching him, with the tears frozen in them, like rain-drops on a spinach leaf. You've heard lastly how the saint leaped up, and what does he do, but push poor Kathleen in the lake."

All this time we had been paddling a boat along the lake, whose waters lay sullen under our keel.

"Here we are," said Dan, "and yonder is the path where Kathleen came down for the last time to St. Kevin. Leap out on that ledge of rock, and take care you don't slip."

I looked up, and saw a shelving wall of rock, scarped and smooth; stubbed with heather tufts here and there.

"There is no way here," said I, "for me, whatever there was for Kathleen."

"Aisy, be aisy," said Dan; "put your first foot in this hole, and your fingers in this slit; now your foot in that broken bush, and your fingers in this corner rock—that's it; there, now your foot on that round block, and your fingers on that ledge, and swing yourself in. This is St. Kevin's bed. Now, tell the saint your best wishes, and maybe you'll get them."

I found myself jammed in a little cave—a regular smugglers' den, twenty feet sheer perpendicular over the sullen lake. That is poor Kathleen's grave—mournful, lonely; no fish springing, no bird flying, no tree growing on the bank. At the end was a ledge for the saint's head.

"Why, what are you laughing at, Dan," said I, "cooped up in this oven of a place?"

"You may call it an oven," said Dan, "for it is here I make my bread. What's your Christian name, your honour? Maybe you'd like it wrote up here on the rock. Will you have it chiselled or whitewashed? Chiselled, a shilling; wash, sixpence. Wash rubs out. Many a shilling I've chiselled the rowlers out of. Here's Sir Walter Scott, you see; and here's Mr. Tommy Moore, and Lady Morgan."

"Thank you," said I, "but how shall I know you ever write it? What do you do in the winter, Dan, when the tourists cease?"

Said Dan, "I sit at home, and invent lies to amuse them in the summer; and when I've done that, I go to Liverpool, and get work at the stone-masing. But the truth is—(encouraged by my fee)—

"This King O'Toole, bedad no fool,
    Had sons and daughters seven;
    To swans and geese, each one of these
    Was turned by good St. Kevin.

The king had sworn by crown and hose
    To give him land and holdings;
    If the old blackguard had been feathered and tarred,
    It might have stopped his scoldings."

With a shout from Dan, to rouse the ghostly echoes, we turned back to the inn.

The next day I started for England.

CHAPTER XX.

TALES IN AN INN-KITCHEN.

'Twas after a long day's ride that, on a January sunset, I leapt from my horse at the door of a small inn, in a village between Ross and Monmouth.

I had been struck at a distance with its sign, which, glistening in the setting sun, like a golden shield, looked like that wayside summons for a feat of arms which in the old days was hung forth as a beacon to the errant knight. A shock-headed ostler, with bowed legs, shambled out to take my horse to its stable, while I, parting company with him for the first time for six hours, followed the landlord, who waddled before me, into the inn's best room. I fairly shook with cold when I cast my eyes round the gloomy and tawdry funeral-plume splendour of the large cavern, in whose grate a newly-lit fire crackled and spitted.

"There's a better fire in our kitchen, sir," said the landlord, apologetically and inquiringly; "but, of course, you wouldn't like to go there."

"I'll go there with all my heart," I replied, "if I shall not intrude on your other guests," my last spark of pride completely extinguished by the cheerful hum of voices and the merry laugh that came in fitful gusts through the opened door, and was followed by a deep lull.

"We've no one there, sir," he said, "but old Watson—who, I dare say, you know—old Watson, who drove the Ross coach, and our village blacksmith and schoolmaster—worthy people all. Follow me, sir;" and with the patronising air of a cicerone, or rather of an old hen introducing her last chicken to the world, he led me into the bar, and drew a seat for me to the fire, which blazed up as brightly as if it had absorbed all the flames of the whole village into one roaring furnace.

I did my best to look companionable and to "the manner born," but there was a smell of cold air about me that jarred with that mirth,—there was a lull. The landlord filled his pipe—the blacksmith eyed the fire as he would his smithy—

Q 2

the schoolmaster whispered in an under-tone to the coach-man—

"Do you ever," I said, addressing the blacksmith, "find any traces of the old battles in these parts?"

"Aye, sir, that we do; flint axes and swords of rough forging."

"And you forget, friend Jenkins, the skeleton discovered some twenty years ago," said the schoolmaster, with an air of authority, "in a cleft of a rock overhanging the Wye."

"How was that?" said I.

"It was found by some quarrymen in a small cave, the aper-ture of which seemed hardly big enough for a rabbit to get through. It was the skeleton of a large man: one bony hand still clutched a spear, the shaft of which had fallen to ashes centuries ago; the legs were drawn up convulsively, as if the soldier had died of famine. He must have crept there like a hunted fox for shelter. Some say he was one of Vortigern's army—yet this seems a baseless fancy; but certain it is that it must have been some British chief who fled hither during the wars that ended in his nation being driven across the frontier, and leaving behind him the beautiful land, with its winding river and its wooded hills, on which Caractacus had struggled for freedom—leaving behind him those mysterious stones on which the rites of his religion had been performed."

"You seem deep read," I said, "in the traditions of this county."

"I'm half a Welshman," said the schoolmaster, "and my mother, Lucy Griffiths, was of a good stock, and claimed descent from a royal tribe; but, as I was a-going to say, this chieftain—for so he must have been—was perhaps wounded here, for there are still signs of a camp, as there are indeed, either Roman or British, on all these river hills; and from these watch-hills a beacon flame would have been seen almost to the mountains of Abergavenny."

"How they could have lived, poor critturs," said the land-lord, "and fought, without a glass or two of humming ale, I can't imagine, for they tell me they only drank a liquor brewed from heath mixed with honey."

"And their iron," said the blacksmith, "was such stuff as I'd be ashamed to hammer on a stithy."

"They beat the Romans with it," said I; "that's more than most men could do with better weapons, and their scythed chariots made dreadful chasms in the rank of the spearmen."

"Vos them ere chariots," said the coachman, taking his pipe from his mouth, and for the first time breaking the silence, "anything like a chariot von sees now turned out?"

"Not at all," said I, with difficulty repressing a smile; "they hadn't yet learnt the art of linking four spanking tits to one vehicle."

"Aye, that vos reserved to a more benlightened age," said the coachman, refilling his pipe, and borrowing a spark of Promethean flame from his friend, the landlord, who, overcome with disgust at the "salvages" who were ignorant of beer, had now dropped aside from the conversation.

There was a momentary hush, for at this instant the storm, which the pale sunset had foreboded, seemed to burst forth at this moment with all its fury upon the earth—a blast, fiercer than its brethren, struck the inn, and shook it as a vessel might when smitten by a head sea. We drew closer round our hearth the more it seemed threatened by the wind that howled deep thunder down its chimney. It seemed muttering up aloft as if a whirlwind was planning a descent that way, but was driven back by the stings of flame that went roaring and shouting up the black orifice. It shook the shuttered window as if enraged at the festivity within, unfitting so wild and chaotic a night. It went moaning down the street and through the churchyard, like the spirit of departed villagers revisiting their homes on some Purgatorial holiday. The village constable, who entered, after slowly disentangling himself of piles of clothing, and unswathing himself of bandages of comforters, like a revivified mummy, seating himself by the fire, said "it was a night in which no dog, much less a Christian, should be out in. It wasn't a night for a decent parish constable to be abroad," he said, "so he had come to keep the peace among his neighbours."

This small joke being much applauded, the landlord proposed a bowl of rum-punch, which he made, and ladled forth with the air of a monarch to a band of perfectly contented subjects. The constable proposed that the schoolmaster should tell a tale, to which proposal, after much pressing, he acceded.

"As we've been talking of Britons of the old times, I'll tell you the story of David Thomas, the one-eyed cobbler, and how from a drunken vagabond he became a thriving farmer, which seems to spring very naturally from our conversation. I was quite a boy when David Thomas came from Caernarvonshire and settled here, but he never got on, for he spent half his time paddling about in a coracle, and the other half in this kitchen. He was a clever, shrewd fellow, and did nothing badly but cobbling. He was a good fisherman, knew every stone in the river, swam like a duck, was shrewdly suspected of poaching, could snare any animal from a mouse to a badger, played the fiddle, and, in fact, was the minstrel at every merry meeting in the two counties. He was the idol of all the boys of the village, of whom he had always a *tale*, soliciting him for whistles, imploring him for mole traps, or bartering with him for rude Pandean pipes. He had the entry of every house, for he was the self-circulating newspaper of the village; and when Boney's battles were toward, he used to read to a congregation every day more numerous and far more awake than ever girded round the pulpit of our minister. He had always a sly joke for the maidens—some allusion from an old Welsh poet, for he was a great reader of the Bards, or some kind word of praise of their absent lovers that sent a blush mantling up to their cheeks, and presenting you in the short space of two moments with the white and the red rose, shifting into hues differing, and yet alike. So have I seen the eastern sky melting its pearl light into the choice radiancy of——"

"Now, none of them ere poetical flights of yourn, mind," said the coachman authoritatively.

The schoolmaster smiled blandly, and proceeded—

"He was a favourite, too, with the village striplings, planning foot-ball matches, making them snares or teaching them all the tricks of the diver in the deep spots of the Wye; or, in an evening, playing his bow all the faster for the 'cog of good ale,' which stood well replenished at his elbow.

" But all this did not make his own fire burn brighter, and his fiddle bow was plied oftener than his awl. In spite of the grotesque cast of his features, there was a something mysterious about the one-eyed cobbler, that kept up the village curiosity about him. He had fits of depression, when he would wander all day among the amphitheatre of woods, from whence the sound of his fiddle, playing strange wild snatches of Welsh airs, could be heard by the distant ploughman. At these times he came home only late at night, and during the day would do such mad freaks that men whispered that David Thomas, if he was not half crazed, had surely committed some crime in his youth for which his troubled conscience wracked him. He would get the key of the old church from his brother the sexton, and shut himself up for hours amongst the tombs in the chancel, or climbing up, for he climbed like a squirrel, to some almost inaccessible chamber of the only remaining tower of the castle on the hill yonder, might be seen looking out from a shattered embrasure like the ghost of some murdered knight in the moon-light ; and some of his dearest intimates said it was particularly about early springtime that he rambled about in those awful places.

"I remember well myself, when I was a boy, coming late one stormy January evening through the churchyard, walking timidly, and with head turned, through the path that led up to the house of God, even in my awe, for the wind was howling through the belfry loopholes, thinking of this Godsacre, where rich and poor met for the first time in real equality, with no richer robe above their cold breast than the green turf, studded with daisies ; when from behind a grave I heard a groan which shook me with fear. I looked ; it was the merry cobbler poring over a grey tombstone, and spelling each letter as one would the Bible's page. A corpse light threw a horrid glow-worm gleam upon his strange features. I was afraid to speak, but a sort of fascination compelled me to crouch down behind a raised tomb and watch him. Presently he rose, looked at the sky, beat his brow, and muttering words which I thought were ' God save her soul,' paced out through the wicket gate that led into the village.

"Then I rose, breathed deeper, and stealing to the stone from which I had never taken my eye, marked it with a cross scratched with my pocket knife, for the momentary light bred from corruption had gone out, and I could only feel its letters. I went home pale and trembling, but saying I felt ill and tired, hurried to bed. To my mother, for my poor father was already dead, I said not a word; a feeling of mystery brooded over me; I felt that I dared not tell what I had seen, and yet I felt that concealment was a sort of crime. Heaven pardon me, if then I first brushed off the bloom of innocence from my youth. I awoke after a night of feverish dreams before daybreak, went down before anyone was stirring, and flew, rather than ran, to the churchyard. The grave lay calm in the grey light of dawn, the weather-cock, like a morning-star, catching the first glimpse of day. I found the spot; I knelt down; there was the hasty cross:—'Lucy Owen, æt. 18, departed this life November 13, 1802.' Below, 'Mary Owen, her mother, November 20. Lovely and pleasant in their lives, in death they were not divided.' Owen—I had never heard the name. The mystery still lay heavier in my heart. I hurried home, and came down to breakfast with clouded brow and troubled eye. My mother's fond eye observed it, but I complained of a slight fever, and she was quiet. Days went by, and though I dreamt of that horrible scene in the churchyard, and of the cobbler, time soon erased it from my young brain, and I drove it from my thoughts. But still I never followed the cobbler as I had done, never dared to ask him for traps or whistles. The church now seemed a dreadful place, and I turned away from the old tower if I heard his fiddle sounding mournfully within its ruined chamber. I saw him often, gay, telling strange tales, and as merry as before, but to my eye there was now a shadow upon him, which seemed to me to give a ghastly hue to his features, and when I saw the glimmer of a cottage fire light up his face, I shuddered as I thought of the stormy January night and the haunted churchyard.

"It was some years after this that as I was reading one day an old fairy story to a crone of a neighbouring cottage, and had just completed, with all the enthusiasm of a youth, the rhapsodical description of my heroine, that the old woman touched my arm, stopped her spinning, and exclaimed, 'Why there was never one in these parts ever like that, but poor Lucy Owen.'

"'Lucy Owen,' I exclaimed eagerly; 'who was she?'

"'Lucy Owen; why the belle of the village twelve years ago, who was found dead in her room the night before her marriage.'

"'And her mother,' I said, 'what of her?'

"'Aye, her mother; there was a mother; why, she died within a week, quite broken-hearted.'

"'And who was to have been her bridegroom?' I said.

"'Why, young Morris, whom you never saw, for he sold his farm soon after that, and started for America, and has never, as far as I know, been heard of since; but the strangest thing of all was (but you mustn't mention it) is that they said the one-eyed cobbler was a suitor of poor Lucy's, and he followed her to the grave.'

"And so our conversation ended; the mystery seemed to grow darker. Could this then be the Lucy for whose untimely fate he mourned?

"I still shunned Thomas, and he seemed to observe it; and again I sought my crone, and having revived her memory, learnt some further and more interesting particulars of the death of Lucy. She told me that she had watched beside the dead, and on the second evening, almost at the dawning, when all were still, and deep sleep had fallen upon men, and one bird singing at the window, gave only a deeper shade to the awful silence and the calm serenity of the corpse, she went down stairs for a few moments to light a fire, which had gone out in a short sleep into which she had fallen. She returned in a few minutes; to her horror, she saw the hand of a man hanging from the sill of the open window. He dropped heavily at the alarm, and she heard his soft footsteps as he crept away under the wall of the house. Recovering herself in a moment, she looked forth, and could just catch the glimpse of the departing form; it was that of a short man; but the light was too dim to distinguish more. On looking round the room, she saw in a moment that it was a thief who had thus entered the chamber of the dead, for a small coral cross, which Lucy had worn since she was a child, and which had been left in an old oak bureau that stood beside the bed, was gone.

"I listened open mouthed. 'Could it have been the cobbler? And what did Lucy Owen die of then so suddenly?' I enquired.

"'The fisherman said as how it was disease of the heart, of which her father had died.'

"Dreadful forebodings filled my mind; an instinctive feeling of horror rose in me. I dismissed it from my mind, and resumed my usual course of lonely wanderings and readings in the woods whenever I could escape from the fields, for even at this time I longed to live and die a schoolmaster.

"It was a November day; I remember it well. It was a day of decay, of rain, of gloom; the leaves new fallen, paved the walks of the woods with sere and withered forms of corruption; a pale sunset was tinting the wood, almost bared, with a faint golden light, that looked like a mockery of summer: it was like the smile on the lips of the dead! I wandered forth by the lonely path which leads from the meadow of the 'battle-heaps,' up to the top of the hill where the 'stone of power,' the rocking-stone of the Druids, rests. I was walking silently and musingly along, making no more noise over the dead leaves than the rabbits that I every now and then disturbed, and that ran bounding through the brake; when I saw in the meadow, not twenty yards from me, Thomas, standing near one of the mounds with a spade in his hand. I was in a sunken walk, hidden from him by a thick clump of beeches, whose red leaves still rustled in the autumn wind. I stood there half frozen with astonishment, as I watched his motions, for those mounds I had been taught to think were the graves of great chieftains who had been slain in battle with the Romans, when the eagle flew on the heights above; and the boys shunned the place after night-fall, for we noticed that no dark fairy rings were ever there, in that field on the border of the wood; and we thought that where the fairies would not trip, no good thing could be; and I thought of stories I had heard of Trojan kings, who slumbered by the light of one gem, or an ever-burning lamp, in enchanted tombs beneath the greensward of a hill, and of demon denizens of caves and mine spirits; and all these I blended, as I stood there trembling at the falling leaf that rustled to the ground, strange thoughts of the cobbler, and the scenes where I had seen him, tinted darker by the shade of fancy: what could he be doing there, in a place as consecrated by village tradition as the very churchyard, that silent city of graves, where the inhabitants come together but speak not, though but an earthen wall divides them? Thoughts of crime, of buried treasure, thronged through my mind. He's digging, he's been digging for half-an-hour, still I lie cowering in my shelter. The moon comes forth, and lights his grim earnest face; he pauses—looks up—looks round—wipes his brow, and digs with renewed vigour. An aperture discloses itself: he works—starts back—again looks in, drags something forth, and puts it in his bosom; recovers the entrance, with care replaces the turf, falls on his knees, lifts his hands to heaven, then looks round like a guilty thing upon a fearful summons, and hurries away with stealthy steps. Then, and not till then, when his shadow was lost in the night of the wood, I arose trembling with excitement, and from my hiding place I, with a dozen bounds, stood beside the chieftain's grave. There it lay beneath the moon, surrounded by that silent multitude of woods, which told by their falling leaves that Death still reigned upon the earth. I looked at the aperture that had been closed so carefully with the sods, that no marks of removal could be discerned. A superstitious awe crept over me at that silent hour, when I felt I was in such a place. Something glittering caught my eye, and amid a heap of seared leaves that the winds, winter's fierce myrmidons, had torn from their parent tree, and driven together. Good God! it was a cross! a small coral cross, tipped with gold, which had caught the moon's rays. A cross like that the old crone had told me of. A thought of guilt flashed through my mind, an instinctive breathing of the God. I felt that I had been marked out from Heaven as the avenger of blood; there was then blood on the hand that had touched that funeral mound. I saw it all, I felt it, I was sure; the sudden death, the gnawing of conscience, the churchyard scene. Slowly I retraced my steps, as if in some fearful dream, past my hiding place, giving one more look at the mound, frosted with the moonbeams that fell upon it like on a pure heaven. Again a form steals forth from the wood; was it some shadow of the dead? It is the cobbler! He sees me not, though he passed me almost close, for his eye was bent on the ground to grope for something lost. He turned over every heap of withered leaves, every knot of rushes, every bunch of dry white grass. He turned his face suddenly. O sorrowing angels! what a face! torn with deep anguish, remorse, and fear. Slowly and stealthily as a beast of prey I stole away, and ran down a lonely lane into the village.

" 'News, Jemmy,' said my mother; 'who do you think has come from America? Who but young Richard, who years and years ago was to have married poor Lucy, a village beauty, whom I dare say you never heard of, who died suddenly in her bed. He is rich, and tells me he means to settle here. He asked after you, and I told him that you were going to be a schoolmaster, and gave your whole life to reading, and wandering about among the woods. He laughed, and said his life had been spent in cutting down woods. The old cobbler too, (I started), why do you start? of course he knows the cobbler, though there is no great love lost between them, as I believe they even interchanged blows before they parted. I believe they were both suitors to Lucy; but what chance had the cobbler, ill-favoured, idle dog, with a youth as straight as a maypole, and so handsome that half the lasses in the place broke their hearts for him.'

" 'Was there any suspicion,' I said, 'of the cause of Lucy's death?'

" 'Suspicion, child! No; she died of a heart complaint, like her father, with whom I have often danced in my young days.'

" I saw no more of the young farmer for nearly a month, for he had friends to see in another part of England. It was the day before Christmas when he returned. During this time the change that came over the cobbler was perceptible to all. The fiddler chided the boys who followed him, or even struck them in his moody fits. He remained in his shop, working sullenly late into the night; for even at midnight a light might be seen burning in his window. Occasionally I met him, but shuddered to see a face so full of remorse and evil passion. You could no longer fancy his grotesque features writhing into a joke, bending over his fiddle, but thought of charnel-houses, and vaults, and death; at least, so it seemed to my wayward fancy always strong, and now doubly excited by the forebodings of crime which I felt sure I had detected.

"Again Richard came to our house, and greeted me kindly. As he left, I went out with him, and whispering in his ear that I had something of importance to communicate, took his arm, and led him to a retired spot near the ruins of the old castle. He turned pale when I mentioned the name of Lucy Owen. After twelve years her love was still warm at his heart. I told him frankly my suspicions, my glimpses of evidence, the scene I had witnessed, and, above all, the cross which I had picked up. He trembled, and would have fallen had I not supported him. He wept over the trinket. I wept too, in sympathy, for I knew the thought it must call up; and I, too, had loved.

"'Bloody murderer!' he cried, starting up like a maniac; 'and yet it cannot be; though I distrust him, and always did, I thought not so ill. Nothing but a fiend could have separated a soul from such a body, and so young——'

"'There are means,' I said, 'by which men even can destroy life, and leave no sign of guilt.'

"'You are wiser than I,' he replied; 'you have thought much. There is truth in what you say, but time may bring forth more: we had best delay. The village would call the story the dream of a crazed lover and a fanciful boy. The villain, hardened in crime, would brazen it out, and we should be branded for ever. But I have not seen him yet: I will go and observe his manner, his eye, his face. I have been accustomed to look for intelligence in the countenance of the Indian, and I know the traces that guilt leaves behind. For once a wretched settler of ours murdered a trapper, tied a stone to his body, and threw it into a rocky stream, where the very rippling seemed the voices of invisible beings: but God sent the beavers, and they gnawed the rope, and the body floated; and the murderer owned the hand of God was in it, and confessed his crime; and we hung him in the Deadman's Hollow, on a withered pine, and there he bleaches now.'

" As he told me this, we had arrived opposite the squalid stall of the cobbler: we looked in—no one was there; we stepped in quietly without chinking the latch, and listened. There was a muttering up the turnpike stair that led from the shop to the poor bedroom above. It grew louder and more distinct. It was the cobbler's voice, as of one in agony and prayer. We listened. The words came to our ears like the last trump—'O God, cleanse these hands from blood! O God, cleanse these hands from blood!' was his cry. We waited for no more; silently we went forth into the street: what a change had come over the face of Richard! There was deep determination in that compressed mouth; energy in that clenched hand. For a moment we looked on each other, but spoke not: that silence expressed more, far more, than speech. 'It is Christmas eve,' I said; 'years back they had a custom here of singing hymns in the church at midnight, to hail the blessed day. The cobbler will be there; there, in the presence of all, I will confront him, and charge him with the deed of blood. Touch not the murderer till then,' I exclaimed beseechingly.

" 'Twelve years since,' he replied, in a voice deepened by emotion, ' when the blood ran hotter in my veins, I could not have foreborne, but rushing in, I should have clutched the hell-birth by the throat, and with a curse have trampled out his horrible and misshapen soul.'

" With a warm clasp of the hand we separated. It seemed a year to midnight. No lover felt the hours creep by at slower pace. I thought the dull grey sky, the frowning heaven, would never veil in the night. It came, night came, and disclosed another world, the mere shadow of that glorious sunny earth in which we live; fairest stars shining where the sun had stood; the moon hid her face, and one star brighter than the rest, shone as red as blood.

"I met Richard at a corner of the churchyard, and entering it with him, we seated ourselves in a dark corner, unlit by the few candles that scattered the darkness in faint circles of light. The cobbler was there, seated in a front bench almost opposite the altar; his head buried in his hands, as if in prayer: one by one, or in small groups, the villagers stole in like shrouded ghosts from the churchyard without—old men, maidens fair as the murdered one, children awe-struck at the darkness of the church, and the novelty of the scene. From the dimly-lit gallery suddenly burst forth a strain of melody, as sweet in that stillness of night as if the choir of angels that the shepherds heard had again sung forth in the heavens. The calm melody contrasted dreadfully with the turbid fever in our hearts. It was like the placid tranquillity that reigns upon the dead, compared with the sorrow that sits upon the mourner's face that bends over the bier. A voice, deep as from a vault below, rang through the church high above the childish choir— 'A voice from the grave of the murdered calls for vengeance!' It was Richard: as he pronounced the words that hushed the praises that were rising to heaven, he strode towards the altar. The cobbler threw himself on his knees, as if some spirit had struck him to the earth. 'Mercy!' he cried; 'let man have pity, for Heaven has mercy!' 'The mercy thou showed to the dead!' said Richard, felling him to the ground. We rushed forward. There were shrieks from the maidens, cries of horror and surprise from the men. 'What means it?' 'Spare him!' 'Keep him back.' I seized Richard by the arm. He would have struck me in his demoniacal rage: Three men held his arms, and he lay foaming and maddened in their grasp. I told my tale to those who crowded around me; I told of the scenes of remorse that I had witnessed; how thoughts had grown into suspicions, and suspicions into proof: I showed the cross. 'It is hers; it was the murdered angel's,' said Richard, and again he struggled to escape. Again rose a murmuring of voices. As slowly, like a corpse revived might rise from a trance, rose the cobbler. He trembled, and the tears poured down on his cheeks.

"'Friends,' he said, 'God has smitten me. I am guilty:

the brand of Cain is here. Hear me ere I go to death, I was not always thus. In my youth I was fair, till disease and vice distorted these features. I loved Lucy Owen, I served her like a hound does its mistress—I ran, I swam, I did all for her: but a handsome stripling came, and I was slighted. The wedding day was fixed. It was in the inn-kitchen that I first heard the news. I rushed forth, and roamed about till midnight, half maddened at tidings which had blighted me, as frost does the early flower. It was a summer night, I crept to the Owens' cottage. Lucy's broad casement was open, though her room was dark. A devil's thought came into my mind, and drove back all recollection of heaven. I clambered silently up the vine, entered the room which was half lit by moonlight, half in shade, lay a moment silent, watched the sleeping spirit; then, like a fiend of hell, stifling her mouth, I suffocated her with the pillow. Again I laid the body of one whom I loved and hated, calm as if in sleep, and crept down as I had come. I felt no remorse; I thought it a just punishment for the cruel rejection of my love. I dreaded that another should share the love of one who despised me. But the devil forsook his victim, and remorse stole in; it was in moments like these that my wounded spirit, not yet entirely lost, found relief in those groans and prayers which you (turning to me) heard.

" ' The mound that I dug in, when I lost the cross which I stole from the room of one whom I could not forget, was a funeral heap, wherein I had heard gold was often found. I wanted to escape to some other land. I found a gold wreath there, round the neck of a skeleton, but I started back when I first looked into that vault, for the glimmer of my own eyes lit it as with a lamp; even in such scenes thoughts of my guilt haunted me, my name seemed written in lines of decay on every leaf, the stars looked down like the eyes of a judge upon me; everywhere the avenging angel was looking.' * *

" With looks of horror we led him from the church, before the morrow he was in the cell of Gloucester prison. I was present at his trial. He was convicted, and was hung, and thus did God discover a crime that had so long lay hid.

'Murder will out,' says the proverb; 'Vengeance is mine, and I will repay it, saith the Lord.'"

We breathed deeper as the schoolmaster concluded his tale, and wiped away something like a tear that hung from his eye.

The old polished clock in the corner, after experiencing the usual convulsions that village clocks experience under such circumstances, struck twelve as we were expressing the interest we had felt in the tale of the poetical schoolmaster; and having distinctly articulated that solemn hour of midnight, and got very satisfactorily through its mechanical feat, it subsided, after a slight agitation, into a quiescent state, its labours for the next few hours being of a much milder character. We were still commenting on the infallible discovery of crime by man, or beast, or bird, or tree, or flower, when the landlady, who had been buzzing about the next room, suddenly burst in, and with a withering look at her alarmed husband, asked him if he knew that it was getting very late.

"There's just half of the last bowl of punch left, my dear," said the landlord blandly, and regarding complacently the rampart of friends that, interposing between him and his angered dame, protected his only exposed flank.

Boniface was a good general in domestic broil, and felt his advantage. The landlady, a gaunt, withered-looking woman, who paid willingly the penalty of treating her spouse with elaborate respect before strangers, for the privilege of keeping the keys of the treasury, and ruling behind the scenes, muttered something very like "pretty hours for christian folk," and slowly retreated from the room, discharging as she retired some Parthian glances at her spouse, harmless for the present, but ominous of future storm. They did not, however, sink very deep into the heart of the worthy man, or abate the relish with which he gave a circular sweep with the ladle and filled the glasses of the company.

"Sorrow is dry," he said, "care killed a cat; so I'll just enliven you a little, by telling you a hanegote of a thing that really happened to my father, good man, who's dead and gone, the year this very rum came into my cellar. He was a coachman, and druv for many a year the Hereford coach, about as good a coach as four spanking tits ever drew along a road. Well now, my father was a man who liked his glass, to keep out the cold, and keep in the warmth, as well as any man, and he was as univarsally respected as any man that ever sat on a box ; he was the busum friend of every landlord in the county, the jarvey best liked by his mate on the road, and a great favorite with all the buxom bar-maids ; but he had one failing, he was a man as had fancies about his health, which was as good as any man could have, and if you'd seen him with his box-coat and his belchers on, with his jolly cheek and merry eye you'd have said, if Methuseley ever druv a coach, he was the mortal picture of that respected patriarch ; he never travelled without a draught in each pocket, which occasionally breaking over a ladies' parcel, made a pretty mess; but, Lor bless you! he was that well spoken, that he generally made it out that such a parcel was peculiarly difficult for such as he to carry, and if it had been any one else it would never have arrived at all. And his waistcoat pockets, which were as large almost, what with the custom of the age and his nateral corpulence, as a small ridicule, were lined with tin, in one of which was lozengers, and in the other pills of a peculiar make ; not that he shirked his glass, but on the plea of health generally looked piteously at the landlady, and desired it, as an invalid, to be made particularly hot; and he had a habit of feeling his pulse at the smallest provocation, so that ignorant persons might have imagined he was undoing a handcuff. All human beings, as the Parson said on Sunday, is liable to error, and this was the error of my guvenor; but the most aggerawating thing was, that when he did come home on Sunday night, he choose that peculiar time, about midnight, especially if it friz, to ring up the house and say he was dying, give us his blessing, and make over to me his silver chronometer and appendages, which I had always to give him back when he recovered the next morning, in time to take a larger breakfast than usual before he started. But 'wolf' was cryed so often that we soon didn't believe it, and after grumbling for some time as we turned out of our warm beds, I got at last restive and didn't go at all, and there was a pretty scene, for the old fellow got up remarkably quiet for a dying person, and coming to my bed with a horse-whip, gave me such a leathering that I never failed after this to attend his dying summons as a dutiful son should do. Well, there were highwaymen occasionally seen along the Hereford road, and one night my father, who had gone out a perfect mass of great coats, so that he had to be helped on his box by the ostler and staff, came into the inn with a hole in his hat, just as if a bullet had passed through it ; and my father, who was just mixing a powder for a stiff glass of grog, could give no further explanation of it, but that about ten miles from Gloucester a man hallo'd out to him, and he, thinking it a passenger, said the coach was full, and drove on. This he thought might have been a highwayman, particularly as he recollected hearing a pistol go off, as he thought, in a field near the road, about ten minutes after. The guard, it appears, as usual, had been asleep, for when they stopped to water the horses, about five miles further on, he blew his horn, thinking they had arrived at Hereford ; not but that he always carried a blunderbuss, which, however, report said had never been discharged within the memory of man, was imperfect about the lock, and not very sound about the barrel.

"My father, thereupon, being a good deal galled with the jokes cut on the occasion, when he next went to Gloucester bought a pair of old cavalry pistols of immense length, and then laying in a bag of bullets and a few dozen charges of powder, announced to his passengers, who assembled in a sort of parliament to hear the harangue that he made the necessity of a defence in case of attack — the good man had, in fact, worked himself up to a pitch of patriotism almost equal to Nelson on the eve of Trafalgar. Most of the passengers quite warmed to the affair ; though some, concluding from the extent of the munition supplied, that there was a chance of not a soul escaping alive, refused to go ; but the rest, concealing their fears under an overdone display of courage, manifested great determination, and, after the third glass of brandy-and-water, expressed their unflinching resolution to cut their way to Gloucester—a promise which, if any one had taken them at their word, they would have been rather puzzled to perform, as the whole company hadn't more than two pocket-knives between them. Like the veterans of a forlorn hope, with consolatory remarks as to the fate of various unfortunate travellers on the same road, the coach started. The ostler drew off the cloths with the same spirited jerk as ever: there was the same throng of chambermaids, hangers-on and admiring townsmen, as ever; but there was a gloom on all, for my father had spread undue alarm by the extra number of pills he had taken, and the ferocious way in which he had flourished his pistols and talked ' of selling his life dearly.'

" But, for my life, I had nearly forgot a material point in the story, which is, that the most prominent of all the passengers, and the one who acted as a sort of prime minister to my father, was a stranger—a man with an immense pair of whiskers and a large drooping moustache, who seemed, by his frogged coat and military air, to have been in the army, had, indeed, his conversation not abundantly shown it; for he talked boldly of skirmishes and cavalry affairs, 'and, stap his vitals,' he was for slaying every mother's son of them. No waiting for tardy justice, but a rope and the nearest tree; a proposition rather 'pooh-poohed' by my father, but applauded vociferously by a wizen little attorney, who said 'he'd have the law of 'em, if they dared to touch him.' Our military friend took a great interest in the defensive preparations, and insisted himself on loading my father's pistols and the guard's blunderbuss, having, as he said, once, by a peculiar system of loading, winged a duellist, who had slain his five men, and thought no more of shooting an antagonist than a proper Christian would of putting a bullet into a mad dog. And then, assuming the generalship, for my father's courage towards the time of starting, if it hadn't decreased, had at least assumed somewhat less of a bellicose character, he advised the secretion of all valuables; and heightening their courage by undoing a sort of box in the heel of his shoe, placed carefully therein a roll of bank-notes, which, as he quite accidentally let out, were of an immense amount. This, and the glitter of a diamond ring on his finger, excited a general communicativeness ; so that from all sorts of purses and rouleaus money was produced, and stowed into hats and wigs, while watches were taken off and stuffed in the interior of cushions—a proceeding which, though it somewhat resembled the prudence of a general who divests himself of his stars before he enters into an engagement, augured badly as far as the giving battle to highwaymen went.

"Away they went, as I said before, and changing horses at Ross about sunset, without anything material occurring, and with a fresh cup to still more stimulate their reviving courage, they started forth, congratulating themselves on their extreme valour, their great prudence, and their still greater good fortune. My father even stopped at one place, and harangued them as to the manner in which they should enter Hereford, as he thought that a show of fire-arms and a determined manner might have a good effect on those highwaymen who heard of it. This proposal was received with loud cheering, particularly by the military passenger, who, collecting the fire-arms, proposed they should take out the balls and leave in only the powder, in order that they might fire off a *feu-de-joie* ere they entered the city. At a turn of the road the coach suddenly stopped, much to the horror of the passengers ; voices in dispute were heard without, and the trample of a horse. Our military friend leapt out, armed with all the defensive weapons. In a moment he had pulled my father from his throne. Our military friend was a highwayman.

"'Valiant gentleman and fair ladies,' he said, opening the door of the coach, with a complacent smile, 'oblige your humble servant by handing me the useless paper and the bullion which you found too heavy for your pockets.'

"There were murmurs and signs of resistance ; but he cared not a whit for that, but drawing a pistol from his pocket, cocked it, and presented it at the window.

"'I have here,' he said, in a bland voice, 'a friend of the most persuasive eloquence, who never fails to convince those whom I cannot.'

"He held his hat ; in a moment it was filled with watches, notes, and guineas. He bowed and withdrew.

"'I've one more account to settle,' he replied, 'before I go. Nimming Jack,' he cried, to a flashily-dressed companion, whom no disguise could have turned into anything but a second-rate knight of the road, 'bring that old gent. there in sight of this window.'

"They dragged my father forward, and put him on his knees between them, a living mass of great-coat. 'I've no money, gen'lemen,' he cried, in a voice of extreme terror, as his tormentors, shouting with laughter, emptied his pockets of pills enough to fill a beaver. 'Open your mouth,' they cried; and, pulling it open, they rammed a fist full down his throat. He rose a wiser, but a sicker man than he had knelt down.

"'Adieu, gentlemen and ladies,' said the military surgeon, bowing a mock farewell; 'and as for you, old Jarvy, don't listen another time to military surgeons. I've a great mind to give you a blue pill at parting, but I'll spare you to kill a coach-full of passengers some day by bad driving.' Then, mounting a led horse of his companion, he galloped off.

"When he was fairly out of sight, there were proposals made to pursue, but nobody seconding it, they determined to fire a salute after him, to intimidate him and prevent his return; and this would have been done, had not it been found that the pistols had been stuffed with pepper instead of powder, in which the bullets lay imbedded, and had been stopped up to the muzzle with paper.

"The coach, lightened of its burden, entered Hereford with a sick coachman and crest-fallen passengers."

CHAPTER XXI.

THE COUNCIL CHAMBER AT BRISTOL.

How many recollections these simple words call up from the dark abyss of memory! We figure to ourselves grave senators in solemn deliberation;—"potent grave and reverend seignors," the great ones of proud Venice, or beauteous Florence, in profound debate. We think of the great republican, or oligarchical senators of the mediæval state, each a prince, discussing solemnly, amidst all the gorgeousness of Asiatic luxury, the affairs of their respective states. Then think we of the Doge, or the still more solemn conclave of cardinals in the eternal city of Rome. With rapid transition we recall the secret tribunals of Westphalia, and the dark mysteries of the inquisitorial assembly, or night meetings of conspirators, the veiled and masked leaders, are remembered by us in a mingling of associations. Dim visions arise before our eyes from the pages of the world's history. Councils held by trembling men as the enemy is before their gates ;—senates receiving their victorious generals ;—and, above all, the majestic senate of Rome, whose every councillor, a Gothic ambassador said, resembled a king. But a truce to the ideal, let us return to the plain " work a-day world."

Leaving, therefore, the motley associations suggested by such places, I the other day, as citizens sometimes should do, strolled into the Bristol council chamber, the room where the civic parliament is wont, at stated intervals, to hold its deliberative meetings. Undisturbed by any parrot guide, my eyes glanced with pleasure over the autograph letters of the great and the brave which depend from the walls. There always seems to me something solemn in a solitary room or an empty chamber—

> " When the festive lights are out,
> And the guests are all departed."

But the chamber is hung with paintings, and we never feel solitary with them, for there is ever a silent, calm companionship about a good portrait. A spirit seems to watch you from the canvass, and those inanimate eyes seem almost capable of beaming with expression. They remind me of the statues of Pygmalion, only remaining for ever unfinished and half animated. And what painting ever had more magic powers on the imagination than that of yonder noble cavalier by Vandyck? We mean the full-length of Philip Herbert, Earl of Pembroke, in his robes of office as High Steward of Bristol. The chivalric-visaged noble wears a red cloak lined with white, and bears in his hand the white staff of office. Near him reposes his ducal coronet. He boasts what Prynne would call the " unloveliness

of love—locks" in the shape of flowing hair. A lace embroidered collar falls over his cloak. His stockings, like Mal-
volio's of comic fame, are yellow, but, unlike that ill-starred
steward, he is not cross-gartered. "It breeds somewhat an
obstruction in the blood, this cross-gartering." His shoes bear
the large ribbon roses of this time. We never saw a more
beautiful painting by that noble artist, Vandyck, not even
his portraits of the unhappy Charles, although in them we
trace so well the deep sorrow and stubborn resignation of that
monarch. It is as admirable for the truth, freshness, and ex-
quisite clearness of its tints, as for its spirited and wonderful
execution, and the lights are brilliant and delightfully modu-
lated by the darker portions of *oscuro*. We realise at once the
tradition which admiring artists tell, that this great painter
always painted on a white ground. Hence proceeds that deci-
sion and lucidity of general tone which distinguishes this
painter's productions from the exaggerated chiaro-scuro of
Tintoretto or Rembrandt, grand masters of colouring as they
may be. Never in his works do we find the senseless *impasto*,
to use a term of the studio, or the daubing on of paint as with
a trowel, adopted by —— and some other modern masters.
How truthful, too, are the carnations, so perfectly aping the
embrowned, ruddy glow of health in a manly cheek. This
picture is so valued, both as a work of art and from its associations, that it is said that the present Pembroke family have
offered to give the city for it as many gold pieces as would
cover its canvas. This same Pembroke family have contributed,
perhaps, more great and brave men from their males than any
noble house in England. Amongst them we find the illustrious
Lord Herbert of Cherbury, whose treatise, "De Veritate," is
esteemed by every philosopher. The tale told by this chivalrous man, in all the ardour of a glowing imagination, and how
he imagined he saw the Divine One in all His majesty, is well
known. Besides various illustrious barons of the middle ages,
intimately connected with this family by marriage, we have the
gallant and the good Sir Philp Sidney, the most chivalrous hero,
and the most generous in his bravery, that England, with all her
noble sons, ever saw. The beauties of his romantic "Arcadia,"

and the sweetness of his sonnets are "oft-told tales." At
Wilton, too, lived William, Earl of Pembroke, the father of
the High Steward, a man of princely generosity, but sullied
by an extreme love of pleasure. This princely noble patronised
Ben Jonson, and, it is supposed, Shakspere. He gave them
money, and they gave him in return for "gold that perisheth,"
IMMORTALITY. Glorious Ben wrote his matchless epitaph on
a Countess of Pembroke, mother to Earl William. Does not
every one know it?

> "Underneath this sable hearse,
>   Lies the subject of all verse!—
>   Sidney's sister, Pembroke's mother.
>   Death! ere thou hast slain another,
>   Learn'd and fair and good as she,
>   Time shall throw a dart at thee."

To this Earl, Ben Jonson dedicated his book of stinging
epigrams. The tone is eulogistic, and therefore honourable to
the earl, for when was Ben insincere? He says—

> " Thou, whose virtues keep one stature still,
>   And the true posture keep in spite of ill;
>   Or what ambition, fashion, pride can raise,
>   Whose life, e'en they that envy it, must praise."

and again he dedicates "to the great example of honour and
nature." "While I cannot change your merit, I dare not
change your title; it was you that made it, not I; I must
expect at your lordship's hand protection while you are con-
stant in your goodness." With respect to Shakespere, a great
cloud of mystery envelopes the Pembroke family. The sonnets
were originally published, dedicated by T. T. (Thorp) "to
their only begetter, Mr. W. H." Critics translate this into
the vernacular as meaning William Herbert, Earl Pembroke.
It is possible that some of his sweet sonnets were written by
Shakspere to his noble patron. They breathe the exaggerated
idea of friendship peculiar to the age, whereon Coleridge,
in his Table Talk, has some remarks, full of his usual sensibility
and sagacity, speaking of the sonnets as generally believed to
be addressed to the Earl of Pembroke, the most beloved man

of his age, although his licentiousness was equal to his virtues. "I doubt this," he says, "I do not think that Shakspere, merely because he was an actor, should have thought it necessary to veil his esteem towards Pembroke under a disguise, although he might if the real object perchance had been a Laura or a Leonora. It seems to me that the sonnets could only have come from a man deeply in love with a woman; and there is one sonnet, which, from its purposed incongruity, I think to have been an intentional blind. The sonnets are, in fact, a poem of several stanzas, of so many lines each, and like the passion that inspired them, always the same." Coleridge proceeds to remark on their harmony, condensation of expression, and considers them, like the Venus and Adonis, the evident offshoots of a young poet. We think no one can differ from Coleridge who has once read the sonnets, and who has not? The 28th, for instance, is evidently addressed to a loved mistress; while others, like the 104th, "To me, fair friend, thou never can be old," are quite consistent with the glowing gratitude of a poet to his beloved patron. So also the 30th, that beautiful one beginning

"When to the session of sweet silent thought
I summon up remembrance of things past."

Some modern writers suggest that Ann Hathaway, Shakspere's wife, may have been seduced by the Earl, but we would not willingly entertain so illiberal a suspicion. The 152nd, "In loving thee thou knows't I am forsworn," would hardly bear this harsh interpretation, and rather refers to some lover's quarrel. A temporary divorce is indeed said to have taken place between him and his wife, who died some dozen years after him. The sonnets were published by Thorpe in 1609, while William Herbert succeeded his father in 1601; this, at all events, makes the dedication to Mr. W. H. rather uncourteous. The first folio of 1623, edited by Hemmings and other fellow-comedians, was dedicated to the Earl, who was known to be of literary taste. This mystery, perhaps never to be solved, adds a thousand-fold interest to this beautiful picture. The mother of this Earl was a daughter of the Duke of Northumberland, his father's first wife being of royal blood, but dying without issue.

Lord Clarendon speaks in the highest terms of this Earl. He says, "he was the most loved and esteemed of any man of that age, and having a great office (Chamberlain) in the court, he made the court better esteemed and more reverenced in the country. He had a great number of friends, and no enemies. He was well bred, and of excellent parts, an excellent-humoured man, and brother-in-law to the Earl of Shrewsbury. His expenses were only limited by his great mind. He was not loved by James. He succeeded in office the famous Carr, Earl of Somerset, the senseless favourite of a pedant, who was more fit to wield the ferule than the sceptre. He had no ambition, but loved his country. He was excessively addicted to pleasure." His mind was injured by these excesses, and he finally died of apoplexy, after a hearty supper,—a retributive death which many epicures have met. Clarendon speaks of his death as happening happily for his fame, just as the flame of civil war broke forth. His brother, we believe, succeeded to his office. He had been, from the beauty of his person, a great favourite with James, but with a prudence peculiar to his family, he gave way to the rising fortunes of Carr. He also endeared himself to the king by his love, real or assumed, for that gentle craft, hunting. He became in Charles's time Governor of the Isle of Wight. but, alas! sullied the honour of his family by treating with the Puritans, and preserving a traitorous sort of neutrality,—trembling for Wilton and his broad domains. His temporizing proceeded rather from fear of consequences than from a disloyal heart; for during the King's residence in Holland, the faithful Clarendon always speaks of the Earl as one on whom they might count. As a Puritan would say, he ever remained a concealed malignant, or as we should reply, the base fear of temporal losses neve extinguished the innate loyalty of his heart. The beautiful seats connected by association with the family are Penshurst, in Kent, sung of by Ben Jonson, and Wilton, where Sir Philip Sidney wrote his Arcadia. A descendant of the family, Lady Dorothea Sidney, was wooed, but wooed in vain by the poet

Waller. His poems addressed to her under the name of Sacharissa (my sweetest) are still preserved. Memorials of all these celebrities are preserved at the two places.

Such recollections did this noble picture call up in my mind.

CHAPTER XXII.

THE DRUIDS' TEMPLE AT STANTON DREW, NEAR BRISTOL.

> " Alter Zeiten alte treue Zengen
>   Schmückt euch doch des Lebens frisches Grün,
>   Und der Vorwelt kräftige gestalten,
>   Sind uns noch, in eur Pracht erhalten."

> " Ye old true witnesses of times long fled,
>   Life's freshest verdure tricks each ancient head,
>   And mighty forms of ancient worlds gone by,
>   Stand round us, robed in antique majesty."
>
> *Die Eichen of Korner.*

> " Four stones, with their heads of moss, are the only memorials of thee; the grass grows between the stones of the tomb; the thistle is there alone shedding its ancient beard. Two stones half sunk in the ground, show their heads of moss. A tale of the times of old—the deeds of the days of other years."—*Ossian.*

COMMEND me to the walks round Bristol, for natural beauty and interest of association. The poet may wander at the foot of thick fairy-haunted woods, by the side of the brown Avon, where Southey, Coleridge, and Lamb have rambled before him; or from the hill of Almondsbury he may admire the lovely landscape that opens to his view, where the silver Severn pouring its tributary flood into the ocean, while in the far distance the blue mountains of Wales melt into the horizon, which is scarcely of an azure less intense than the sky which floats over the scene; or he may saunter on the Down, whether it be decked, as the seasons change with the snowy May blossom, the golden gorse, or the purple heather, and gazing from the beetling crags, or far across the plain, he may think of bygone times, when British huts covered that area, and in the distance was heard the tramp of the legionaries and the rumbling of war-chariots, while the Roman eagle might be seen as if ready to pounce on its prey. Then to the mind's eye blaze up ruddily the signal-fires on the top of Brandon's hill, which are answered by a flash from some distant cliff, as through the wood gleams a fire on an opposite headland, and the painted Britons grasp their hatchets, and leap into their scythed chariots, and——but does not every walk open fresh tableaux of history? And whether we watch the silent Avon stealing on its way to the sea, glance at some old grey tower, or pass through a street of old fantastic houses, all here seems more redolent of the past than the present.

But of Stanton Drew:—The walk from Bristol is pretty enough, were there even no witnesses of the past awaiting you at the goal as a reward for voluntary labour. The high road winds like a river, at " its own sweet will," amid wooded hills, through quaint villages, to which old Elizabethan houses give an antique character, and prepare the mind for those " ancient of days," the Druidical stones of which you are in quest. At the very outset, there is a beautiful view of the city and environs from a commanding point. In the hollow of an amphitheatre of hills lies our miniature Rome, the city on seven hills, the city of churches. Near, but below us, rises the battered gray tower of Temple, nearer still the truncated spire of old Redcliff, while even now, its chimes comes sighing towards us in the wind, and blending with the hum of the great city. Beyond lie in a cluster the Grecian towers of Christchurch, and the old Gothic ones of St. Werburgh, All Saints, and Mary-le-port, and far above all rises the airy beauty of St. Stephens. Below, in dark and almost an indistinguishable mass, lie the four cross streets, the ancient nucleus of the city, the old city gate of St. John's, the Avon we see flowing through all, and that black Lethe-like stream, the Frome, once called the fair; around lie white villages dotting the hills, looking like colonies from that one great black swarm, and amidst them

rise many heaven-pointing spires. Over all, although it is
September, and the leaf is rustling down, the sun shines
sweetly, and the sky is blue overhead, while the lark pipes
aloft at "heaven's gate." Autumn seems to be mimicking
summer, and aping, with her withered cheek and wrinkled
brow, the smiling joyousness of youthful summer.

But we must on our way. It is Autumn, reader, a season
which we love, and all around, in Nature, seems to harmonise
with the association of bye-gone ages. These monstrous tomb-
stones of the past, these monuments of departed centuries
should be seen in autumn. We venture to lay this down as a
most oracular *dictum*. Spring, with its budding leaf and
springing flowers, is too joyous a time to think of the dead;
summer, again, is all too merry, and too full of "gauds." But
melancholy Autumn is the time, when the berries shine ruddy
on every hedge, and the brown leaf rustles to the ground, and
its companions turn crimson, and golden, and brown, and a
thousand other colours, as if they could escape the grasp of icy
winter by these Protean changes. Now, too, we hear by the
roadside the little brooks rippling louder, and they seem to be
prating musically to pray cold, chilly Winter to tarry, if but for
one little week longer, in his snowy palaces of the north. But
he comes relentless, and the swallow prepares for his flight to
burning Africa, and the robin alone pipes, and sweetly too, from
yonder hedge, which, though it has all the summer been a
beautiful entanglement of eglantine, and hawthorn and wild
flowers, now begins to look dreary, as the cold bleak, piping
winds, winter's *avant couriers*, whistle through it. This is the
time for thoughts of the past, now that the sunsets no longer
tint the clouds with a thousand gorgeous hues of fiery and of
golden light; and there is but a chill, ruddy farewell gleam in
the West, while in the pale morning the East is drear and
grey.

In this dim light, at a season when the sky is but a
mass of dull leaden-coloured cloud, did we sally forth for
Stanton Drew, or, in other words, "the stone town of the
Druids." There is no flat monotony about the road, which
winds snake-like as a river, through quaint hamlets, and cot-

tages with the rose still blooming round their diamond panes, and past old hostelries too, with signs representing obscure naval heroes, whose fame and bodies have long since been gathered to their fathers' mausoleum. Here the road is half-shaded by trees; for the golden-leafed elm, and the silver-shafted birch, and the giant oak, its trunk of a dusky brown, and the alder, with its stem of frosted silver, and the primeval pine are all there; and then we catch glimpses of sloping meadows, which are each, mayhap, the whole world of some rustic boy, and perhaps, if he has a sense of the poetry of life, a world filled with a thousand forms of beauties. Another winding, and we see a little brook ripple over its pebbly bed through entangled shrubs, and even this tells of Autumn, for its little current is strewed with yellow leaves. Here is a lone meadow with a dark pond, over which a willow hangs; such a place as we dream of, and think of poor Ophelia's fate. Bridle paths here and there lead from the road, into wooded recesses, where one might expect to find none but the monarch Pan or some attendant Dryad. Around us and about us, on all sides, as far as the horizon, are hills and sloping fields, which blend in the distance.

And over all these scenes which our imagination may have coloured, there is impending like a thunder cloud the solemn stillness of Autumn. The only sounds are the fall of the whirling leaf and the robin's mournful note. All nature seems preparing for her winter's sleep.

"Is this the turning to the Druidical temple?" said we, majestically, to an old animated skeleton, who, in accordance with England's admirable system of relief, was kneeling breaking stones by the roadside. The poor old wretch, half in his grave, should rather have been enjoying the genial heat of his own hearth, surrounded by half-a-dozen chubby grand-children.

"*Temple?*" said the animated skeleton, evidently pozed, but not liking to show it, resting on his hammer, and scratching his head, and speaking after awhile in a tone of savage rebuke. "You mean the *stauns* at Stanton? First turning to your right from *my* next stone heap."

We thanked the old man and plodded on; the animated

skeleton's hammer we could hear feebly chipping for half-a-mile. Not many persons did we meet; a few old couples, regular Baucis and Philemons, going on their weekly visit to Bristol, *their* great metropolis; a recruiting sergeant, with two entrapped bumpkins with ribbons on their caps. We walked two miles and met not a soul. But we have passed through some pretty dells, where the tops of the trees have been level with the road, and we have passed a deserted house, which is always food for conjecture. The pathway to the door was grass-grown, and the garden had run wild, but, amidst all the ruin, a few roses were still blooming profusely. Now we quicken our steps, for just at the bend of that hill in the distance we discern a pedlar, one of a craft which we have loved ever since we read, at ten years of age, of the doings of that merry knave, Autolycus, "the picker-up of unconsidered trifles." That stiff hill has pulled him up, for his pack is heavy, and we are now upon his heels. Ha! that is a French *vaudeville* he hums—

> "Mais le plus grand plaisir
> Que le Printems me donne,
> C'est quand le vigne bourgeonne."

We have come up to him now, and find he *is* a Frenchman. We enter into conversation, and get familiar on the lonely way. He tells us, with all the gaiety of a ruined Gaul, that he was born in beautiful Le Vendée, that seat of ancient loyalty, and had finally settled as a jeweller in the Palais Royal, and having married (*telle femme!*), and was prospering, too, when that *revolution maudite* broke out. He described to us the "*silence triste et morne*" of that horrible night of blood, when nothing could be heard but the wail of the tocsin, the rumble of artillery and caissons, and suddenly the thundering clang of cavalry. Then he rose and joined the National Guard, and fought at the barricades against those "Coquins and larrons," the Rouge Republicans. He had received a pike wound while storming one of those obstacles to peace in the Faubourg St. Antoine, and fell. A republican hag stabbed him, but his brave comrades bore him off, and he soon recovered. But, alas! since the peace, trade was gone, and he was, after all, compelled to shut up his shop, send his wife and children to "dear La Vendée," and trudge to England, pack on back, and visit the land of " milords " and rich millionaires, as a pedlar.

" C'est tout, me voila," said our companion, smiling good-naturedly, as he left us, for he wanted to offer his wares at an old farm-house on the brow of a neighbouring hill.

We parted from him with the less regret, when about half-a-mile further on we found an Italian organ man sitting on a heap of stones by the way-side. We passed him with a " Buon giorno."

" Parlate Italiano, Signor ?" he said, getting up smiling and trudging on with us.

We said " Si," and began talking to him, in *la dolce farilla*, the mellifluous language of his country, of the state of Italy, and of its patriots Garibaldi and ——. He seemed delighted, for he had left before the outbreaks, and had heard but very incorrect accounts of them at his nightly meetings with his countrymen, in trampers' lodging-houses ; and how his eyes sparkled with delight, as we recited in an enthusiastic tone that beautiful sonnet of Filicaja's :—

> " Italia, Italia, tu cui feo la sorte
> Dono infelice de bellezza,
> Deh fossi tu men bella o almen più forte."

" O Italy, Italy, to whom, in unhappy hour, the fatal gift of beauty was given, would thy beauty were less, or thy power more."

At first he grasped his organ staff like a sword, and again looked more mournful than ever when we came to the final line—

> " Per servir sempre, o 'vincitrice, ò vinta."

He had heard of Filicaja, for his *padrone* would have brought him up as improvisatore, had he not disliked the 'dolce far niente' (the sweet pleasure of doing nothing), and preferred a wandering Bedouin sort of life. He then told me that he was born near the Ghetto, or Jews' quarter, in Rome.

S

"Ah!" said we, "Roma, Roma, non era piu com era prima," quoting a song of the Campagna.

This touched too tender a chord by far, he stopped and sat down on the bank by the road-side, and burst into tears, burying his face in his hands.

We passed on. Reproach him not, reader, for you know not what deep thoughts of home and his loved ones those simple words may have awakened.

One winding lane more, then past a mediæval thatched, conical, comical turnpike-house, and we are landed in Stanton. A pretty and clear trout brook runs through the village, which in the summer is greatly haunted by urchins, who dabble about and scare away the speckled trout with crooked pins, much to the rage of old Izaak Waltons. Then here and there, on the right hand and on the left, are tranquil-looking mansions, possessing in the highest degree that mixture of ugliness and comfort in which a true Englishman rejoices. There is one with an old dial on the lawn in front, and another of an Inigo Jones sort of air, and besides these there is a one-roomed "public," (so called by courtesy), "house," where the best "apple wine" and home-baked bread are to be procured. An Elizabethan house, a fine farm yard, some old cottages with arched doors; and, above all, an old mediæval grey church, full of monuments, and surrounded by a "God's acre," in which "the rude forefathers of the hamlet sleep," complete the village. If every cottage were an alms-house for an ancient Druid, the place could not be more quiet. A whisper reverberates through the village, a loud footstep attracts as much attention as a troop of cavalry would in a city. Every house looks unaltered since the days "when good King Charles was king," and no great effort of the imaginative faculty is required to picture a troop of cavaliers or Ironsides riding through in hot pursuit. We asked for the "stoans" of a very pallid baker, who was slowly driving on foot a cart containing a pretty rosy-cheeked child, seated on a pile of quartern loaves, like a victim on an altar. We found them, after receiving an ironical round of cheers from a party of juvenile Somersetshires, who expressed it audibly, as their private opinion, that we were "a spinning along like anythink."

The old monsters of the past stand in a tranquil field adjoining an orchard and a farm-yard, and the first view of these stony skeletons is very impressive, although the blocks are at a considerable distance from each other. The Druids had planned three distinct circles, forming the *circus*, emblematical of the sun's supposed revolution, and composed of stones, some of which are four yards square. The first great circle is of five stones, many of which the local savages, aided by that great savage, Time, have considerably injured. Then there is a circle of eight, with a diameter, says Seyer, of 96 feet, the circumference of which is just 150 feet distant from the other. Next, is the south-west circle, or lunar temple, also emblematical of planetary revolutions. It is composed of eleven stones, having a diameter of 110 feet, and being distant from the centre of the great circle 714 feet. There is also, about 100 yards to the north-west, a cave, so called, ten feet wide, and eight feet deep, formed of three large flat stones, eighteen inches thick. North of this are two large stones, lying flat in a field; and beyond an adjoining brook, is a very large stone, called, locally, " Hachell's Quoit," being, we presume, the supposed work of a giant.

Local intellect is undoubtedly highly mystified as to these relics. The children of the hamlet don't play at " hide and seek " about them after dusk, and if public-house oracles are infallible, groans, &c. are not unfrequently to be heard in the stone-close, " when the moon is out," towards the sma' hours. One gaping rustic told us, " as how some do zay that it's a wedding, and that the fiddlers and the bride and groom were all petrified as they went to church." Now this idea is probably a fable of the seventeenth century, when music always preceded a couple to church. Another old dame said, " Others do zay, nobody can't count 'em ; certain 'tis a baker did try with loaves on each, and they never could come right. But there 'tis, some do zay one thing, and zum another, that there's no believing none of 'em." So we thought, reader, don't you ? An intelligent old farmer told us he had seen men dig several yards down without getting to the foundation of one of these stones. The stone is certainly not of the neighbourhood, being chiefly old red sand-stone, half

vitrified with intense heat in some great convulsion of our globe.
Some of them, however, were of limestone, and have been used
to pave the roads. May the bones of those who did it be mixed
with their dust. One or two of these antique giants have now
fallen from their high estate, and others are tottering to their
ruin; we saw no Druidical rock basins in any of them, but
time had cloven in all of them vast gaps and fissures, which
were full of rain water; all were covered thick with various
sorts of lichen, and on many grew wild flowers, blooming,
as if mocking at decay; we need hardly tire our readers with
the natural association of such a scene. The centre altar-stone
of the chief circle is a gigantic block as large as an Egyptian
obelisk, on which, doubtless, human blood has often been shed,
when the Prince of Cornwall, before the time of Stonehenge,
ruled over Cavenodor and all the west of England.

We thought—who could help it?—of the Druids, those white-
robed believers in one God, those teachers of a pure Sabaism,
of a metempsychosis, and a future state. All the lays of the
bards their attendants rang in our ears, for does not old
Taliesin say :—

"They talk of the proud and magnificent circle round which the majestic
oaks, the symbols of Tayreny, the God of thunder, spread their arms."

And again, when he is watching the rock-basin, he says—

"A cormorant approaches me with large wings; she assaults the top
stone with her hoarse clamours; there is wrath in the fates, let it burst
through the stone."

Then we think of the priests of Baal, so often mentioned in
Scripture, who cut themselves with knives in honour of their
God. Aneurin, too, says, like Taliesin—

"Let the thigh be pierced in blood."

And again—

"In honour of the mighty king of the plants, the king of the open
countenance. I saw dark gore arising from the stalks of plants, and on the
clasps of the chain; while the circular evolutions were performed by the
attendants and the white bands with graceful extravagance. The assembled train were dancing after their manner, and singing in cadence with the
garlands on their brows."

We have no doubt that the Druids first taught a pure Deism, in temples of stone, intended to represent the sun, the supposed abode of God. But soon this faith became corrupted, and the belief which they had brought from Tartary changed into the worship of Hertha, and the god of war, and the oak god, or the quickener, &c. Indeed, Oriental scholars trace a strong connection in Druidism with the faith of the Hindoo; the very names of their deities can be detected; their symbolic circle is the emblem of Brama; their crescent, of Siva; their crucial cross is Egyptian; their magic rod resembles that of the Brahmins; their reverence to oxen is like the worship of Apis; their beads, and lustrations, and tiaras, are all Oriental; their astrology is Chaldaic. What a pure morality did they teach. These were their laws—"The universe is eternal—the soul is immortal. Honour thou nature, defend thy mother, thy country, the earth. Admit women in thy counsels. Honour the stranger, and put aside his share in thy harvest. Let the infamous be buried in mire. Do not raise temples, and trust the history of the past to thy memory alone. Man, be free—be without property. Honour the old man, and may never the young one be a witness against him. The brave will be rewarded after death—the coward will be punished."

The stones which form these temples are covered with lichens and a grey moss, which seems to furnish a soil for numerous plants.

A local historian sums up the statistics of this rare old place, which are too unromantic for us. He says, "There are altogether three circles of stones, the largest of which, like Stonehenge, is in reality a sort of ellipsis. Within is a great altar-stone, as at Stonehenge, placed towards the east; the greatest diameter of the large circle is 126 yards; the largest stone is 9 feet high, and measures 22 feet in circumference; thirteen stones remain, with foundations of others; the original number is supposed to have been thirty. The circle of eight, on the eastward, is 96 feet in diameter, and the moon's temple 120 feet across. Mr. Phelps, the Somersetshire historian, says, "These remains may be classed with Abury, in Wiltshire, from the rudeness of their execution, and they bear a close resem-

blanco to those of Carnac, in Britanny,"—that land of forests
and Armorican tradition. Near Dundry we also observed a large
cistvaen, or sepulchral mound, beneath which repose, perhaps,
the bones of some ancient British prince. It covers the area
of a whole field. The soil all around Stanton is impregnated
with iron, and its rich red hue gives a fine tone to the landscape, cheering to the heart of the farmer, as it tells him of
hidden geological riches.

We have no doubt that these monstrous stones were dragged
thither by the united strength of a whole tribe; indeed, some
of the Welsh triads distinctly refer to such efforts when they
talk of great undertakings being "like the labour at the stone
of strength."

Just a little below these remains of Paganism, stands the old
church, founded by the holders of a purer religion, which was
unknown when these stones were first dragged to their present
position.

But a chapter on the Druids would involve a volume. So
imagine us, prithee, good reader, plodding home, and, when
arrived there, sitting down to our desk and writing the above.
Farewell, "a word that has been, and that must be," 'tis
spoken with regret, but still,—FAREWELL.

CHAPTER XXIII.

A SOMERSETSHIRE WALK.

"But here no more soft music flows,
No holy anthem's chanted now;
All hush'd, except the ring-dove's note,
Low murmuring from the beechen bough."

WHAT a dismal thing is an Autumn morning. So we thought
as we looked out from the diamond-paned window of an old-
fashioned inn in the pretty monastic little village of Banwell.
Our hostelrie, reader, was one of those which are eulogised in
so sweet a manner by old patriarchal Izaak Walton—"Where
the bed with its clean sheets smells of lavender, and the walls

are decked with some simple ballads." Or, as Keats says, more poetically—

> " Where azure-lidded sheep
> May rest on beds, all blanched and lavendered."

It was a little before dawn when we looked out towards the Mendips, which, covered with a blue mist, stretched away towards the sea, their outline looking fainter and fainter, till they blended with the cold grey mist of the morning. Almost at the very instant we looked forth the dawn commenced, with a faint, pallid glare in the East, which anon turned into a pale crimson glow, and soon subsided into the misty, leaden-coloured obscurity of an October morning. It was a very ghastly imitation of a July morn, and a miserable aping of the aerial pageantry of summer. We were getting quite abusive against autumn, when suddenly the sun gleamed forth through the chill air and lit up the whole scene before us, the hill-tops in the distance, the old towers of many churches that rose around us gleaming coldly, while its rays gave a look of cheerfulness even to the trees, clad in their golden-coloured foliage of autumn. We took a hasty breakfast, and sallied out through the hamlet, which antiquarians say is so called from *Bann* (deep) and *Weilgi* (sea), having been in former ages covered by the waters of the sea and the Severn. The village, situated in a rich valley, is about six miles from Axbridge, and thirteen from Bristol. Nothing can be more interesting than its legendary and historical recollections. Like most of the Somersetshire hamlets, its associations are of great antiquity, a monastery having been founded here by one of the West Saxon kings, at the time when England was split up into little kingdoms. The great Alfred appointed to this ecclesiastical establishment his well-known favourite Ayser. It was destroyed during the Danish wars, probably by piratical bands, who landed on the adjacent Somersetshire coast, but was, however, soon restored, for Edward the Confessor took it from that ambitious chief, Earl Harold, and bestowed it on Dudaco, the Lombard Bishop of Wells. In the fifteenth century, about the time of Henry V., an era when many of the beautiful and richly-decorated churches of Somersetshire were built, this bishop erected an episcopal palace here, which was pulled down many years since, after having been first turned into a modern mansion. The monastery once belonged to the Duke of Somerset, but after his attainder, ruthless Queen Mary restored it to the bishopric of Wells. This same munificent prelate built the fine old church of Banwell, dedicating it, we believe, to St. Andrew. The tower, richly decorated, is 100 feet high. There is some good painted glass within the holy pile, and a fine brass, dated 1554. There are, besides, part of a rood loft, an old font, some parish records, commencing 1805, and other objects of interest. The village is, in fact, full of monastic reminiscences, and there are still remains of parts of the old monastery, and a market cross. Bishop Paul Bush, of Bristol, whose skeleton monument is in Bristol cathedral, was once connected in some way with this place. There is also a mineral spring in the village. The adjacent hamlets are Rolston, Westwick, Towerhead, Knightcot, Yarborough, &c. It is in a place like this that we forget all the errors of the monks, and think of them only with gratitude as the heralds of civilization in these wild districts, and the precursors of a purer religion. As we give a parting look at the old tower, we think too—

> "How many hearts have here grown cold,
> That sleep these mouldering stones among;
> How many beads have here been told,
> How many matins have been sung."

Passing on, we wended our way to the antediluvian caves, which are situated in the grounds of a cottage built by the late Bishop of Bath and Wells, the grounds of which are laid out with much taste, on the western side of a hill above the village. A beautiful view from the summit repays the traveller for a clamber up a steep ascent, and an unrivalled panorama lies before us in a bird's-eye glance. Behind us lay the dark chain of the Mendips, among which Bleadon (Bleakdown) rises boldly towards the sky, and Brent knoll is hardly less conspicuous. To the south the splendid spire of Bridgwater church points its stony finger to the sky. To the north rises the spire of the old Bristol hamlets of Congresbury and Yatton, and towards the west lie Weston and Worle. Beyond the Severn sea, which stretches, gleaming in the sun like molten silver, in the furthest horizon, extends the dark line of the Monmouthshire coast, broken by the Abergavenny mountains. This beautiful spot on which we stand, some thirty years ago was nothing but the bleak hill side, occasionally quarried for its hidden treasures of lapis calaminaris, ochre, and lead. While blasting some immense piles of mountain limestone, the astonished miners accidentally struck upon a cavern, which, in times before the flood, is supposed, by fair induction, to have been the den of the wolf and the grisly bear. This immense orifice, consisting of a large area, with two diverging galleries, was found filled with loose alluvial earth, intermixed with the bones of the buffalo, the stag, the rein-deer, the fox, the wild cat, and the bat, and of the older tenants mentioned above. Following the gardener as our guide, we explored the cavern, lighted by torches. Nothing could be more impressive than its dark recesses, lighted by a feeble glare that hardly disclosed the dark, irregular masses of rock which formed the roof. The great geologist, Dr. Buckland, who wrote without visiting the place, calls them, in his *Bridgwater Treatise*, one of those caverns which are filled by the bones of animals which fell in or crowded here together for safety at the deluge. But the immense quantity of these bones, which were piled up in large heaps and columns on the floor of the cave, prove that it was the haunt of bears, who preyed on the buffalo roaming in the wooded valley beneath, and whose carcases they dragged hither to gnaw at leisure. Indeed, many of the ox bones appear gnawed at the place where the cartilage joined the bone. Our guide seemed to have a personal acquaintance with every bone, and talked as glibly of the "ulna," "radius," "humerus," and "tibia," as a young surgeon would of the contents of his dissecting-room. Many of the bone relics are quite colossal in proportion. Mr. Beard, a clever antiquarian of the neighbourhood, has preserved some very fine specimens, which prove the animals to have been of quadruple the present size; one leg bone of an extinct species of elephant is as large as a man's

thigh. In a curious cave in Bleadon-hill, the bones of elephants, hyænas, rhinoceri, and other tropical animals, have also
been found, but no remains of man. Who can imagine the
Mendips haunted by monsters, against whom all the strength
of man would have been ineffectual.

The roof of Banwell cave drips with liquid carbonate lime,
which tends to preserve the bones, and some of the oozings
from the rock have already petrified into stalactites. These
interesting remains have been carefully preserved almost exactly as found, by the wish of the late Bishop. On the wall
of the garden are some marble tablets inscribed with appropriate lines of a devotional character—alluding to the hill
having once been a spot devoted to Druidical rites. The only
drawbacks to the *tout ensemble* are two Cockney-looking
grottoes, which are whitewashed and decorated in the worst
possible taste, and on a mound of turf near is a sham Druidical
altar. A short walk through the grounds brought us out on a
bridle path on the bleak fern-covered hill, and we turned our
faces towards "Maxwell mills." Before us lay many ranges
of hills, stretching as far as we could see on either hand, occasionally broken into dells by mutual intersection. Many
of them are partially cultivated, and the stubble gleamed yellow in the sun on the dark hill side. Some of them, the highest of the chain, rose far in the distance, and were tinted by
the sun's mellow golden light, while those nearer still were
dark and over-shadowed, as if by the vast black wing of some
evil spirit. Here and there, on the side of a hill, a man might
be seen ploughing on places so steep, that it seemed problematical whether in some unlucky lurch, plough and ploughman
might not roll together into the valley below. We traversed a
rough field path, pushed through a picturesque field or two, and
passing some tranquil-looking cottages, and a public-house
with a great elm-tree before the door, under whose shade, and
under the sign, as if under the banner of their liege lord, Sir
John Barleycorn, sat some sages, discussing a capacious pot of old
ale, and the newest news, we got into the main road. We passed
through some pretty lanes, turned up a high road, at the side
of which a spectral sort of sign-post pointed its lank-black

finger, and we reached Maxwell. There a little stream, dammed up till it had formed quite a miniature lake, turns a mill, and having performed that piece of industry, wanders about among the meadows in a very reckless sort of way indeed. Autumn's rule was evident in every tree and bush, even in the sallow flags and rushes that peered out of the brooks, that rippled cheerfully by the wayside. Every tree had lost its gay livery of Summer, and seemed as golden as if Midas, in a freak of regal fancy, had coined each leaf into a little plate of the precious metal. One might fancy that we were in the realms of the Arabian Sorcerer, or those regions of Mammon, where the trees bear jewels instead of leaves.

These are the beginning of the enchantments of that aerial wizard Winter, who after turning them to gold, tinting them with a thousand ruddy hues, and stamping them with the livid plague-spots of decay, sends his "piping winds" to strip them from their parent tree, and to drive them with a cruel persecution over the hill and the moor, and the ploughed field and up the lane, and over the high road, wherever they assemble in little knots, these withered leaves, as if whispering conspiracy, these savage myrmidons of the icy king rush at them and send them rustling to the four quarters of Daven. And the sun, too, that great alchemist, now tints the already golden leaves with a deeper yellow, and the great fanlike leaves of the chestnut. The carvelled leaf of the eastern sycamore and the flowerlike keys of the ash, and in the orchard by the wayside, the ruby-dyed foliage of the apple, whirl in the wind and come eddying to the ground, and every now and then, across the hard, dry road, a leaf crackles driven by the breeze, and that is the only sound. Banwell is a sort of nucleus of field and road, where at night you might expect some will-o'-the-wisp with his livid torch might beguile you to muddy death in the horrible depths of some dark swamp. But enough of Autumn; a few more turns, after a judicious enquiry at a cottage window, of a blooming Somersetshire maiden, bring us to Winscombe Hill. After passing through an irregular street, with a few cottages, and a ruined barn, &c., which form the village, you see an old church that stands at a little distance to the right of the road. It is a lofty decorated building, with a beautiful tower all carvelled and enriched in the most gorgeous manner that stone is susceptible of. Some fine old trees, emblems of immortality, stand in the "God's acre," "where the rude forefathers of the hamlet sleep." We were slowly toiling up Wiscombe Hill, which runs through a pretty defile, we had just reached the top, we say, and were listening to the rushing of the wind amongst the branches of some funeral-looking pines which deck its brow, when we were overtaken by a cheerful-looking old farmer, with a scarlet waistcoat, on his way to Axbridge. We gathered from a chat with him, and his broadest "Zummerzetshire" dialect, full of "zurs" and "thicks," &c., that he had just sold at a very satisfactory price, to another farmer, an old white mare, which for many years had alternately pulled at the plough, and bore him once a week to Wells market. Now this very satisfactory sale had thrown our friend into a state of great placidity, and had given him a very good opinion of the world in general. An ominous jingle in his pocket at each step told us of "hid treasure," and the shadow of a smile of ill-concealed self-complacency lurked about the wrinkled corners of his mouth. After having, in the bubbling over-warmth of his heart, pulled out a sort of portable bracket-clock, *alias* a watch, which he carried in his pocket, and then offered us a pinch from a huge sarcophagus, which we courteously called his snuff-box, he fell unsolicited into an amusing gossip of his youthful recollections. We won't trouble the reader with his tales about his "old missus," or his opinion of the minister, whom he thought "a great scollard, and a good Latiner," but we will briefly relate what he told us he had heard his grandfather "zay" about the highwaymen that once haunted that pass. The stages used to be frequently stopped there, and single travellers were often robbed in the winter as they passed over Axbridge Moor by night. Once, he said, a gentleman who had "taken the road," let the passengers of a stage pass on trust, on condition that a pretty lady inside would dance a minuet with him on the moor. "And he was quite the gentleman, and never would rob the poor, but would give them a guinea or two now and then, when he called at their houses for anything by night." This anecdote reminded us of something we had heard of Claude Duval in Charles II.'s time, but we did not interrupt the worthy farmer.

While our garrulous friend was thus haranguing on "the tales of the days of other years," we had reached Axbridge Moor. A Roman road is here half visible amongst the grass on one side of the road, while the little river Axe flows at a little distance below. The great Bridgewater road crosses to the right, and the Mendips stretch nobly away towards the sea in the distance. Here the poor people believe the "good folk" (fairies) still linger and gambol by the light of the moon, under the shadow of the hills. We catch a view of a wooded slope, rich with the tints of autumn, and we enter the long street which forms the village of Axbridge. But this, although it is very quickly written on paper, took us some considerable time in walking; and before this we had met an old, lank man in seedy black, a friend of my new companion, who, making a rustic bow to us, entered into conversation with him. He proved to be the "Croquemort," *alias* sexton, of some adjacent hamlet. Our good-humoured farmer drew him out for our especial amusement, and for about half-an-hour we talked of nothing but "graves, and worms, and epitaphs." He told us several curious anecdotes of his ghostly craft, one of the most curious of which, and the only one worth repeating, was his digging up, some years back, the wedding-ring of his wife, whom he had buried sixteen years before. Not a bone of her body could, however, be found, and he believed that it had been carried off by resurrection-men; the ring dropping from the shrunk finger, had probably been trodden into the loose soil. He knew the ring, he said, well, by a mark he had himself made upon it at his marriage. Just then we entered the interesting old village, and our farmer turned off to refresh himself with a cup of cider at a friend's house with the sexton; and they were received, as we could see through the window, by a pretty dark-eyed maiden, who, we doubt not, is the belle of the village!

WRINGTON.

A few miles further brings us into Wrington, after wandering through some pretty lanes, after passing an old posting inn which was shut up long ago, and which looks like some vast mausoleum reared to the genius of coaching, an effete science; and above all, some orchards, where the trees are bowing down with the weight of ruddy apples, and where some urchins, with cheeks as rosy as the apples, are pelting each other with the fruit, in spite of all the remonstrances of a gray-headed grandfather, while the orchard re-echoes with their silver-toned laughter.

A long lane leads us into Wrington; the houses begin to thicken, hostelries get more numerous, and above them the fine tower of the village church peers over all, the streets thicken and diverge as from a nucleus of four. We anxiously enquire for the house of the great Locke, who, we know, was born here in the year 1632. To our great delight, every boy in the street, even the group playing for " dear life" at leap-frog near the chief inn, knew all about " Mr. Locke ;" and under the guidance of the head boy, who volunteers to pilot us, with an ultimate eye to a prospective penny, we sally on. A short turn up a little half-paved lane, past a row of clean cottages, in many of which a pleasant fire is glowing, and we arrive at the object of our pilgrimage. It is an humble, clean, thatched house, close to the churchyard, the last of a row leading from one of the principal streets. It consists of two stories, and, in our own day, might be the fit abode for a gardener or higher order of labourer ; although Locke's father was a man of some landed property, and of Dorsetshire extraction. A man who could afford to send his son to college, and train him up to one of the liberal professions, would hardly live in such a cottage at the present day.

Never did saint feel more devout when he reached the shrine of his patron saint, never crusader at the sight of Jerusalem, than we did at the sight of a house so connected with the memory of the greatest philosopher of England in modern, or, perhaps, any time,—that great man, who first made an intelligent use of the sublime principles laid down by Bacon ; who earnt from that sage to watch nature in her laboratory, and trace her works; he who first cleared the science of metaphysics from all the barbarous jargon of the schools; and, as Shaftesbury says, "brought philosophy into the use and practice of the world, and into the company of the better and politer sort, who might well be ashamed of it in its other dress;"—the great man, who, first clearing the science of the mind on the one hand from the ideal obscurity of the Platonists, and on the other from the debasing materialism of the disciples of the Stagyrites, taught us, as if with the voice of a god, that all our ideas proceed from two simple sources—sensation and reflection. The senses furnish the raw material to the brain, which by its reflection and contemplation is worked up into innumerable thoughts.

That great authority, Sir James Mackintosh, says, "Locke's works have contributed much to rectify prejudice, to undermine established errors, to diffuse a just mode of thinking, to excite a fearless spirit of enquiry, and yet to contain it within the boundaries which nature has prescribed to the human understanding. He has left to posterity the instructive example of a prudent reformer, and of a philosophy temperate as well as liberal, which shares the feelings of the good, and avoids direct hostility with obstinate and formidable prejudice. If Locke made few discoveries, Socrates made none. Yet both did more for the improvement of the understanding, and for the progress of knowledge, than the authors of the most brilliant discoveries." Perhaps few men have led a life so happy as our philosopher. Neither Plato with his dreary years of sorrow and suffering, or Aristotle with the toil of his disciples, could boast such advantages. Locke learnt toleration in the school of persecution, acquired liberality from the doctrines of the Independent divines, and a love of freedom from his dissenting friends. He was born in an age when experimental philosophy was making rapid strides, and the Royal Society was only lately established. He was an intimate friend of Newton's, of Le Clerc, and other continental men of science. The generous liberality of the Earl of Shaftesbury enabled him to devote his life to study; he studied wisdom in men as well as in books, and mixed with every rank of society. His life glided on peacefully towards eternity, like some mighty, silent, flowing river. He realised those fine lines of old enthusiastic Crashaw :—

> "Sydneyian showers
> Of sweet discourse, whose powers
> Can crown old Winter's head with flowers.
>
> Soft silken hours,
> Open suns and shady bowers,
> 'Bove all nothing within that lowers.
>
> Whate'er delight
> Can make day's forehead bright,
> Or give down to the wing of night."

His was

> "A happy soul, that all the way
> To heaven had a summer day."

He died at the seat of Lady Masham, at Ongar, in Essex, while his patroness was reading him a chapter in the Psalms. We will not say a word on the absurd imputations of materialism once thrown out against this great Christian philosopher; for no writer in the English language is more pious or devout. It is difficult to say whether Locke did most for the cause of true science, religious toleration, or education. He found them all hidden in Cimmerian darkness, and besmeared with corruption; he left them almost restored to their pristine beauty.

The most delightful trait of Locke's private character is his behaviour towards Sir Isaac Newton, who became insane from grief at the destruction of some MS. by fire. Pepys alludes to it. Newton, soon after this dreadful visitation, wrote to his friend a letter, beginning strangely thus :—

"SIR—Being of opinion that you endeavoured to embroil me with women, and by other means, I was so much affected with it, that when one told me you were sickly, and would not live, I answered 'twere better if you died," &c.

Newton then apologises for this, and also for having said that Locke's principles "struck at the root of morality." Our philosopher answered with all the Christian charity of an apostle and the affection of a true friend thus:—

"SIR,—I have been, ever since I knew you, so entirely and sincerely your friend, and thought you so much mine, that I could not have believed what you tell me of yourself, had I heard it of anybody else ; and though I cannot but be mightily troubled that you should have so many wrong and unjust thoughts of me, yet, next to the return of good offices, such as, from a sincere desire of good will I have ever done you, I receive your acknowledgment of the contrary as the kindest thing you could have done me, since it gives me hopes that I have not lost a friend I so much valued ? . . . . Give me leave to assure you that I am more ready to forgive you, than you can be to desire it, and I do it so freely and fully, that I wish for nothing more than the opportunity of convincing you that I truly love and esteem you," &c.

Locke then alludes to Newton having signed himself "your most humble and *unfortunate* servant," and concludes. Newton soon after this wrote a letter to Pepys, reproaching him with treachery, and then the next week apologised. This wonderful man never fully recovered his intellect, and died with a clouded brain, before he had finished his great theory of light. In heaven he will see God with undimmed vision, and to him will be revealed all those great mysteries, of which, even he, saw but a faint glimpse while on earth.

We should like to have every village in England raising a fund to rear a statue to their worthies, to excite its youth to a noble and generous emulation, to ornament their streets, and to encourage science : then would Bristol boast its Chatterton, its Cabot, its Colston, its Sir T. Lawrence, its Canning, &c.; Berkeley its Jenner, and Wrington its Locke and Hannah Moore. We cannot imagine a nobler encouragement to patriotism, and a desire for glorious fame, than this would give throughout all England.

This interesting village, Wrington, has many legendary associations. It is said to have been given by the Saxon king Athelstane to the Abbey of Glastonbury, and the savage Queen Mary bestowed it on a favourite courtier.

The church is one of the most elaborate specimens of the last glorious sunset of Gothic architecture to be met with in

T

all Somersetshire. The edifice is 120 feet long, and 52 wide; the tower 140 feet high, and every little ornament of the building is elaborately finished. We particularly noticed the east end, on each corner of which are niches for statues; while above, gurgoyles, in the shape of dragons, seem to scramble down the wall, and vomit the water from their stony mouths. There is also a nave, chancel, and porch, comprising every requisite of this architectural period. The tower contains a good peal of bells, which sound musically as the traveller catches their chime faintly on the distant Mendips. A new church has been built in the adjoining hamlet of Redhill. The well-known Waterland once lived here; and there is a free school in the parish. The teazel is grown largely for the uses of the cloth trade in this neighbourhood, towards Broadwell down; and zinc and caliminaris are found in abundant quantities. The village, situated near Burrington, is about twelve miles from Wells, and eleven from Bristol. We were sorry to learn from a villager, that the inhabitants of this rich village have been for half-a-dozen years collecting subscriptions to buy an organ for their beautiful church, and have not yet succeeded.

The great object of interest here, after the birth-place of Locke, is *Barley Wood*, a pretty little cottage, where the excellent Hannah More resided with her band of loving sisters, after she gave up their school at Stapleton. Here, after publishing *Bas Bleu*, her plays, and "Caleb in search of a Wife," that novel so "saintly and solemn," she retired as to a hermitage; and here, after having acquired a vast deal of literary fame, and having contracted friendships with Dr. Johnson, Reynolds, Burge, Garrick, &c., she devoted herself to works of charity and mercy. Penetrating the wilds of the hills, like a nun of old, she established schools in the rocky fastnesses of Cheddar; and before her death had that inexpressible delight, which only the virtuous can conceive, of seeing above a thousand children, with several female clubs of industry, assemble at an annual fête on those rocky heights. Then might this excellent woman have said, "Now let thy servant depart in peace, for mine eyes have seen thy salvation." Of £30,000 made by her writings, she left legacies to charitable institutions amounting to £10,000.

Was ever money got by purer means, or spent to a more holy purpose? To the rough miners whom she visited, living in districts as uncultured as the wilds of Africa, that pious band of sisters must have seemed like ministering angels. She died on the 7th of September, 1833, aged eighty-eight, full of years and full of hope. She was gathered in like a sheaf of the ripest wheat into her Saviour's garner. A merry, plethoric, old land-lady at an inn where we took dinner remembered all the family. They were carried to the grave, she said, all five, one after the other, and poor Mrs. Hannah More, "dear soul," the last. "There's her grave, sir, with the weeping willow over it." It stands, reader, near the road, and a willow does bend its leafy branches over it. "And," continued the good Mrs. Boniface, "there's a grand monument to her in the church, with such a hepitaph, it would take you a quarter of an hour to read it." This is vulgar fame. The worthy hostess would have suffered death at the stake, if she could have insured herself a hepitaph that would take half an hour reading, beating Mrs. Hannah by a good quarter; ladies said she came down and prayed the villagers to copy it, as they haven't time to wait. We got quite chatty with the old lady; and having praised Locke and Han-nah More in a flowery oration that consumed half an hour by the great inn clock, that ticked lugubriously, we so won her heart, that having unfortunately made an observation on the crop of apples being deficient, the old lady forcibly and power-fully convinced us of the contrary, by not allowing us to depart till we had filled our pockets to repletion with the ruddy pro-duce of her own orchard. We left as heavily ballasted as a Dutch East Indiaman; and having taken a stirrup cup of ex-cellent cider of this year's brewing, went on our way rejoicing, light of heart but heavy in pockets.

Like Autolycus, we sang on our way to Congresbury, pro-nounced cachophonously Coomesbury,

"Jog on, jog on, the footpath way,
And merrily hent the stile a.
A merry heart goes all the day,
Your sad tires in a mile a."

T 2

Just as you get on any of the heights here, a mansion half hidden with foliage meets your eye —

> "Bosom'd high in tufted trees,
>   Where perhaps some beauty lies,
>   The cynosure of neighbouring eyes."

We believe it is called Mendip Lodge. A more beautiful situation could hardly be conceived.

CONGRESBURY

is associated with the legendary of a hermit named St. Conger, who is said in very recent times to have come to England, after being a monarch of the East. This benefice was given by the tyrant, John, to Joceline, Bishop of Wells. There is a beautiful view from hence of the vale of Glastonbury and its monastic ruins. Travellers should always visit a place where hermits are said to have lived; for both that pious fraternity as well as the founders of monasteries had a wonderful keen eye for the beautiful and sublime, and none felt more keenly the loveliness of unadorned nature—

> "When unadorned, adorned the most."

A long walk through a devious lane and winding road brought us, after a careful consultation of the half-obliterated hieroglyphics on many a sign-post, to

BROCKLEY.

Let us bury for ever in dark oblivion our conversation with a miner, our chat with a collier, and, lastly, although we drop a tear as we wipe it off our tablets, the meeting with an old man and his wife, who were going to an adjoining workhouse. They wept as they went along; because they knew that, after living together for thirty years, and sharing the world's smiles and frowns, the showers and sunshine of fortune, they were to be torn asunder for ever, and not to meet, no, not even in the grave. We were still thinking over the *prison-relief* system, that inflicts such deserved punishment on the atrocious crime of poverty, when we entered the wooded COOMBE, and its wild beauty soon swept away all thoughts of the suffering of our fellow-men. It is wonderful, by the bye, reader, how soon the misery of *others* vanishes from the mind. The Coombe is a beautiful glen, with crags on either side, now frowning and precipitous, now sloping into a plain, through which the road glides. Every tree known to our land seems to grow on these heights with all the luxuriance of the tropics—the chesnut, the horse-bean, the oak, the ash, the elm, the beech, the lovely birch; and over the shingly grey pebbles, which cover the banks, hang wild flowers, among which the brambles cling everywhere. Beautiful is the scene in summer, but in autumn it is matchless. Wood nymphs might sport and not miss Arcadia. Fairies, we have no doubt, love the spot and nightly revel here. Decay was already stamped on every leaf when we passed, and winter seemed to have begun its triumphant march, like an icy conqueror as he is, through this lovely glen.

A short walk through a village, over which the Mendips seem to impend, brought us to the Nailsea station. We were just in time for a train. We plunged into the recesses of a first-class carriage; and in a few minutes the fiery monster, panting as if his iron heart would burst, and vomiting fire like the Hippogrif of the magician, *Aldiborontos phosciphornio*, bore us through a dense cluster of tiled roofs and smokey chimneys to old Bristol. The stars had

"'Gun to pale their ineffectual fire"

when we reached our domicile.

CHAPTER XXIV.

A WALK OVER THE MENDIPS.

"The chilly close of an Autumn's day,
  When the leaves fall thick on the wanderer's way;
  And rustling pines with a hollow sound
  Foretell the tempest gathering round;
  When the skirts of the western cloud are spread
  With a tinge of wild and stormy red,
  That seem, through the twilight forest bowers,
  Like the glare of a city's blazing towers."—*Mrs. Hemans.*

"When Autumn has laid her sickle by,
  And the stacks are threepit to keep them dry;
  And the sapless leaves come down fra' the trees,
  And dance about in the fitful breeze;
  And the robin again sits burd alone,
  And sings his song on the auld peat-stone."—*Captain Gray.*

CHEDDAR.

"And Cheddar for mere grief, his teene he could not wreake,
  Gusht forth so forceful that he was like to breake
  The greatest banks of Ax, as from his mother's cave,
  He wandered to the sea."—*Drayton.*

THIS gem of a village is interesting alike from the natural magnificence of its scenery, its manufactures, and its antiquities. Like Axbridge, it was originally a royal demesne belonging to the Saxon Kings. King John gave it to the Bishop of Wells, from whence it derives its name of Cheddar Episcopi; the former name being derived from the British word *Ced*, a height, and *Dwr* (Dwvr), water, as Dover, &c. In the reign of Edward VI., it was sold, and finally came into the possession of the Marquis of Bath, to whom it now belongs. Passing an old market cross, only the shaft of which remains, we go through one or two irregular streets, passing several picturesque water-mills, and a dark den, whence the red sparks are flying out under the ponderous hammer of a stalwart smith, we arrive at the cliffs. A road by the side of a clear brook, here and there dammed up for the use of mills, leads you into a rocky ravine. On one side is a gentle hill, well wooded, and glowing in the

varied colours of autumn, at the foot of which are some miners'
cottages; on the other rise the cliffs, 400 feet high, frowning in
awful grandeur. The grey rocks are here clothed with nature's
tapestry; the dark yew, the clinging ivy, the fiverwort, and
the fengren. At the foot, and on little ledges below, everywhere blooms the sweet-scented basil and the wild rue. At
some seasons of the year, too, these dark grey rocks are covered
with red clouds of the rock pink, and in summer by the blue
hare-bell, which blossoms in every crevice and fissure of the
cliffs. In some places the rocks swell forth with bold pro-
minences, like the bastions of some ruined keep, and at others
sink into dark chasms. Many deep caverns are found in various
parts of the rocks. In one of them an old woman lived for
twenty years. Another abounds with the most beautiful
stalactites, and in a third, human bones, as well as those of
beasts and oxen, have been discovered. At one point the cliffs
rise to a height of 420 feet, nearly 100 feet higher than those
of St. Vincent, at Clifton; and nothing can surpass their
sublime grandeur at this spot. A winding ascent of two miles
brings you through this rocky pass to the summit, which is
still 100 feet below that of the highest Mendip. Here five
sister-springs gush out of the rocks, and, uniting together, pour
their crystal stream, which is filled by dark green aquatic
plants, and the blue shells of limpets below.

As at Clifton, the geological strata point out, by their resemblance on either side of the defile, the dreadful convulsions
which tore them asunder. The delighted visitor is tormented
in this place by guides, who insist on pointing out what they
imagine to be objects of interest, and "beautiful jimpses," with
the monotonous voice and whining tone of the craft. The
stones and spar they offer for sale are dug some miles off.

An interesting legend appertains to these crags. An old MS.
in the possession of the Axbridge Corporation, of the eleventh
century, mentions that Edward the Confessor, A.D. 975,
came here to hunt, during his retirement at Glastonbury, soon
after the disgrace of St. Dunstan. In the ardour of the chase,
the stag and the hounds were carried together over the cliffs,
and dashed to a thousand fragments. The king's horse was

following them at the height of his speed, when Edward, suddenly breathing a vow of repentance and forgiveness of Dunstan, was preserved by his horse suddenly stopping on the edge of the yawning chasm. Struck with awe at God's goodness, he returned to Axbridge, and restored St. Dunstan to his former honours. So says the monkish chronicler.

We tore ourselves away and turned back to visit the church, which is dedicated to St. Andrew, and was probably built in the fourteenth century, by Sir Robert de Chedder, the son of a Bristol burgess, who lived in Broadmead; his tomb still stands within the communion rails, and a fine brass on this monument represents the knight " clad in complete steel :" while a figure of Isabella, his lady, is on the floor below. There are also in the church two piscinas, a fine stone pulpit, painted and gilded by the monks of old, a lectern with a half-destroyed copy of Foxe's Martyrs, part of a rood-loft, and a gilded and carved roof. The vestry is an old chantry, and another chapel of this rare old church contains a statue of some saint, much mutilated. In the windows are some good fragments of early-stained glass, one or two of the faces in which have a holy, placid expression, rarely found at so early an age. An old tombstone, A.D. 1593, of Ed. Roe, with an English inscription, is on the floor, and the remains of a stone with a floriated cross.

There are two chapels, dedicated to the Holy Virgin and the Trinity. In one of them is part of a very old defaced monument, on which the arms are a "heart between hands and feet." The tower, adorned with pinnacles, and an elegant parapet, is 100 feet high. The nave and aisles have pierced parapets, and the ceiling of the belfry is richly decorated. As we were in the church, a pale ray of sunlight lit up the tombs with a beautiful, yet melancholy light. One of the Cheddar family was married to Lord de Lisle, who perished in the battle of Nibley Green, in the reign of Edward II., when William, Lord of Berkely, was his opponent. The church is 129 feet long, and in the north and south porches are stone seats and niches, where the images of the patron saints once stood; a fine yew-tree grows in the churchyard. On Cheddar Moor, many battles are said to have taken place between the British and the Saxons; and the bones of the slain are often found in the caves of the rocks. From the stone signal stations, the British sentinels could see over the whole vale, from the sea to Glastonbury. There were once forty-three mills in this parish, now there are only three—two of paper, and one of corn. The cheese made in this village is known all over England. Camden says, "that it is like that of Parmesan." There are some excellent local charities, including a school, established by the excellent Hannah More.

There are several feudal remains of old mansions round the hamlet, and traces can be seen on the Wells road of an old episcopal palace. One of the Cheddar mansions is now a farm-house, another is occupied by a gentleman named Birch, who has published a very clever and interesting little work, full of antiquarian lore and general erudition, on the lions of his native place, which estate was originally granted to Cheddar Fitzwalter, by the Conqueror, and afterwards to Malherb, by the usurper Stephen. Although partly rebuilt in the last century, it is still a quaint and interesting old-fashioned mansion, with a spacious hall hung with family pictures.

Quitting Cheddar, repassing its old market-cross and beautiful church, we turn back towards Axbridge. Now turn up to the Bristol road towards Shipham. Bleadon, or Bleakdown, rendered interesting by the residence of the great Casaubon, and its connection with the celebrated Earl Godwin, we did not visit. The silence of Autumn prevailed; the only sound was some robin "whistling from a garden croft," or the winds piping o'er the moor. The hedges were decked with clouds of ruddy berries. The road here lies through deep ravines of rock, occasionally sloping to a plain, and humble cottages are seen here and there along the road-side. Near Rowberrow, the rocks on one side of the road, on a distant moor, rise up to a great height out of the earth, like the grey battlements of some old British fort. The wind whistling against this rocky barrier, sounded like the roar of some distant ocean. The moor by the road side was covered with fern and gorse.

> "Beside the straggling fence that skirts the way,
> Blossoms the furze, unprofitably gay."

Every now and then there is a plantation sloping to the road-side, or the road itself winds down into a valley, or stretches across a plain. Here and there is a fine view of the channel, which stretches wide in the distance; and just away from the high road there are some pretty snatches of scenery—the rocks become precipitous, and a rivulet gushes forth, as the mining population would say, like silver ore when it is molten. And this pretty village is associated with Bristol, for Henry VIII., with all the generosity of a royal robber, gave this vicarage to Bishop Bush, the skeleton effigy of which worthy man rests in the chancel of Bristol Cathedral. The vulgar tradition there is, that he was starved to death by the Roman Catholics; but skeleton effigies, having a figurative meaning, are frequent in old churches. Antony à Wood gives a good account of this prelate. A short walk brings us on to

SHIPHAM.

Just below the road, the rocks sink into a wild, craggy valley, most picturesque and beautiful. A more charming spot for the pencil of a Salvator Rosa cannot be imagined. From hence, on a clear, cloudless day, can be seen all the coast of South Wales, and the "rock of the chasm," and other mountains near Abergavenny. The Saxons and Danes once fought here, and stained this spot, where nature seems so wild and beautiful, with blood. Lapis calaminaris is found in considerable quantities in these rocks; an industrious man quarrying for it can, I am told, earn *a guinea a-day*. This stone, when powdered, is used in the manufacture of brass; when fused, the metal is considerably increased in weight. This mineral is probably nothing but lead in an oxidized form, being always found over a vein of that metal. The subterranean riches of Somersetshire are yet but half developed. A new church, possessing a good deal of simple beauty, has lately been built in this parish. St. Leonard was, we believe, formerly the patron saint of the hamlet.

A mile or two further, after enquiries from a throng of chubby children, who are absorbed in the delight of a game of "ring-taw," and again, of a corpulent, merry-looking old land-lord, who stood at the door of his inn, as if to show passers-by what capital effects his XXX produced; so have we seen a fat old spider, lying *perdu* in a corner of his web, waiting for some intrusive flies. Several anxious questions of stone-chippers by the road-side, who served us as animated mile-stones, brought us to

CHURCHILL.

One thing, however, did we notice in an adjoining hamlet, which afforded us an inward smile. In the principal part of the said village stood an attorney's house; its varnished door and ponderous knocker spoke of flocks of litigious clients. The house looked purse-proud and important, and looked down at you with its great glass eyes, quite contemptuously. A few doors further on, however, we came to the humble house of a junior limb of the law, evidently an unsuccessful practitioner, for the house looked emaciated, and weeds were growing round the door. The business of John Doe seemed evidently to have been absorbed in the whirlpool of Richard Roe. So have we seen a black corpulent spider live for a long time in the corner of a window-pane, enjoying a bloated state of prosperity, till a rival practitioner has established himself in an opposite corner, and speedily first drawn away, and then swallowed, all his clients. We pitied the absorbed practitioner, and passed on.

The village of Churchill lies near the great Bridgwater Road, and under the north brow of Doleberry Hill. This fine old rugged eminence has served as a place of encampment for every nation that has ever invaded England. The Britons have built here their wattled huts, and on it, and from hence, have blazed their beacon fires, gleaming over the vale of Glastonbury; and the eagle of the Romans, and the white horse of the Saxons, have alike waved from its summit. The peasants still believe the height haunted, and imagine that vast treasures lie concealed beneath its rocky surface.

> "If Doleberry digged were,
> Of gold should be the share"—

runs the local adage. Traces of encampments still remain, many acres in width, parallelogram in shape, and open at either hand.

CHAPTER XXV.

THE SUBURBS OF BRISTOL.

"The knowledge of scenery which is achieved by such excursions is all clear, unalloyed, and priceless gain, for it not only enriches the chamber of memory with pictures which can be expanded at will, but nourishes the power of appreciating all other kindred scenes, and redoubles the charm of those we may afterwards enjoy."—SERJEANT TALFOURD'S VACATION RAMBLES.

THE enterprising pedestrian who sets out with intent to visit the hamlets which form the text of our present chapter, must leave the city by the side where the tower of Lawford's Gate once commanded the town wall. Passing along a dull and uninteresting road, he will first arrive at Easton, a scattered village, chiefly inhabited by miners from the adjoining coal-pits. There is nothing here to detain the eye for a moment, if we except the old manor house of the village, an erection of the time of Queen Anne, or perhaps older, which is now divided into two houses. A sun-dial still remains over one of the doorways, and the old-fashioned terrace is ascended by a few steps, on each side of which, like guardian deities of the soil, grow two enormous bay trees. A little further on, down the same lane, away from the road to Stapleton, brings you to a modern church, a massive building of the early Norman style. The architect, in his love for the Gothic ideal, has retained even the barbarities of other days, for down the roof of the tower sprawl uncouth monsters, half beasts, half fiends, who do not answer even the excusable purpose of gurgoyles. This church seems quite like a missionary station among this rude and neglected population, who, for so many years, with the exception of a small chapel, of some fanatical sect, have lived in as savage and uncared-for a state as could any tribe of unwashed Ethiopians, whom, by-the-bye, this begrimed population exceedingly resemble.

Leaving Stapleton, with all its Hannah More associations, to the left, we cross some dreary waste-looking fields, just such as might be found in the vicinity of a great city, and which constitute that unpicturesque "debateable land," where you cannot tell where town ends and country begins. To our left looms in the distant fog a great bastile sort of building, which, once a repository for French prisoners, is now turned into an equal penal place—a union workhouse. Here those wretched beings, whom the heinous sin of poverty has reduced to beggary, draw out the last weary moments of an unhappy existence. Here they ply, stupefied with misery, the wretched toil which Charity demands as the pay for their miserable pittance of food. Here the only welcome sound to their ear is the sullen harsh bell, which tells of the hour of rest. Here the poor indeed learn by bitter experience what is

"The cold charity of man to man."

In this palatial, gloomy house, half mansion, half prison, are huddled the depraved and the virtuous, the vicious and the wretched, in one festering mass. Here the aged couple who have borne for so many long years all the buffets of time, are torn asunder, as if even the miserable comfort of sympathy in wretchedness must be forbidden. But as it is exceedingly problematical if we shall ever get to ABBOTS TOWN if we once get into an harangue against the cold-blooded Poor-laws, we will conclude by saying that from this building the French officers, dismissed on their *paroles d'honneur*, used to sally forth, and visit the adjoining villages, forgetting in the short-lived pleasures of the moment all the sorrows of a prison life. These poor fellows were in the habit of putting up their watches and other articles of value, for raffle, as a means of raising a few shillings; many of them broke their paroles, escaped to France, joined their own ranks, fought against us, and were again captured before the war ended. We believe that it was here that the celebrated General Lefebre was imprisoned.

Escaping from these fields we strike back into the road and proceed on towards Kingswood, the centre of the colliery district. The whole of our way to Abston lies on the summit of a *plateau*, the road the whole way winding along the level summit of a ridge of hills, which, beautifully wooded, stretch below us, before, and on either hand. We seem to be entering into the veritable realms of old KING COAL, the great grim monarch of nursery fable; the roads are paved with coal, the leaves of the trees that fringe the road are black! the men that pass us with candles in their caps are very dark, so are the donkeys they drive; the children that shout along by the way-side are "black as Erebus;" the houses are as dark as if they had been cut out of blocks of coal; the stones we walk on, seem coal; and the air, as far we can see, is blackened with dark wreaths of smoke.

Colliers are evidently an ardent and bibulous set, for public-houses seem innumerable; there are the Mason's Arms, and the Royal Arms, and everybody else's arms, enough to tire the Clarencieux king of arms himself to enumerate.

Amongst this strange semi-barbaric population Wesley began his labours; his fervid enthusiasm and homely style made thousands of converts. Among a race, to whom to speak of "Christ, and heaven and hell," were unheard-of things, dissent gained ground, because the Church had never raised her banner. Whether dissent still prevails we cannot say; but we only saw one chapel by the side of the road, and a more hideous defiance of the ungodly law of beauty we never saw. It was devoutly ugly. A great part of the low lands of this parish are devoted to market gardens, a purpose for which its dark, friable, alluvial soil well fits it. The produce is brought to Bristol by the female inhabitants, chiefly the wives of colliers, who affect a most primeval dress, and rejoice in peculiar and rather picturesque bonnets, which seem derived from the gipsy hat of George II.'s reign. The village of St. George contains nothing of interest. A part of the hamlet, bearing the mysterious name of Don John's Cross, derives its romantic title from a cross formerly erected here, in the time, we believe, of Elizabeth, to commemorate the halting of the funeral possession of Don Juan, a rich Spaniard, whose body was brought to Bristol to be exported to its native country. Remains of its shaft are said to be still somewhere preserved.

The houses about Kingswood have an uncomfortable, unrural air; about some of them there is an ill-maintained air of respectability, and about all of them there is *dirt*. Colliers loll round the doors smoking, looking dingy out of windows, and the roads are perpetually crowded with waggons full of coal. The juvenile part of the population seem to grow up colliers precociously. Infant carters, clad in profuse ancestral waist-coats, "a world too wide," and more like great coats, drive along carts, looking like little models of their fathers, who walk before. Itinerant vendors of different commodities fill the air with their hoarse cries, in rival eagerness to tempt the inhabitants to purchase. We pass two neat modern churches, and breathe a little pure air as we approach Syston. Here mysterious-looking chains cross the road, belonging to some coal works; a brook ripples by the way-side, it sounds romantic —but it is of boiling water, and flows from the engine-shed. Unearthly clangings are heard, the only sound is the throbbing of the steam-engine; the yards are filled with miners' "picks." Who would think that this unromantic mining district is the seat of numerous historical associations. To Syston Queen Anne used to come, to drink of the water of some medicinal spring, which here wells up from the ground. At Pucklechurch, adjoining, is an old farm-house, which stands on the site of a palace of the Saxon Kings, one of whom, Ethelred, as far as we remember, was stabbed here, at a great feast, by a famous robber, who enraged the monarch by his intrusion, in defiance of his authority.

Every now and then we pass some picturesque old gable-ended house, redolent of the days of Teniers. One of the inns, "the Maypole," was probably built on the scene of the village festivities.

At Bridge Yate the road passes through a pretty common, and near a most picturesque hostelrie. The house is gable-ended, with those ornaments on the ridge-front which are peculiar to the age of Charles II. A vine clambers over the walls, and round the windows, and over the old porch. And here, by-the-bye, a word about the porch as a peculiarly English adjunct to a house, most suitable to our climate, and well worthy the attention of all modern architects. Well managed, it might be made a great ornament to the house of a man of middling rank.

The common here is a beautiful little bit of English village scenery; the high road traverses it, while on one side it is edged by a group of old-fashioned houses, and on the other by wooded hills; and you can just see the heights of Lansdown. Diverging to the left, and traversing a hilly road, which is now sunk between high embosked banks, all yellow with the death-tint of decay, and now rising higher, leads you over the summit of a hill, on each side of which, below, the country rises and falls in beautiful irregularity.

A sudden turn of the road brings you at once into Abston, opposite the church, which rears its grey head on some rising ground, above the few scattered houses that now constitute what once was so important a place. It derives its name, "Abbot's-town," from the circumstance of there having been once a monastery here; and few villages, perhaps, in the wide realm of England have been the scene of so many events. Zealous local antiquarians even assert it to have been the *Abone* of Antonius. Though this may be more justly claimed for our own Clifton, or Sea-mills, it cannot be denied that Abston was a well-known halting-place for the Roman legionary on his way from the Severn, *ria* Clifton, to Aqua Solis (Bath).

Here, and at Wick, Roman coins and other remains have been found; footpaths can be partly traced here, and a field, called the "Chestles, or Castles," is still pointed out as the scene of a great battle between Ceaulin, a Saxon chieftain, and three British kings, all of whom fell beneath his sword. It took place about the year 577. The church, dedicated, we believe, to the flayed St. Bartholomew, is of plain architecture. The tower is, however, rather elaborate in its last story, and has a door adorned with quatrefoil. The whole building, however, derives beauty from its commanding position. Some old yews flourish in the church-yard. A steep path, on one side of which are houses, brings you to a deep wooded glen, through which the Boyd, a pretty rippling stream, hastens to join its waters to the great Avon which flows above. The rocks on either side fall back from the river, and form on the one side a sort of mountainous country for the space of a whole field which is richly wooded.

Diverging from here by some hilly field paths, you emerge into the high road from Marshfield, and striking up an unfrequented-looking lane, which is paved like an old Roman road, you arrive at the Chestles field. The three monumental stones, honey-combed and moss-covered with age, rear their old heads from a sepulchral mound. The whole erection bears traces of the greatest antiquity, no inscription or chiselling being visible on their surface. The farmer to whom the field belongs is a great enemy to antiquarians, and has rendered the field, by a malicious sort of ingenuity, almost inaccessible. The living of Abston is said to have been given to the Abbey of Glastonbury by Edward the Confessor; afterwards it went to Joceline, Bishop of Wells. A brook near the village, Holy Brook, was formerly dedicated to the Virgin Mary, and is supposed to possess miraculous powers of healing. This was the scene, too, of the great battle between Lord Hopton and Waller, the poet general. Hopton, after the battle was gained by the courage of the cavalier pikemen, was blown up and severely injured by the accidental explosion of an ammunition waggon, and was carried off to Bristol, of which place he afterwards became governor. A division to the right of the road brings you to the summit of some high crags that edge the river Avon, just above its confluence with the Boyd. The rocks here rise eighty feet above the river, and their broken surface is covered with a profusion of beech and other trees. A little damsel, whom we had hired as a guide at the first cottage we came to, seemed to think all the interest of the scene lay in a particular point of rock from which the much-respected donkey of a carrier had once fallen. So much for diversity of opinions respecting the beautiful. The rocks furnish lead ore, serpentine, belemmites, &c. The latter part of our scene lies in the parish of Wick, a small hamlet which lies above the great Bath road.

We retraverse the domains of "Old King Coal," and arrive at length at Bristol.

CHAPTER XXVI.

A WALK TO TAUNTON.

TAUNTON, or the station on the river Tone, called by the Romans who settled there Thonodonum, is as picturesque an old English town as any in Somersetshire. It boasts of much that can give interest to the antiquary or delight the lover of the picturesque.

It has all the associations of a little city; and its old alms-houses, its castle, and, above all, its two beautiful churches, furnish materials from which the imagination, as from some inexhaustible treasury, can weave the legend and the romance. We might conjecture, even if we were not supported by tradition, that in the very earliest age some British tribes chose the fertile vale of Taunton Deane as a station in which to rear their huts. The keen eye of a savage would readily see the advantages of a place so adapted by nature as a site for a settlement. Protected on all sides by the vast marshy tracts around the source of the Parret; having a river flowing through the vale, from which they would fish, and not very distant, the great forest of the Mendip Hills, the haunt of the wolf, the badger, and all those other animals, whose skins, in that early period of civilization, furnished clothing, while their flesh furnished food to the fierce hunter. There, too, at a later period, the rich alluvial soil, washed from the hills, and carried down by the stream that watered the district, must have attracted the Roman settlers and the civilized Saxon. In this valley, as far as the eye can reach from the fair tower of St. Mary's, did the White Horse and the Red Dragon once struggle for conquest and for life. Here, if tradition may be trusted, did the patriot Arthur spread havoc amongst the followers of the traitor Horsa. Here, too, how inspiring to reflect, on this very ground, thought we, as we paced up the principal streets of the town, did the great Alfred, perhaps, animated by the recollection of the glory of a hero, although of a hostile nation, after his long conceal-ment in the neatherd's hut, amidst the dreary marshes, dis-comfit the Danes in a terrible battle, after they had already been driven back with the loss of their great magic Raven standard, which was woven by the hands of wierd women. Now, again, the pageant changes, and we hear from St. Mary's the hymn of praise, the beauteous building echoes with the sound, for since the days of Alfred has sprung up a strong castle, which is a fortress held by some great baron, and instead of the war-like Saxon citizen, ever ready to repulse the Danes, who land on the adjoining coast, there are plump, well-fed burghers here, men who work the silk and the wool, and they the first, too, who have practised those arts in England.

Taunton, even at the Conquest, seems to have been rather an important place, as it was then made a fief of some favourite noble. It afterwards became an appendage of the Bishopric of Winchester. It stood a siege from the forces of the impostor Warbeck, in Henry VII.'s reign, who was taken before its walls, after a short skirmish with the royal troops. In Elizabeth's age Drayton says—

> "What care so empty is that hath not heard
> Of Taunton's fertile vale?"

As in most of the facts advanced in that wonderful repertory, the *Polyolbion*, Drayton is correct.' In the civil wars Taunton endured a siege from the royalist forces, it being then a centre of a very Puritan district. Colonel Goring, one of the bravest and most licentious of the royal party, commanded the beleaguering troops. They were still lying before the town, which held out stoutly, when the fatal battle of Naseby was fought. The want of that Colonel Goring's troop gave that victory to Cromwell and Fairfax. A letter from Goring, an officer as fierce and dashing as Rupert, saying that he expected to take the place in three weeks, and intreating the king to delay giving battle, was unfortunately intercepted by Fairfax. To this siege, therefore, may fairly be attributed, if not the fate, at least one great defeat of Charles. Fairfax, relying on this letter, raised the siege of Taunton with three thousand men, and having defeated the Royalists at Lamport, took Bridgwater by storm. We believe it was at this siege by Goring that the citizens were encouraged in their resistance by the exhortations of a brave Independent minister.

But perhaps the most interesting and well-known event connected with the history of this town is the active part it took in the Duke of Monmouth's rebellion. Soon after he had landed at Lyme, he visited Taunton, which had been reckoned on by his partizans as one of the towns most zealous for the Protestant cause, the defence of which furnished him with an excuse for aiming at the throne. All here was for him, and his star, so soon to set for ever on Sedgemoor, seemed now at his zenith. The townsmen presented him with a stand of colours, adorned with Protestant emblems; twenty maidens of the town, dressed in white, in a solemn procession, gave him a Bible and a sword; and great was the applause and deep the admiration, when this wretched impostor, in a theatrical speech, promised to defend the one by the other. In less than a month his head had been held up by a bungling executioner amidst the execrations of a London mob.

Then came the terrible retribution; for this hour of folly about twenty townsmen were hung by Jeffery, and the damsels who had compromised their loyalty were only pardoned after paying a very heavy fine, which a man named Penn, acting as agent of the queen's maids of honour, wrung from the terrified burghers. In this town, too, the butcher Kirk exercised his most horrible cruelties. Hanging some of the rebels, he employed fiddlers to play while the wretches were writhing in their death agonies, and then he laughed aloud at the "rogues dancing."

The town has had numerous charters from nearly all our kings, and seems during the reign of Edward III. to have been considered by that great monarch as the centre of the cloth trade, the citizens being aided by settlers from the great commercial districts of Flanders.

The town is intersected by several streets. At the end of one stands St. Mary Magdalene, the great glory of the valley. By the side of another, towards the river, is the castle, standing in the midst of a court-yard, the entrance to which is by an old gateway, on whose scathed front may still be traced some inscriptions, carved there by the abbots of yore. Across one street runs the Tone, and in another, which rambles away towards the country, are some old almshouses, still in excellent preservation.

But the great glory of the town, after all, is the splendid edifice of St. Mary Magdalene, one of the most elaborate specimens of the "pure perpendicular." The hard, bluish grey stone, of which it is built, seems perfectly to resist the slightest inroad of time—not the minutest tracery on the elaborately carved porches has crumbled at the breath of the great destroyer. There it is, rising up towards Heaven, in matchless beauty; destined, by all appearances, to remain for ages a monument of ancient piety. We often linger with delightful musing over the defaced capitals and obliterated tracery of some old abbey: they speak to us of eternity and a thousand solemn things; but far sublimer is a building like St. Mary's, which seems to smile at the puny efforts of successive centuries, as they fleet round its walls, roam through its aisles, and pass on. We feel that permanence of beauty which strikes the mind in seeing a Grecian statue, or the frieze of the Pantheon. Not but that all things of beauty, in their effects, at least, are indestructible. Not but that the wonder of Adam in Paradise is not still on the earth, embalmed, perhaps, in Homer, or floating about to be embodied by some bard yet unborn; yet still an apparently imperishable beauty does strike us with delight, mingled, not unpleasingly, with awe. The church consists of a tower, a nave, two aisles, and several chapels, formerly dedicated to the Trinity, St. Andrew, and the Virgin Mary. The chief entrance is at the westward, under the tower; but there is a very beautiful porch in the north side. Over the west door, which is richly moulded, are, on either hand, curious carvings, emblematical, it is said, of our Saviour on the lake of Genessaret; but, perhaps, merely intended for some monkish legend, or traditionary tale. Every arch springs from a corbel, of exceedingly various and grotesque design, yet never ludicrous or irreverent. Some of the faces express the deepest awe, some terror, and others the most heavenly piety. There are no monuments of knights in the church, but those of the rich citizens are exceedingly curious. One, to the memory of Henry Mills, once Mayor of the town, boasts a statue of the worthy man, dressed in the decent attire of a rich burgess of the time of Elizabeth, and painted to represent life. The epitaph is long and curious; it begins, "Taunton bore him, London bred him, piety taught him, religion led him, Taunton blessed him London blessed him, &c." Another is to the memory of Richard Naish, who endowed almshouses in the town, still existing. Some of the seats in the church under his monument are still devoted to the use of his descendants. An elegant modern marble monument perpetuates the memory of the soldiers who fell in the Afghan war. Some of the windows contain beautiful stained glass, wrought out in legends.

> "Innumerable of stains and splendid dyes,
> As are the tiger-moth's deep damask'd wings,
> And in the midst, 'mong thousand heraldries,
> And twilight saints, and dim emblazonings,
> A shielded 'scutcheon blush'd with blood of queens and kings."

The whole building has been lately beautifully restored. The old timber roof looks well, chastening down, with its dark sober hue, the splendour of the illumination. Over the north porch there is a room with a window, from whence you can see into the church; here, probably, a charity priest connected with one of the shrines once lived. What a solemn and awful habitation must that have been. To look forth at night from the one side on to the cold " God's acre," on to the graves of his brother monks who had died before him, or into the church, as the moon-beam fell through the storied window, and poured with a pale crimson light on the floor of the aisle, or to look again, on a summer's evening, and to see the last ray of the sun stealing in, and irradiating the altar or some monument with its effulgence, as if an angel had accompanied the beam on its passage from the world of fire. Then, at the appointed hours, at matins, or vespers, or complines, would that holy man go down, and breathing forth his wonted prayer, return again to his dim chamber. What a life for man, shut out from all the joys and sympathies of his kind, and yet that very isolation invested with a strange, peculiar interest! The old sexton, who showed us the church, told us he should like to live there. We heard

after, on inquiring his history, that he was a man alone in the
world, a widower, and childless. Worthy old fellow! he seemed
to know every stone in the building, ay, and to love it, too.
The tower is beautifully decorated in its third story. The
gurgoyles, which seem like fiends flying from the sacred harmony of the bells, are strange monsters, very elaborate in form.
The north porch is peculiarly rich in adornment. Angels support shields covered with various heraldic emblems. Amongst
them we recognised the *gypcier*, or purse of the middle
ages, and priests, with all the emblems of the passion, beautifully carved. The crown of thorns, the nails, the hyssop, the
ladder, the lance, &c. St. James's, the other old church in
Taunton, is a very humble building, compared with its lovely
sister, yet the tower is good, and seems of greater antiquity
than St. Mary's. We ascended its cork-screw staircase, which
was worn away by the tread of several centuries, worn by the
sandalled shoes of the monks, and the boots of the Puritan
soldier. The view is worth the ascent, for the whole valley lies
before you. Taunton boasts its mayor and corporation;
and in the round tower of the old castle, the assizes are still held.

Alas! for the corporation! On the 5th of November, ——,
a grand edict forbade the burning of a "Pope" or "Guy
Fawkes" in this once Protestant town. If the Puritan
burghers could rise from their tombs, they would surely ex-
claim, with the nasal twang of a true devotee, "Ichabod, Ichabod,
the glory is departed from thy house!" *

* The following fact relating to the town, which would only interfere
with the general narrative, we throw into a note. The tower of St. Mary's
is 153 feet high. The population of the town is about 10,000. It still
returns two members to Parliament. A king of the West Saxons first
built the castle in the year 700. The castle was destroyed by his queen,
Ethelarga, and a new one was raised by Bishop Langton, of Winchester.
The gateway of this building, built in 1406, still stands. There are on it
the arms of Bishop Horn, who repaired it. Taunton boasts of a free
grammar school, founded by Bishop Fox, in 1552. There are also the remains of a convent, founded by Franciscan monks, in the thirteenth century. The Cornhill is pointed out as the place of Jeffries's legal murders.
The suburbs of the town are, Bishop's Hill, Staplegrove, and Wilton. The
latter church was originally a branch chapel of St. Mary's.

CHAPTER XXVII.

BRISTOL AND ITS SIEGES.—NO. I.

Urbs hæc, sublimis, spatiosa, fidelis. amœna,
Dulcit et insignis, prisca, benigna, nitens.
Jura, Deum, Regem, Regionem, Crimina, Pacem,
Servat, adorat, amat, protegit, odit, habet.

Motto to Millerd's Map of Bristol, 1671.

BRISTOWE is very badly off for historians—there is no denying it. Barrett is choked with Rowleian lies, and therefore useless;—Sayer remains incomplete, and what is finished is a mere skeleton of dry antiquarian facts, so unvivified and left so confused by the author, that they might almost as well have remained in the old archives from whence they were drawn, covered with the dust of oblivion. The natural consequence is, that nine burghers out of ten know no more of the history of their venerable city than the stranger who passes through it. Its ancient importance, and the great historical events which have taken place in its streets, are only known to a few old antiquarians, who seem determined to shroud all they discover in as oblivious a darkness as they first found it. (We need hardly allude to "Travellers' Guides," and other ephemeral hand-books.) A singular fatality for a city so long the second in the realm, so long a mart for all nations, a city tracing back its foundation to the hoarest antiquity;—a city, moreover, full of historical reminiscences, old churches, old houses, old streets, and everything of which legend and tradition love to tell;—a city which has contributed a large quota to the illustrious of past centuries, the good and the great; and finally, a city the remoteness of whose foundation entitles it to the reverent attention of the antiquarian.

In our present chapter, we do not profess to have raked up any moth-nibbled, time-worn memorials; our extracts are taken chiefly from the diurnals and historians of the seventeenth century, and we garnish our "*pièces de resistance*" with sundry anecdotes and contemporaneous allusions. Let our reader recall to his mind the features of the age we are going to describe, its physical, at least, if not its moral aspect. Remember that our great-great grandfather, even, might have seen the very event we describe. Bristol still retains, of course, the great features of those days. The Frome then, as now, crept sluggishly on with its dark, silent stream, and at the foot of the cathedral the Avon rolled its waters. The churches, dedicated to St. Peter, St. John, St. Werburgh, St. James, St. Thomas, lifted up their then venerable heads towards the clouds. The former of these churches stood near the castle, which, of Norman erection, and added to by various rulers, towered above, in all its pride of place. Then, as now, near College Green, formerly the burial-ground of the great Gaunt family, stood the cathedral, shorn of its glory;—its nave demolished by the fierce Henry. The streets were few and narrow, and the quaint projecting houses, with gable ends and wide diamond-framed windows, which now stand in the Pithay, Maryport, Redcliff, and Thomas Streets, and other old localities, were then, perhaps, the new and fashionable mansions of the day. Those rooms, now the habitation of want and poverty, were then thronged by staunch burghers, whose hearts throbbed for the cause of loyalty, or longed for the ideal liberty of the Puritan. Round the gaping fire-places, surmounted by grotesque carvings and heraldic fancies, sat proud families, where now the shivering mendicant creeps to his nightly pallet of straw, fireless, starving, friendless. Let our readers imagine the narrow street, of the high cross, thronged with people; the town gallant, with his silken doublet, short cloak, and dangling rapier;—the foot soldiers, with their calivers or musquets, others with the halberds, partisans, or pikes (the bayonets of the period), the steel skull-caps; the troopers with their petronels, or horse-pistols, steel breast-plates, and wearing scarfs gaily fastened at their sides; the gallants, with their locks flowing over their shoulders, or tied up in fantastic love-knots, in very contempt of the Puritan's cropped head, their white lace collars falling over dark steel cuirasses;—the 'prentices and burghers in their more homely and less costly dress;—the Puritans, in sombre garments and steeple-crowned hats, contrasting with the gay plumes of the "swash bucklers" of the day. Imagine yourself gazing, as a spectator of the seventeenth century, from a window of a house in Wine Street, on the motley crowd. You distinguish at once, mixed as they are together, the two great parties of the day, as different in their dress as in their opinions. Hardly can they suppress the hatred and contempt which they entertain for each other. Yonder, see, is a puritan;—how solemn he looks in his dark cloak and high hat, with no hair showing beneath it. He is, verily, chanting to himself a devout psalm, with somewhat of a nasal twang. And see yonder spruce cavaliers, how contemptuously they eye him; and, marking his fair rotundity, quote to themselves Ben Jonson's exclamation of zeal in the Land Busy :—

> "I shall eat exceedingly, and prophecy."

They have passed, and are lost in the distant crowd. Now passes before us a trim abigail, who hurries along, glancing furtively back in a most coquettish manner. No wonder; for close behind are riding two young cornets of the garrison, restraining the wanton curvettings of their spirited chargers. One is telling the other of the glories of the Globe theatre, and lamenting his banishment in the dull west. Then, with the volatility of his age, he directs his attention to the above-named damsel, and, alluding to her attire, smiles as he quotes those lines of a poet of the day—

> "Hair loosely flowing, robe as free,
> Such sweet neglect most taketh me."

Anon they fall to discourse on rare Ben and immortal Will. Then comes by—but we must leave our rhapsody, and fall to facts.

A traveller who visited the city early in this century, describes the goodly city, with "its fayre cross, between both bridges, as not much inferior to that in Coventry. To it come four large and fayre streets from the four chief quarters of the city, viz., High Street, which is the fairest from the great bridge in Somersetshire; Broad Street, from the great bridge in Gloucestershire; Wine Street, from the Castle; and Corn Street, from the Marsh (the locality of Queen Square)."

The writer proceeds to describe the Marsh, which, he says, "is a very pleasant and delightful place, with as much art added thereto as could well be, for walks or bowling ground (a great amusement of the day, even among the higher classes), and other recreations for the rich merchant and genteel citizen, adorned with many a fair tree, wherin constantly the city captains drill, and muster, and exercise the city forces." The writer dilates on the seventeen churches, and the "fyne and strange fabricke of the cathedrall." "The merchants," he says, "are rich and numerous, using traffic to every part of Christendome; the citizens pious, and vying with each other in adorning their churches. The city," he adds, "is a sweet city, and compassed in with a strong wall and gate. The Castle is of great extent and bulk, and hath formerly been a most fayre and strong hold; but now it is almost quite demolished."

In addition, the reader must imagine the walls round the city, bearing, as now, their Norman names; Mont-pelier, Mont-aigu, and the British, named Brandon, almost bare, but occasionally used for outworks. Clifton was at this time known only for its hot springs.

The ancient walls extended to Park Row, Stoke's Croft, Lawford's Gate, and Redcliff Church, with a redoubt on Brandon Hill, and one in Tyndal Park. The great breach mentioned was made in the wall near Park Row. At the commencement of the great struggle, when an English king, for the first time since the death of the crook-backed tyrant, was compelled to set himself in battle array against his rebellious subjects, Bristol was in the hands of men attached to the Parliament, who openly threw off the royal authority, as soon as their party unfurled the banner of rebellion. The Royalists were, however, a powerful body, and were aided by the Cavalier gentry of the environs and adjacent parts of the country. The tragical fate of two of our loyal citizens is briefly alluded to by Lord Clarendon. The extract shows the importance of the city at that time.

He says—"There had been some months before,"—he dates May—"a design of Prince Rupert upon the city of Bristol, by correspondence with some of the chief inhabitants of the city, who were weary of the tyranny of the Parliament: but it had been so unskilfully or unhappily carried, that when the Prince was near the town, with such a party of horse "—the Prince was a dashing cavalry general—"and foot as he made choice of, it was discovered, and many principal citizens apprehended by Nathaniel Fiennes, son to the Lord Say."

(This nobleman, a statesman unfitted for his post, was one of the few of that class who were suicidal enough to join the Republican party, partly from ambition, and partly from considering themselves neglected at court; he did not escape the imputation of cowardice), "and the governor of that city for the Parliament at this time, special directions and orders were sent thither, that he should, with all severity and expedition, proceed against these conspirators, as they called them; and, thereupon, by a sentence and judgment of a council of war,"—it was ever short shrive with the crop-heads—" Alderman Yeomans, who had been high sheriff of the city, and of great reputation in it, and George Bouchier, another citizen of principal account, were—against all interposition his majesty could make—both hanged, and all other imaginable acts done, to let all the world see that there was no way to peace but by the sword."

The account of this plot, given with all the minutiæ of a coroner's inquest in a daily paper, is nearly all Sayer says of this memorable siege of the city in that civil war, when fair England's soil was drenched with the blood of her best and bravest sons. These ill-fated gentlemen were hung, we believe, in Narrow Wine Street. Their place of sepulture is disputed by local antiquaries. This public execution (the first during the war) must have struck terror into the hearts of the vanquished Royalist party: for, hitherto, the Puritans had carefully kept up that sophism, i. e., that their intention was only to remove evil councillors, "malignants," in the language of the times, from the person of their sovereign. The retribution, however, was at hand, and Royalty, before finally sinking on the scaffold, was destined to achieve a signal triumph in the capture of our ancient city, the capital of the west.

Lord Clarendon, the faithful historian, from whom we quote, says :—

" The Cornish army, levied chiefly from the loyal counties of Devon and Cornwall, reinforced by Prince Rupert" and Lord Wilmot, took Bath, which was soon quitted by them, after Waller's (the poet general) overthrow at Lansdown, (where the brave Hopton, afterwards Governor of Bristol, was blown up by the explosion of a powder tumbril ;) " the garrison (of Bath) being withdrawn to reinforce Bristol. At Bath they rested and refreshed themselves till they might receive new orders from the King : who upon full advice, and consideration of the state he was in, and the broken condition of the enemy, resolved to make an attempt upon the city of Bristol, to which Prince Rupert was much inclined, for his being disappointed in a former design, and where there were many well affected to the King's service from the beginning, and more since the execution of those two eminent citizens."* (The unfortunate Boucher and the Yeomans.)

We can imagine the fierce Rupert was burning to revenge his friends, to atone for his carelessness in the arrangements of the plot. The cruelty of the stern, and it is said cowardly Fiennes, produced doubtless, as cruelty often does, a re-action in the minds of the people. " And the disesteem generally had of the courage of Nathaniel Fiennes, the Governor, made the design to be thought the more reasonable, so the Marquis of Hertford and Prince Maurice (Rupert's brother) returned to Bath, and upon agreement to appear on such a day, with their whole strength before Bristol, on the Somersetshire side,

---

* Prince Rupert's party were in ambush in a house at Redland, when the plot was discovered, and the conspirators seized. They were all distinguished by a white badge on the arm, and were to be let in by St. John's gateway—the bells of that church were to be rung as a signal. The prince instantly rode off with his troop on finding that all was lost ; and during his march over Durdhamdown, a shot from a redoubt in Tyndal's Park struck down one of his men and two horses.

when Prince Rupert, with the Oxford forces, would appear before it on the Gloucestershire side. On the four-and-twentieth of July, (1643) both armies sat down before it, quartering their horse in that manner that none could go out or into the city without great hazard of being taken; and the same day, with the assistance of some seamen who were prepared before, they seized all the ships that were in Kingroad, which were not only laden with goods of great value, as plate, money, and the best sort of all commodities, which those who suspected the worst had sent abroad, but with many persons of quality, who, being unwilling to run the hazard of a siege, thought that way to have secured themselves, and to have escaped to London; and so all were taken prisoners. The next day Prince Rupert came to his brother and the Marquis, and a general council of all the principal officers of both armies being assembled, it was debated "in what manner they should proceed,—by assault or approach." There were in the town five-and-twenty hundred foot, and a regiment of horse and dragoons; the line about the town was finished, yet in some places the graff was wider and deeper than in others. The castle within the town was very well prepared, and supplied with great store of provisions to endure a siege. The opinions were several: the officers of the Cornish army (very natural that the Cornish troops, miners from their youth, preferred regular approaches) were of opinion "that it was best to proceed by way of approach, because the ground being very good, it would in a very short time be done, and since there was no army of the enemy in a possibility to relieve it, the securest way would be the best, whereas the works were so very good they must expect to lose very many men, and if they were beaten off, all their summer hopes would be destroyed, it not being easy again to make up the spirit of the army for a new action. Besides, they alleged the well-affected party in the city, which was believed to be very great, would, after they had been closely besieged three or four days, have a greater influence upon the soldier, and be able to do more towards the surrender than they could upon a storm, when they would be equally sensible of the disorder of the soldier and their own damage by plunder, as the other and the too late example of the executed citizens, would keep men from offering at any insurrection in the city." (Sensible, and, as it appeared after, correct advice, for the storm was attended with great loss of life, and their friends in the city must have suffered by it.) On the other hand, Prince Rupert and all the officers of his army, very earnestly desired to assault it, alleging " the work to be easy and the soldiers fitter for any brisk attempt than a dull, patient design, and that the army would be more weakened by the latter than the former; that the city not having yet recovered the consternation of Sir William Waller's defeat, was so full of horror, that it would make a very weak defence; that there was no soldier of experience in the town, and the Governor himself would not like to endure the terror of a storm; whereas, if they gave them time to consider, and to look long upon them with a wall between, they would grow confirmed and resolute, and courage would supply the place of skill, and having plenty of all kinds of provisions within the town, they would grow strong and peremptory, whilst the besiegers would grow less vigorous and disheartened." These reasons and the Prince's importunity, with some insinuations of knowing more than was fit to be spoken, as if somewhat would be done within the town that must not be mentioned, and a glorious contempt of danger, prevailed so far that it was consented to on all parts to assault the town the next morning at three places on the Somersetshire side and three places on the Gloucestershire side at the break of day. (The High Street side of the city was the Somersetshire side, and on the Gloucestershire side, down Broad Street, stood then, as now, the old gateway of St. John's, defended by its portcullis and drawbridge, and flanked by redoubts and other external works. There were several redoubts on the opposite hills.) The truth is, both opinions, with regard to their different circumstances, were in themselves reasonable. For the Gloucestershire side, were Prince Rupert was, might be stormed, the graff (ditch) being shallow, and the wall in some places low and weak, which could not be easily approached by reason the ground being rocky and the redoubts very strong which overlooked the ground. On the other side, the ground was very difficult to approach, and as inconvenient and dangerous to storm, by reason of a plain level before the line, and a broad and deep graff, and the line throughout better flanked than the other. The next morning, with little other provisions fit for such a work than the courage of the assailants, both armies fell on. On the west side, where the Cornish were, they assaulted the line in three places, one division led by Sir Nicholas Hanning, assisted with Colonel John Trevannion,

> (By Pol, Tre, and Pen,
> You may know the Cornish men,

runs an old distich), Lieut-Col. Slingsby and three more field officers, too great a number of such officers to conduct so small a party as five hundred men, if there had not been an immoderate disdain of danger, and appetite of glory. Another division on the right hand was led by Colonel Buck, assisted by Colonel Wagstaffe, Colonel Bernard Ashley, who commanded the regiment of the Lord Marquis Hertford, with other field officers; and the third division on the left hand led by Sir Thomas Basset, who was Major-General of the Cornish. These three divisions fell on together with that courage and resolution as nothing but death could control; and though the middle division got into the graff, and so near filled it that some mounted the wall, yet by the prodigious disadvantage of the ground, and the full defence the besieged made within, they were driven back with great slaughter; the common soldiers, after their chief officers were killed or desperately wounded, finding it a bootless attempt.　　　*　　　*

On Prince Rupert's side it was assaulted with equal courage, and with almost equal loss, for though that division, led on by the Lord Grandison, a brave young cavalier, Col.-General of the foot, was beaten off, the Lord Grandison himself being hurt; the other, led by Colonel Bellasis, likewise had no better fortune. Yet Colonel Washington with a party, finding a place in the curtain (the general term in fortification for an extended wall) between the place assaulted by the other two, weaker than the rest, entered, and quickly made room for the horse to follow. The enemy, as soon as they saw the line entered in one place, either out of fear or by command of their officers, quitted their posts; so that the Prince (Rupert) entered with his foot and horse into the suburbs. Sending for one thousand of the Cornish foot, which were presently sent to second him, he marched up to Froom gate, losing many men and some very good officers, by shot from the walls and windows, inasmuch as all men were much cast down to see so little gotten with so great a loss, for they still had a more difficult entrance into the town than they had yet passed, and where their horse could be of no use to them, when, to the exceeding comfort of generals and soldiers, the city beat a parley, which the Prince willingly embracing, and getting their hostages into his hands, sent Colonel Gerrard and another officer to treat. The treaty began about two of the clock in the afternoon, and before ten at night these articles were agreed on, and signed by all parties :—

1. "That the Governor, Nathaniel Fiennes, together with all the officers, both of horse and foot, now within and about the city of Bristol, castle, and forts, may march out to-morrow morning by nine of the clock, with their full arms, bag and baggage, provided it be their own goods; and that the common foot soldiers march out without arms, and the troopers with their horses and swords, leaving their other arms behind them, with a safe convoy to Westminster, and after not to be molested in their march by any of the King's forces for the space of three days.

2. "That there may be carriages allowed and provided to carry away their bag and baggage, and sick and hurt soldiers.

3. "That the King's forces march not into the town till the Parliament forces are marched out, which is to be at nine of the clock.

4. "That all prisoners in the city be delivered up; and that Captain Eyres and Captain Cockaigne, who were taken at *the* Devizes (the old name for that town, as Bath was called the Bath), be released.

5. "That Sir John Horner, Sir John Seymour, Mr. Edward Stevens, and all other knights, gentlemen, citizens, and other persons that are now in the city, may, if they please, with their

goods, wives and families, bag and baggage, have free liberty to return to their own homes or elsewhere, there to rest in safety, or ride and travel with the Governor and forces ; and such of them and their families as shall be left behind by reason of sickness or other causes, may have liberty, so soon as they can conveniently, to depart this town in safety, provided that all gentlemen and other persons shall have three days' liberty to reside here or depart with their goods, which they please.

6. "That all the inhabitants of this city shall be secure in their persons, families, and estates, free from plundering, and all other violence or wrong whatsoever.

7. "That the charters and liberties of this city may be preserved, and that the ancient government thereof and present governors and officers, may remain and continue in their former condition, according to his Majesty's charters and pleasure.

8. "That for avoiding inconveniences and distractions, the quartering of soldiers be referred to or left to the Mayor and Governor of the same city for the time being.

9. "That all such as have carried any goods into the castle may have free liberty to carry the same forth.

10. "That the forces that are to march out are to leave behind them all cannon and ammunition, with their colours, and such arms as is before expressed."

The next morning, if not before, for the truth is, from the time that the treaty was first offered, they in the town kept no guards, nor observed any order, but the soldiers ran away to the Prince, and many of his soldiers went into the town, his Highness was possessed of Bristol, the enemy then marching away. Here the ill example of Reading in the breach of the articles was remembered, and unhappily followed, for all that garrison was now here ; so that they, with some colour of right or retaliation, and the rest by their example, used great license to the soldiers, who should have been safely conducted, which reflected much upon the Prince (Rupert), though he used his utmost power to suppress it, and charged Colonel Fiennes to be accessory to his own wrong, by marching out of the town an hour before his appointment, and thereby his convoy was not ready, and at another gate than was appointed or agreed on ; and as the articles were thus unhappily violated to those who went away, so they were not enough observed to those who stayed, and to the city itself; for many of Colonel Fiennes' soldiers, taking conditions, and entering into the King's army, instructed their new friends who were most disaffected. Just like the zeal of new proselytes, and still more like the mercenary soldiers of that day, who sold their blood to the highest bidder. The soldier has in all ages been rather reckless of friend or foe. As Schiller says in his "Wallenstein"—

> "Their life is 'tween a battle and a march,
> Like the wind's blast, never resting, homeless,
> They storm across the war-convulsed earth."

So that one whole street upon the bridge (there were formerly houses on the bridge itself—this was common in London and other cities), the inhabitants whereof lay under some brand of *malignity*, (this word was used by both parties in the civil war, like "rogue" in a quarrel, you must believe it applied to both sides equally, or neither,) though no doubt there were many honest men among them, was totally plundered, which, because there was little justice done upon the transgressors (Rupert would not have visited such an offence with much severity), was believed to be done by the connivance of the officers, and more discredited the King's troops and his cause than was then taken notice of or discovered. The King's cause was marred by the licentiousness and factious intrigues of the undisciplined officers. The high discipline and good moral conduct of Cromwell's "Ironsides" first endeared them to the peasantry. The reduction of Bristol was a full tide of prosperity to the King, it made him master of the second city in the kingdom, and gave him undisturbed possession of one of the richest counties, and rendered Wales more useful to him, being freed from the fear of Bristol, and restored the trade with Bristol, which was the greatest support of those parts. . . . . The victory was, however, dearly bought. There were slain in the assaults five hundred common men and abundance of excellent officers. Of the Cornish regiment fell—Colonel Buck, who was knocked

x 2

by a blow of a halbert from the wall into the graff, and there perished, Major Kendall, Colonel John Trevannion, and Sir Nicholas Hanning, Governor of Pendennis Castle (Cornwall), both shot in the thigh with musket bullets. On the north side of Prince Rupert's army, Colonel Harry Lunsford and Lieut.-Col. Mayle, both shot out of a window after they had entered the suburbs. There were wounded Lord Viscount Grandison, nephew to the Duke of Buckingham, who was Col.-General of the King's foot; he died from his wounds; Colonel John Bellasis, Colonel Bernard Ashley, Colonel Sir John Owen, and many other officers of name.

(The old farce of this date describes some Royalist officers obtaining refreshment from the Puritan peasantry by pretending to bargain for the bodies of their children.)

Colonel Lunsford was much dreaded by the Puritans. He was one of those who drew their swords in self defence in Westminster Hall, which afforded a subject of much invective against the King's party. Absurd reports were spread that he ate children; and this charge, ridiculous as it may seem, was believed by the ignorant peasantry to affect all Cavaliers. A ballad of the day says—

> "From Fielding and from Vavasour,
>   Both evil affected men;
> From Lunsford eke deliver us,
>   That eateth up children."

Cleveland jokes—

> "The post that came from Banbury,
>   Riding in a blue rocket,
> He swore he saw, when Lunsford fell,
>   A child's arm in his pocket."

The vulgar depicted him in the act, for Cleveland also says—

> "They fear the giblets of his train, they fear
> Even his dog, that four-legged Cavalier;
> He that devours the scraps that Lunsford makes,
> Whose picture feeds upon a child in stakes."

Butler, in Hudibras, says—

> "Make children with your tones to run for it,
> As bad as bloody bones or Lunsford."

Echard, in his History of England, says the maligned one was "a person of extraordinary sobriety, energy, and courage.")

As soon as the news of the taking of Bristol reached the King at Oxford, a solemn thanksgiving for the success was immediately publicly performed. And the next day the King issued a public declaration, exhorting his subjects to return to their obedience.

(This shows how elated the Royalists were with their success, and at what value Bristol was estimated. There is no doubt that even at this time Charles would have gladly made peace with his subjects.)

Jealousies (the ruin of the royal cause, the nobles of that party thinking only of their private interest) began amongst the principal officers concerning the government of Bristol.

Prince Rupert, indignant at serving under the Marquis of Hertford, and the Marquis, disliking the interference of the Prince in his councils, and that when Bristol was taken, where the Marquis took himself to command in chief, being a town particularly within his commission, and of which he was besides Lord Lieutenant. And he was angry that Prince Rupert should have concluded the treaty without his knowledge, and therefore with little ceremony he declared he would appoint Sir Ralph Hopton governor. Rupert, thinking he had gained the city (he certainly bore the heat and toil of the day, saving his royal descent, should have obeyed his commander-in-chief), considered himself entitled to the government, and writing secretly to the King, obtained it. Shortly afterwards, the Marquis wrote that Hopton was appointed, which determined the King himself to visit Bristol to quell the disturbance. He made a joyful entrance into Bristol, which was performed with all decent solemnity. He established Prince Rupert in the government, and Hopton his lieutenant-governor, with the real power.   *   *   *   *   *

Lord Hopton, who had been blown up at the skirmish at Lansdown, was left at Bristol to recruit his health and form that new garrison, which was a magazine for men, arms, and ammunition, and all that was wanted.

We have seen an engraving of Hopton as governor of Bristol, copied, we believe, from a unique print in Lord Spencer's collection. Sir Ralph is in the dress of peace, and has the flowing locks and lace collar of a Royalist gentleman. He wears an embroidered coat, with a scarf across his breast, jack boots, and immense spurs. In the background are a regiment of foot soldiers, with their pikes.

In proposing the reduction of Gloucester, it was argued that the garrison of Worcester and Shrewsbury might be supplied from Bristol, and the trade of the city thereby so advanced, that the customs might bring a notable revenue to the king, and the wealth of the city increasing, it might bear the greater burden of the war. At Bristol the army lost many, as those who had plundered would no longer serve.

After the taking of the city, the Cathedral was visited by Charles I., accompanied by his sons, Charles and James, the future kings, who attended divine service on Sunday.

This was in 1643, one year after the royal standard had first been unfurled, and the capture of Bristol was one of the first, and, perhaps, the only important success gained by the Royalist party. In 1649, King Charles's head rolled on the scaffold.

CHAPTER XXVIII.

BRISTOL AND ITS SIEGES.—NO. II.

" Then came the lusty Froom, the first of floods that met,
Fair Avon entering into fruitful Somerset,
To Bristol her to bear, the fairest seat of fame,
    *   ◦   The prospect of which place,
To her fair buildings adds an admirable grace ;
Well fashioned as the best, and with a double wall,
As brave as any town, but yet exceeding all,
For easement, that to health is requisite and meet,
Her piled shores to keep her delicate and sweet ;
Hereto she hath her tides, that when she is opprest
With heat and drought, still pour her flood upon her breast."
Drayton's Polyolbion, B. 3.

"Let the high praises of God be in their mouth, and a two-edged sword in their hands "—*Psalm* cxlix. 6. The favourite text of the Puritan military saints, the true church militant.

In our last chapter we attempted briefly to bring back to our reader's mind the appearance of Bristol in the seventeenth century. But a few years after the first siege the city was still walled round, from the present Park Street to Stoke's Croft on one side, and Lawford's Gate and Redcliff district on the other. Redoubts commanded those important positions for the safety of a city, girt in by a strong belt of hills, Tyndall's Park, the hill of St. Brandon, &c. The Castle towered above the present narrow Wine Street: the Avon "winding at its own sweet will," in a line of silver, and the Froom, the lusty Froom, as Michael Drayton calls it, creeping through the city like a dark lethe. But two years had elapsed, and the central republic, or rather London, the focus of rebellion and fanaticism, found Bristol, the Monarch of the West, a serious annoyance to the traffic of the provinces they had subdued. In the autumn of 1645, three years after the royal standard was unfurled, with ominous circumstances, the brave, but phlegmatic Fairfax received orders to march on Bristol, the faithless city of the malignants; the Jericho which they little expected to win so bloodlessly. The Prince lay there with a strong garrison, supported by the train bands of the city, a well-disciplined body even in Elizabeth's time, and accustomed to handle the pike and the caliver. To prevent the enemy from foraging, the stern Rupert burnt down Westbury and a few adjacent hamlets. This made all the club men, or neutral body, go over to Fairfax. Thus says our authority, a Parliamentary paper, the *Mercurius Britannicus:*—

"On Thursday, Sept. 4, 1645, our general, Sir Thos. Fairfax, sent a trumpeter with a summons to Prince Rupert for the surrender of Bristol; but the trumpeter was at first something loath to go, because he had heard that Rupert should swear that if any trumpeter came into him with any message from Sir Thomas Fairfax, that he would hang him; but seeing our resolution that if he should offer any such thing we should retaliate, Sir Bernard Ashley being with us, and others of note, he passed over these doubts, and went with his message into Bristol; and so soon as the Prince received the message paper, he looking in it, *swore, God damn him*, it was a summons, and called for a cup of sack, truly cavalier like, and sat down and read it, and detained the trumpeter in Bristol until Friday. We wondering what he was stayed so long for, not knowing but that Prince Rupert might have done as he had vowed before; but he did not, for our trumpeter returned with an answer to our general, in which the Prince only desires so much favour from him as to give him leave to acquaint his uncle therewith, and then he would send a speedy and plenary answer, which did not at all give any satisfaction to our general. On Saturday, Sept. the 6th, the general sent again another trumpeter with his resolution to proceed; and to certify Prince Rupert that he would wait no longer, nor admit of delay, and therefore to require his answer one way or other The meanwhile Sir Thos. Fairfax marched from his quarters into the field, and had his dinner brought him out of his quarters, so careful was he to follow the business closely; he dined in the fields, on the Somersetshire side, towards Redcliffe Church (which was guarded by cannon); and after dinner, having given orders to Colonel Ireton (afterwards Cromwell's son-in-law, and one of the King's judges) to draw out two regiments of horse, to be left to wait at the bottom of the hill, near the Sally Port, to be ready in case the enemy should attempt to sally out. Sir Thomas Fairfax went then in.

(This Ireton was originally a lawyer's clerk, and, like most of the followers of Cromwell, of humble origin. From his skill as a clerk, he was chosen as one of Cromwell's secretaries, and with his master, and one or two more of the ultra-military fanatics, was cognisant of Charles's death. He was a great preaching colonel, and was "powerful in the word," as the cant of the day termed it. Pride, another fellow-colonel of Ireton's, was a brewer's drayman, and a foundling. Ireton afterwards distinguished himself in Ireland, and as an ardent and visionary republican, was much dreaded by Oliver when he assumed the supreme power.)*

* The records of Bristol citizens during these stirring times consist in a

Sir Thomas Fairfax then went in about himself in person, with Col. Birch, Col. Rainsborough, Col. Ireton, Adj.-Gen. Eveling, Adj.-Gen. of the Horse, Major Bethell, and other gentlemen attending upon him, to view the enemy's works, and sometimes the general viewed the works by himself, and sometimes with the gentlemen, but no soldier was to show obedience to him as general, lest the enemy, seeing it from their works, should take notice of it, and make shot against him to endanger his person. And when the general had viewed all, he came to his own cannon and viewed them all, to see how they were and how levelled, particularly the great twisted piece; he viewed that, and observed all things, and what was not well caused to be altered, taking such careful notice of all things himself that he went so near to the enemies' works that in viewing the Great Fort he was within pistol-shot of their breast-work near the Little Fort, which is by the Royal Fort, and thus he did venture to take exact notice of their work elsewhere also. And we do now keep the enemy so close in that they have not been able to make a sally out since Col. Okey was taken. On the said afternoon, viz., Saturday, the

few half-obliterated stones and battered monuments. In the Cathedral there is an effigy, " in complete armour clad," of Sir John Newton, Bart. who died 1665. In the Mayor's Chapel, monuments of Mrs. Baynton, a Wiltshire lady, about 1667; of Thomas Aldworth, and his son John, Newfoundland merchants—the former died 1615, the latter 1628. The Throgmorton family, 1635. Sir Baynah Throgmorton, in 1611, bore the King's message to the Mayor of Bristol, commanding him to hold the city for him. The Rev. Richd. Standfast, chaplain-in-ordinary to Charles II., was turned out of the living of Christ Church, and a taylor inducted thereto. In St. James's Church is a brass tablet to the memory of H. Gibbes, mayor, who died in 1636. The Rev. W. Towgood, vicar of St. Nicholas, was imprisoned by the parliamentary forces. He was afterwards rewarded for his sufferings by being made dean. In 1668, Sir Henry Creswick, who resided at the "Bristol Mirror Office," was buried in St. Werburgh's Church. The murdered Bowcher is said by Barrett to have been buried in this church. The long epitaph he gives attributes the capture of the city by the Royalists to the power of a guilty conscience in their enemies. He lived in Christmas Street. The illustrious Whitson was spared from "the evil to come," for he died in 1629; and his monument, is it not with his townsmen to this day? His name has a monument in every Bristol heart.

6th September, Lieut.-Gen. Cromwell viewed the horse, and gave order to their quarters. On the Lord's day, September the 7th, there came divers fresh club-men into us with such arms as they had, protesting to live and die with us, because they say that the cavaliers plunder and are barbarous, therefore they will stand on their guard against them; but Sir Thomas Fairfax carries himself so well (they say) to them, that they will never leave him, but assist him to the utmost of their abilities. Neither is it these club-men only that take notice of our general's fair and orderly carriage, but the very enemies themselves acknowledge it, and some colonels in Bristol sent word by our trumpeter to the general that they remember their service to him, and from them to give thanks for showing him so brave and well-bred a gentleman, saying that he is a true and well-disposed gentleman, and that it is a pity he is for the Parliament; the truth of it is, he is so worthy and absolute a well-bred gentleman, that malice itself cannot tax him of ill. Sir Thomas Fairfax sent the last summons into Bristol to Prince Rupert on Sunday night, September the 7th, he having all things in readiness to storm, and intending to fall on the next morning; received propositions from Rupert that if he would permit him to march away with 20 pieces of ordnance colours flying, 20 carriages, arms and ammunition, bag and baggage, and all his soldiers and bishops (*strange collocation*) and prebends and choristers, gentlemen and others, with a safe conduct, that then he would deliver up Bristol with all the forts, castles, &c. To this Sir Thomas Fairfax returned answer that for the terms of honour he would do what was fitting for his degree, that is to march away, with three pieces of ordnance, colours, arms, &c. But for the other propositions, viz., concerning the protection of the bishops, &c., he desired to be excused.

Sir Thomas Fairfax was resolved, if Rupert would not agree, on Monday, Sept. the 8th, that he would storm, being resolved to admit of no delay. Tuesday was the day nominated for the surrender of Bristol, and commissioners of both sides were chosen.

" Dated at the Leaguer, 8th September.

" But all this time what's become of Goring? He, they say, appears about Exeter, 7000 strong, if we allow him more 'tis no great matter, for the galliant Massey (who was routed last week in Ely House) jostles with him for quarters, being lustily recruited by a grand body of club men out of the counties of Devon and Somerset, some say no less than 8000. If they go on thus, I will call them Knaves of Clubs, no more. Especially if they continue to do as well as they promised at Mendip Hill, where the High Sheriff of Somersetshire appointed them a general meeting also near Bristol (the very city of Bristol, O ye malignants!) is taken, they will be better than their words. For we have received absolute, excellent intelligence of the storming of Bristol, and taking the town, castles, forts, ordnance, ammunition and arms, by his excellency Sir Thomas Fairfax, on Thursday, the 11th of this instant, Sept."—*Merc. Brit., Sept. 8 to 15.*

" Sept. 15. By a gentleman of note from Bristol, it is certified that Prince Rupert (according to the articles of agreement) went out of the Castle of Bristol on Thursday last, towards Worcester, with his lifeguard of about 300 horse and 700 foot, most of the Welch refused to go along with him, being *pressed* men, and they, as well as those which were raised in the counties adjacent, either desire to return into their own counties, or join Sir Thomas Fairfax, so that they were most Irish that went with the Prince, and we hear that Lieut.-Gen. Cromwell is appointed to attend the King's motion with 400 horse, on the one side, and Col.-Gen. Poyntz on the other ; but of his Excellency's design we hear nothing as yet ; the council of war being not called, in which regard we shall not make any conjectures thereof."—*King's Weekly Intelligencer, Sept. 9 to 16.*

A letter from Lieut.-Gen. Cromwell to the Parliament, dated at Bristol, the 14th of September, was to this effect :—

CROMWELL'S DISPATCH TO THE PARLIAMENT.

" About one o'clock of the morning, Thursday, the 15th instant, Sir Thomas Fairfax stormed the city. The general's signal when to follow was the burning straw, upon which the

men went on with great resolution, and very presently recovered the line, making way for the horse to enter. Colonel
Montague and Colonel Pickering, who stormed at Lawford's
Gate (very near the site of the present gaol) where was a
double work well filled with men and cannon, presently entered,
and with great resolution beat the enemy from their works,
and possessed their cannon without any considerable loss, and
laid down their bridges for their horse to enter. Major Des-
borough commanded the horse, who very gallantly seconded
the foot; then our foot advanced to the city walls, where they
possessed the great gate against the Castle Street, wherein
were put 100 men, who made it good. Sir Hardress Waller,
with his and the General's regiment, with no less resolution,
entered on the other side of Lawford's Gate, towards Avon
River, and put themselves into an immediate conjunction with
the rest of the brigade. During this Colonel Rainsborough
and Colonel Hamond attempted Prior's Hill Fort (Stoke
Croft), and the line downwards towards Froome; Colonel
Birch and the Major-General's regiment being to storm towards
Froome River, Colonel Hamond possessed the line immediately,
and beat the enemy from it, and made way for our horse to
enter. Colonel Rainsborough, who had the hardest task of all
at Prior's Fort, attempted it, and fought very near three hours
for it, and indeed there was great despair of carrying the place,
it being exceeding high, a ladder of thirty rounds scarce reaching to the top thereof; but his resolution was such that he
would not give it over. The enemy had four pieces of cannon
upon it, which they played with round and case shot upon our
men. Here Lieut.-Colonel Bowen and others were two hours at
push of pike, standing upon the pallisadoes, but nevertheless
they could not enter. Colonel Hamond having entered the line,
and Captain Ireton with a forlorn (*en fains perdus*, as the
French say) of Colonel Birch's regiment, interposing with his
horse between the enemy's horse and Colonel Hamond, received a shot with two pistol bullets, which broke his arm, by
means the entrance of Colonel Hamond did storm the fort on
that part which was inward. By which means Colonel Rainsborough's and Colonel Hamond's men entered the fort, and

immediately put to the sword almost all in it. And as this was the place of most difficulty, so of most loss to us on that side, and of very great honour to the undertaker. Being thus far possessed of the enemy's works, the town was fired in three places by the enemy, which we could not put out, which began to be a great trouble to the general and all his officers, that so famous a city should be wasted: but whilst they were viewing that sad spectacle, the Prince sent a trumpet to the General, desiring a treaty for the surrender, and so the fire was quenched and articles agreed on, as you have formerly heard. A list of what loss and hurt was sustained on our side at the taking of Bristol, as it was certified under the hand of Lieut.-General Cromwell, (then in his 46th year):—Colonel Fortescue's lieutenant killed; Colonel Hamond shot with a brace of bullets in his arm; Major Cromwell dangerously shot; two of Colonel Engleslie's brothers shot; some other officers wounded; 200 in all was the most lost in the storm and from the beginning of the siege; one dead of the plague; many common soldiers wounded. In the city was taken 140 pieces of cannon mounted, and many unmounted; 300 muskets, besides a good quantity of shot, ammunition, and other arms; 100 barrels of powder, besides much not yet brought to the magazine; 320 days' victuals in the Royal Fort for 150 men, 15 days' victuals in the Castle. The Prince had in the garrison 1001 horse and 250 foot, and 1000 auxiliaries, besides the trained bands of the city."

The *Mercurius Vindicus*, another London puritanical organ and a staunch advocate of the Parliament, writes:

" On the Lord's Day, Sept. 21, according to order of Parliament, Lieut.-Gen. Cromwell's letter of the taking of Bristol was read in several congregations about London, and thanks returned to Almighty God for the admirable and wonderful reduction of that city. The letter of that worthy councillor is well worth observation, and especially those *pious and self-denying expressions* therein, are very remarkable, viz.; ' It may be thought that some praises are due to these gallant men, of whose valour so much mention is made, their humble request to you, and all that have an interest in this blessing, is that they may be forgotten. Its their joy that they are instruments of God's glory, and their country's good; it is their honour that God vouchsafes to use them. Sir, they that have been employed in this service, know that faith and prayer obtained this city for you; I do not say ours only, but of the people of God with you, and all England over, who have wrestled with God for a blessing in this very thing. Our desires are, that God may be glorified by the same spirit of faith, by which we ask all our sufficiency, and having received it, its meet that he have all the praise.' "—Sept. 16 to 23.

The *Mercurius Britannicus* of March 17 to 24, 1644-5, says:

"A most remarkable piece of service, it was performed by Sir William Waller (the court poet) and Oliver Cromwell, near Lavington, Somersetshire, where they killed 10, took 800 prisoners and 400 horse, gallant horse, and their best horse, being the same which conducted the Prince (of Wales) to Bristol, besides their mock sheriff, Col. Long, who now may return by Tom Long, the carrier. Since this action, we may presume they were joined by Rolborne, for then they were within two days' march of him."

The *Perfect Diurnal* of March 24 to 31, 1644-5, says:

"The forces of Sir William Waller and Colonel Cromwell dividing upon an eminent design about Shaftesbury, Sir William went towards Bristol."

Cromwell, in a letter, dated Basingstoke, 14th October, addressed to the Speaker of the House of Commons, Lenthall, after alluding to the taking of Basing House, says:

"If you please to make a strong quarter at Newbury, Wilts, inasmuch as Newbury lies on the river, it will make the trade most secure between Bristol and London for all carriages."

The *Moderate Intelligencer*, under date June 29 to July 6, 1648, the year before the execution of Charles I., and when he probably was in Carisbrook Castle, Isle of Wight, says, alluding to the intended attack on Pembroke:

"Our guns, for want of wind, are not yet come from Bristol; we expect them hourly: had they come, we had done ere this." (How truly laconic and soldier-like.)

In the year 1649, the Parliament decided that a magazine of

provisions should be settled at Bristol, as an *entrepot* for the West, which was accordingly done.

The surrender of Bristol by Rupert (Roberto) will always remain one of the unexplained mysteries of history. We would wager our lives he was brave, we are sure he was honest. Surmise alternately suggests some political jealousy, as the cause of the ignoble surrender to the exulting Roundheads. Rupert was the dashing Murat, le beau Sabreur, the brave, hot-headed, swearing, truly loyal, faithful, vicious cavalier of the day. He hated a siege, he loved the hot charge and the clash of squadrons meeting; he would rather, like Douglas of old, hear the lark sing than the mouse squeak. Perhaps impatience at the prospect of a long and tedious siege, while his sovereign was unaided, or the fear of treason in the leaguered city, may have conduced to the unhappy result. Certain it is, from our extract, that only a few Life Guards left the city with him. The cowardly body who hung the unhappy men, Boucher and Yeomens, may have been plotting but too successfully. Charles never forgave Rupert this unhappy affair, although he pleaded that the city wall was not defendable, being in some parts only three feet thick and five feet high. Prince Rupert was ever the daring partisan general of his age, indefatigable in cutting off convoys, beating up quarters, night surprises, ever in the saddle, his foot as frequently in the saddle as his hand on the sword's hilt. The nephew of Charles, and son of the unhappy Elector Palatine, he was accustomed to the alarms of war from his infancy. Making his first campaign, at the age of sixteen, under the Prince of Orange, he had fought like a knight-errant for fame and pastime. No man relished more keenly what Fletcher calls the "fierce delight of war." To his ears, the drum's rattle was the sweetest music. His despatches, published by Mr. Warburton, "bear witness," says that gentleman, "to his fiery and impetuous daring, his perfect indifference to danger, moral and physical, his fertility of resources, his promptitude and zeal for the cause." Some of these despatches are stained dark red, with the life-blood of the bearers; one has a bullet mark through it. Many are inscribed "*Haste, haste, post haste!*" and one is endorsed by the various officers through whose hands they passed. Mr. Warburton attributes the surrender of our city to him as rather an error of a statesman's judgment than the defeat of a commander. May it be so. Peace to his manes. He was as a fiery spirit as ever rode in saddle.

The royalist Mayor and Town Council were deposed on the first entrance of the enemy, and soon after the Republic was declared at the High Cross, as so many kings had been in former ages. The churches suffered the usual spoliations, the tombs of the Cathedral were broken, and the brasses stolen. The nave was turned into a stable; the three altars were plastered up, and the 'idolatrous' paintings of the prophets on the organ screen were purposely hidden from sight. The goodly pile, sufficient to strike a fanatic with awe, was defaced. Some pinnacles were knocked down; the organ was broken up; monuments were destroyed, to hurry the dead into a quicker oblivion. Local historians say that the fanatic mob burnt all the furniture of the church, and marched through the streets blowing the broken organ pipes in derision of their fallen enemy, and carrying white banners made of shreds of surplices. In the chapel of the Gaunts, the altar was partially destroyed. In All Saints the altar was removed to the centre of the building. St. Peter's Church had a few years before been declared dangerous in its propinquity to the Castle, and it is said orders had actually been given for its demolition. Soon after the occupation a cutler was made curate of St. Philip's.*

A few years after, and Charles II. passed through the city disguised as a retainer, and seated behind Mrs. Lane. The lady came from Staffordshire, availing herself of a parliamentary pass, under pretence of a visit to Mrs. Norton, of Abbotsleigh. The king tells the story himself in the Boscoble papers; it was

---

* The speech of Major Shippon, one of those brave fighting preachers, may amuse the reader:—" Come on, my boys, my brave boys; I will run the same hazard with you. Remember, the cause is for God; come, my honest, brave boys; let us pray heartily and fight heartily, and God will bless us!" As laconic as the soldier's prayer before Edgehill.—" For what we are going to receive, the Lord make us truly thankful. Amen." And he rushed to the charge.

one of his favourite stories, for the king was a great "button-holder;"—how he ran much risk in his anxiety to make a dé-tour, and see the royal fort, where there had been of old so much fighting. The king was to have embarked at Bristol, but finally left for the Dorset coast. It is worth noticing that, during his wanderings he was entertained at King's Newton, Derbyshire, by Sir Robert Hardinge, connected with the Fitz-hardinges of Bristol history. The witty monarch wrote with his diamond ring on the window of the hall, "Cras, ero lux;" There'll be "light anon;" an anagram for Carolus rex. Enough for our present chapter.

"To-morrow to fresh fields and pastures new."

CHAPTER XXIX.

A DAY'S FISHING AT KILLARNEY.

SCENE.—A boat moored not far from O'Donohue's Library, Lake of Killarney.

DRAMATIS PERSONÆ.—*Vaughan*, a tramping artist; the *Author*; *Darcy*, a medical student, just plucked; and *Phil*, the boatman.

TIME.—A July evening: the blue sky bedappled with sleeping flocks of white fleecy clouds; the water of a deepening sapphire colour; a wild deer every now and then belling from the green-wood caverns of high Glena.

AUTHOR. Try the green drake, Darcy, the spotted darlings don't bite here as they did in that little curling ripple off Paddy Blake's rock. I suppose you would think it breaking the law to try the German plan of a cherry with the stone out, or the old Gloucestershire poacher's receipt of a fleshy grass-hopper?

Darcy. (Reproachfully, with an *ex tu* Brute look.) Is it murther you mane, you pot fisher you, with your lazy head on a square altar of novels. They shall never say that Bob Darcy didn't treat all the fish he ever played with like a gen-tleman. Lind me the fly-book there, it's on the well by the whisky-bottle, which, like a solemn barometer, tells us by its green lapse of the progress of time. What's o'clock?

Phil. (With tremendous violence, and enthusiasm.) It's turned four, your honour. I know it, because the four o'clock fly, your honour, is just gone.

Author. Nonsense, Phil. Don't bamboozle me. There's no fly that's quite so punctual as that. They don't read Bradshaw.

Phil. (Winking violently and putting on the innocence of an unborn babe.) Why, I meant the four o'clock fly that goes from Muckross to the station. By the same token, I just hear the guard's bugle. Oh, it's as purty as Kitty's dancing, to see his fingers run over the keys; they're no sooner on than they're off again. Try a black and orange, Mr. Darcy, the wind is going down.

Vaughan. (Waking up, and humming the angling song of Göthe). How this cool, deep water, Mr. Critic, makes one long to dive to some mermaid's cavern, and study fly-fishing with lines made of the golden thread of her errant hair.

Darcy. What! study fishing from the fish's point of view—learning by the way the great salmon language, and the trout's *patois?*

Vaughan. Exactly. Waking up drowned knights, and suicide monks, and having small tea-parties of respectable banshees, in their blue flannel bathing dresses and shrouds *sine crinoline.*

Author. Now don't let your fancy become ghastly.

Vaughan. I must say, Darcy, with all his bull-finch riding, tumbler smashing, and frolics at Flynn's, has a tender heart, and a high sense of sporting honour. He refuses to catch but on equitable and scientific principles. He is the Bayard of the fist, and the Sir Philip Sidney of the rod.

Darcy. You be hanged.

Author. Don't. He's blushing.

Vaughan. (Taking up Darcy's fly book.) Did it cost you much money to make this collection of natural history?

Darcy. Pots, sir; pots, by Jove.

Vaughan. Why, old fellow, here's a leaf like a tulip bed, or

Benjamin's coat and Disraeli's conscience. Why, my palette, new set with its carmine, cobalt, and chromes, is nothing to it. I believe it's a tailor's pattern book, or snips from a ribbon shop. The devil fishes with ribbons sometimes, eh?

Darcy. Och! you sucking Raphael, you big ignoramus, (pull a bit on, Phil,) what have you been wasting your time at? Why, those are the best salmon flies to be had at Limerick—butchers, by Jove. This is the golden pheasant, that the red ma-caw; beauties both, and devilish killing.

Author sneezes.

Phil. God between you and all harm.

Vaughan. Sings :—

> " Oh, Gra Machree,
>   You don't love me,
> Or else you would not linger
>   To slip this ring,
>   Which now I bring,
> Upon your little finger—
>   Your purty little finger."

Author. (While Darcy and Phil are weighing that big silver flapper.) Tell me, Vaughan, as you finish that sketch, if you agree with my last severe remarks on modern historical novels. As to historical novels, I do not think the best men should confine themselves strictly to their own times. He who knows the human nature of to-day surely knows the human nature of yesterday, and if he choose to place his scene a century or two back, he has the advantage of a large scope for his imagination, picturesque dress, and stranger social contrasts. One cannot always be describing clever tailors, like Alton Locke; wonderful governesses, like Jane Eyre; ingenious reporters, like Young Copperfield; kind, simple-hearted officers, like Colonel Newcombe; or even inspired coal-pit proprietors, like Mr. Kingsley in Miss Craik's clever book, *Riverstone.*

Vaughan. No, nor, bedad, Vespasians, like Dr. Croly; Sir Richard Steeles, like Mr. Whitehead; Osmonds, like Thacke-ray; Queen Elizabeths, like Scott; or Richelieus like that clever charlatan, the negro Frenchman, Dumas. The pre-sent is a fashion now, as the past was some years ago, just as

Leach is, and Bunbury was—as Giotto is, and Guido was ; it is only a turn of the wheel.

Darcy. The reel? I don't want to stop all night playing him—you fellows, mind your talking. I could catch the sea sarpint himself if I only knew the right sort of fly.

Vaughan. We wern't talking to you—so shut up. We said wheel, not reel.

*   *   *   *   *

Author. Mind your fishing, Darcy. If your heart was only as soft as your head——

Darcy. Och, you omodhaun,—pass the bottle,—if I had ten thousand a year, I would erect twin statues to Jameson and Kinahan.

Author. You must feel a good many pulses before that, and shake that death-rattle of a head of yours, Mr. Doctor, some thousand times, you legal homicider; but put the brake on, Darcy, and let us rattle on with our palaver. As I was saying, Vaughan, and I would enunciate it with the twitch and power of Johnson, it is better for a book to be antiquarian, which is, at least, instructive, than to be of no age, which is unmeaning. The authoress should have looked at our old flint axes and dagger brooches, the arrows and horns, the spears and pipes, the crowns and maces. With her pleasant fancy and easy style, she might soon study carefully the set of old robes and the slouch of old hats, till she knew them as well as our own beavers and bornouses. The balance and shot-silking of manners, politics, and religion, she should have also mastered.

Vaughan. Why, you would not turn her into an encyclopedist, or one of those small omnisciencies you meet with at clubs.

Author. Six months' hard reading and note-taking would have done this.

Vaughan. O authors don't read ; they write : reading is not thinking.

Author. No, no more is writing : but reading is a stimulus to thought, and some people with small concentration can only think over a book. This is a novelist we are talking of and dissecting, Darcy.

Darcy. I begin to long for a dissection again; I gave my last body to old Mouser: bedad bodies are deuced dear. Bad luck to his father's grandfather, that's the second time he has refused to take me.

Author. What, still thinking of the man who would not back the bill?

Darcy. Trash! The bill be hanged. No backbiting now, it's the salmon I'm talking of,—ten pounds if he weighed an ounce. There he goes off, sulkily, like a big whale as he is, into deep water;—and I could fling the whisky bottle at him in mere spite.

Vaughan. Fling something less precious to you, my dear Darcy. Try one of O'Dwyer's pills for a bait, gulls take them fast enough. But to return. The antiquarian novel, Mr. Author, to say the best of it, is but a mere wax-work exhibition. The novelist must learn that it is only after long prayers and vigils to the gods that the artist's cold statue begins to throb and heave with life; that it must be by the long embraces of faith that the cold stone warms, and the stony heart lifts and beats. It is only after long wrestles with the angel of fiction, that we win his blessing. It is our own life's blood that we must pour into the veins of our Frankensteins. It is only by the magic of great offerings, that the dead teraphim we worship will deign to speak: we must lay face to face, and heart to heart on the dead child, before it will arise and thank the prophet for giving him life.

Author. True, Vaughan, true. It is only when the pangs of the crucifixion day have fallen on the great writer, that the graves open, and some, who have been dead, arise and appear unto many. You know me too well to believe this metaphor irreverent. Now, Darcy, the end of your song of "The Nate Goold Ring," of which you gave us the first verse a while ago. Now, no spitting.

Darcy. Sings :—

> " Colleen asthore,
>   My heart is sore,
> Too long I have been waiting ;
>   We've feed the priest,
>   And cooked the feast,

It is no lies I'm stating—
It's truth, bedad, I'm stating.

Mavourneen, then,
Be one in ten,
And do not look so tazing :
The pig is bought,
The fowls are caught,
The day and hour are plazing,
O, Kitty, a'nt they plazing?

You smile at me,
O, Gra Machree,
Sure, dear, you will not linger.
'No blarney, Tom,
'I'm deaf and dumb.'
The ring is *on* her finger—
Whoop, boys, it's *on* her finger."

Vaughan. A very pretty bit of rustic dalliance—not classical, yet mighty rural and tender. * * * * Let us rest a moment and cry *pax*, dear Mr. Author, before we summon our next culprit to the bar; just watch those broad white-sailed Argosies of clouds, piled up with Indian amber, bearing down towards us, fanned by the west-sou'-west, from the bluff shoulder of Tore mountain, where the great trumpet-snorts of the cascade's trumpet sound perpetually, and will sound till they be silenced by the judgment trump of God himself. Now shot to pieces and pierced by the artillery of an unmasked battery of sunbeams, they sink and fade away into the blue clouds of the July ocean of wandering air.

Darcy. Take your hog-brush, man, and paint—you don't live by words.

Author. Just watch Darcy, Vaughan, it's really quite a treat, you should have seen him ten minutes ago.

Darcy. Is thy servant a dog that you should do this thing?

Author. He draws out of various mysterious leathers, envelopes, packing cases, and wooden repositories, three of the most favoured pipes of his harem : first, an amatory French pipe, with a Pompadour head upon it—no Lucretia, to judge by her kindling eyes, unless haply she might be Lucretia Borgia ; secondly, an immense china well, holding a pail-full of bird's-eye, brought from Heidelberg, and grown black in many a student's beer-battle; thirdly, a meerschaum skull, convivially moral, and professionally sociable. He selects the last, and fills it gravely, with head on one side, like a magpie.

Darcy. Can't you lave a fellow alone with the comfort of his life? Isn't old blood, like the Darcys, to do what it likes?

Vaughan. Yes, even to get plucked—falling at a drain, when it could clear a five-bar. A pity the fine old tap isn't cooler. Now see him how he lashes the quiet lake water lightly with his taper whip rod springing from the very wheel, and twenty yards of line out. The great tulip flower of a fly falls light as thistledown. It's the Darcys know how to do the old beguiling game: you would think he expected to hook a water-fairy, or to fish up a crock of old king gold. Click, click, goes the merry reel; flip, flip, goes the water from the line in a thin, silvery dry dust over our heads. Darcy is happy in the indulgence of hope and tobacco unlimited. Darcy descended from a great line of kings.

Darcy. You may say that, and a fishing-line too.

Vaughan. The spasmodic novel is a remote descendant from such verbal epilepsies as Smith's " Life Drama." It makes a dew-drop and a world of equal consequence. It rains on us stars, suns, fires, and Paradises. Pre-Raphaelitism came from Wordsworthianism, just as the Lake school emerged from old ballads and revived Elizabethanism, when the French Revolution, and its consequent freedom of opinion, had led us rebelliously and heretically back to nature. Bronteism was the twin of Spasmodism and pre-Raphaelitism, and led us to the love of common, and even at first almost repulsive things. The same reason that made Mr. Millais paint scrubby, red-haired girls, made Miss Craik select a plain governess for a heroine, and Miss Mulock make a hero out of a tanner's boy, in "John Halifax," though she does at last artfully redeem him by proving his gentle descent.

Vaughan. Well, thank God! the old Leigh Hunt Cockney enthusiasm and sickly affectation of new words has gone by. The new school is sounder, deeper, and truer.

Author. Still, though they do not blow out a Hampstead daisy till it becomes as large as St. Paul's, there is about them a feverish and false tone of exaggeration which destroys the balance of parts, by enlarging one part and leaving the other a sketch. "The earnest," too, has grown into a cant all but intolerable—"The mission," "The human," are their great phrases. It was foolish to make a hero an Adonis; but why run to the other extreme, and make him a humpy Æsop?

Darcy. If you fellows don't let me speak, I shall burst from repletion, of imagination. We are just off the Man-of-war Rock now, and I am going to stir up Paddy Blake with a rapid succession of incoherent questions, which that great dull bluff of rock, that holds the mocking spirit, will answer pat off the tongue. Paddy Blake never trips at his lesson. Listen, quick as lightning—

How do you do, old Paddy Blake?	*How do you do, old Paddy Blake?*
Where were you last Easter Monday?	*Where were you last Easter Monday?*
Driving home the pigging-rigging,	*Driving home the pigging-rigging,*
You, and Tim, and Mike, and Darby.	*You, and Tim, and Mike, and Darby.*
Coming down the long boreen	*Coming down the long boreen—a*
All fell over the dyke together;	*All fell over the dyke together;*
Some broke legs and some broke noses.	*Some broke legs, and some broke noses.*
Good night, Paddy Blake, you rascal.	*Good night, Paddy Blake, you rascal.*
Parley vous Franchez, Mademoiselle?	*Parley vous Franchez, Mademoiselle?*
Hurrah! Paddy Blake, you rascal.	*Hurrah! Paddy Blake, you rascal.*
Ha! ha! ha! ha! whoop—hurrah!	*Ha! ha! ha! ha! whoop—hurrah!*

And while we fell back, laughing at the demon-like humanness of the voice in the rock cavern, the echo laughed and gibbered still about us.

Author. Well, not all the fairies that fly in the summer dust, or that trip round mushrooms, can match that.

Darcy. Can't they?

He dropped his rod and seized his bugle. Enchantment of sea and earth, were ever such sounds that, with fairies trooping after them, broke forth from the great mountain side, till the Reeks called to Derrycunihy, and Tore shouted to Glena! Nearer, farther, deeper, sweeter, louder, prouder, nearer, clearer; ringing from mountain unto mountain—silver-springing, like a fountain—fainter, fainter, fresh and fainter, from some blue and distant glen, far beyond the keenest ken; then a low Æolian wail—dying down some distant vale—far away— O, far away.

Darcy. You may look, but that's nothing: you should hear a band play here, as they do sometimes in Lord Kenmare's state barge, with its glittering flag dragging in the water. You'd think O'Donohue was passing to his castle on a May morning.

Vaughan. I've heard it. The mountain breaks into music, like a great hive awakening. The great silent, lonely, woody rocks, that have listened so long, break forth and sing—bright, strong, and sweet as fairy harps from hidden cave and tree. Then, all at once, a cannon is fired with a bursting shock and thunder-split that seems to crack the very navel of firm-set earth. It is sublime.

Darcy. As Tom Moore says, you would think that at one time—

> " Fairies, with a silver chime,
> Shook the heather bells, till tune
> Broke from every flower of June.
> Then, to break the spell, the shock
> Of the cannon rent the rock."

" And what was Vaughan, the artist, doing, all this time?" says a grisly, inquisitive reader.

I will tell you: Vaughan, who will wear a black velvet skullcap, like Inigo Jones, and a black velvet coat, like Raphael, is sitting with a canvas on his knees, sketching in colour the shifting glories of the purple mountains above our heads. Rows of bottle-golden fluids, ambery, rich, transparent, are on the seat beside him. In his hand are a sheaf of brushes, one or two tipped with sky azure—on his thumb is a round mahogany shield of a palette, tinged with colours from vermilion and flake-white to orange cadmium and brown-black. He is sketching, with a loving smile, as we would paint the smile of one we love. Now he looks up with knitted brow, then down again, and so on. Thin, gold, waving leaves, floating up in heaps in the eddies and bays—rough crimson sorbs of the dark-leaved viscid-flowered arbutus—misanthropic herons, and motherly ducks—he has them all. Vaughan alone can paint Killarney, for he loves it.

Author. Now, Darcy, a song.

Darcy. What shall it be? Rebel, as, "The night before Larry was stretched," "Croppies, lie down," such as Corporal Moonbeam, of the Shanavasts, or the Hearts of Steel used to sing, or a rouser for the lively end of a wake, like "Moll in the Wad," "Rattle the Hasp," and "He's a neat Hand for a Grinder;" or merry and convivial, like "The Black Stripper," or "Nell Flaherty's Drake;" or shall it be pathetic, like "Savournah Deelish," or the old Jacobite air, "The Wild Geese?"

Author. O, botheration! give us those two new versions of old tunes you hammered out last night at the landlord's.

Darcy. Well then, without the usual cold in the head, here goes.   Call this

A CUSHLA-MACHREE.

The blue's in the sky, and the flower's in the thorn,
But the brightness, and freshness, and sweetness of morn
May be blackness, and foulness, and silence for me,
When I meet at the chapel door Cushla-machree.

There is Kitty in scarlet, and Norah in blue,
And Nelly, her black hair all silvered with dew;
But what are their ribbons and trinkets to me,
When I look on my Aileen, my Cushla-machree?

There's the girl at the brewer's, and Kitty at Tim's,
And that neat-footed coleen, who is cousin of Jim's;—
Let them ogle and dance, it's all nothing to me,
All I want is the love of my Cushla-machree.

Author. Now the other.

Darcy. Stop a bit, Vaughan has got a rise! Play him! play him! quick with the landing-net, or, by jingo! he'll be off. Keep the top joint down—drown him! hurrah! ten pound if he weighs an ounce. Well done, Raphael! now paint him, and then eat him.   What shall I sing?

Says he, Katty?
Says she, Patty?

or "The Bould Soger Boy." Sentimental? Very well, here's my half-new words to "Savournah Deelish."

The plover was calling, the snow it was falling,
   Savournah deelish, Shighan oh!
Feathery white it's falling, falling,
   Savournah deelish, Shighan oh!
Wan was her cheek, which lay on my shoulder;
Damp was her hand, no marble was colder;
I felt that I never again should behold her,
   Savournah deelish, Shigan oh!

The snow it was drifting, the wind it was sifting,
   Savournah deelish, Shighan oh!
Silvery snow-dust, sifting, sifting,
   Savournah deelish, Shighan oh!
Under the long wave wreath they found her,
Dead and cold, for the snow chain bound her
But she lay smiling, the cold snow round her,
   Savournah deelish, Shigan oh!

Author. Bravo! but how did she get there? Lost her way, or smothered, or——

Darcy. Don't ask questions; it is quite enough she *was* found there. To be obscure is to be grand!

Vaughan. Just look at this rose-tint on this last cloud. Rose madder, where are ye?

Author. What a pity you could not brush off some of the rose bloom from the cheeks of an Irish girl; some of that transparent, shifting, pulsing, quickening carmine, that a kiss turns to warm crimson, and a tale of pity softens to the pale pink of a winter rose.

Darcy. Three cheers for the girleens, with black eyes and red cheeks. God bless them! Was that a rise? Yes. Try him with a dun badger. Where's the whisky bottle? I've got another attack of that horrid wind in the heart.

Author. Is that a new complaint?

Darcy. Faith, it's down in all the materia medicas; but some call it tympany, and others anemozœa.

Author. Thank you for the information. You'll do the examiners yet.

Darcy. Of course I shall, as sure as a *bonoveen* has two

flitches. But how deuced polite you are; you're getting like old Baron Roper, who I saw once bow and apologize to a Ribbonman, at the Clomel assizes, for having forgotten to sentence him to death. "By ——," says the fellow, who had shot three landlords running, because they were too particular about the rent, "don't mention it, your honour;" and the whole court broke out into a thundering guffaw.

Author. Why, that's as good as the story of Charles II. apologizing to the ribboned men round his bed "for being such an unconscionable time dying;" or that varnished old humbug, Lord Chesterfield's, last words to his valet, "Dessolles, give the gentleman a chair."

Vaughan. Look at

"That great mountain rent away
From some white Alps of yesterday."

It now changes into a fiery dragon, and presently into a mountain of roses.

Darcy. Or strawberry ice, Vaughan.

Vaughan. Just squeeze me out a twisting worm of that crimson lake, and I'll have a fling at it—just a glaze of madder. Thank you. Now for it.

Author. This is our last evening, Vaughan, so do your work. Blue lake—fiery sky—Tomies—Glena, too, with thy battalions of pines defiling to the lake—and thou, eagle's nest, with thy long lines of burning lances, farewell! to-morrow the 9.20 from Killarney bears us on white, cloudy wings to Dublin, and the blue mountains of Wicklow.

Darcy. No I'm not (sings) :—

"Yes, Aghadoe,
I must say no
To thee, Killarney's daughter;
To Torc so tall,
Glena and all,
And Derrycunihy's water.

"The deer may bell
On rock and fell,
Where birch trees nod and feather;
Yet we must go,
Farewell, Dunloe"——

Bedad, I've got him! Quiet: get the net. He's a fourteen-pounder, as I'm a slayer of men, just plucked. Play him, and I'll keep the boat down.

Such a scene! Apollo and the Python was child's play to it. Hat blown away—that's nothing; bottles upset—a trifle. Whiz runs the line, forty yards out; still as a log, then off like a rocket; at last, worried, worn out, baffled, tired by Darcy's iron wrist and cunning play, the monster, a lump of dripping silver, is dragged into the boat, to flap himself disconsolately on the bloody planks till a blow of Vaughan's maul stick gives him the quieting *coup de grace.*

Author. Bobbing for whale, or trolling for the great sea sarpint, Darcy, will soon be an easy matter to you.

Darcy. Now I'll finish the O'Grady's farewell to Killarney:—

"O *Coom a Dhur,*
Far, far above
Genera's lake I prize thee.
Not Holland's sea,
Though strong it be,
In my esteem could rise thee.

"The first of May,
When sunbeams play
Before the chieftain riding;
When Ross's tower
Becomes the bower
O'Donohue took pride in.

"Then golden bridge,
From ridge to ridge,
Joins towers of pearl and beryl;
With banner, sail,
And shining mail,
They ford the waves of peril.

"Tore waterfall
Will roar a call
Unto his fellow yonder;
The wind, the waves,
Drives over the caves
As I would drive a gander.

" The deer in a flock
Swim round the rock,
To see the king of Erin,
In his golden crown,
Just fresh from town,
And the fairies after him cheering."

(Laughter.)

Author. That bathos is thoroughly Irish, Darcy. It's only people who are able to be earnest who can afford to be funny.

Darcy. Why not afford it: it don't require £10,000 a-year and a pinery? When they sent about the world offering a prize for the happiest man, didn't they find him digging as a Connaught boy, with no shirt on the back of him?

Author. *Veramente,* which means true for you; but it is time to take the rod to pieces, screw up the tin tubes, and wind the fly hook—we shall be late for dinner. Suppose, on our pull home, we improvise a grand *ologawa,* as a keening for Killarney we are about to bid farewell to.

Darcy. Bravo! Three cheers for Joe Smith and all successful blackguards, crowned and crownless. I'll take the comic side—the prosaic—the material; to use the words of that illustrious poet, proverbially dull Tupper's friend, Higginbottom, to whom, I am disgusted to say, his ungrateful nation has not yet erected even a sign-post—" *the prosaically and unpleasantly true,*" I may say, the shadow side of life.

Vaughan. I, the neutral tint ; the poetical colour, the artistic.

Author. And I, the light—the full sunshine of whatever poetry my rush pipe can produce.

Darcy. Well, now then, fire away. We've got half an hour, from the old buffer here—the Weir Bridge—what a run we are going with. Keep steady, or we shall go a mucker, and thirty is not a pleasant age to be drowned in. Now it's quiet water, the troubadour begins. It's your first move. Where's the whisky bottle?

Author. I sound trumpets, then. Farewell, a long farewell

to thee, lake of the milk-white horse and the kingly rider, of
the wood, the waterfall, and the mountain, and the eagle, of arbutus and oak, of wild deer and heron.   Farewell, ye rocky
islands, where the blue wave frets and laps; where the bee,
on the heather flower, sings sleepily all the June day to the
tide that gurgles in and out the little sand-cove and the narrow
bay; where the wild ducks float and gabble, and where the
moping heron poises like a timid bather in a brown study.   No
more I tread the spongy green turf of Innisfallen, where the
great hollies throw aloft their thick clusters of blood-drops;
and the blackbird, with the golden bill, flutes and pipes like the
soul of some old monk just liberated from purgatory.   There
the ash feathers in the sky, and the oak twists its serpent arms.
Farewell, dear island, on whose grassy shores I can see the
hooded monks at sunset time, watching night darken over the
lake.   Farewell, Tore, with thy spilling silver, tossed from
ledge to ledge; passing, yet never passed.   Black valley, purple cliff, broad lake, high mountain, beneficent, all-covering,
and all-guarding sky, farewell!

Darcy. Time's up!   Now I must put in my oar; and you,
too, nimble-footed Tim, the waiter, who, in thy irrestrainable
philanthropy, watchest the ignorant Saxon, and suddenly digging thy fork into his unmanageable potato, offerest to divest
it of its splitting jacket, much to his delight.   Thou who, with
the innocence of the golden age, readest the newspaper and ex-
changest jokes behind our chairs at dinner; who toilest in
with unwieldy kishes of fresh turf: who runnest for ponies;
who hurriest for the bag-squeezing, noise-compelling piper.
Farewell! ye, too, bare-legged girls with the goat's milk and
mountain dew; who ran, nymph-like before us up the boulder-
strewn paths of Mangerton; who clung to our bridles like
delaying fairies; who hung unto our perpendicular horse's tail
with pretty recalcitrance and reluctant feet; who, with flushed
faces, covered with wind-tossed hair, laughed and sang, and
teazed us for the slow-coming halfpence.   Farewell, thou not-
to-be-forgotten wizen little *Jim of the Eagle,* who, as a babe, an
eagle bore to its gory nest, up near the Tomies; who, with thy

squeaky bugle and cracked voice, nearly killed us by declaring
that thou wert, as Mrs. Hall said, Jimmy, the enchanted knight
of Mangerton.   Thou who, for the not-to-be-mentioned sum
of fourpence, offered to strip and swim on that chilly October
day round the cold tarn, called the Devil's Punch Bowl.
Farewell! and thou, Jemmy O'Donohue, most sturdy and resolute of guides, who led the hot gallop and charge of the
redoubtable Kerry ponies through the astonished street of
Muckross.   Farewell!——

Vaughan. Hold a while, Darcy, put a stopper on; where is
my colour to come in, and we just at the jetty? O, farewell,
then, ye green-blue skies of Kerry, navigated by those piles of
silver fire that move slowly burning into the gold and torrid
orange of such a sunset as we see yonder—with long veins of
quivering purple, and bars of golden russet.   Farewell, the lake
that burns at this early twilight into a great level sea of new-
spilled blood, far away towards the west where the red light
glimmers through the trees, and the returning birds wing to the
darkening wood—the hotel windows shine like those of a lighthouse, and acquaint us that dinner is ready.

Darcy. Hurrah! then, for Muckross! there's the salmon
down here longing to be boiled.

Author. Give way, then.

Vaughan. Now, then, Author, with a will.

Darcy. Altogether.

Author. One and all.

OMNES. Hurrah! put your backs to it.

And we *did* go.   I thinking of life and its changes in my
own dreary way (I could suck melancholy from a sugar-cane),
thinking of how I should never again see that grand block of
cloudy amethyst, they call the Tomies mountain, as we leaped
and shot along, as if propelled by steam, the water gurgling
and smoking under us.   Together the oars dipped, turned,
and feathered, in quick pulses.   The boat went cleaving on
past darkening rocks, and trees, and wood, and island, past the
old Ross Tower, past the great stone and rocks of fantastic and
enchanted shapes.   Nearer, nearer—we drive on land, the
boat grinding into the wet silt, and oozy, gritty sand.

Instantly that his foot touched the shore, Darcy put his two hands, trumpet-wise, to his mouth, and roared out, with the voice of an agonized bull, "Is the dinner ready?"

Tim, still more jovial, from the far-off LAKE hotel door, answers, "It's just being dished, Surr."

Says Darcy, ferociously grinding his teeth, "I could eat a horse's leg off."

THE END.

FILLING, PRINTER AND STEREOTYPER, GUILDFORD, SURREY.

www.ingramcontent.com/pod-product-compliance
Lightning Source LLC
Chambersburg PA
CBHW021114270326
41929CB00009B/881